PENGUIN BOOKS

RUSSIA

David K. Shipler worked for *The New York Times* from 1966 to 1988, serving in Saigon from 1973 to 1975, Moscow from 1975 to 1979, and Jerusalem from 1979 to 1984. In 1982 he was a co-recipient of the George Polk Award for foreign reporting for his coverage of the war in Lebanon. He was a guest scholar at the Brookings Institution from 1984 to 1985, after which he joined the Washington bureau of the *Times*, where he served as chief diplomatic correspondent. In 1988 he became a senior associate at the Carnegie Endowment for International Peace. *Russia* won the Overseas Press Club Award, and Shipler's latest book, *Arab and Jew*, won the Pulitzer Prize for nonfiction in 1987. He and his wife, Deborah, have a daughter and two sons.

RUSSIA

Broken Idols,
Solemn Dreams

REVISED AND UPDATED

David K. Shipler

PENGUIN BOOKS

PENGUIN BOOKS
Published by the Penguin Group
Viking Penguin, a division of Penguin Books USA Inc.,
40 West 23rd Street, New York, New York 10010, U.S.A.
Penguin Books Ltd, 27 Wrights Lane,
London W8 5TZ, England
Penguin Books Australia Ltd, Ringwood,
Victoria, Australia
Penguin Books Canada Ltd, 2801 John Street,
Markham, Ontario, Canada L3R 1B4
Penguin Books (N.Z.) Ltd, 182–190 Wairau Road,
Auckland 10, New Zealand

Penguin Books Ltd, Registered Offices:
Harmondsworth, Middlesex, England

First published in the United States of America by Times Books,
a division of The New York Times Book Co., Inc. 1983

This revised edition first published by Times Books,
a division of Random House, Inc. 1989
Published in Penguin Books 1989

1   3   5   7   9   10   8   6   4   2

Copyright © David K. Shipler, 1983, 1989
All rights reserved

LIBRARY OF CONGRESS CATALOGING IN PUBLICATION DATA
Shipler, David K., 1942–
Russia: broken idols, solemn dreams / David K. Shipler—Rev.
and updated ed.
p.   cm.
Previously published: New York: Times Books, 1989.
ISBN 0 14 01.2271 0
1. Soviet Union—Description and travel—1970–   .2. Soviet Union—
Social conditions—1970–   .3. Soviet Union—Civilization—1917–
4. Shipler, David K., 1942–   —Journeys—Soviet Union.   I. Title.
DK29.S524   1989b
947.084—dc20   89-36297

Printed in the United States of America
Set in Garamond No. 3

Except in the United States of America, this
book is sold subject to the condition that it
shall not, by way of trade or otherwise, be lent,
re-sold, hired out, or otherwise circulated
without the publisher's prior consent in any form
of binding or cover other than that in which it
is published and without a similar condition
including this condition being imposed on the
subsequent purchaser.

For my mother,
Eleanor Karr Shipler

and my wife,
Debby

Contents

Foreword to the Revised Edition

Soviet customs officials have confiscated many copies of this book since it was first published in 1983. Readers have written to tell me the gruesome details: the menacingly polite request, "Do you have any books? May I see them?" followed by a glance at the cover and a flip through the pages and the judgment that the book is "anti-Soviet" and may not be carried into the Soviet Union.

Occasionally, travelers have been told that the volume will be held and then returned when they leave the country. One man's copy was seized when he arrived in Moscow and was returned to him when he left from Leningrad; another's was taken at Leningrad and given back upon his departure from Moscow.

Such reports grew less frequent after Mikhail S. Gorbachev became General Secretary of the Communist Party's Central Committee in March 1985. As he gradually opened the range of permissible debate and criticism, the Soviet borders became more permeable to ideas from the outside world. Therefore, I was curious to see what would happen when I took the book along on a visit to the Soviet Union in April 1988.

"Do you have any books? May I see them?" They were still checking, and thoroughly. As I pulled out books, magazines, and newspaper clippings, the customs officer behind the counter summoned two young plainclothesmen, smooth-faced English speakers. They looked through all the printed material with a chilling calm, spending more time with unfamiliar items than with my *Russia*; one of the men picked it up, read the title, flipped it open to make sure that the inside corresponded to the cover, and gave it back to me.

Indeed, everything was returned. Nothing was confiscated. And as I spent the next three weeks exploring the altered political landscape of the Soviet Union under Gorbachev, I kept thinking of this first encounter as a telling introduction to what I was finding there: The rules had been relaxed considerably, but the machinery of state control remained firmly in place, to be activated with ease if desired.

The Gorbachev era will enter history as a bold effort to revise some of the deepest political and cultural reflexes in Soviet society, an effort led by a man who displays only a dim understanding of the principles of free speech and democracy toward which he struggles to pull his country. Since the old political reflexes form the central theme of this book, which was written before Gorbachev, my task here is to revisit the attitudes I observed, to test my earlier conclusions, and to measure the force of the society's conservative instincts against the power of liberalization set loose by Gorbachev.

This I do in an epilogue, which becomes the final chapter of this new edition. The rest of the book remains substantially unchanged, since it focuses on durable features of Soviet society that have proven resistant to reform. They are characteristics that must be understood to grasp what Gorbachev confronts as he tries to drag the Soviet Union away from many of its own political traditions. The epilogue, therefore, is designed to add depth to the original by throwing those durable attributes into relief and by imparting a sense of motion to the portrayal of the Russians' search.

I am grateful to *The New York Times* for agreeing to my requests for a three-week working trip to the Soviet Union. It was the fourth and longest of six visits within two years, allowing me to contribute to a series of articles, from which some of the material in the epilogue is drawn.

D.K.S.
Washington
January 1989

Foreword

I set out for Moscow without thinking specifically of a book; it seemed sufficiently overwhelming to try to cover the Soviet Union for *The New York Times.* But as I worked there day to day, catching the most visible, transitory events for the headlines, I began to develop a strong feeling that, despite the broad opportunities for reporting provided in a newspaper like *The Times,* something was being left unsaid. Gradually this sense grew into a driving need to write in a more coherent and, hopefully, more durable manner on the themes of Soviet life, on the values that shaped the society as it entered the last quarter of the twentieth century. I wanted to look beneath the surface, past the leadership changes, dissidents' trials, economic statistics, and diplomatic negotiations, to dimensions of attitude and culture where the task was not so much to answer questions as to ask them, to find the right points of curiosity and wonder, and to give them reasonable voice.

Those who helped me the most in this were Russians, not only those who became friends, but many more with whom I crossed paths fleetingly, and who took the risk of giving me a flash of insight before moving on. Because of the danger to them and their families, I must avoid naming any of them here, as much as I would like to give them thanks. Those who can be identified are mentioned in the course of the text; others, who need to be disguised, are either left anonymous or are introduced with fictitious names, which on first reference are placed in quotation marks. All other details are accurate; some I have blurred into vagueness, but none have been changed or mixed together to make composite characters, which is a device I oppose absolutely.

Living and working as a correspondent in a foreign country is an experience of total immersion, and so your family becomes crucial to your own interaction with the place. When there is also hardship, their solidity and good cheer are essential to well-being. My wife, Debby, and our children, Jonathan, Laura, and Michael, all deserve enormous gratitude. Looking through my children's eyes, I saw much of what I never would have seen alone. And Debby's perceptions as a skilled teacher were essential to the first two chapters, on education, for she visited schools and kindergartens with me and helped analyze much of what we saw. She made valuable suggestions on the manuscript.

My appreciation goes to Marshall Shulman, who arranged for me to spend a semester of study at Columbia University's Russian Institute before going to Moscow, and lent me his office during his sabbatical; Nathalie Nabokoff, who forced me to learn Russian grammar before setting foot on Soviet soil; Hedrick Smith, who generously shared the contents of his address book, providing me with a long list of stimulating Russians to meet; Stephen F. Cohen of Princeton, whose perceptive assessments of Soviet society helped organize my thinking and focus my questioning; Christopher Wren and Craig Whitney, who became good friends as we shared the Moscow Bureau; and my other colleagues, whose insights were important, including especially Hal Piper, Kevin Ruane, and Chris Catlin. Harold Isaacs, whose thinking on group identity and other elements of human behavior has influenced me greatly, read the manuscript and made particularly helpful comments, as did Inessa Rubin, Valentin Turchin, and Anthony Austin. Julie Fallowfield and Ned Chase provided patient encouragement, which was instrumental in seeing this work to completion.

Russia today is only 1 of 15 republics in the Union of Soviet Socialist Republics, the Russians only 1 of more than 100 national, linguistic, and ethnic groups living across the face of that vast land. But because the Russians are the dominant group, numerically and politically, I have made them and those assimilated into their culture the focus here, allowing whatever variations exist among ethnic minorities to recede into the background, except where they take on significance for a specific subject at hand. Similarly, I have sometimes used "Russia" to mean the entire country. And since this book is for the general reader, I have given in to the convention of using the noun "Russians" to mean Soviet citizens of all national groups, while usually sticking to "Soviet" as the adjective. The exceptions to this come where the text clearly speaks of ethnic Russians, as distinguished from the general array of the Soviet population.

In transliterating Russian words and names, I have used the system employed by *The New York Times,* which omits soft signs and combines some double vowels. Occasionally I have deviated from the style by putting some proper names in forms more familiar to a non-Russian reader: Israel instead of Israil, for example, Herman instead of German.

For the titles of Chapters Two, Three, and Four, I owe gratitude to Samuel Taylor Coleridge, Ivan Turgenev, and George Orwell, respectively, with a caveat of apology to Coleridge, who meant his "willing suspension of disbelief" as praise for what he called the "poetic faith" of the creative mind. I have taken the liberty of giving his line a caustic twist.

Bits and pieces of some sections have appeared in other forms in my articles for *The New York Times,* including fragments of the following: the reporters' visit to the Azerbaijani village, the Siberian picnic, medical care, juvenile crime, Christianity, Stalinism, Russian nationalism, images of America, and social mobility. Aside from an occasional passage, however, this material is freshly written and analyzed, with little resemblance to the treatment I gave it in the news columns.

Despite the indebtedness I have to those who helped me, the judgments and perceptions are, ultimately, mine alone. And they must rely on my bias as well as my tolerance, for I am devoted to freedom of thought and word beyond any other principle. I cannot approach any society, including my own, divorced from this conviction. In the Soviet Union, it chafed against the pull of personal friendships with many Russians, against the fascination that I found in probing all facets of that great country. It drove me to try to unravel things, to seek to explain why. It left me unable to escape with only a single emotion; my feelings were too complex to be contained in either a plain affection or a simple distaste. I was always relieved to get away, and nostalgic when I left for good. In some measure, this book has been fashioned out of those contradictions.

D.K.S.
Jerusalem
February 1983

RUSSIA

INTRODUCTION
Russia Without Heroes

Every traveler is indiscreet, so it is necessary, as politely as possible, to keep track of the always too inquisitive foreigner lest he see things as they are—which would be the greatest of inconveniences.

—The Marquis de Custine, 1839

Autumn is the saddest season in Moscow. It comes too soon, furtively, dissolving the fleeting summer warmth in a haze of grey and rain. In the collective farmers' markets the crude wooden counters begin to lose their splashes of bright greens and reds, shifting into somber shades as squashes and nuts and potatoes appear, heaped in front of peasant men and women who have come on crowded trains and buses in the aching hours before dawn. In coarse, padded jackets, they stoop over their wares, their faces the color of burlap. Occasionally a gold tooth flashes in a clucking, coaxing smile of salesmanship, like the glint of gilt on a church's onion dome against the sunless city. The smells of the aging summer turn musty.

On such a day in September 1975, less than a week after I had arrived in Moscow, the sky seemed as if it would be forever sheathed in lead, and the city was cast in a chill gloom that confirmed the worst stereotypes I had brought with me, images of

3

overpowering drabness and cheerlessness. From my second-story office window I looked across a narrow street to a wall of bleak dun buildings, a view of what I imagined to be the monotony of Russian life.

Suddenly down the small street poured a stream of little school-girls, running, laughing, tripping, pulling at each other's long braids, all in matching brown dresses with pinafores starched and gleaming white in honor of the first day of school, all with pristine, elegantly tied ribbons in their hair. They were like fresh blossoms bursting out of a field of slate, their neat prettiness testimony to the devotion of a dozen mothers somewhere behind the austere walls of the city.

It was a surprise, a quick glimpse at a richer, warmer vein of Russia. And just as quickly the girls were gone, the street again grey and quiet. Of course, they were an illusion, too, a mirage of uni-formity and orderliness and gaiety, a neat veil prettily masking the diversity and hardships of Soviet life. Even the meticulously dressed schoolgirls, as I learned much later, wear subtly patterned stockings with their uniforms—a technical violation of the rules, overlooked by teachers—as a faint form of rebellion into individual expression. At an early age they acquire the technique of dodging and weaving in and around authority without confrontation, a skill vital in their adult lives.

As the illusions and images are peeled away one by one, Soviet society reveals itself as having grown more complex than it appears from outside. The variety of political thought is more extensive, the literature and theater and film more creative and truthful, the press more critical than many Americans imagine. It took me a full four years of living and traveling in the Soviet Union to arrive at some understanding of how minds are shaped, of how political values and social attitudes are absorbed by the young, of how it is to grow up in Russia long after the zeal of revolution has died. I encountered the anguish of men and women fighting to carve out for themselves some small zones of intellectual freedom, and I watched a few of them slide into either compromise or bitterness, either succumbing to the system's stifling demand for complete loyalty or pulling back and finally breaking painfully with the country they loved.

These private dramas are played out on a broad stage, where some of the most potent forces of modern civilization come together in turmoil. It has always been a paradox of Russia that despite its great isolation and inertia, it has been strangely vulnerable to ideas, and today stands at the confluence of conflicting currents of communism and Christianity, patriotism and materialism, an urbanization as anonymous as America's and a passion for order and authority alien to anything in the contemporary American experience. Remarkably, even beneath the state hierarchy's tough rules of debate and belief, many Russians have lost their heroes and their faith, their faith in their ideology and in their future. Some respond by retreating into their personal lives, neglecting the collectivism that is supposed to govern the country's social structure. Others idealize an irretrievable past rooted in rural simplicity and moral purity, a search for Russianness. These are more than drawing-room philosophies nourished by small handfuls of Moscow intellectuals; they catch a groundswell of tension and yearning that runs across the full sweep of Soviet society. How they bear on individual lives is a theme of this book.

Officials and ordinary Russians go to lengths to foil such discovery. Every foreigner who approaches Soviet life, whether journalist, scholar, diplomat, or businessman, inevitably finds himself like one of the blind men in the parable who grope against an elephant and draw conclusions from what they happen to touch: the tail like a rope; the leathery ear; the leg as thick and rough as a tree. Digging into a closed society requires humility. And so, "Once again," as George Feifer writes in *Our Motherland,* "a book about Russia begins with an apology."

Nothing in Communist rule has diminished the old instincts of insularity that thrived under the czars; nothing in the scientific, futuristic doctrine of Marxism-Leninism has reduced the distaste for introspection and the compulsion to mask unpleasantness, which were abiding features of Russian culture long before the Bolsheviks took power in 1917. Americans and West Europeans are invariably befuddled when they confront these traits face-to-face, regardless of how much they have read about them in advance. I was no exception, and I oscillated between being infuriated and amused. It took me some time before I realized that the art of dissembling was much more than mere censorship from above; rather it was a profound aversion to the Western habit of turning the darkest defects of society into the sunlight for ruthless scrutiny. Our delight in self-criticism, and our guilt when we fail to dissect ourselves with sufficient honesty, bring to Russians something close to visceral revulsion.

This once came home strongly when Yelena Aksyonova, a gifted Russian teacher who performed a miracle by getting me to the point where I could speak her language, scolded me for a criticism I made of a United States government exhibition in Moscow, which I thought put a misleadingly good face on American life. Yelena was no dissident. On the contrary, she was blindly loyal to her country and her system, a deep patriot so warmhearted that her countrymen felt like family to her. Every saccharine short story about Soviet suffering and heroism in World War II (and these were my steady diet of readings until I rebelled and insisted on Chekhov) brought tears to her eyes. Every good word from me about the attractiveness of a city I had just visited or the kindness of a Russian I had met had her reaching for her handkerchief and blinking in pride. She was not a limited woman. She was well traveled, having lived in India with her husband, a Communist Party member and expert in Indian dialects. She was well read, though she found Dostoyevsky rather gloomy and uncomfortable. Plump, neatly dressed and in her fifties, I would guess, she carried herself with an air of propriety, not stiffly or remotely, but possessed of an impervious confidence that discouraged discussions about weakness or injustice in Soviet society. When I returned from visiting the Moscow exhibit on America put on for the Bicentennial by the then United States Information Agency, I told Yelena, who was planning to go, that the displays had been less than candid. Life in America was presented as an endless run of suburban luxury, and while old photographs of Depression bread lines were included, there was almost nothing about present-day poverty, little hint of the corrosive difficulties of drugs, crime, racial discrimination. If I expected Yelena, the diehard Soviet partisan, to deplore the attempt to hide American problems, I could not have been more ignorant. She was horrified at me. This was supposed to be a celebration, she said, the 200th anniversary of my country's founding. Why should a government, celebrating such a momentous occasion, publicize problems? It was simply unthinkable.

A Western journalist deals constantly in the unthinkable, making him something less than a welcome guest in a country where taboos encompass subjects of the most routine newspaper reporting at home. Ask a simple question on an unspeakable topic, and you might as well put a live grenade on a coffee table: Everybody in the room dives for cover. This happened to me soon after I arrived. I made a trip to Murmansk, a bleak city of prefabricated apartment houses, which are eating away at the quaint neighborhoods of weathered wooden *izbas,* peasant bungalows put up in a massive rebuilding effort after the war. Murmansk is the world's only full-fledged metropolis north of the Arctic Circle, and it never sees the sun in the depth of winter. The perpetual darkness is softened only for a few hours across the middle of the day, when the sun hovers just below the horizon and casts a thin grey light, as in the first trace of dawn. Temperatures are kept about the same as in Moscow, nearly 1,000 miles to the south, by the Gulf Stream, which spends its last warmth in the Barents Sea. But there is an icy wind that rips in from the water, driving needles of frozen mist stinging against the skin. With wan humor the city's residents paint their buildings in pastels, adorn schoolhouse walls with murals of beaches and palms, and fill lobbies with houseplants kept lush by sun lamps.

For several days I had been guided around with utmost courtesy by a local newspaperman from *Polyarnaya Pravda* ("Polar Truth"), who had answered all my questions except one. I had wanted to know something about the breakdown of the city's working population among service industries, manufacturing, fishing, and navy. The Murmansk area is well known as a major base of the Soviet Navy, but somehow local officials, usually armed with bushels of meaningless statistics to dump on visitors, could not come up with data on this point. The mayor, Viktor Romanyenko, didn't bother to include sailors in his breakdown of the work force, though they were all over the streets in uniform. I thought it was important to know sociologically, just as it is important to know it about Norfolk, Virginia, or any other navy town, because it affects the character of the place. So I pursued the question.

I had invited a sociologist, a newspaper editor, and the city's chief architect for a discussion in my hotel room over a table loaded with *zakuski,* assorted platters of sliced fish and salami, chopped beet and cabbage salads, globs of red and black caviar smothering halves of boiled eggs. These form the mainstay of any Russian cocktail, washed down by small glasses of vodka and cognac, which must be thrown back in fiery gulps and laced with effusive toasts to peace and friendship and understanding. We were well along in this ritual and having an animated talk until the moment I asked how many Murmansk residents were in the navy. The men fell into silence. They suddenly found fascinating things to stare at on the floors and in the far corners of the room. The stretch of quiet lengthened. At last the sociologist, Grigory Benkevich, tossed the grenade back into my lap, asking menacingly what such a question had to do with life in Murmansk, supposedly my subject. The architect, Feliks Taksis, followed with a disingenuous soliloquy on his frequent travel in the Murmansk area to plan new towns, "and I have never once seen any navy," he declared. I gave up and passed on to the next topic. The group relaxed.

Military secrecy is so broadly defined that Westerners need to develop a whole new set of instincts when they get to the Soviet Union. Officials and much of the population proceed as if they were in the midst of a conventional war, one predating the high technology of reconnaissance satellites and intercontinental nuclear-tipped missiles. No pictures may be taken of bridges, ports, railway junctions, men in uniform, police stations, or military installations, except with special permission. No photography whatever is allowed from airliners, as if the Pentagon's satellites were not repeatedly recording every visible detail of Soviet territory. I once met an ex-Aeroflot stewardess from Soviet Armenia who said she had worked for the KGB, the secret police, fingering foreign tourists who broke the rules on her flights. She was barred from emigrating because of this work and because, one KGB man told her, "You know the map of the Soviet Union."

Even the weather is considered a security item with military implications—and rightly so, as Napoleon discovered. Only in the late 1970's did Soviet newspapers begin publishing weather maps. An American reporter on a story about Russians' New Year celebrations once called the Meteorological Service to find out how much snow had fallen in a storm that day. His question was met with suspicion. "Why," he could almost feel the person thinking at the other end of the line, "should an American imperialist propagandist wish to know such a thing?" Finally he was told that if he wanted the information, he must write a letter to the Protocol Department.

It is a flexible paranoia, though, tempered by momentary considerations of politics and public relations. A possibly apocryphal story went the rounds of the Moscow press corps that in the full bloom of détente, when Soviet officials were trying to avoid any unpleasant incidents with Americans (even correspondents), an American newsman was traveling in some provincial capital, idly taking pictures of street scenes, when he was grabbed and hauled to the nearest KGB office by four or five irate Soviet citizens. They brought him before the duty officer and pronounced "this foreigner" guilty of photographing something that he shouldn't have —a soldier on the street, perhaps, or an unmarked building that had a military function. The KGB man asked for the foreigner's identification and, discovering that he was an American correspondent accredited by the Foreign Ministry, knew this was a problem. So the resourceful duty officer gave the conscientious citizens his warm praise for their vigilance and handed them a stack of complicated forms. "You have served the motherland nobly, comrades," he said. "Please go into the next room and fill these out in triplicate." When they had left, murmuring to each other in satisfied tones, the KGB man turned to the American. "And you," he commanded, "get out of here."

I was not allowed to fly to Murmansk. As a foreigner I was permitted to go only by train, two nights and a day each way. Why? "There are no flights," said the Intourist clerk.

"There are Aeroflot flights every day," I protested.

"Not for foreigners," she said.

I supposed that this was a precaution against foreigners' seeing the immense naval bases in the vicinity, and I told a middle-aged party member in Murmansk how silly it seemed, considering the proficiency of satellite technology. He replied, "You know it's stupid, and I know it's stupid, but . . ." and then he smiled and shrugged a wonderful shrug that contained all the inner contradiction of an official's simultaneous loyalty to the system and to his own common sense. The rule was later changed, and foreigners could go by air. But I had only the train, and it was delightful.

Called the *Arktika,* it left in the evening from Moscow's Leningrad Station, from which all northbound trains depart. Snow was falling, and the narrow platforms were filled with jostling men and women, bumping past each other in their heavy coats, pushing along with overstuffed shopping bags and bulging suitcases, the snow like powdered sugar dusting mustaches and dark fur hats and curly astrakhan wool collars. The train was long. At the door of each pine green car stood a uniformed attendant, usually a woman, checking tickets, watching impassively as friends and family hugged and kissed each other in fervent good-byes. The crystal smell of the winter air was swept from time to time by pungent coal smoke from the samovar and heater at the end of each car. Inside, water was being boiled for tea.

I had a cozy compartment, called "soft" rather than "first class" to avoid ideological complications. It contained only two bunks, while "hard" contained four. I was alone. The train began to move, and the streetlights, each catching a globe of swirling snow, slid by silently outside the window. Even in the daytime there would be little to see for the next thirty-six hours but the soothing northern forests of Russia, a quiet green cut by snowy waves of blinding whiteness, spotted now and then by tiny villages—collective farms, mostly—clusters of wooden *izbas* huddled together in the deep snow, smoke puffing from their chimneys.

In the dining car, over a dinner of stroganoff (the only choice) the second evening, I shared a table with Volodya, a twenty-one-year-old bricklayer with blond hair over his ears and a gaping hole where two front teeth should have been. Married with a four-month-old daughter, he had quit school in eighth grade because he found it dull and wanted to get out and work, do something useful. "There are a lot of engineers and so forth," he said, "but where do they live? In houses. And who builds the houses? I do." And he flashed a scraggly grin.

He was my first encounter with Russian generosity, which can come suddenly like a flash flood and then dry up quickly, leaving barely a trace. And he was my first lesson in how I would have to probe Soviet society, catching the bits and fragments as they came, saving them for later, hoping that when added to others, they would eventually form a mosaic that would give some coherent picture. Volodya was on his way from his small village to Murmansk, where his mother lived, with some raw cranberries he had picked before the autumn frosts and had kept frozen since. On the train he stored them between cars where sub-zero winds roared. He asked if I'd like to taste some, and when I said sure, he appeared after dinner in my compartment, carrying about a kilogram wrapped in old newspaper. The car's attendant brought steaming tea in two glasses resting in silver-handled holders, *podstakanniki,* and we sat eating the frosty, sour berries, drinking sweet tea, and talking.

Volodya had a lot to say. He admitted that Soviet construction was shoddy. He said that despite his youth, he felt the pain of the war strongly. He declared that he thought men should help women more in the house, though he admitted that he didn't come up to his own standards on that score. And he described his image of the United States as a place with "lots of murders, big cities, many robberies—at least that's what they write in the press. I don't know whether it's true or not." On his lapel he wore an interesting little blue and white *znachok,* one of the pins turned out in the thousands by factories, city councils, schools, sports teams, collective farms, and on every conceivable occasion and anniversary. These lapel pins fuel fads and feverish trading among kids, who collect them and bargain for them as hotly as I did for baseball cards years ago. The *znachok,* Volodya said, was for sharpshooting. He belonged to a rifle club, and the pin was obviously a treasure to him. He took it off and handed it to me so I could have a closer look. But when I tried to give it back, he wouldn't take it. "You keep it," he said. I objected. He insisted. And there was nothing I could do. I have it still.

We talked some more, and when it grew late and the sway and click of the train on the rails began to make us sleepy, Volodya got up to leave. There was a mound of cranberries left on the open sheets of newspaper, but he wouldn't take them either. They were a gift, he said. What about his mother? "Oh, I have more," he said, and with his scraggly grin he disappeared into the corridor.

He would be in Murmansk when I was, but he did not take up my suggestion that we get together there. It was safe to cross paths with an American by chance on a train; to pursue the relationship further would take him beyond an invisible line into a danger zone, not a danger of arrest anymore, as under Stalin, but a risk of losing access to some privilege or position. Perhaps he would want to join the Communist Party someday or take a trip abroad. It would be better to have a clean record. The less prudent sometimes find themselves actively discouraged by KGB agents who summon them for a round of uncomfortable questions, a technique most effective against loyal citizens who are integrated into the society's official values. These are people, called "straights" in the idiom of the Moscow press corps, with a stake in the rewards and security that the system can provide or withhold. They are vulnerable, therefore. An American exchange student told me of a straight he met on a train, a tough, polemical man whose conversation was laced with invective against the United States. At a stop the man got off to stretch his legs and was approached on the platform by a plain-clothesman. When he returned to the compartment, he asked the student for the piece of paper on which he had written his address and phone number in case the American wanted to look him up sometime. When the student returned it, the man tore it up, then moved to another compartment.

My most disappointing experience of this kind occurred after an evening at the apartment of a film critic who had become a friend to my wife, Debby, and me. He and his wife invited us to their new flat in a colorless neighborhood of enormous high-rise buildings at the most distant edge of Moscow. It was a district reminiscent of the gigantic American urban renewal projects of the 1950's, when architects and planners seemed oblivious to the need of people to feel some relationship with their structural environment, lest they see themselves as dwarfed, insignificant. Every older city in the Soviet Union is now encircled by these mammoth high-rises, marching into the countryside, usually well ahead of telephone cables, movie theaters, department stores, and other amenities, which are destined to follow only years later. But our friends were happy there: The air was clean, and the small apartment was entirely theirs, without the grinding friction common in the crowded flats of the city center, where several families often share a single apartment, each cloistered in its own room and using the kitchen and bathroom in shifts.

The critic had invited some of his other friends, among them an actor who did card tricks by mental telepathy and "Furtsev," a former Soviet diplomat presently on the staff of the Central Committee of the Communist Party. This was extraordinary. The Central Committee, along with the Secretariat and the Politburo, is the inner sanctum of Soviet political power. It is not accessible to Westerners of any sort except on a highly controlled basis in the form of rare and often rigidly formal interviews. Certainly for an American correspondent to spend a social evening with a staffer, who may know as much as many committee members themselves, is practically unheard of. That dissidents openly critical of the regime feel freer than party officials to form friendships with Western journalists is one of the bizarre ironies of a system sensitive to its public image. People who would give it a positive report are cut off in effect, forcing journalists to work for some years cultivating contacts, building up sources, and hoping—usually in vain—that some relaxed relationships can be found with Russians who exist wholly and happily within the system.

It had taken me a long time to get to the evening with this man Furtsev. He was in his mid-forties, precisely dressed, very poised and polished, with a well-rehearsed manner of easy charm and careful control which I had come to know as a fairly typical feature of the party *apparatchiki* I had met. He wanted to talk mostly about cars. He was quite an auto buff and drove a Ford, which he had somehow, through his pull, managed to get into the country. He wanted to know much more about the latest American models than I was able to tell him. Only eventually could I pull him away from this favorite subject of his and turn the conversation to other matters.

We had some interesting talk on his perceptions of Western democracies, where he had served as an embassy officer. We spoke of the war's effect on the Russian psyche, and we talked of film and theater. But it was just a tantalizing appetizer, and I wanted more. I suggested that we get together again, and he said sure, fine, love to. The invisible barrier seemed to have been overcome. When the party began to break up about midnight, there was some talk about Furtsev's catching a ride with us since his beloved Ford was in a garage for repair. In the end, as we walked downstairs, our host maneuvered him into the actor's car, we promised to contact each other soon, and Debby and I gave a lift to another guest, a young relative of the critic.

I did not move quickly enough. A month or two later Furtsev was summoned by his superior, according to our mutual friend. He was sternly reprimanded for meeting with me and especially for riding in my car, where he had presumably had a private conversation whose contents he had never reported. Of course, he had not been in my car; only in the apartment on the way out had there been some discussion of his going with me. Probably the flat was bugged, and the KGB did not catch the conversation on the stairway down. Or the building was staked out and the agents misidentified the bundled figures emerging into the black winter night, saying their good-byes, and getting into various cars. Whatever the reasons for the inaccurate surveillance, the authorities' concern over an alleged, unheard conversation in my car seemed to reinforce what I had believed for a long time—that my little orange Zhiguli, a Soviet-made Fiat, had not been equipped with expensive eavesdropping devices.

Furtsev was threatened with the loss of his post, the disintegration of his career. But he was evidently as tough as his boss, in the version I heard. He denied being in my car and said that after years of serving in Western capitals he did not need lectures on how to converse with Americans. He also promised, if his dismissal were attempted, to fight it into the upper hierarchy of the party. This was a canny move by a well-seasoned political professional who knew the passion with which his colleagues avoided bureaucratic conflict. So he kept his job. But they had their way, too: He would never see me again.

I puzzled over what the authorities thought this man might tell me. He was no liberal. From the Soviet Communist perspective, he had a healthy distaste for Western pluralism, and he displayed a mystical, almost angry patriotism for Russia. He was very articulate and adept at explaining the Soviet view of the world, and the view he offered was of a planet shaped by its two political poles. Virtue was on the Soviet side, which America had tried again and again over the decades to wound. The West, in whose democracies he had lived for some years, whose technological gadgets he adored, whose languages he spoke with enviable fluency, was profoundly alien to him. He seemed beyond reach, somehow, and so did I to him. That is why we intrigued each other. And perhaps that is what the authorities did not want us to explore.

Most of my efforts to establish lasting relationships, even formal ones, with Communist Party officials did not succeed. There were Soviet journalists and editors who were, in effect, licensed to see American correspondents regularly for stiff discussions of foreign policy, but even they turned these relationships on and off according to higher instructions. Casual social encounters were discouraged. A relatively candid conversation with a straight had little chance of happening more than once, and it was wise to make the most of it, not to assume that a relationship would have an opportunity to grow and deepen over time.

Encounters with Russians fell into several categories. There were official contacts, including scientists, schoolteachers, economic planners, doctors, factory managers, mayors, farm directors, and others in many fields who would grant cautious interviews upon the approval of their superiors. There were dissidents in great variety, not only the best-known Jews who wished to emigrate and rights activists, such as Andrei Sakharov, who wished to stay and humanize the system, but also less visible ethnic nationalists such as Ukrainian and Georgian separatists, devout religious believers in the Russian Orthodox Church and various fundamentalist Protestant sects, "underground" artists whose work was officially unacceptable, writers who could be published only in the West, and blue-collar workers with bitter complaints about authoritarian bosses and corruption. There were down-and-out people well outside the ranks of the dissidents but anxious to tell an American a personal story of suffering. There were those met by chance, the Volodyas on the trains to Murmansk, who were willing to have some good conversation. There were, finally, those suspended between open dissent and normal adjustment, working in approved roles by day and by night engaging in astonishing political irreverence, enjoying the company of Americans and Western Europeans with whom they could speak freely. Every one of these relationships, no matter how lasting or transitory, carried a special burden: No casual banter, no searching talk was ever free of the fact that I was an American. The fact inhibited some and relaxed others, with some growing more circumspect with me than with fellow Russians and others delighting in the excuse to examine their society through the critical eye of an outsider.

Foreigners, and Americans in particular, have a special place in Russians' emotions. We are fascinating and frightening, embodying the forbidden and forbidding world outside. Anxious to impress us, afraid of what we will say, nervous about our contaminating effect on the population, officials pamper us and try to isolate us. The result is that we live neither wholly within Soviet society nor completely outside it. At the gates of most apartment buildings where foreigners are housed—in markedly better conditions than Soviet citizens—a "militiaman," as Russians call their policeman, stands guard on rotating shifts, twenty-four hours a day. He is there ostensibly to protect us and our property from unwanted intruders, but of course, his function is to monitor our movements and screen out casual contacts with Russians. The fiction that he is there for our benefit is so important to the authorities, however, that it takes on a reality firmer than reality itself, just as many fictions in Soviet life do. Whenever we invited a Russian to dinner, I had to meet him out on the street and escort him past the mili-man, as Americans called the guard. Because of the fiction that we were being protected, our escort was enough to get any guest in. Even if he was a prominent and outspoken dissident openly critical of the regime, just the sort the authorities would rather we did not have to dinner, the mili-man would usually let him pass with nothing more than a hard stare. After all, he could not be an unwanted intruder if he was being brought in by a building resident. Otherwise the fiction might begin to appear fictional.

Once, a Russian managed to slip past the mili-man and into my office by dressing up like his image of an Englishman. He carried a pipe, which Russians rarely smoke (his was unlit), donned some thin-rimmed antique spectacles, and pushed out the top of a felt hat to make it look like a bowler. He simply strolled confidently past the guard, went into the first entrance he found and into the first news office he came to, which happened to be mine. He said he knew Philip Short of the BBC and left some statements for him on a dissident theme. Oddly, Philip, it turned out later, had never heard of him. And he could not find the man's name on a list of people his predecessor had given him.

One of our mili-men, tall with a close-cropped brown mustache, used to engage us in conversation as we walked by, and although some of my colleagues felt he was trying to worm information out of them on their activities, I enjoyed stopping and passing the time of day. He once asked me about *The New York Times*—the biggest American paper, he said. I corrected him on that, explaining that it was not the largest in circulation or income, though it probably was in influence. Ah, he said, it's your "central newspaper." In the Soviet Union the central newspaper is *Pravda*—the paper of the Communist Party's Central Committee. So I went through my patient explanation—already well tested on dozens of other Russians who thought that our world looked like their world—that we have no state-run or party papers to articulate government views. Understanding came slowly into his eyes. "You mean anybody can just start up a newspaper, any private person, without permission?" Yes, I said, if he's got the money. He was genuinely fascinated; you could almost imagine gears and ratchets clicking into new patterns inside his head. Within several weeks he was transferred away from our building to the West German Embassy, where diplomats hurried busily by without time to talk.

Much Russian insularity can be explained by an aversion to alien ideas, especially those in which the competing system appears more attractive than Soviet socialism. Much also results from the universal bureaucratic instinct for self-preservation, which operates as effectively in Moscow or Omsk as within any corporation in New York or Omaha. Nobody who wants to keep his job is going to make public criticisms of his superiors in any of those places. But at least in New York there are competing hierarchies and sovereign, disparate interest groups; if one cannot expect criticism of AT&T from inside, it will come from outside. In Moscow there is no outside. The hierarchy is totally enveloping, and the chain of command from the lowliest assembly-line worker to the Stalin or the Khrushchev or the Brezhnev or the Andropov at the pinnacle is unbroken, deriving from comprehensive government ownership and party control. Even putting aside the emotional winds that have blown through Russia for centuries and have shaped its secretive reflexes, no Russian acting wholly rationally today would see his personal interest advanced by talking to a *New York Times* correspondent about problems on his job, any more than that correspondent would gain the favor of his editors by talking with the *Columbia Journalism Review* about the problems on his job (in the unlikely event that there were any). The difference is that if it comes to a matter of integrity, there is no place for the Russian to go. He is trapped forever, and he speaks truthfully at great sacrifice.

The well-honed skill for avoiding self-injury was displayed by two officials I interviewed in the Ministry of Health, physicians who had become consummate bureaucrats running vast governmental programs. A few weeks earlier the health minister, Dr. Boris Petrovsky, had published a brief article in the Soviet paper *Trud* complaining about inadequate manufacture of medical supplies such as thermometers, surgical instruments, and X-ray equipment. This was typical of the carefully channeled and sanitized criticism that strikes at inefficiency and middle management, but never at the system or its highest officials. As safe as it was, having been scrubbed and cleared for publication under the minister's name, the two doctors refused to discuss the subject. They would rather have had me quote the minister from an approved statement, already published, than be quoted themselves, even if they said precisely the same thing. Such careful cultivation of greyness and invisibility is a key to success in the Soviet hierarchy.

The Russian suspicion of inquisitiveness has deep roots, as the Marquis de Custine discovered in his nineteenth-century travels, and as Maxim the Greek found even earlier when he arrived in Moscovy in 1518. Maxim, a monk, had been invited by Grand Prince Basil III to revise liturgical texts, but he was never allowed to leave, being told, "We are in fear: thou, a man of learning, comest to us and hast seen here of our best and worst, and when thou goest hence thou wilt tell of everything." In 1556 poor Maxim died in a monastery near Moscow. In 1977 a Moscow police lieutenant stopped a newsman from filming the giant Rossiya Hotel after a bad fire in which at least twenty people had been killed (though no official figures were ever released) and told the offending correspondent, Fritz Pleitgen of German television, "We do not want to let foreigners laugh at our misfortune."

Russians reveal themselves in such remarks more completely than by relaxing and letting the foreigner see what he may. In all my experience in the Soviet Union, through more than 40,000 miles of travel and thirty-six cities, that policeman's statement remains with me as one of the most haunting expressions of the dark agony in the Russian's sense of himself and of the larger world. To imagine that foreigners are eager to laugh over a tragic hotel fire must require an extraordinary measure of self-persecution, an anger and fear and loneliness of unfathomable pain. To see a facet of the mind laid bare is certainly worth the momentary inconvenience of a picture untaken or a question unanswered.

I once attended a criminal trial of three teenagers in the small border town of Brest, where about $1,000 worth of my personal belongings had been stolen from a moving van en route to Moscow. The three boys, sixteen, seventeen, and eighteen, had confessed to this and three other burglaries; the proceeding was being held to determine sentence.

Apparently the authorities wanted no slipups in the presence of an American correspondent. Presiding in the small courtroom, beneath a looming black-and-white drawing of Lenin, was none other than the chief judge of the People's Court of Brest. Attorney for the people was the town's chief prosecutor, decked out in a neatly pressed prosecutor's uniform, which is rarely worn to routine court appearances. The trial went two full days, much longer than usual in such cases.

As a victim I was given the right to question the defendants and the witnesses and to make motions, as were the boys, their parents, and their lawyers. This is customary in Soviet courts, but there was one major deviation from normal practice: When I was called to testify, the judge asked me what punishment I thought the boys should receive. I was unprepared for the question and flabbergasted that an American should be asked to advise a Soviet court. But after having heard their teachers, Komsomol leaders, and others talk about them for two days, having heard how they stole things and then became afraid of having them and so burned them or dumped them in the river, I felt they needed skilled and intensive help of whatever sort the society could provide. I told the court that prison, which often produces people who then repeat their crimes, was not the answer. I hoped the judges would not send them to jail. I said I did not want to see young lives ruined.

When it came time for summing up, the prosecutor began by telling the court how rare such cases were (not true) and then asked for suspended sentences, citing my testimony in the most flowery terms, "taking into account that David Shipler, who suffered considerable material damage, showed high humanitarianism as man and father and asked the People's Court not to deprive the defendants of freedom. . . ."

The first defense attorney (each boy had his own) then opened by arguing that "crime is alien to our socialist society," thus removing any mitigating social reason for his client's actions. "Why did he steal all that food and clothing?" the lawyer asked. "We know he is well clothed and is provided with everything he needs for study and life." No economic causes there. No attempt to explain and thereby soften the guilt. When the third attorney rose to make his final argument on behalf of the eighteen-year-old, the one most likely to get a prison sentence because of his age, he was obviously more interested in defending his country than his client.

He was an older man, grey-haired in a yellow shirt and an orange and blue tie, and a forceful orator. The case, he said, had international implications because one of the victims was an American citizen. Such cases were rather infrequent "because the majority of our youth behaves correctly—all their thoughts and actions are aimed at becoming true builders of communism in their country." So these three, he stressed, did not characterize Soviet youth. This was an isolated instance. Brest's young people were exemplary. Some, he declared, had even been invited recently to participate in an art colloquium in Paris. The Soviet circus with its many young people had been to America, he observed, where it had been applauded. And he was sure that Mr. Shipler had applauded it in Moscow, too. Then the climax: "I do not agree with Mr. Shipler when he says that when a man gets into prison, he is not a man any longer. Our system is not like yours in America. We do not have the problem of repeated crime." Having made a good argument for why his client should be sent to one of those nice, humane Soviet prisons for rehabilitation, he then asked perfunctorily that the boy be kept out of jail. And despite the good case the defense attorney had made for the virtue of Soviet prisons, the court pronounced suspended sentences on the three boys.

There were several other occasions on which I learned more from the contortions aimed at preventing me from learning anything than I would have by seeing what I was not supposed to see. Once I was met at the gate of a collective farm by the deputy director. "What's the full name of the farm?" I asked.

He stiffened. "Please ask all questions of the director," he said, escorting me inside.

Part of the treat of this learning experience was exposure to a Russian form of behavior that can actually become endearing if you approach it in the right spirit, much as bargaining in a Mediterranean or Middle Eastern marketplace can be enjoyable even while you are being cheated, provided you begin with a smile. This is the notorious custom of *vranyo,* which dictionaries translate inadequately as "lies." Really it is something closer to "leg-pulling, ribbing, or blarney."* A Russian friend explained *vranyo* this way: "You know I'm lying, and I know that you know, and you know that I know that you know, but I go ahead with a straight face, and you nod seriously and take notes."

Once, in the Transcaucasian republic of Azerbaijan, there occurred a vivid combination of *vranyo* and another art known as *pokazukha,* which is a phony show or a snow job usually put on for people of high standing. Nearly 200 years before I saw it attempted in Azerbaijan, it was perfected by Prince Grigory Potemkin for the benefit of Catherine the Great. She was anxious to see that some newly won southern territories in 1787 were well populated, so the prince obliged by erecting stage façades to look like villages as she passed by at a distance. Hence the epithet "Potemkin village." The Azerbaijanis, a Turkic people with a century of domination by the Great Russians behind them, have produced officials with similar impulses.

We were about thirty Moscow-based journalists from the United States, Japan, Western Europe, and several Communist countries on a tour organized by the Foreign Ministry. We rode one day into the countryside for a visit to a sleepy and pleasantly shabby provincial town called Kuba, the center of a state farm. We might as well have been a high-powered delegation of diplomats or senators. The policemen in the town all wore shiny new epaulets. Schoolgirls were waiting with flowers. Along the roads our bus was to take, the first several rows of the fields and orchards had been newly harrowed for the sake of neatness. If our goal was to have a look at Soviet rural life, we failed in the face of the impenetrable courtesy and theatrical proficiency of the reception.

The welcome was generous and friendly, falling somewhere between a military inspection and a chamber of commerce presentation. Wine was abundant, but candor was scarce. Questions were invited, but answers were evasive. Problems were never mentioned. The farm director, Ismail Udumov, who was dressed incongruously in a gleaming white shirt and dark suit and tie as if he were

*In the words of Ronald Hingley, who devotes fourteen pages to *vranyo* in *The Russian Mind* (New York: Charles Scribner's Sons, 1977).

off to a funeral, took us to an apple orchard whose earth had just been turned over that morning, for no obvious purpose except appearance. Down the rows a bit, almost out of sight, the weeds began.

We were taken to a farm worker's house, an enormous place with endless rooms laden with brand-new carpets, crisp new curtains, blankets so fresh from the shops that they were still in plastic wrappings. "This is the home of a 'typical worker,' " a Hungarian reporter said to me under his breath, his eyes rolling in sarcasm. He was later bawled out by his ambassador in Moscow for the remark, even though I identified him only as a nameless Hungarian in a story for *The Times.*

We went into the kitchen, to be confronted by a gleaming new refrigerator. I opened the door. It was completely empty except for a pitcher of water and a small plate of greens. It seemed entirely possible that it had been brought in just that morning and that when the busload of reporters had rumbled out of sight, burly men would clump into the kitchen and carry it away.

I had another revealing encounter with a refrigerator a couple of years later and a couple of thousand miles to the east in a handsome log cabin on a collective farm near Siberia's Lake Baikal. A group of us were again treated to a display of workers' comforts when Kevin Klose of *The Washington Post,* remembering my story about the refrigerator in Azerbaijan, spied another new one here in the wilderness, winked at me knowingly, and opened the door. There, stacked solidly inside, were piles of old newspapers, leaving not a single cubic inch for anything resembling food.

The officials who put on these grand tours of Soviet achievements often have a marvelous stage presence. They greet every visitor with a brisk friendliness, whisking him in chauffeur-driven Volga sedans to appointment after appointment, showering him with smiles and handshakes and toasts, a warmth that once led Peter Osnos of *The Washington Post* to observe rightly, "If a Soviet journalist showed up in Kansas, I don't think he'd get much better." Occasionally the hospitable veneer cracks, however. The visitor suddenly slips from his exalted station as honored guest to his truer position as the day's number one nuisance. Everything was fine in Azerbaijan until the typical worker took some of us outside his typical house, back to a small barnyard that was typically dirty like barnyards in all the world. When I began taking pictures of him and his daughter, Udumov, the dark-suited farm director, raced up, shrieking, "Why are you taking pictures here? Why here? Take them back at the house!" and shoved me roughly out of the barnyard. He had panicked because some unpainted wooden outbuildings stood in the background of my scene. And he shot the worker an extremely mean look.

We were all then herded onto the bus (amid protests from some reporters, who wanted to talk to random workers rather than typical ones) and taken back to town for a feast of a lunch that went on and on, course after course, into the afternoon. A few of us ducked out between dishes and tried to have a look around Kuba. It was a slow-paced town with dull brown stucco buildings and ambling streets lined heavily with trees. Local people waved at us cheerfully, and a cluster of kids playing soccer in a dusty lot invited a couple of us to join their game. All the while smartly dressed security men scampered after us nervously, calling us smilingly back for the next course. When I finally set off alone down a dirt road past run-down shacks reminiscent of rural poverty in Appalachia, an agent ran up behind, yelling merrily, "They want you back at the restaurant!"

The Foreign Ministry officials from Moscow, a trifle more worldly than our local hosts, had the good sense to be embarrassed. But in other places this was not always so. Sometimes the worldly diplomats displayed a skill of their own in such affairs. On a trip to a scientific pig-producing farm, a group of journalists—mostly from Eastern Europe, Mongolia, Cuba, Vietnam, and other points in the Soviet sphere—were first lectured at for an hour or more and then put directly back on the bus without ever laying eyes on a pig. The two or three Westerners in the group raised a fuss. How could they visit a pig farm without seeing a single pig? The schedule, said the Foreign Ministry escort, would not allow it. The schedule must be kept. The objections continued. The official explained that to keep sanitary standards, the visitors would have to shower and change into sterile gowns before entering the barns, and that would be time-consuming. The earnest reporters said they would be happy to do that. So the Foreign Ministry man turned to the American who had been making the loudest noise and suggested that perhaps the decision should be taken by an American-style democratic vote.

The American knew what was coming, but how could he disagree? He was supposed to be the advocate of democracy. The Foreign Ministry man was smiling. How many wanted to stay and see a pig? Not one Hungarian or Pole or East German or Vietnamese or Cuban raised his hand. "It seems you are in the minority," the official said pleasantly. And the outvoted Westerners took their seats as the bus rumbled off.

At other times officials seemed less nervous, more considerate of a reporter's need to get the feel of a place, interview people, dig a bit, and understand. The result was an odd mixture of latitude and control, cooperation and interference. Occasionally the conflicting gestures put officials at odds with each other.

About a dozen American correspondents once toured the rich Tyumen oil-producing area in Western Siberia, a trip that had taken months to arrange and required extensive coordination by various government ministries. We were seated around a table laden with the inevitable bottles of mineral water, trying unsuccessfully to get some answers about oil production from a balding bureaucrat who was sweating under the cross-examination but evading the questions relentlessly. Finally a local Soviet television journalist, who was evidently much more than a reporter, cut into the repartee and said firmly and loudly to the poor bureaucrat, "Apparently you have not understood the question." Then he repeated the question in a tone that left no doubt that it should be answered. It was.

At a bridge-building plant in the grimy industrial city of Ulan-Ude near Lake Baikal, the factory manager, Vladimir Chernobylsky, engaged in a bit of *vranyo* and was caught up short. He told a few of us that he didn't have figures yet on the plant's production for the previous year. We all knew that the data had already been collected nationwide and published some weeks before. To make matters worse for him, I had spotted a chart in the corridor outside his office showing serious shortfalls in output. When I quoted the numbers to him, he succumbed and gave us the full totals. A few days later, as we were set to leave Ulan-Ude, an extremely bright party official, Lev Pokhosoyev, the chief of the district party committee's science and education department, told us that he and the Foreign Ministry escort from Moscow had scolded Chernobylsky for his lack of candor (or, more probably, for getting caught). It is easy to imagine the factory manager's complete bewilderment at being criticized for playing the game, even if sloppily.

The target of *pokazukha* is often more exalted. When President Gerald Ford visited Vladivostok in 1974, officials decided to make the route he would take in from the airport picturesque, so they moved people out of wooden *izbas* along the road and burned the buildings. Then they cut down fir trees from a nearby forest, brought them in, and stuck them upright in the deep snow along the road. When Pierre Trudeau, the prime minister of Canada, visited the remote northern city of Norilsk in 1971, a team of waiters from the Prague and Metropole hotel restaurants in Moscow were flown up and outfitted in blazers labeled "Norilsk" to look like local folks. As Mr. Trudeau motored around the city, he attracted enthusiastic crowds, which must have flattered him. But the reason was that the authorities had shipped a big black Chaika limousine up to Norilsk, where such fanciness does not exist, and residents were out on the streets, gaping and shouting to each other, "Look at the Chaika! Look at the Chaika!"

Every outsider who lives in the Soviet Union for a time has his own realms of access and frustration and, consequently, his own special picture of the society. A businessman selling computers or bulldozers, exposed to the commercial facet of the power structure, accumulates a certain knowledge of the exceedingly slow machinations in Soviet industry and foreign trade. A historian teaching a semester's course at Moscow State University quickly gains insights into the intellectual abilities and limitations of contemporary youth. An exchange student at Leningrad University absorbs a good deal about young people's tastes, hopes, ambitions, and values. A scientist studying earthquakes in Central Asia learns something of the technological prowess and research capabilities of the Soviet system.

Americans and Europeans have done all these things and many more in recent years. As their scholarship and firsthand experience have been recorded, the literature on the Soviet Union has expanded to a scope impossible for any but the most serious lifetime academician to digest. Yet because of the cultural chasm, the closed nature of the society, the Russian propensity for *vranyo* and *pokazukha,* and the highly compartmentalized system in which Russians from one discipline rarely see the problems of their compatriots in another field, the results of outside observation have usually been something less than definitive.

The American, German, Japanese, French, and other businessmen who have set up offices in Moscow see a good many factories and construction projects from the inside, and they learn the hardships of negotiating with an unwieldy bureaucracy manned by tough, no-nonsense bargainers. But they never catch a glimpse of the most important and efficient dimension of Soviet industry—the military production lines that turn out tanks and missiles and sophisticated aircraft—so whatever conclusions they rightly draw on the lackadaisical approach of blue-collar workers, on the counterproductive impact of certain incentive mechanisms in factories, on the suffocating restrictions and demands handed down by ill-informed planners in faraway offices must be suspended when discussing the invisible military sector.

Similarly, American professors who have taught courses on American history and economic problems have usually seen only carefully screened students, a select group of uncommonly bright, well-read, and often politically reliable young people. Western students who live with Russians their own age are, again, usually exposed to aware, achieving youngsters, frequently from well-educated and well-placed families. Scientists doing joint research are not placed in Soviet institutions where funds are the scarcest and equipment the most backward. All our images of Soviet society, then, must be accepted with deep caution as only pieces of the whole. Vast regions remain beyond reach. These include not only the military establishment with its extensive network of industrial support but also much of the lower socioeconomic level of collective farmers, coal miners, textile workers, ex-convicts, and others living at the edge of poverty; many remote rural areas of the country that are off limits to foreigners; and the most rarefied strata of the governing elite, whose special stores and party schools are inaccessible to outsiders.

This would be cause for despair if the country were still as tightly closed as in Stalin's day. But some Russians will talk to us now, as the society has slowly liberalized. We ourselves may not see the inside of a special store, but we hear about it, and in some detail. We may not see firsthand the style of life on a collective farm, but we can find those who have, just as we can now know something of winter in a Siberian village where the wells freeze and the wood stoves, blazing constantly, cannot keep a cabin's inside walls free of frost. Some of my friends have been exiled to such places. Others have joined the flow of émigrés who can speak most openly about their country once they leave it behind. So even if no systematic studies are possible, occasional glimpses beyond the normal limits can be had secondhand as Westerners and Russians are thrown together by the rise of the dissident and Jewish emigration movements and by the proliferation of East-West exchanges.

Our contacts with dissidents have sometimes carried us into the more normal Soviet world where people keep their heads down and fulfill accepted roles. The dissidents are often from the elite themselves or have acquaintances who are. A few come from rural and working-class backgrounds. Most important, the line between the dissident and the straight is not always well fortified, but is often blurry and porous; Russian friendships seep back and forth from one side to the other. An evening around a Russian kitchen table is likely to include both the outspoken and the cautious, the man with integrity and the man without. This again puts the foreigner who uses his time well into broader contact with the society.

The research and academic exchanges have also brought large numbers of Russian-speaking Westerners into the Soviet Union, and even when their formal work confines them to a single facet of investigation, their travel and their close relationships with Soviet colleagues expose them to something more—again, bits and fragments but enough to give me the impression that the passage of just a few years between Hedrick Smith's assignment in Moscow (1971–74), which produced his excellent book *The Russians,* and my tour there (1975–79) saw a continuing, subtle process of relaxation. The pendulum began to swing back after I left, as the exchange programs were curtailed following the Soviet invasion of Afghanistan, Jewish emigration was cut to a trickle, and the Russians pulled inward during the upheavals in Poland. But even if the term "détente" passes permanently out of fashion, as seems likely, I do not yet know whether to write of this process of relaxation in the past tense, for moods are cyclical, Americans have short memories and hold grudges badly, and the habit of contact created its own constituency inside the Soviet Union.

The phenomenon known as détente bred a class of America fanciers, especially among experts whose careers were made by studying the United States and writing policy papers for various think tanks, notably the Central Committee's Institute of U.S.A. and Canada Studies. These are generally hard-nosed and politically loyal middle-aged men who stand at the front line of any reception committee for distinguished American visitors. They have had a stake in decent Soviet-American ties and have often acted as brokers in promoting contacts. Svyatoslav Filippov, a legal expert in the U.S.A. Institute, told me once of his efforts to arrange a discussion for a U.S. customs agent who was traveling with a group of Citizens Exchange Corps visitors and asked to meet his counterparts in Soviet Customs. Filippov, knowing that Customs had quasi-military overtones and corresponding secrecy, gulped in discomfort at the request. But he agreed to try. He called Soviet Customs. At the other end of the line, a disbelieving silence. He prodded. Finally an officer said a reluctant yes to receiving the American, adding, "But we won't answer his questions, and we won't ask him any questions." At the appointed hour, around a table laden with bottles of mineral water, the silence was so heavy and gave so little sign of breaking that Filippov finally ridiculed his compatriots in Russian. "We can all sit in silence for half an hour," he remembered saying, "then we'll leave." The barb failed to pierce the Russians' poker-faced reticence. At last the American began talking about his job, discussing the drive to intercept narcotics, explaining techniques being used, and describing cases. As he spoke, the Soviet customs officers listened with growing interest and suddenly jumped into the conversation with some cases and techniques of their own. They ended up comparing notes on the details of training dogs, in which the Soviet officials, Filippov believed, learned a great deal from the American.

The power of the KGB to disrupt Westerners' contacts with Russians is formidable. Every foreigner who lives for a while in Moscow develops an added sense of prudence, a wariness akin to paranoia. He sniffs the air to try to smell the difference between an innocent encounter and a KGB-laid trap, a *provokatsiya*. Following the arrest of Robert Toth of the *Los Angeles Times* in June 1977, moments after a "scientist" he had come to know handed him a paper on extrasensory perception in front of the puppet theater on Sadovo-Samotechnaya Street (our favorite place for meeting dissidents out of microphone range), we all immediately became reluctant to accept any piece of paper from anyone on the street, and we began to pick our acquaintances more carefully. Toth, accused of receiving state secrets, was interrogated, badly frightened, and then released. It was an unpleasant experience, only one of a long series of dirty tricks played over the years on newsmen, diplomats, businessmen, and others. A French woman reporter was quietly accused of selling drugs in the hope that she would leave the country. She stayed, and the accusation was never pursued. Two British correspondents were unofficially accused of homosexuality. An American bureau chief was summoned to the Foreign Ministry's Press Department to be told that one of his correspondents was spying for Israel. The department director, Vsevolod Sofinsky (later to be expelled from New Zealand, where he was Soviet ambassador), tapped a thick file folder as he made the charge. The bureau chief, feigning grave concern, asked to see the dossier. Sofinsky refused to show it to him, whereupon the American declared, "Well, I guess you have no case then," and walked out. Nothing further came of the matter. On a trip to Soviet Central Asia, Robin Knight of *U.S. News and World Report* was fed a mickey by an "Intourist guide" who had just returned from Afghanistan in 1979 and knew nothing about Tashkent, where he was supposed to be an expert on tourist attractions. Knight passed out, and his wife was pawed by the "guide" and his pals.

The assortment of bluffs and menacing pressure tactics seemed designed partly to get a little something on everybody, just as the authorities liked to have a bit of dirt on every Russian for use at the appropriate moment. Partly, too, they were aimed at stimulating our paranoia, for if we began to distrust casual acquaintances with Russians, then we cut ourselves off, doing the KGB's work. From the Soviet perspective, the most gratifying response must have come from Malcolm Toon when he was American ambassador; he blocked many American diplomats from friendships with Russians by requiring that anyone wishing to meet Russians outside his own apartment get clearance in advance from embassy superiors. The purpose was to reduce the chance of setups; the result was to stifle easy relationships that did not have strictly professional dimensions, and I felt that embassy officials were poorer for it.

I fought hard against my own impulses to be overly suspicious. If I never knew when I might be set up, I also never knew when I might miss an interesting look into Soviet life. As time went on, the phones in my apartment and office rang with greater and greater frequency. Unknown voices asked if I would meet them. Usually they would not want to give their names and would not talk on the phone. So I met them, more often than not. Many were down-and-out people for whom the American press was a last resort, who wanted to plug into the circuitous chain of communication: We would write their stories, the Voice of America would see our articles, and the broadcasters in Washington would translate the stories into Russian, beaming them within hours to the Soviet Union. It was this access to publicity, this voice to their fellow countrymen and to the officials who could solve their problems, which many sought. Some callers we termed smoky, usually with an unorthodox or illegal favor to ask. Others were just crazy.

I once had a call from an official-sounding woman who said the composer Iosif Arshakovich Andrasian had some material for *The New York Times,* and could someone pick it up? I assumed she was his secretary, and I went to the address she gave me. It turned out not to be his office or his studio, as I had thought, but his apartment, and the woman was not his secretary but his wife. Andrasian was an intense, friendly, rotund man, who sat me down in his living room and made me read a long *zayavleniye,* a declaration typed single-spaced in Russian complaining that the authorities would not let him leave Moscow and live in his native Yerevan, the capital of Soviet Armenia, that his apartment was unsuitable for composing music, and so on. When I had gotten through the bulk of the reading, he began telling me his problems. First, he said, he had discovered morality in music while writing his second symphony and had done a book on the subject, a monumental work that Soviet authorities would not publish. He began reading aloud from the heavy manuscript in a kind of chanting catechism. The book had been sent to a friend of a friend who was a distant relative of somebody in the Politburo, he explained, and Brezhnev had plagiarized a section of it in a recent speech. Plagiarized? "Yes, this section here," he said, grabbing a handful of pages. "He plagiarized. But he got it all wrong!"

I made my move to go, but no, he said, there was more. "They have put me in this apartment right near this factory," he declared, gesturing at the window, "where a machine goes bang, bang, bang at forty beats a minute, and another machine goes *hmmmmmmmm,* on the note D. Now how can anyone compose music with that going on?" I listened. It was a weekday afternoon, a working day. But I heard nothing. It was as quiet in that room as it ever gets in a Soviet apartment house. He saw my face; I must have had a quizzical look. "Oh, they knew you were coming," he said, "so they turned it off."

In the absence of a free press and extensive advertising, word of mouth has developed into such a rapid and reliable form of conveying information that when a shipment of couches or a stock of imported shoes arrives in a neighborhood store, crowds are there in an instant. In the same way, the studied refusal of the authorities to list foreign news bureaus in the Moscow telephone book or with the information operator makes little difference to the determined. My office and home numbers and those of other journalists were passed hand to hand through city after city. When officials changed our numbers without asking us how we felt about it and without putting a recording on the old numbers to direct callers to the new ones, it took only a month or two before the phones began to ring again with Russians wanting stories on their housing problems, their clashes with their bosses, their thoughts on Soviet foreign policy, their insights into the chronic shortages of meat and furniture. Sometimes they would come from far-off towns and cities to what they called "the center"—Moscow—just to make contact with the American press.

A woman from Yerevan called me on an icy winter day. She sounded almost frantic. We arranged to meet in a small park near my apartment, and when I arrived bundled in a sheepskin coat and muskrat fur hat, she stood stamping the ground with cold, her nine-year-old daughter by her side. Neither of them had gloves, and had brought clothes suitable only for the southern climate of Armenia. She had fallen into trouble with the authorities by organizing tenants to complain about housing. Harassed and miserable, she had finally applied to emigrate and was refused.

Another woman, bony and hollow-eyed, came to Moscow with her infant daughter to make an appeal on a housing problem. She said she had been evicted from a new apartment because she didn't have the money to pay bribes to officials and was back in a terrible house where the water didn't have enough pressure to reach the fifth floor. She had spent time in prison, and her baby had been born behind bars. Now the authorities were threatening to take her child away.

These meetings were always punctuated by hands digging into sacks and folders stuffed with official documents, some yellowed and limp from being thumbed and folded. The papers were spread out on snowy park benches, broken chairs in cheap hotel rooms, kitchen tables littered with dirty teacups, as if we, too, would be impressed by the collages of official seals and stamps so vital to the Russian sense of authenticity.

Again and again people kept appearing in my life who seemed to exist in a netherworld between the KGB and normality. Some of them may have been agents; some may have been used by agents; some were merely the stuff of any big city: the eccentric; the neurotic; the psychotic; the creative misfits; the supremely sane in a society where an insane inability to tell the truth marks the norm.

Then there were the transparent setups. An obvious KGB caper unfolded in my office about a week or two before I was scheduled to leave Moscow for good—the secret police's prime time for pranks, just before departure. A young man walked past the mili-man without bothering to attempt a disguise, entered the office, and said in Russian that he had a "present" from Andelman in Belgrade. David Andelman was then *The Times*'s correspondent in the Yugoslav capital, but I happened to know that at that moment he was filing stories from Warsaw. I questioned the man. Where was the present? He hadn't brought it with him, of course, in case he was stopped by the mili-man. It was back in his hotel, the Hotel Belgrade! And would I come now to get it? What was the present? Oh, he couldn't tell me, and he pointed knowingly at the ceiling.

I said I was too busy to go just then, which was true. I had been working in my apartment upstairs on a series of farewell pieces, and I had dashed down to the office briefly to get something from the files. By sheer lack of coincidence, I'm sure, this man had appeared in the office during the minute and a half I was there—I was almost on my way out when he materialized. I suggested meeting the next day or the day after, figuring I could get in touch with Andelman.

No, he said, he was leaving Moscow that night. We agreed to meet at his hotel at 5:00 P.M., and he left the building in complete calm, without a request that I escort him past the guard, without the slightest betrayal of uneasiness.

I had no intention of keeping the appointment and did not. A day or so later I managed to have a telex conversation with Andelman, who was still in Warsaw. He had never sent me a present. "I thought I might have missed something," I typed on the machine.

"You did," Andelman typed back. "A night in a cold cell."

I had to admit to feeling slightly insulted that the KGB, after watching me for four years, thought I was so stupid.

He was a huge barrel of a man, well over six feet tall and built like a linebacker, with closely cropped hair and a tough, unfriendly face. His voice on the phone had had a deep resonance, and his English was practically flawless. He stood calmly on the sidewalk in front of the puppet theater, towering over a sea of small children who were waiting for noon, when an elaborate clock high on the face of the theater would crow and ring and open doors to reveal comical mechanical figures dancing and bowing and twisting to a recorded tune.

I was not sure he was the man I was supposed to meet, and as his eyes scanned the sidewalk, he gave no flicker of noticing me. So I waited. The hour came, the clock went through its performance, the crowd of youngsters and parents dissolved, and we two were the only ones left standing in front of the puppet theater. We shook hands and walked toward Central Army Park, talking as we went.

His name was Valery Yakovlevich Korotich, and he wanted me to write his story, which he told in booming English. His fluency in languages, he said, had tempted the KGB to try to hire him, but he had refused, a rejection that angered his suitors. They had begun to harass him, making it impossible for him to get a steady job, forcing him to take only badly paid part-time work, which he found translating foreign religious articles for the Russian Orthodox magazine of the Moscow Patriarchate, a slick journal authorized by the state as a showpiece of religious freedom. The police were accusing him of being a "parasite" without a recognized job and were tailing him ostentatiously, sending thugs to threaten him on buses, and occasionally beating him up, he said. In the manner of a man used to pushing people around, he demanded that I write about him. Something bothered me here, and I told him I wanted to talk to him again, later. When he called in a week or so, it was a busy period, and I put him off. He grew insistent and rude, badgering me in repeated calls for another meeting. Finally I saw him again and took detailed notes on his tale, but somehow the instincts of suspicion were operating. I wrote nothing, and when he pursued me again, I told him flatly to get lost.

Months later I saw him appear in a crowd of dissidents and relatives standing outside the Moscow courthouse where Yuri Orlov, who had organized a group to publicize Soviet violations of the Helsinki human rights provisions, was on trial. He approached me with a friendly handshake, said he had come to show his support for Orlov. But his presence sent a chill through the crowd. Dissidents started asking him angrily why he was there, telling him to move off from their conversations. Some of my dissident friends told me that he was always hanging around the synagogue, eavesdropping, and they assumed he was a *Kah-Geh-BEYSH-nik,* a KGB man.

"You don't seem very popular." I grinned at him.

"Tell them who I am," he pleaded with me.

"Well, who are you?" I asked.

He tried to explain. He hung around the synagogue because he had a girlfriend who went there, he said. And well, he hadn't told me the whole truth before, but yes, he had once worked for the KGB as an informer inside the Moscow Patriarchate. But he'd given it up, and that was why they were out to get him.

A few days later, toward the end of the Orlov trial, Korotich made his last appearance. The dissident physicist Andrei Sakharov got into a shoving match with policemen outside the courthouse, and during the fray Korotich suddenly leaped on the crowd of cops surrounding Sakharov, pummeling them with his huge fists until he was wrestled into submission and taken away in a paddy wagon. I never heard from him or of him again. Perhaps he was an agent assigned to establish credentials as a victim and dissident. Or was he a genuine target for harassment? Maybe he was just a man who did not know who he was. There are more than a few of those in the Soviet Union.

34

The voice on the phone was sultry, sexy. Would I meet her? She had some interesting things to tell me. I tried to find out who she was, what she wanted. Her name was Anna, but that's all she would say. I put her off, asked her to call back next week. Too often I had heard tales from diplomats and military attachés about entrapment attempts by seductive women under KGB employ. An American naval attaché once got misty-eyed, telling of a pass he had dutifully resisted. "It was done very tastefully, I must say," he recalled with an obvious tinge of regret.

Anna called again. I was torn between curiosity and an instinct for self-preservation. Finally the curiosity prevailed. Why should I let them scare me into cutting myself off? I agreed to meet her in broad daylight, outside a bookstore on Gorky Street. Just before she hung up, she said, "And come alone, David."

So I did not go alone. I took my colleague Craig Whitney. We waited for a while at the store, but no woman was standing there, nobody approached us. By the time I returned home Anna had called my wife, scared and breathless, saying she had seen two of us and had run, thinking the two men might have been secret policemen. She said she wouldn't call again. Debby tried to calm her down, and in the end Anna agreed to phone the next day. This time I went alone and stood on the sidewalk against swirling currents of midday shoppers, waiting. Then I felt a touch on the arm from behind and heard a half-whispered "David?"

She had the cheap look of a prostitute. She was very young, but heavily made up and slickly dressed to look older. Her hair had been done in a dime-store permanent of loose curls, and she kept fingering the top buttons of her coat, opening and closing them. As we walked up Gorky and began to talk, she took my arm, and I imagined a KGB photographer with a long lens somewhere in a car or a window snapping frame after frame to be used in some "exposé."

She was nervous, trembling, and the conversation was rambling, nearly incoherent. Pieced together, it amounted to a bizarre offer of insight into an underworld of Soviet society. She had been listening to the Voice of America, she said, and had heard translations of a couple of my recent articles on juvenile crime. They were good, she allowed, but they did not go far enough. There was more. Homosexuality. Her brother, for instance, was a homosexual. Narcotics. Her brother was an addict. I should write about these things. We came to a small park and sat on a bench in the sun. She sat too close to me, still holding onto my arm, still trembling.

I questioned her closely. She refused to give me her last name, explaining that she was married to a high party official, an older man, although she was only nineteen. (I wondered if she had been reading George Feifer's *The Girl from Petrovka.*) I asked where she got my phone number. From Christian Schmidt-Hauer, a German radio correspondent, she said, "but please don't tell him I told you." (Christian later said he knew nobody named Anna, nobody fitting her description; he had given my number to no one.) I asked if she had ever taken drugs because I suspected from her tension and disjointed speech that she was either on uppers or needed a fix. She said no. I asked what she proposed to do to help me write about addiction and homosexuality. She looked puzzled. I explained that a reporter had to have something solid. Could she introduce me to some addicts?

She stared at me, wide-eyed and disbelieving. "What for?" she said.

"To talk," I said.

"Talk?" She dissolved in a torrent of giggles. "They don't talk; they just hum and mumble."

"OK," I said. "I'll listen to them hum and mumble. But I can't write anything without something firsthand." I asked if she could bring an addict or two to our next meeting. She hesitated, turning the idea over and over, and finally said that she doubted that anyone would come, but she would try. Could she come tomorrow? No, she said, smiling, she had to get an abortion tomorrow. Saturday, she proposed. Saturday at noon. Here at the same park bench.

I left the house a bit early on Saturday, drove in tight circles through back streets to make sure I wasn't being followed, and parked a good distance from the rendezvous. Then, ten or fifteen minutes before noon, I began a slow circuit on foot around the edges of the park. I had little confidence in my ability to spot a stakeout by real professionals, but I felt better taking some precautions. I was looking for unmarked cars with two, three, or four men in them. I was looking for people in the back seats holding cameras. I was looking for women with big shopping bags, who would wait at bus stops but never get on buses once they came. I was looking for young men with the meticulously dressed, scrubbed, disgustingly clean appearance that marks an agent. If addicts were being brought to this meeting, I could easily be photographed and picked up on a phony charge of buying or selling drugs.

I saw no one suspicious. Nor did I see Anna. She did not appear. I walked past the bench several times, sat on it for a few minutes, ostentatiously checking my watch. Then I went back to the office.

She had called before I returned and had had a strange conversation with our Soviet translator, Boris. She asked him why I hadn't kept the appointment, saying on the tapped phone that I had been interested in narcotics addiction. Of course, Boris knew nothing of this and said so. "Oh, I know why he didn't come," she blurted. "He had nothing to wear. Why don't American men know how to dress? Why do American men always run like rabbits? Where is he?" Boris said truthfully that he had no idea where I was, and she shouted at this loyal, upright Russian, "Oh, you American pig!" and slammed down the receiver. She never called again.

Such mystifying experiences are so common that they threaten a Westerner's equilibrium, robbing even the most casual chance encounters of their sense of innocence. Whether in trains, planes, or restaurants, "there is a confounding ambiguity about many of those meetings," Peter Osnos wrote in *The Washington Post*, "a sense that they are not nearly as spontaneous as they seem, that something unpleasant may be in the offing." In Kishinev, the capital of Moldavia, where in earlier years thousands of Jews had been murdered or driven out in pogroms, Osnos and his wife, Susan, arriving at a restaurant where they had made a booking through their Intourist guide, were placed at a table with an elderly couple who "greeted us warmly, barely flinching when I said we were Americans. They were not, I am certain, surprised."

The couple were Jewish and entirely happy in Kishinev, of course. "We heard about their cozy new apartment, their three successful children and their plans for retirement. Life was a bowl of sweet raspberries." Sure enough, some months later, an article appeared in a Soviet paper with a detailed and largely false "account" of that evening, in which the friendly elderly couple accused Osnos of urging them to emigrate.

A KGB agent also worked his way to my dinner table—in my apartment. He was Sanya Lipavsky, a grey-haired doctor with a twinkling eye who had befriended prominent Jewish dissidents by posing as one. Among those he fooled were Vitaly and Ina Rubin, who were trying to emigrate and who later made it to Israel, where Vitaly was killed in an auto accident. The Rubins were coming to dinner, and Vitaly called to ask if he could bring a friend. I said sure, and I went out to the street to escort all three of them past the mili-man.

Lipavsky made little impression on me, except that he had such virulently anti-Soviet things to say that I dismissed him as too extreme to be reliable. I forgot about him completely, forgot even that he had been in my home until nearly two years later, when he surfaced as the chief accuser of Anatoly Shcharansky, the Jewish activist who was tried for treason and sentenced to thirteen years in prison and labor camp. It was Lipavsky's carefully woven fabrication that provided the "evidence" the court required to come to its predetermined verdict and sentence. Later, when I got to Israel, I met the former Soviet prosecutor, a recent émigré, to whom Lipavsky had first offered his services as an agent and informer in the 1960's. He could just as easily have fabricated something about me, and I waited for it to happen. But it never did.

It is not easy for a Westerner to exist in such conditions. When Karen DeCrow was president of the National Organization for Women, she visited Moscow for an international conference on women's rights and had an eye-opening experience. Officials forced her to delete from a speech a brief, critical remark about the Soviet Union's own inadequate record on women's rights. It was the first time in her life that she had been censored, and it was not a good feeling. She told me that she felt a bit like Alice in Wonderland. "I stepped off the plane and fell into the hole," she said. I can testify that the surreal quality of life does not fade, even after years of living there; it remains as debilitating as a fever.

What is so enervating is that the danger comes in large measure from inside your own mind. Enveloped in official lies, swathed in *vranyo* and ironic smiles, smothered in warm and generous friendliness that can turn cold at an order from above, you exist in the knowledge that at any moment of the state's choosing it can manipulate your surrounding environment gradually or dramatically to cause slight discomfort or excruciating pain. So you begin to take a defensive posture. You feel guilt over ordinary acts of courtesy and goodwill toward Russians who want books they cannot get, for instance, and who ask your help. If you hesitate in the simple act of giving a Russian friend a book, because you know that you are technically breaking an oppressive Soviet law, you feel dirty and unworthy of your own belief in free inquiry. And if you go ahead, you feel a knot of tension.

Early on I realized that if the KGB wanted to fabricate some case against me, it would do so no matter how I behaved. But I saw also how much it seemed to need, or want, just a tiny kernel of fact on which to mold its monster. So I resolved to make it as difficult as possible, without compromising my integrity. I did not fully realize until I left Moscow for good, and the tension slowly drained out of me, how exhausting this had been.

Much of the strain came from protecting Russians, who were naturally more vulnerable than we. Dissidents and other well-educated adults have been buffeted enough by the system to know the risks thoroughly and to make their own judgments on how open to be about seeing correspondents. But Debby and I felt obligated nonetheless to avoid flaunting our acquaintance with various people, believing that the risk was theirs to calculate and not ours to impose. So we developed a hilarious set of hand signals for use in our bugged apartment, presumably making the KGB's transcripts read like a censored manuscript. "You want to go see [pause] tomorrow?" "OK, how about stopping there [pause] on the way?" We became adept at twisting our hands into the first letters of our friends' names. And it took a few weeks after leaving Moscow for us to kick the habit and begin to speak freely again.

Sometimes we took this to extremes and felt foolish about it. Shortly after I had arrived, Chris Wren of *The Times* took me to the apartment of Valentin Turchin, a mathematician and human rights campaigner who later emigrated to the United States. Chris warned me not to speak any English inside the building on the way up so neighbors wouldn't know that Turchin was seeing Americans. I obeyed and kept my mouth shut until we got into the apartment, where we had a good long talk. When we left, Turchin came out into the corridor and said loudly, in a good English that echoed through the building's stairwell, "Thanks for coming! See you!"

Similarly, I bent over backwards to honor a request by Andrei Amalrik, the dissident writer, not to phone him at his communal apartment unless absolutely necessary. One night it was absolutely necessary because an article of his for *The Times* needed some last-minute editing. I had bumped into him just a few evenings before at a concert, so I thought he would recognize my voice.

"Andrei, hello. Can we meet?"

Silence.

"Andrei, don't you know who this is?"

"Not exactly."

"Well, we saw each other the other evening."

"Where?"

"Uh, at the concert, the symphony, don't you remember?"

"Oh, David! *Privet!* Greetings! How are you?"

Good grief, I thought. When I saw him later, he teased me for being so conspiratorial.

Nevertheless, there are Russians, especially young people, who are kept so ignorant about their own country, and are so thoroughly wrapped in a political cocoon where they are taught to see only the benignity of the system, that they are truly unaware of the vast role of their secret police. They never happen to bump up against the limits of acceptable behavior, so they do not encounter the KGB. They are too young to have experienced the terror of Stalinism, and unless their parents tell them about it (and many do not), they have no idea what happened then and little sense of their government's capacity for cruelty. And so on occasion I had to warn them. I asked a young woman from a language institute if she and her husband did not feel nervous coming past the mili-man with me to our apartment. She looked completely baffled and said she was doing nothing wrong—why should she be nervous? On a trip to Soviet Central Asia I cautioned a law student embarking on a promising career that if he did call me when he came to Moscow on vacation in a few months, as he proposed, that fact and our subsequent meetings would certainly be known to the authorities. Maybe that didn't matter to him, I suggested, but he should realize it anyway and conduct himself accordingly. He was astonished and indignant, insisting that foreign guests should not be watched as if they were enemies. But I never got a call.

Oddly, it always seemed to me that while the party apparatus was highly sensitive to everything written about the country and quick to criticize offending correspondents (I can proudly point to about a dozen vicious assaults on my character, motives, discretion, integrity, and the like in *Pravda, Izvestia, Novoye Vremya, Literaturnaya Gazeta,* Tass dispatches, Moscow television broadcasts, and local newspapers in various outlying republics), the KGB was less bothered by what a reporter wrote than by what he did. A KGB general heading the division that monitors foreign correspondents once told a Soviet acquaintance of mine that the reporters' questions in various bugged apartments are fed into a computer and analyzed over time to see whether a pattern of repeated questions emerges. They are looking mainly for military-related questions that may recur, which would lead to suspicions that a certain fellow is a spy. One assumes that similar techniques are used with businessmen, scholars, and diplomats.

Beyond the obsession with espionage, official resentment is also directed against foreigners whose Russian is good enough and whose experience in the Soviet Union is lengthy enough to give them access to wide circles of Soviet friends and contacts. As a general rule, the longer a correspondent is in Moscow, the more difficult his life becomes. If his "private" remarks are virulently anti-Soviet, that makes him a candidate for dirty tricks. And if he openly sympathizes with dissidents, for example, giving them moral support or helping them communicate with people in the West, his chances of becoming a target of harassment or expulsion seem to increase.

But not always. The pattern is often broken. A reporter sometimes appears as nothing more than a target of opportunity in a larger KGB purpose. Once in a while a correspondent whose behavior is clearly distasteful to the authorities is left untouched. The moves, or lack of them, seem partly the product of the prevailing mood in Soviet-American relations at the moment. And about the best one can do is keep his sense of humor, as Hal Piper of the *Baltimore Sun* did when he put three baskets on his desk—not "In," "Out," and "Priority" but labeled with the stock invectives used by the Soviet press to describe our work. "Slanderous Fabrications," said Hal's first basket. "Routine Anti-Soviet Lampoons," said the second. And the sign on the third read: "Fables Interweaving Blasphemy with Calumny."

Despite the pressure, I never knew a journalist stationed there who pulled any punches. Censorship of correspondents' outgoing dispatches was ended by Khrushchev in 1961, and although the self-censorship of individual and official Russians remained a formidable obstacle, the reporters I knew worked honestly. In my own conscience, I had resolved before getting to Moscow that I would not be intimidated in my writing, and the periods of greatest calm and freedom came when I was at the typewriter. There the hand signals and the cryptic phone calls, the constant eye on the rearview mirror, the guarded initial meetings in the streets and parks—all these receded into a distant, misshapen nightmare. I was left in a cleansing solitude with the truth, as well as I could perceive it.

I decided also that to be uncompromising in my professional work as a journalist, I would be wise to give the authorities no opportunity to catch me overstepping the boundaries of a reporter's role. So when I met a small, intense, chain-smoking man who called himself Nikolayev, I was on the defensive. We walked around a park and talked. He had a thin, pockmarked face and a nose like a needle. His eyes never stayed focused on a single object for more than an instant but darted to and fro as if he were following a tiny bird flitting from branch to branch, to park bench to trash basket. He wanted to be a "local correspondent" for *The Times,* making me immediately suspicious about either his authenticity or his sanity. I said no, explaining that under Soviet law, no foreigner could hire a Russian except through a specific Soviet government agency known by its initials, UPDK. He had never heard of the agency, as most Russians haven't. The full title is Upravlenniye Obsluzhivaniya Diplomaticheskogo Korpusa ("Administration for Servicing the Diplomatic Corps"), and it provides carefully screened translators, drivers, violin teachers, piano tuners, maids, handymen, and the like to all foreigners, including nondiplomats.

Nikolayev pressed me, asking if I weren't interested in information from the grass roots. Sure, I said, and I'd be happy to interview him anytime. He drew unhappily on his cigarette. Could I help him get a visa to the U.S.? I said I had no way of doing that. Could I put him in touch with Sakharov or other dissidents? (Sakharov, living at that time in Moscow with his phone still connected, was inundated with appeals for help from strange characters all over the country.) I explained that my job was to report and write for *The Times,* not to be a middleman for dissidents. As the conversation wound on, I grew steadily more certain that this man was a rather awkward agent, trying to lure me into one illicit form of behavior after another. Yet something about him fascinated me. He talked at length about how bad things were in the Soviet Union, how much he wanted to leave, though he was neither Jew nor dissident. He was an architecture buff, and he saw beauty and history in Moscow's greyest quarters. He seemed bright. I didn't trust him, but I was interested in him. When we parted, he asked if he could call me again. I said yes.

Over the next two years we met perhaps six or eight times. He turned out to have spent six months in jail for showing a black-market pornographic film in his apartment to "friends," one of whom happened to be an informer. A lot of his acquaintances were ex-convicts, and some of them wanted very much to meet a real live American. One was a man with a little enterprise, and he thought he might be able to do business with me. The enterprise was buying and selling Western goods—jeans, rock records, books—an illegal activity for both Russian and foreigner. Alarm bells again. I said I had no desire to deal with the fellow, but if he just wanted to talk, fine. Nikolayev was honest enough to say he would have to ask and see, and some weeks later he passed the word that his friend would still like to meet. "Just to talk?" I asked.

"Well, he has high hopes," he said. I told him to forget it.

But Nikolayev eventually opened important doors into the seediest side of Moscow life. I spent time in the fetid single room of a communal apartment with an alcoholic newspaper deliverer who admired Stalin; in another single room laden with faded lace and quilts belonging to a wispy white-haired lady who had had some poetry published in 1918, which she kept in brittle clippings and read aloud, holding the pieces in trembling hands while her guests sipped tea and jam; in the tiny apartment of a young man who had served time for speculating in foreign goods and wanted a visa to the United States, where he figured he could make a fortune and possibly sign on as a mercenary in southern Africa. "He wants to shoot black people," Nikolayev explained. Nikolayev never gave up trying to get me to give him Sakharov's phone number. Every time he met me he prodded, always in vain. I was faintly suspicious of him until the day I left Moscow.

A week or so before leaving I divided my notes from four years into several piles, not by subject but by their value to me in writing this book. The most vital I resolved to carry with me in a shoulder bag through airport customs without letting them out of my sight, the others to be sent out in various ways, mostly with my shipment of clothes, books, records, and such. It was this carton of files, mixed into a huge truckload of household goods, that provided the final, telling episode in my exploration of Soviet society.

The boxes, packed in our apartment by the West German moving company Interdean, were taken to the old stone Moscow customshouse next to the Leningrad Station. There they were transferred one at a time from one truck to another, enabling a customs officer to select those to be opened and inspected. I was informed politely that my presence was not required during this lengthy process and that I would be called only if a problem arose. The call came a few hours later. There was no problem, I was assured, but could I just come sign the customs declaration?

When I appeared at the appropriate desk and gave my name, I was sent immediately into a supervisor's office and from there into the office of one of the highest-ranking customs officials in the country, Boris Borisovich Klyucharev, head of a section called the Department of Diplomatic Cargo. He oversaw all foreigners' shipments. This seemed a bit too much royal treatment for filling out a customs declaration. Something was up.

Klyucharev was a short, stocky, friendly-faced man with a trimmed brown mustache and thinning grey hair. He had the sort of build that could not possibly look neat in a uniform no matter how hard he tried, and it was clear that he tried. He shook my hand warmly, as if I had just come to his house for tea, and had me sit down across from his small wooden desk, fill out a form, and sign it. He asked some routine questions about two decorative Turkish plates, which he thought might be antiques, but were not. Then, holding his head worriedly, he said that there was "a box of problems."

He closed and locked the door to his office, walked to the window, and pulled back the curtain. He smiled impishly. There on the windowsill was the cardboard carton of notes. He hefted it over to his desk and patted it. "Problems, problems," he said with regret and sadness. "You should have mailed this; then there wouldn't have been any trouble." He meant that I should have mailed it out through the American Embassy in the diplomatic pouch, a remarkable suggestion for a customs officer.

Over the next several hours we fenced like practiced swordsmen, steadily courteous, even gentle, and ruthlessly alert to an opening for a thrust. Klyucharev had pulled from my files a few pages typed in Russian, open letters to government agencies from a group of workers who had formed a "free trade union" to complain about corruption and safety hazards before most of them were bundled off to prisons and psychiatric hospitals. The documents had already been made public, both to the Soviet government and the Western press, so they would come as no surprise to the KGB. (Such was the case with all the dissident appeals and essays in that carton; I had carefully culled from the files sensitive material posing potential danger to Russians.) But the items were brand new to Klyucharev since of course they weren't publicized in the Soviet press. He was fascinated.

He bent over the workers' petitions and letters on his desk, running his finger down the lines of typescript, murmuring sympathetically. "Poor people," he said. "Poor people." He shook his head in dismay. "They suffer." He straightened and looked at me over his shoulder. "We have illness, our society. Everywhere there is illness." He hunched over the pages again. "But you don't cure the wound by rubbing salt in it." He punched the long typed list of signatures with his finger. "Now why did they go to the Western press? Why?"

"Because they had nowhere else to go," I said. "Their own press and their own officials wouldn't hear them." Klyucharev frowned and said nothing. He knew it was true.

Then he explained the problem. Customs, he said, would have to look through my handwritten notes to see if there were any that were related to these typed materials. I reminded him of the European security accords signed at Helsinki in 1975, under which the Soviet Union pledged to create conditions conducive to foreign correspondents' work. Certainly if the agreement meant anything, a journalist should be entitled to take out his own notes. He rubbed his thinning grey hair, pulled at his ill-fitting uniform, adopted the puzzled, unsure pose of a rumpled television Columbo doing detective work by throwing his suspect off guard. Yes, he conceded, Helsinki permitted the export of a journalist's notes. But not necessarily things written by others.

"Well, then, there is no point in your looking at my notes," I said.

"Ah, well," he replied, "I do have a right to read the notes."

"Good luck," I said. "I always got bad marks in handwriting in third grade and deserved them. Nobody can read my scrawl."

"We'll try," sneered his assistant, a harder man who had said nothing until then.

It would be a shame, I countered, if just ten days before Carter and Brezhnev were to meet in Vienna to sign SALT II, the strategic arms treaty, the Soviet government violated an earlier agreement with Brezhnev's signature on it—Helsinki. It would just play into the hands of those in Washington who doubt Moscow's word and want an incident. I was trying a political language I thought this man would understand.

"Yes, yes, I know," said Klyucharev, holding his head in his hands. "There are people who want a return to the cold war. I know." I proposed that he just return the notes to me and not send them out if he felt unable to do so. Playing the role of the tormented, he sat at his desk, stood again, paced the room, rubbed his head, and said finally that he would have to take the formal position of a customs officer and say no to that. But what was my position, he asked, on his right to remove the material written by others (the dissidents' appeals)? I said that I would have to take the formal position that this was an interference in a correspondent's work. If he were going to hold my notes and read them and perhaps confiscate them, then, of course, I would have to complain to the Foreign Ministry and the U.S. Embassy, and news stories would be written about the matter, and that would be a shame just ten days before the Brezhnev-Carter summit. But if he wanted to take such a heavy burden of responsibility on himself, then that was his decision. If he would postpone the decision, I would postpone the public noise, I offered. The quiet complaints to the State Department and the Foreign Ministry would go ahead.

"Please come back tomorrow," he said worriedly. This was my hope. Decisions not yet firm in the Soviet Union are decisions that can be reversed with pressure in the right places. I did not want to lose my own notes. It would be a matter to fight out between my government and his, Klyucharev said with a smile, pointing at the ceiling.

We then embarked on a farcical debate over what to do with the notes overnight. Technically, according to the Soviet passion for the appearance of legal propriety, an *akt* should have been written, listing in detail every page being held in custody or at least giving a precise count of the pages. Klyucharev's deputy, who had a mind like a bulkhead, insisted on following this procedure, but Klyucharev waved him off impatiently. There were thousands of pages. "It would take all night to count them," he said.

I suggested that he put a customs seal on the carton. But then, he countered, "We could break the seal, take papers out, and reseal it, and you would never know."

"I hadn't thought of that," I said.

"If we keep it," he added, "you could charge that we took things out." ("Or worse, put things in," said a dissident friend who heard the story later.)

I suggested that he seal it, let me take it home overnight, and bring it back the next morning. He rubbed his head uncomfortably again and said that he had a gut reaction against allowing such a thing. Then, after a good long time of wrangling over this, there popped into his head a solution that lit him up like a comic-book character underneath a light bulb. The carton would be placed with the rest of my goods in the West German moving van—"A third country!" he said with delight—and sealed. Then it would come back in the morning—he pointed at the ceiling again—after a decision had been made. He was immensely pleased with himself for having found a solution that would have done Gromyko proud. "Another SALT agreement," I said, and we both laughed and shook hands on it.

It was early evening now, and the truck had already gone off to a parking area. It was called back, and in an hour or so it rumbled into the customshouse courtyard, an enormous orange, black, and white van with a long trailer. An officer supervised the breaking of the seal and the opening of the high doors, which were as huge as a barn's. A solid wall of packing cases reached from the floor of the trailer to the roof, solid except for a tiny gap near the top about the size of the offending carton. One of the German crewmen clambered up while another handed him the box, and like a basketball player stretching for a rebound, he slipped it into the high hole. The doors were swung closed with a clang, and a new lead seal was put in place. My notes were in the custody of a "third country." Hilarious.

Back in the office I got on the phone to the American Embassy and the Foreign Ministry and sent a message to my editors in New York asking for complaints to the Soviet Embassy and the State Department. Soviet officials seemed embarrassed, for the incident came at a moment, shortly before the summit, of relatively warm relations, which nobody wanted to spoil. I was virtually assured by Foreign Ministry people, almost immediately, that at least my notes would be returned.

And that was the happy news that Boris Borisovich had for me when I showed up in his small, stark office the next day. He smiled a bit less than the day before, and he seemed to wear his uniform more soberly. He explained that he must remove the material written by Russians and hold it "temporarily" while it was read and a final ruling made. "Temporarily" meant forever, I knew, but with my notes cleared and left unread, it was an 80 percent victory.

With great ceremony the truck's seal was broken, the carton removed and handed to me, and I carried it to Klyucharev and put it on his desk. He pulled out the file folders one by one, leafed through them quickly, and took only pages typed in Russian. He read everything written by the dissidents with the intense hunger of a man who has never tasted prime sirloin. He was so swept up in the chronicles of anger and despair and injustice that gradually his guard came down and he began punching the pages with his finger. *"Nu, pravilno* ["Well, that's right"]," he said. "Yes. Right. Yes. *Nu, byvaet* ["Well, it happens"]." And on each line of these contraband documents, Boris Borisovich Klyucharev, trusted head of the Department of Diplomatic Cargo of the Moscow Customs Administration, found something to agree with. Jews wishing to emigrate were protesting violations of Soviet pledges to reunite families. Georgians who wanted to preserve their national culture were resisting Russification. Tatars were pleading for a right to return home to the Crimea, from which Stalin had exiled them during the war. Workers were condemning corruption. From time to time a particular page on a particular theme would set him off into a passionate soliloquy on the failing at hand. Occasionally something would make him mad. The Tatars were deported to Central Asia because they killed Jews and Communists, he said—he knew, he had been stationed in the Crimea during the war.

"Then why aren't they allowed to go back now?" I asked.

"Ha. Of course they can go back. You see them every day at the station here, going back."

"No, they have tried from Central Asia, and they can't get permission to live in the Crimea. Did you ever hear of Mustafa Dzhemilyov?" I asked. A blank look. "He's now in prison for the second time for speaking out for the Tatars' right to return."

"Yes? *Hmmp.*" And he flipped to the next page of the typescript. Once he came across a clipping from *Pravda* that included a photograph of Brezhnev. It sparked a startling expression of resentment at the recent spate of honors and medals and titles that had been heaped on the aging party chief. Without once saying the name "Brezhnev" aloud, Klyucharev jabbed at the picture and commented acidly on the sycophants around the leader, accusing them of currying favor with the old man by excessive flattery. *"Eto ne khorosho, ne khorosho* ["It's not good, not good"]," he said.

It took him a long time to go through the material. Often he seemed lost in the storm of grief he was reading. Even though he agreed with much of it, said that he knew it was happening, believed it, didn't like it, worried about it, he also became bothered by the candor in these pages. It set him off on a discussion of Solzhenitsyn, and I asked him if people of his generation knew the full scope of Stalin's crimes as described in *The Gulag Archipelago* and by Khrushchev in his "secret speech" to the Twentieth Party Congress in 1956.

Yes, he said thoughtfully. But it is not necessary to expose all these ills. If you are sick, he said, what do you do, ask anybody to treat you or go to a doctor? You need skilled treatment, and that could be obtained from the party, from the country's leaders, from those trained to heal wounds.

Khrushchev moved too fast, he explained. Why don't we allow *The Gulag* to be published here? "Because we're not used to it. We have to go slowly. We didn't know anything. We lived behind a curtain. And suddenly the curtain was lifted, too fast, and we had all this mixture with foreigners and foreign ideas."

Patiently he tried to explain to me. "If one pornographic movie were shown in Moscow, people would kill each other trying to get to it. In the West it wouldn't happen because you're used to it. It is as if you went to the tropics and just drank from a river—you couldn't handle it. You would get terribly sick. You need an injection first. Our people need an injection, too."

He was finished with the Russian-typed material, which he stacked on his desk. We counted the pages and drew up an *akt.* My notes were replaced in the carton and returned to the truck for shipment out. Somehow we did not feel like hurrying to the goodbyes, but there was little excuse for lingering.

"I enjoyed talking to you," I said, "despite the unpleasant circumstances."

"Yes." He looked at me steadily. "Too bad we didn't meet before."

"Yes, too bad." And we shook hands.

ONE

Smothering Love: Children's Hands Tightly Held

Our children are our future.

—A MOSCOW JANITOR, 1977

Authority and Creativity

On a grand square in Moscow named after the first head of the Soviet Union's secret police, Feliks Dzerzhinsky, there stand two massive stone buildings, each in its way a monument to deeply rooted instincts in Russian culture. One is Lubyanka, the notorious prison and interrogation center of the KGB, whose basement cells once echoed with the cries of countless men and women en route to Stalin's labor camps and firing squads. The other, diagonally across the square, is the country's largest children's store, a dingy, cavernous place called Detsky Mir ("Children's World"), where parental indulgence becomes a national cult, where the earliest values take shape in plastic and tin, the little dreams and fantasies bought and wrapped and registered with a melancholy jangle at the counters of a hundred bored cashiers.

To get to Lubyanka, you must begin at Detsky Mir. From the shelves stacked with centrally planned playthings, the newest members of the society are introduced to the physical world, guided in their games, taught the rules. Taken into the kindergartens and through the schools and young Communist organizations, this is a journey of some ambiguity, fraught with detours and contradictions, complicated by the frequent twist of a question without an answer. But it exposes lines of continuity between the realms of childhood and adulthood, connections between the beginning and the end.

In the weeks before the New Year, which Russians celebrate with the same frenetic buying and gift giving that we do Christmas, Detsky Mir is thick with crowds of heavily bundled men and women, sometimes with children in tow, pressing and jostling and sweating in long lines, craning their necks for the attention of exhausted, disheveled salesclerks. The sacrifice of stamina and good cheer which buying anything in the Soviet Union demands attains a high pitch here, yet the ritual is observed unflinchingly. A young father in a grey overcoat, having battled one line to select three battery-operated plastic phones, a second line to pay for them, and a third to turn over his receipt and get the phones from behind the counter, has now taken them aside to check them out and finds to his enormous dismay that one doesn't work. He is trying to catch the saleswoman's eye, which is studiously trained to slide quickly past the pleading gazes of the clientele. He smiles wanly and turns to a fellow customer. "There will be tears," he says. "There will be crying."

The toys at Detsky Mir and other children's stores around the country are heavy on military themes and educational functions, and their display is organized to define unambiguously the roles of boys and girls. Beneath a large sign that reads: "Toys for Boys," the counters in Detsky Mir are laden with plastic fighter planes, tanks, antiaircraft guns on eight-wheel vehicles, mobile rockets, green plastic artillery pieces, toy soldiers (some on horseback carrying red flags), metal submachine guns that go rat-tat-tat-tat when the trigger is pulled, and remote-controlled armored personnel carriers with guns and searchlights. There are also cowboy pistols and holsters that could be straight out of Macy's, electric trains made in East Germany, electric hockey games, and space guns that shoot rubber-tipped darts. The girls' section has tea sets, cradles, washing machines, toy stoves, tops, little washboards, toy vacuum cleaners, and sewing machines.

In other departments and other stores, shelves are full of wonderful stuffed animals that make you smile—soft brown hippopotamuses with orange stomachs, pink curly dogs, yellow pigs, orange and white foxes—and toy pianos, drums, and accordions. There are hard plastic dolls in various native costumes, including stereotyped blacks with big lips, grass skirts, and Aunt Jemima-type bandannas.

In Moscow at least, where material standards are considerably higher than in most of the rest of the country, the stores are stocked with good manipulative toys, not as pretty as Western versions but often modeled on them. They involve small eye-hand coordination, reading, matching shapes and colors and building skills, and they include games with telephones, letters, and other features of the surrounding world. There are Soviet and Eastern European variations of metal Erector sets and plastic Lego, the building blocks with buttons and perforations that fit together. There are games like lotto, with cards and boards on which pictures and numbers must be matched; chemistry sets; electric construction sets with lights and switches; traffic games using little cars and dice; and electric question-and-answer games, in Russian and various foreign languages, whose lights go on when an electrical contact is touched to the correct answer. One of these is a very good one for teaching English. Many of the educational toys are made in Estonia and Lithuania, the most Westernized of the country's fifteen republics. And unsurprisingly, the crowds of shoppers usually pass them by, forming most heavily at the counters where the electric battery-run cars and planes and armored personnel carriers are sold.

The common denominator of the toys is that they break easily. Made mostly of flimsy metal and cheap plastic, these first possessions rarely last long, and as they crack and bend and splinter, they teach something about the child's powerlessness over his world, fostering a sense of material things as expendable and unworthy of strong attachment. These are bitter lessons, accompanied by terrible disappointment and anger. But they have their usefulness in promoting ultimately a numbness and a fatalism conducive to later contentment within an adult system that is also physically deprived and unresponsive to individual desires.

More than the brittle result of shoddy merchandise, the inability to control externals is woven into the texture of a childhood that is softly unyielding, lovingly inhibiting, soothing in its certainty.

The child is smothered in anxious affection, like a puppy on a street corner, lest he stray dangerously beyond bounds. Swaddling, a traditional Russian practice that is gradually being abandoned by some young parents, still exists as a metaphor of human relations, in which the child is wrapped in a comforting restraint whose bonds of warmth allow him little independence.

You can see this in the parks, where parents and grandparents badger their children and grandchildren affectionately, intervening constantly in their play, rarely leaving them to get dirty, to skin knees, or to find solitude. One sunny, cold November Sunday, while two of my little ruffians, Jonathan and Laura, were in Sokolniki Park poking sticks into a big puddle covered by a thin sheet of ice and breaking the ice into glassy panes and flinging them to watch them shatter on the ground, neatly dressed Russian children were standing properly with adults at the edge of a nearby pond, politely tossing breadcrumbs to ducks, staying within safe limits, never wading into a new situation. Though most of the children who walked by the puddle showed no interest, occasionally one or another cast a fleeting look of longing. Two small boys stopped, watched for a few moments, and then tiptoed toward the puddle. They reached down to touch a piece of ice and pick it up tentatively, being careful not to get their feet wet. Their grandfather, grumbling constantly, told them gruffly to come along. The boys hesitated. The grandfather stalked off, saying, "Do what you want. I'm going." And the boys dropped the ice and scampered along behind him.

A child is everybody's business. Complete strangers are forever scolding and cajoling when children seem insufficiently bundled or inadequately supervised. Take your little one out in a Moscow winter with a fragment of skin exposed, and you are likely to be swooped down upon by finger-wagging *babushkas,* who make you feel like a naughty child yourself. When my Laura was four and we were being whisked up out of a deep subway station by a high-speed escalator, a hawk-eyed grandmother racing down on the other side spied my daughter in a nylon parka (warmer than it looked), fixed me with a devastating glare in the instant that we passed, and declared, "Isn't she cold, young man?" Then the woman was gone, like an apparition.

Laura went skating a couple of years later in a pleasant little park near our apartment. She had one of those arctic hoods that unrolled into a long tunnel shape, and she was skating around cheerily, peering out through her elongated hood, when I noticed from across the pond that a chunky *babushka* had stopped her and was bending over her, doing something. Finally released after a few moments, Laura skated over to me, her face crinkled into unhappiness. Her hood was rolled back.

"Did she say anything?" I asked Laura.

"She said it was too hot."

In a glassware shop an American diplomat was subjected to withering denunciations when he put his daughter on his shoulders to prevent breakage. "Women came at me from every corner of the store," he reported, "telling me I shouldn't do that, saying, 'She'll be a hunchback.' "

I once saw two boys trudging across a patch of open space knee-deep in snow near the Kremlin. Two hefty women street cleaners in orange vests shouted at them angrily to stop, to go back, not to cross that place. The boys ignored them and continued on their way, but it seemed to me that this was simply another example of a ridiculously stern restriction—not being permitted to romp through the snow in the shadow of the Kremlin—until I overheard the real reason for the women's concern. One said to the other disgustedly, "They'll get their boots full of snow!"

The imperious concern for one's fellow man—grown-ups as well as children—pervades Soviet society and rapidly becomes a blend of natural behavior and social control. A man once pulled up next to Debby at a red light and reproached her for having a dirty car (something policemen can fine you for). And at the diplomatic wing of Vnukovo Airport, when Secretary of State Henry Kissinger was arriving in Moscow in January 1976, a middle-aged American diplomat and political counselor of the U.S. Embassy in Moscow, Marshall Brement, was scolded for standing out on the tarmac without a hat. The man who issued the reprimand was Foreign Minister Andrei Gromyko.

Of course, this is all done out of kindness, especially where children are involved. Even the most officious Russians seem to melt into helpless, cooing blobs at the sight of a tiny baby, shifting into a wonderful language of diminutives—the word for "wet," *mokry,* becomes *mokrinky;* the word for "good," *khoroshy,* turns into *khoroshinki;* and the vocabulary fills up with purring *sh*'s and *ch*'s. I cannot even count the times my family and I were ushered through Soviet customs without a bag being opened as our little ones whined and cried from exhaustion after a long trip. A small, tired, unhappy face was enough to soften the sternest inspector.

Institutions are also solicitous of children. On school vacations, daytime television switches heavily to children's shows, and the country's 106 puppet theaters and 77 permanent circuses put on extra afternoon performances. Enormous resources are spent in every city on vast networks of hobby clubs, handicraft classes, music schools, and other uplifting after-school activities. Subways throughout the land have signs instructing passengers to give their seats to veterans and parents with small children. Outside railroad stations one often finds separate taxi lines for those with youngsters.

A most dramatic personality transformation was rendered by children in our apartment house about two years after we had arrived. The chief janitor, who went under the elegant title "Commandant," wore a suit, and had a bulbous red nose, rarely did much about leaky roofs and cold radiators. But when the residents got together and turned a small parking lot into a playground, the Commandant, without even being asked, stirred himself into a frenzy of enterprise and efficiency. Suddenly there appeared an array of playground equipment—two rotating carousels, a big swing, and some benches—which he promptly detailed two of his helpers to paint in bright colors. When I thanked him and told him how amazing it was that he was able to get such things so quickly, no easy task in the Soviet Union, he just smiled and said, "Our children are our future."

The phrase crops up also in conversations with principals and teachers, in official speeches, in pompous newspaper articles as a solemn expression of the society's vital interest in shaping young minds into accepted patterns. Here is where two streams of attitude intersect and reinforce each other: the natural bent for affectionate, bossy attention to the behavior of all its members, especially the young, and the more calculated effort at manipulation, which emanates from above. The high value placed on children's conformity is a hallmark of both, generating sanctimonious pronouncements by ranking officials on the moral and political obligations of those who manufacture toys, make cartoons, write stories, and formulate curriculum.

The secretary of the cinematographers' union, L. Kulidzhanov, for example, stood before a membership meeting called to discuss films for children and declared with embarrassing melodrama, "Our youth—this is the future of the country, to whom the baton will be passed by several generations of revolutionaries and builders, called by history to take onto their shoulders the task of the creation of communism, the responsibility for its full success. As everyone knows, the child-rearing task of cinematographers in developed socialism is a dialectical interdependence, in which they interact in the formulation of the world view, the political outlooks, and the moral principles of the builders of communism." The platitude may be empty—though not quite—but the message is clear, and it fosters a close watchfulness over the development and growth of small Soviet boys and girls.

Lidiya Aleksandrovna Agaryova was a chunky, grandmotherly veteran of twenty-two years in the kindergarten business, and she chattered warmly to the swarms of little ones as she took Debby and me proudly through her Detsky Sad ("Children's Garden") No. 104, off Profsoyuznaya Street in one of southwest Moscow's new high-rise neighborhoods. The building was nothing to look at from the outside—a dull ochre box, scarcely distinguishable from the taller boxes around it and separated from them by muddy and weedy lots—but inside, its design revealed a skilled hand. Every class of twenty-five children, grouped by age, had a complex of rooms: a large, airy playroom with huge windows that allowed a flood of daylight to wash over them; a big changing room for shedding sopping boots and snowsuits, with benches arranged so each child could sit in front of his own cubbyhole; a spacious bathroom with a rack of cream-colored potties (in the section for two-year-olds), each painted with black numerals designating a particular child; and finally, for those still in the nap-taking stage, a fourth room full of beds. The layout was so conducive to easy functioning by teachers and children that it was hard to believe they had not drawn it up themselves, and it reflected such obvious high expense that it was tempting to see it as a false showcase for foreign visitors. The most privileged and creative American or European educator would have been seized with envy.

No doubt it was better kept and better equipped than many others. (A Russian friend later said sardonically that he wished I'd visited his daughter's kindergarten so they would have fixed it up for my benefit.) But throughout the country I encountered the identical physical design, a rare virtue of the centralized and authoritarian system in distributing something positive nationwide. Less attractive to a Western eye that values individual creativity is what takes place inside these beautifully planned kindergartens—the function also of centrally dictated procedures, including uniform curricula and even holiday skits and songs that are the same from Moscow to Central Asia.

The tour with Mrs. Agaryova began in the clinic and the kitchen. "A doctor is here three hours a day, a nurse full time," she said stoutly. "The children eat three times a day—they're here from seven A.M. to seven-thirty P.M. At eight A.M., breakfast: a salad of carrots, potatoes, tomatoes, something hot, usually porridge, and weak coffee with lots of milk. Four hundred grams of milk, that's a must. At twelve, lunch: meat or chicken soup, one hundred grams of meat, *kisel* [a thick drink of fruit juice and potato flour or cornstarch], compote or fruit. At four P.M., a snack: macaroni, tea or buttermilk or milk.

"We teach them love, respect for other national groups," said Mrs. Agaryova as we poked into classrooms full of houseplants and tropical fish in bubbling tanks, blocks stacked neatly in sunny corners, shelves of stuffed animals, sailors' and doctors' and cabbies' hats for highly organized dramatic play. "We tell them a lot about collective farms. We teach the child to dress himself. We have a garden in the summer and grow things. We develop the children's diction. We take children to construction sites so they can see different professions—carpenters, masons, et cetera—and take them to the library. We cultivate love toward our respected Vladimir Ilyich Lenin—that is most important. Each group has a portrait of Lenin. The children read verses, sing songs, decorate the rooms. They sing songs about the motherland.

"A *metodist* oversees the educational aspect," she continued, "works out the plans for the *vospitatelnitsi* [teachers; literally "upbringers"]. The plan is the same throughout the Soviet Union"—and she held up a little white book—"two-week plans for each age-group."

The atmosphere is less regimented than it sounds. There is time for casual play and opportunity for misbehavior. In fact, some parents complain of too little supervision. Young mothers who feel economic and moral pressure to hold full-time jobs, and virtually all do, often contrive to have grandmothers watch small children at home rather than use the kindergartens, where youngsters seem always to be coming down with colds and sometimes suffer from outright neglect.

A Russian friend I'll call "Sergei" complained once that in the kindergarten where he had pushed so hard for his daughter's admittance, she was being sent outside with her coat half-unbuttoned. "It's nothing but a place to deposit your children where they won't get run over by a car," he said angrily. One day she came home with scratches on her eyelid, the result of a fight with another girl at a moment when the upbringer was not paying adequate attention. Both girls were put on the "guilty bench," the equivalent of standing in the corner.

"The trouble is I don't give the upbringer gifts, so she doesn't look after my daughter," Sergei explained. "I gave a box of chocolates to the director to get my daughter in—otherwise she would have said there was no room, et cetera. But I just got tired of giving bribes. The teacher obviously expected it on the eve of the November Seventh holiday [the anniversary of the Bolshevik Revolution]. When I went to pick up my daughter, the teacher looked at me expectantly, and when she saw I was empty-handed, she just turned her back on me and walked inside, very erect. Since then she doesn't speak to me and turns her back when I pick up my daughter." Sergei noted that the upbringers earned salaries of only 85 rubles* a month, about half the average industrial wage, and probably assumed that little presents from parents were part of their due.

He finally set out to have his girl moved to a better kindergarten, but that wasn't easy. "To get her transferred out, I would have to write some sort of document explaining the reasons," he said. "The real reason is that the upbringers don't pay the kids enough attention. But I can't say that. Otherwise the upbringers at the new place would think me a haughty guy, and there would be trouble again. So I have to figure out some other way, some other explanation." What he managed was to get his wife's boss to contact a factory manager with whom he deals and ask as a personal favor (with the

*During the period covered by this book, one ruble equaled approximately $1.35 to $1.50.

assumption that it would someday be repaid in some form) that the little girl be admitted to the factory's own kindergarten, which was of high calibre. This was done, and when Sergei was desperately searching for a special gift to give his wife's boss in thanks, he asked if I could get him a Pan American World Airways wall calendar before the New Year. I did, and I heard it was a hit.

These inner foibles of the system exist within a crust of neat orderliness and prim propriety where the child is given little latitude to find his own means of personal expression. Walk into any Soviet kindergarten, no matter how well stocked, and you will see immediately that the activities are essentially teacher-directed. In one corner, big blue blocks have been stacked into the shape of an elaborate boat, far beyond anything that the five-year-olds in this room could do. In another, blocks for building a city are used to copy a plan or picture, but there is no evidence of kids building, building, building the tallest tower they can. The nature corners, each with a parakeet in a cage, a fish tank, and a few plants and posters, look so perfect that no small child could have had much of a hand in making them.

A stranger going into a good Western classroom could probably get a fairly clear sense of a particular child by strolling around the room, examining drawings and stories and other pieces of work on the walls and bulletin boards. But in Soviet classrooms almost nothing made by children appears on shelves or walls, and there is no way of obtaining a picture of a given child by exploring the classroom, looking at favorite colors or self-portraits, as American parents are accustomed to doing.

There is not much to get fingers dirty, to get hands molding and shaping. There is nothing experimental, no material that says to the child, "Look at me. What am I? What can you do with me?" There is no table with hard things and soft things to touch and talk about, for example. There are no books for younger children in a corner or on a table so they could walk over at a whim and browse through pages and pictures. Debby observed after our visit to Kindergarten No. 104 that there was no room to investigate the environment in a creative way that said to the child, "Gee, *your* perceptions are extremely important."

Nowhere in the younger years are the style of education and the matrix of expectations more clearly visible than in the approach to art. The stress is on drawing, painting, or modeling realistically, often according to a rigid prescription. In one class, youngsters made clay roosters all looking the same. The teacher was quite proud. In another, stacked on a back shelf—not hung—were drawings of a curled plant stem. Again, all were similar except for one rather pathetic scribble, which the kindergarten director said embarrassedly was by a small girl who had just arrived three or four days earlier but would soon be drawing just like all the others. As is customary in Soviet schools, the pictures did not have the children's names written boldly on the front but had them penciled lightly and discreetly on the back, where they could not become personal statements.

Teachers display considerable uneasiness about artwork that is out of the well-defined groove. An American friend, watching a class of eight-year-olds in Moscow copy a drawing of a snowman with such precision that their work might have been paper tracings, noticed one boy coloring his snowman yellow. The youngster received a stern reprimand. In the Central Asian city of Dushanbe I was shown kindergarteners' pictures of trees made from pasted bits of paper. Much to the teacher's dismay, one tree had black leaves —the only unusual creation in the lot—and she laughed nervously. "Look, a black leaf one did—an Afghan," she said in a confidential tone, as if I were supposed to wink and understand that one could not expect more from an Afghan. In the same kindergarten I looked through a stack of drawings done by a class that had visited a construction site and was instructed to reproduce the scene faithfully on paper. With varying degrees of drawing skill the children had done what they were told. But one had introduced what seemed at first glance to be an element of lovely fantasy into the picture—a fairylike blond princess right in the middle of the construction. I stopped and held it up and pointed it out to the teacher, who immediately thought I was being critical and hastened to assure me that it was all right because there really had been a blond girl there at the site.

Fantasy exists in well-defined formats such as old Russian fairy tales, circuses, and cartoons, but it is often discouraged by adults when children try to practice it in drawing, storytelling, or make-believe play. The dramatic games in kindergartens seem most highly valued if they approximate reality; they are conceived as lessons in understanding the larger world, not in releasing individual emotions or acting out fears. Brennan and Nina Klose, whose father, Kevin, was a Moscow correspondent for *The Washington Post*, told me after two years in a Moscow elementary school populated mostly by children of the elite that they had seen no fantasy games, no make-believe play. "They're not all that creative," Brennan said of his Russian classmates. "Not at all, not a thing. I don't think they have much creative imagination." Good grades in art, he said, came on the basis of two criteria: accuracy and neatness.

I am less certain about what happens in homes, which are as varied in intellectual level and social behavior as in any society. The rhymes and stories of the children's writer Kornei Chukovsky and the fairy tales in verse of Pushkin are read with enormous joy. But it may be reasonable to think that parents are basically in tune with the values expressed in the schools. Debby and I drew some blank looks from highly educated people when we asked about their children's make-believe play, and in a couple of cases parents told me that they intentionally derided their youngsters' fantasies as if they were somewhat unhealthy. This may grow out of a general aversion to introspection. Dostoyevskian searches into the subconscious find little favor in modern Soviet society, except in the great Russian classics themselves, which are read so hungrily that every new printing disappears instantly from the bookstores. In everyday life there is no taste for sociological and psychological analysis in handling children, nothing akin to Western self-consciousness. The attention focuses on the outward performance and behavior, not on the causes below, where a cauldron of emotions can boil and hiss and heave with no notice taken as long as it does not quite bubble over.

Such is the case at Children's Home No. 23, an orphanage in the First of May District of Moscow's eastern periphery. The building is a duplicate of the spaciously designed kindergartens with their sleeping rooms and dressing rooms and playing rooms. There are fish tanks and houseplants and colorful blocks. But in the early evenings no parents come to gather the children into their arms and take them home. Born to young women out of wedlock, cast out of homes full of drunkenness and mental illness, abandoned on the street or as their parents are taken off to prison, the youngsters live and grow under the tender gazes of 85-ruble-a-month upbringers.

Since officials encourage adoption of infants only, few of these older children are placed with families and for the most part are raised in institutions. Their clothes are uniform. The girls' hair is cropped short, like boys', except that when a visitor comes, starched hair ribbons are pinned on top of their heads.

When I walked into a room, their great, hollow eyes grasped mine longingly and followed me steadily, just as the eyes in Vietnamese orphanages had locked onto mine years before.

Fira Sergeyevna Dobrovetskaya, who runs this orphanage and has twenty years of experience working with homeless children, ought to be either hardened or incisive. But she is neither. She approaches her job with a relaxed kindness, an earthy peasant warmth as natural and unrestrained as a summer wind across the steppe. She wants to think the best of everything, and if children without parents are tortured somewhere deep inside with a hidden emptiness, she tries not to see it.

"The children seem not to feel they lack real love," she told me. "They call the upbringers mothers. They don't even know the difference." Don't they? I pushed her a bit. "Yes, maybe deep in the soul they may develop some kind of sadness—they are such sensitive children," she said. "But they become so used to the regime here they don't feel the lack of parents. They don't have spare time to become engaged in deep thoughts. They don't ask questions about their parents." Some protective blind spot had evolved in this woman, though she was not insensitive. We walked through the rooms of the orphanage, letting the eyes fasten upon us, stopping, crouching, watching the children play, and when we returned to her office, I asked her if she did not ever go home in the evenings and sit alone and feel an overwhelming sadness. "Of course," she said. "Every day. It's a difficult mission. It is sad to see the mists in their eyes. It is a very sad establishment because with all the funds and attention being paid by the state, we would like to have fewer children. Sad," she said quietly. "Sad."

Without dissecting thought processes or throwing issues open to free analysis, Soviet schools approach academic subjects in much the same way as they approach crayon drawings. There are right answers and wrong answers. And very early on youngsters develop an instinct for knowing which is which. In the reading textbook for the third grade, which is used in every school in the Russian Republic, the questions following each few paragraphs of reading are not designed to stimulate creative thought: "Why in czarist Russia was it profitable for the rich to hold the people in ignorance and submissiveness? How did the situation of the people change after October 1917? What is the main strength of our multinational state? How is this explained in the article? What is the main idea of the article? Find the answer in the text and read it." Since Soviet children enter first grade at age seven, third graders are already nine and ten, old enough to begin absorbing the political messages.

Youngsters are drilled in a catechism of memorization and correct response. At School No. 35 in Dushanbe, almost 2,000 miles from Moscow near the border of Afghanistan, I poked my head into a tenth-grade social studies class. About twenty-five teenagers sat at scarred wooden desks bolted in rows to the floor. The teacher, a matronly-looking, sharp-tongued polemicist, was lecturing and shooting rapid-fire questions at her pupils, not waiting for them to volunteer but picking on them for quick one-sentence answers.

"We were discussing the general crisis of capitalism," she said. "What do we mean by 'general'?" She pointed at a red-haired girl in the front row, who sprang to her feet.

"It means it is multifaceted, involving political, economic, and cultural life."

"Correct," said the teacher. "Be seated. And when was the first crisis of capitalism?" She selected a pretty girl at the side of the room.

"The First World War," said the girl.

"And the end of that crisis?"

"The Second World War."

"No," snapped the teacher. "The end of the first crisis." She pointed to a boy, who rose confidently.

"The October Revolution and the formation of the first socialist countries," he declared.

"Correct. And the second crisis?"

"The Second World War."

"Correct," said the teacher. "The third crisis began in the 1950's and continues to this day, marked by inflation, unemployment. But the working class in the United States of America has become less revolutionary because the owners have had to make concessions to the workers." She went on to talk about the working class's rising in technological level and asked if Soviet workers should get advanced technical training, as those in the United States receive. From the back of the room, someone said, "No!" and the whole class, including the teacher, burst out laughing in a refreshing touch of irreverence.

Hanging a map on the board, the teacher went on to divide the world into spheres of certainty, explaining that the third crisis of capitalism had been characterized by an end of colonialism, with more and more ex-colonies turning toward socialism. She asked the students to name some of the countries that had made the switch. The first mentioned was Ethiopia, then Angola, then Laos. They forgot Vietnam.

Certainty is such a solid foundation of Soviet education that by the time many Russians reach their teens they have already developed a virulent allergy to ambiguity. I saw it in action once in a Moscow school's select tenth-grade English class, the only case I witnessed during my four years of visiting classrooms in which students were being asked to do their own thinking. The fourteen youngsters in the room were painfully uncomfortable with this unusual exercise. Their teacher, a middle-aged woman with smart eyes, was the sort you remember your whole life: cheerful and demanding, creative and precise.

She was inviting the youngsters to give their own reactions to the behavior of a character in Arthur Hailey's novel *The Final Diagnosis,* which they were reading as an insight into contemporary English usage. They had been studying the language since second grade and spoke fluently.

"Do you approve or disapprove of Dr. Pearson's behavior in this situation?" she asked. The students were dumbfounded. Nobody spoke. They searched the teacher's eyes for clues to how they were to react. She gave none but prodded them smilingly to say what they thought. They looked at their fingernails, fidgeted with their pencils. Had she asked, "Why do you approve?" or "Why do you disapprove?" there would have been a flurry of raised hands.

Finally she had to point to a boy and force him to speak. "I disapprove, but I understand his feelings," he began, and when he had finished, a girl rose to take slight issue.

"It is impossible to understand . . ." she said, and the discussion was begun. The teacher managed to bring out a variety of contrasting ideas about personal relationships without subjecting any of them to autocratic value judgments. And having accomplished that to the bewilderment of her students, she then divided the class in half for a small debate: One side of the room was to defend Dr. Pearson, the other Dr. Coleman, two characters whose antagonism did not rank among the momentous in English literature but provided a decent way of limbering up the brain.

The youngsters did not take to this easily. They giggled and squirmed and played their roles with excruciating self-consciousness, winking and smirking at one another across the room as they formulated their arguments ponderously, without much forensic skill or enthusiasm. One would have expected about the same delight from a class of seventeen-year-olds who, placed on ice skates for the first time in their lives and told they could swoop like free breezes across the lake, just fell flat. At the end the teacher summed up. "Sometimes you should think about the people around you," she said, "not to think only of yourself. Old, experienced people and young, talented people with great ideas must respect each other." The bell rang harshly, and the students leaped for the door.

This was a rare teacher in any school system, especially in the Soviet Union, as the discomfort of her students testified. Even in subjects without the heavy political baggage of social studies and history, the style is usually pedantic, and the response is to regurgitate what has been taught, as if the student were that empty vessel into which and from which knowledge could be poured at will. Irina McClellan, who taught English in a Russian school until she lost her job for marrying a visiting American professor (whom she was then not allowed to join in the United States), remembers growing increasingly appalled as her daughter, Yelena, worked her way up through the grades. What had seemed normal from a teacher's perspective became intolerable from a mother's. "When Lena started literature and I tried to discuss ideas with her, she couldn't," Irina said. "Our director [principal] taught literature. I never heard of discussions during the lecture. She would ask them to open their notebooks and copy what she said. When I saw my daughter's notebook, I was amazed. There were no ideas. They sounded like laws."

Pushkin's poems are committed to memory even in the second

grade—for the purpose, I always suspected, of providing pleasure to grown-ups who enjoy hearing the silvery words ring out in the clean, clear Russian of a child's voice, untarnished by the slurs and slang of adulthood. The verses also keep a continuity among the generations and a soothing connection with a history transcending the politics of the Revolution. As Hedrick Smith reports in *The Russians,* identical passages are learned by heart over decades; his daughter had to memorize one from Gogol, the same one, he found, that two Russian acquaintances aged twenty-six and fifty-five had been required to learn in their schooldays: "What a wonder is the Dnieper River in tranquil weather when, smoothly and freely, it speeds its generous waters through forests, hills and dales . . ." There is an old Russian saying: *Povtoreniye—Mat ucheniya* (Repetition is the mother of knowledge).

The method of drill works well in many fields, producing technically proficient linguists, dancers, and violinists. If you happen to walk along one or another back street in Moscow or Leningrad or any of dozens of other cities at a time of year when windows can be open, you may suddenly find yourself outside a music school where sprays of delicious dissonance shower down in lemony minglings of notes and scales and tunes from the separate lessons of piano, flute, clarinet, violin. Seven- and eight-year-olds in these afternoon and evening music schools, which conduct classes and individual lessons after normal school hours, hold the violin or the viola or the cello perfectly, their elbows and wrists at just the proper angles, their bow arms moving with trained gracefulness to draw the bows across the strings at the correct speed and pressure for a given note and volume.

All but a fraction of these youngsters will remain amateurs; they are pushed by their parents into music lessons, as I was forced to take piano from a nice old woman named Mrs. Murphy. But there is none of the American dedication to having fun in such pursuits. It is a more serious and intensive endeavor. Until one step or exercise is mastered completely and boringly, no teacher will allow the pupil to skip ahead to play a pretty melody just because it would be enjoyable and motivating. Nor does one think of approaching Mozart before the required études can be done flawlessly. The gratification comes later, in the desperate nervousness of an examination well played and a recital well performed, in the buzz and hum of an auditorium of parents and siblings and fluttering teachers who are on trial with their students.

The results of the discipline are well known. Battalions of fine musicians are produced, among whom an occasional David Oistrakh, Mstislav Rostropovich, Svyatoslav Richter emerges from the ranks. Yet professionals in the United States and Israel, where many Soviet émigrés have settled recently into new musical careers, often find the usual Soviet professional bland and wooden in his performance—precise and technically superb but cold and unfeeling in his interpretation, a triumph of prowess over meaning.

Even where a teaching situation cries out for students to react individually, they are rarely asked to do so. The afternoon music schools, which are sprinkled in large numbers throughout all the country's cities, normally require youngsters to study the history and theory of music as well as their particular instruments. But the history courses concentrate on the memorization of dates, names, pieces, composers' biographies, and the recognition of passages of music played on a piano or a record player. The teacher analyzes musical form, explaining why it is a rondo or a sonata, and during exams the children are expected to define the form and the identity of the particular passage, usually selecting from multiple choices listed on the blackboard. In one course every class began with one pupil after another standing to recite the lesson from the class before, while his deskmate pushed his open notebook over so he could look down and crib the answers while everybody giggled and snickered. It was a relaxed atmosphere, but never were the children invited to talk about their own attitudes toward the music they were hearing; never were they asked to describe its mood, to explore how it made them feel.

The deficiencies of such an education are less visible when Russians are in the protective environment of Soviet society than when they emigrate and plunge into the open societies of the West. Although those who leave are hardly representative of the Soviet population as a whole (most are Jews, courageous and strong-minded enough to defy accepted mores and risk retribution by speaking critically or applying for exit visas), many have intellectual difficulties when they get out. The combative political debates in the two countries where most of them go, the United States and Israel, are completely bewildering for a good proportion, who attempt to resolve their confusion by superimposing a familiar Soviet-made grid of categories onto the hurly-burly of free ideas—something Aleksandr Solzhenitsyn has done eloquently during his involuntary exile in the United States. Nor do many acclimate easily to the Western demand that they do their own thinking on their own feet. A professor of education in Jerusalem told me with dismay that his Russian students in a course on teaching handicapped and retarded children followed instructions exquisitely but just could not come up with their own thoughts on how an unexpected problem should be tackled. A professor of Soviet and Eastern European studies in Tel Aviv said that Soviet émigrés who write for a journal he publishes are constantly looking to him for guidance on what they should say, with more regard for finding the line than the truth.

An apprehension about the unknown, a discomfort about the undefined become the common denominators of life. The outside world is safe only if it is well ordered in the mind; the personal world is manageable only if it is relieved of uncertainty. It is crucial to be able to see clearly where you stand.

From elementary school on, no child can ever have any doubt about his elders' evaluation of his performance. He is graded every day on his classwork, and the small notebook in which the daily grades are written must be carried back and forth between home and school so that parents are kept apprised. Test scores and other marks are posted on bulletin boards for all to see, and every school has its central display of photographs of *otlichniki,* the "excellents" who get all 5's, the top grade, equivalent to straight A's. Neither success nor failure can be accomplished in privacy.

Even children's entertainment often observes the safe frontiers of certainty, carrying moralistic messages about the frightening unknown and placing the deviant or the adventurous at grave risk. The endings are not always entirely happy either; the hero or heroine is not always given the opportunity provided in traditional fairy tales to conquer danger and emerge victorious over an external threat that is frequently a metaphor for an internal fear.

At eight-fifteen every evening millions of Soviet children are placed in front of their television sets for the nightly performance of *Spokoiny Nochi* ("Good Night"), a fifteen-minute show of puppets and songs. It's cute, and children love it. But it can be annoyingly preachy. One episode starred three hand puppets—a little bear, a rabbit, and an unidentifiable animal of some sort that acted as an adult-approved spoilsport. The bear wanted some ice cream; the unidentifiable animal said no, it was too cold outside. The bear wanted to walk in the woods; the unidentifiable animal said no, he might get lost. The little bear went to the rabbit to ask about going to the woods, and the rabbit said it would be fine if he were a big bear, but since he was little, he would have to ask somebody to go with him so he wouldn't get lost.

Somehow the three got hold of a magic chunk of glass with the power to transport them all to the woods together. They counted one, two, three and materialized in a deep forest, where they proceeded to have a very educational conversation about pine trees, mushrooms, and berries and how they grow. As they walked and talked, they eventually realized that they were lost. But the magic glass took them home safely.

Well, not entirely safely. Because at the end somebody sneezed, setting off a big discussion about how he had probably caught a cold out in those damp woods. Then the little bear asked for ice cream again, and the unidentifiable animal said no, it was too cold outside. And on that unsatisfying note the program was over. Even the fantasy wasn't freeing, but stifling and enveloped in rules. There was no real high-flying fun.

Debby once saw a cartoon that struck more deeply at unapproved behavior. It was in the form of a filmstrip that could be bought from toy stores for showing at kindergartens and birthday parties. A rather unlikable boy was portrayed going around greedily asking for animals to give him things, and he acquired a rabbit's ears, a peacock's tail, an elephant's trunk. As he put on each of his new possessions, he came to look more and more like a monster until, when he went home, his mother screamed with fright and slammed the door in his face. At the end, he was left sitting alone outside.

If it had been a more therapeutic version on the themes of traditional fairy tales, the boy would have shed his appendages, learned his lesson, and finally been embraced by his mother. But here there was no forgiveness. The boy was left rejected. And the effect on children watching must have been terribly frightening. It was good preparation for the real world of larger Soviet society, where serious deviance would also be punished by the withdrawal of the affection and protection of the motherland.

The most popular cartoon series was an endless chase of a rabbit by a wolf, modeled on the Roadrunner and Tom and Jerry cartoons. Called *Nu Pogodi* ("Just You Wait!"), it was sheer laughter, pure release, entirely free of the moralistic pounding found elsewhere. The smart-pants rabbit was forever making narrow escapes, running up and down mountains and swimming through streams and lakes and building elaborate contraptions with which to render the poor bumbling wolf senseless. Originated in 1969 by three artists, one of whom, Feliks Kandel, later emigrated to Israel, the films were still going strong a decade later, guaranteeing packed houses anywhere in the Soviet Union and bringing in hard currency through sales abroad. Kandel told me that only once did he remember a higher official in the state-run film studio trying to give the series an ideological cast, by making the rabbit into a brave young Pioneer with red neckerchief and the wolf into some symbol of evil capitalism. "We beat him," Kandel recalled, mainly, he thought, because the cartoons brought huge income to the studio—not something to be ignored even in the centrally planned economy of the World's First Socialist State. To some extent, though, children saw in the rabbit the good Pioneer anyway, the studious intellectual, the bright, upstanding citizen their teachers wanted them all to be. And therefore, it was the wolf they loved, Kandel said, as a statement of their resistance to the expectations. At occasional showings the audience of youngsters would be asked whom they liked more, "and they all cried, 'The wolf!' " he recalled. In schools, when pupils were invited to draw their versions of a *Nu Pogodi* story, about four out of five portrayed the wolf sympathetically, putting him in the hero's role. "He's not cruel," Kandel explained. "He's just a fool."

The Collective and the Individual

An important function of Soviet fantasy is to convey the ethic of collectivism. The sense of individual desire and personality submerged in the broader group—whether that group is a row of schoolchildren, a department of factory workers, a scientific institute, or the entire nation—is much more than a fragment of Marx and Engels polished by Lenin and stuck like an irritating splinter into Russian flesh. It has been absorbed into the structure of values and mores so that its violation stimulates genuine revulsion in many people. If a scientist goes against the stream and pushes for the financing of unorthodox experiments, he is likely to be considered an egotist rather than an achiever—which is precisely what happened to a man I knew who developed a method of implanting artificial lenses in human eyes afflicted with burns or cataracts. As a young scientist he went out too far on his own, his laboratory rabbits were ordered destroyed, and he was transferred to a small Siberian city until, over many barren years, he painstakingly worked his way back into the main line of the scientific establishment and ultimately became a leading eye surgeon commanding an institute. If an architect draws an innovative plan, he may find it politic to avoid claiming authorship lest he be accused of heaping credit upon himself—which is what happened in Murmansk, where "microdistricts" of apartment houses were being built in huge horseshoe-shaped configurations carefully positioned to form solid walls against the relentless winter wind; inside the shelter provided by the high-rise buildings, schools and playgrounds were situated. The architect who thought this up gracefully demurred. "It is science that dictated this idea to us," he said. The head of the Foreign Ministry's press department, Vsevolod Sofinsky, gave an explanation of why officials rarely grant interviews: "It is not a modest way. It is considered self-advertisement."

The enforced humility is a device of social control, of course, but it also accords with Soviet notions of good taste and proper behavior. Not only do political dissidents and would-be émigrés and defecting ballerinas and chess players represent a confrontation with state authority and a challenge to the country's mystical patriotism, but they also commit the sin of self-aggrandizement, in which each of them somehow regards himself as better than, and apart from, the *kollektiv*. This is an affront to elementary morality; few Russians seem to question the morality itself. Many appear ready and anxious to believe the official condemnations in *Pravda, Izvestia,* and elsewhere that those who criticize the country or want to leave it are interested only in acquiring personal fame and material luxury. In milder form, the same basic accusation is often leveled at loyal citizens who complain quietly within their places of work about a defective procedure or decision. "You are trying to call attention to yourself," they will be told. Similarly, children of high school age who seek part-time jobs to earn money for themselves are frowned upon, and their parents are considered uncultured. This is beginning to change, slowly, but the old ethic still holds in many households that any money earned is the property of the whole family, and children are expected to turn it into the general pool—that is, give it to their parents. Any little one who set up a lemonade stand, as American kids do to learn the virtues of private enterprise, would be shut down immediately and scolded for engaging in an activity seen as simultaneously demeaning and self-centered.

A friend who is not a party member, but is one of the few real, believing Marxists I encountered in the Soviet Union, once recited to me what he said was an old Russian proverb expressing the collectivist idea: "In a field of wheat, only the stalk whose head is empty of grain stands above the rest." To him, this was a beautiful statement, one that touched the essence of human affairs and reflected the transcendence of traditional communal impulses over modern communist doctrine, thereby rooting the ideology firmly in Russian soil.

How much Russia was changed by the Revolution is a subject of debate by historians and other scholars, many of whom in the West have come to see strong lines of continuity between the autocracy of the czars and of the Politburo. In the matter of communalism the threads reach back to the ancient Slavs, who were organized in blood-related tribal communities that worked as teams. Later most of the Russian peasantry owned farmland jointly with others in the communal village, called an *obshchina* or *mir*. But as Richard Pipes points out in *Russia Under the Old Regime,* there are few similarities between this and the present-day collective farm, for each village household in the nineteenth century owned the fruit of its own labor, even if it did not own the land individually, whereas the Soviet collective farmer must give his product to the *kolkhoz,* the collective farm (except for what he raises on his small private plot), which turns it over to the state and pays the farmer a share of the return, less certain contributions to the *kolkhoz* fund for social benefits, capital expenditure, and the like. Pipes acidly notes the similarity between this and the *mesiachina* under Russian serfdom, in which "the landlord enclosed his land and placed the peasants on full-time labor on his own behalf, paying them a wage to support themselves."

The collectivist ethic today finds expression in diffuse forms, as well as in the sharper features of the society's social and economic organization. On the job, in trains, and even on hikes through pristine forests, Russians tend to congregate, to mingle, to find solace in what is sometimes the necessity of bumping against one another and rubbing shoulders—unavoidable in crowded stores and tiny apartments. Aside from the friction this inevitably creates, and the tension within families jammed into small rooms with new-lyweds and in-laws thrown under each other's ruthless scrutiny, a certain taste also develops for the gritty contact and the sense of belonging it provides.

One October dawn I waited for a train from Kishinev to Odessa. There was a heavy, steady rain. The spacious station with its cold stone floors awoke ponderously from the lingering night, first to the shuffling of the *kolkhozniki,* the stocky men and women from the collective farms, faces still chalky from sleep, lugging stuffed sacks and packages of shoes and dresses and cheese of a quality they could buy only in the city. Then came the random click, click of the boots of sleepy soldiers going back from leave, girlfriends leaning against them as they wandered a few steps at a time, looking at watches and at each other's eyes. Slowly beneath the high, echoing ceilings the station filled until 6:50 A.M., when the train glided in, the automatic doors slid open, and the crowd pushed and shoved frantically, afraid that every place of hard slatted wooden bench would be taken. Stout women with their bulky, odd-shaped packages muscled into cramped seats. "Who put things here?" one shouted at a stack of bundles in front of a vacant bench. A young soldier in uniform, his hat with the red band and the gold hammer and sickle thrown back haughtily to reveal a shock of curly black hair, said they were his. "Well, why did you put them there?" yelled the woman. "I have a lot of things!"

"I have a lot of things, too!" he shot back nastily.

Strangers, jumbled together on the uncomfortable seats, facing each other, fell into instant familiarity. I was next to a window. Across from me sat a mother with a deeply lined grey face and her daughter, a plain country girl of about twenty. On my left was a jovial fat woman, and next to her on the aisle a thin elderly grandmother.

"Slava Bogu!" the fat one said as she settled into her seat. "Glory to God, we found a place," and she crossed herself. The grey-faced mother facing her made the sign of the cross also. "We were lucky to get places," boomed the fat one. "On the train from Odessa, one day no places, the next day no places."

The train had not yet moved. A young woman appeared in the doorway in the back of our car, shouting at her husband, who was seated nearly at the far end, "Where are the keys?"

"I gave them to you!" he yelled back.

"No. I don't have them," the woman replied, patting her pockets, digging into her purse, dancing nervously in fear of the train's leaving before she could get off.

"I don't have them either!" her husband shouted. All conversation in the car ceased. All eyes turned as the man stood up and plunged his hands desperately into the pockets of his overcoat, his pants, stabbing wildly at his shopping bags. Time was running out. He looked at his wife helplessly. "You must have them!" he yelled. She shrugged and jumped off the train just as it began to move. A wave of rich, earthy laughter rose in the car as it gathered speed.

There was something both tough and soft in the mother's face. Her daughter had a sparkle and a gaiety in her eyes when she was talking, but it quickly drained away when she fell silent, leaving an awful glaze. Everyone spoke to everyone else—small talk mostly, about the weather and the time, about this person or that they might have known on one collective farm or another years ago. The train stopped at a tiny village; the thin grandmother on the aisle got off; a fat, ruddy man took her place, barely squeezing onto the end of the bench, pressing against the jovial fat woman, who said to the mother, *"Baba luchshe* ["The grandmother was better"]." We all giggled except for the fat man, who didn't know exactly why everybody was snickering at him. "She was thinner," said the fat lady with the perfect timing of a professional comic. We all chuckled. "Much thinner," and a widening group of us broke into guffaws. Finally, with the poor man looking puzzled and left-out, the mother explained that the passenger before him had been very thin, and he howled with laughter and joined in the string of wisecracks.

"Closer and closer," he said, nudging against the fat lady, who whooped and laughed. "Closer, closer." This went on for a long, wonderful time. Among strangers, a warmth, as the train sped through the wet green countryside, blurred through rain-streaked windows like Impressionist canvases.

Few seek solitude. On Sundays, in the woods around Moscow, hikers travel the trails in long, sinewy lines of twenty to thirty; whole clubs are organized for the sport. "Don't you ever go alone or just with a friend or two?" I asked a middle-aged woman.

She was baffled by the question. She loved the people and the babble of conversation in the woods. "It's a collective," she said proudly of her group, as if that answered everything.

"Collective" has become a catchword. At the office, in the classroom, on the assembly line, the individual is expected to blend in without any rough edges, to flow smoothly with the collective. And if he does not, if he has his idiosyncrasies, if he is a loner, if he is shy, if he is unusually able and doesn't mind showing it, if he does not go out of his way to drink with the boys, if he is disliked for any reason, people begin to say that he does not really fit into the *kollektiv,* that he somehow doesn't quite belong where he is. What can begin with a petty rivalry and a personality clash can grow into a damning insult—"not a good collectivist"—and like a stain, it is almost impossible to wash off.

Consequently, it was surprising to see that a Moscow theater for children included in its repertoire Rudyard Kipling's "The Cat that Walked by Himself." It is hardly a story for the collectivist. Set in ancient times, when the Cat, the Dog, the Cow, and the Horse are still wild, it is in part an approving appraisal of aloneness and independence, an appreciation of the Cat, who cannot quite be domesticated by the Woman's clever bribery or by the brutality of the Man and the Dog. The Woman offers the Dog roasted mutton bones if he will hunt with the Man and guard the cave; she promises the Cow fresh grass if she will give milk, and she provides grass to the Horse if he will wear a halter and carry the Man hunting. "This is a very wise woman," thinks the Cat, "but she is not so wise as I am."

As the embryonic society begins to form, the Woman and the other members develop a disliking for the Cat as he declares haughtily, "I am the Cat who walks by himself, and all places are alike to me." So when the Cat wants to sit by the fire and drink warm milk, the Woman rejects him, throwing his self-reliance back in his face. Only when he flatters her, calling her beautiful, does she begin to relent. She makes a reluctant promise: If she can find a word of praise for him, he may enter the cave. If she can find two nice things to say about him, he may sit by the fire. If three, he may have warm milk three times a day forever.

The Woman is determined to say nothing good about the Cat, but the Cat is cunning. When the Baby cries, he caresses it with his paw and tickles it with his tail until it laughs. When the baby is cranky, he amuses it by chasing a spindle whorl across the floor and playing with the little one until it falls asleep. When a mouse appears in the cave, the Cat catches it. So he gets to the fireside with his milk, figuring he will never have to do anything more.

But then the Man and the Dog return from hunting. They have made no deal with the Cat, they say. The Cat must always be kind to the Baby, says the Man, or he will throw his boots and his axe at the Cat; the Cat must always catch mice, says the Dog, or he will chase the Cat up trees. The Cat agrees but adds, "I am the Cat who walks by himself, and all places are alike to me." And because they are angered by these words, the Man throws things and the Dog chases the Cat for all time, even though the Cat is kind to the Baby and catches mice. "But when he has done that, and between times," Kipling writes, "and when the moon gets up and the night comes, he is the Cat that walks by himself, and all places are alike to him. Then he goes out to the Wet Wild Woods or up the Wet Wild Trees or on the Wet Wild Roofs, waving his wild tail and walking by his wild lone."

Not so on the Soviet stage. An enterprising team of rewriters and actors took Kipling's story, melted it down, and recast it in the appropriate mold, retaining the author's name and the original title, but little else. The Baby was a child, fussed over by the Woman, suffocated with protective attention, argued about at length when the Man wanted to take it hunting. More important, the allegory was gone. The Cat was female, feminine, almost sexy. The Dog and the Cow were comical. The dialogue was heavy on how good it was to be part of the group, and there was nothing positive in the Cat at all, nothing enviable or free or soaring. She was simply unpleasant and arrogant and vain.

The power of the collectivist ethic was documented by some interesting research in 1966 on the comparative strengths of peer-group authority in the Soviet Union, the United States, Britain, and West Germany. Soviet schoolchildren were found to be highly responsive to the expectations of their classmates for good behavior.

The results are described by Urie Bronfenbrenner in his book, *Two Worlds of Childhood: U.S. and U.S.S.R.*; he headed the research team, which also included Robert R. Rodgers and Edward C. Devereux, Jr. They presented more than 150 twelve-year-olds in each country with a set of situations in which the youngsters could choose between correct and immoral behavior—cheating on a test, for example, or denying that they had damaged property. The tests were run in three different conditions: In one, the children were told that the results would not be seen by parents, teachers, classmates, or anyone else they knew but would merely be fed anonymously into a computer; in the second, they were told that the results would be posted for a parent-teacher meeting but that their classmates would not see them; and in the third, they were led to believe that only their classmates, not parents or teachers, would be shown their answers.

"The results indicate that, under all three conditions, Soviet children are much less willing to engage in anti-social behavior than their age-mates in three Western countries," Bronfenbrenner wrote. "In addition, the effect of the peer group was quite different in the Soviet Union and the United States. When told that their classmates would know of their actions, American children were even more inclined to take part in misconduct. Soviet youngsters showed just the opposite tendency. In fact, their classmates were about as effective as parents and teachers in decreasing misbehavior." A companion study "showed that Soviet youngsters placed stronger emphasis than any other group on overt propriety, such as being clean, orderly and well-mannered, but gave less weight than the subjects from the other countries to telling the truth and seeking intellectual understanding."*

A few cautionary notes are in order. First, as a Soviet sociologist once lamented to me, it is almost impossible to convince a Soviet

*Urie Bronfenbrenner, *Two Worlds of Childhood: U.S. and U.S.S.R.* (New York: Pocket Books, 1973), pp. 82, 85.

citizen that an anonymous questionnaire he is about to complete will, in fact, remain anonymous. He knows that the study could not be done without the approval of the local party committee in his factory or his institute, and he is sure that it is some trick by the authorities to gain access to his innermost attitudes. Secondly, as Bronfenbrenner's companion study indicated, even children acquire canniness—an emphasis on overt propriety, as he termed it —and they know what the expected answers are. Finally, even if Soviet school officials are not told the contents of the study in advance, they are adept enough to make sure their most exemplary schools and their most exemplary pupils are used as the focus of the research; in the Soviet context this means the children who are most active in Young Pioneers and Komsomol, where collectivist ethics are practiced most intensively. This would naturally give the results Bronfenbrenner obtained.

Far from undermining the research, however, these caveats tend to demonstrate how vital collectivism is in the formal value system of the society, leaving only some question about its effectiveness in determining behavior. On this point contradictory evidence exists. In some schools I found an aversion to invoking the collective as a vehicle of discipline. Elsewhere young people often explained that their peers had the real authority in inducing proper behavior and good study habits. "The collective is more influential than the parents," said a law student. "We are more concerned with what the collective thinks of us than what our parents think." In secondary schools, collective "persuasion" is used routinely, he and some of his college friends reported, followed by collective "punishment" if necessary.

Teachers' manuals are clear on the desired methodology. Each class is to be divided into groups or rows of five to eight pupils, which compete with each other like teams, seeking the best scores for deportment, neatness, academic performance, and the like. Each team is called a *zveno*. The team leaders, usually chosen by the teacher or under her heavy influence, tend to be what my generation called teacher's pets or administration finks, good students who never got out of line and invariably took the school administration's side of issues. Every morning the team leader is supposed to rise and report to the class on the shortcomings of his group: Masha did not finish her homework again; Viktor did not do his neatly; Boris has a dirty shirt. Although this sort of self-criticism is not practiced religiously in many schools today, the basic structure of competing teams does create what to an American eye is an odd chemistry in the relationships among children. Because a laggard or an unruly youngster holds back the entire *zveno* and because a brilliant and well-behaved student pushes it ahead, classmates react with inordinate intensity to each other's performance, scolding the lazy, helping the slow, admiring the talented.

The result is a diffusion of authority. The recalcitrant finds it difficult to point to the source of pressure; he has no ready target. Like a diver submerged, he feels the weight of the water everywhere, from every direction. Collectivism becomes an imposition of authority indirectly; the peer group becomes the medium through which officialdom controls individual behavior. The class is manipulated by the teacher into taking the teacher's position, by electing the leaders it is expected to elect, by criticizing the youngsters it is expected to criticize. "We try to produce good behavior through the collective," explained Yevgenia Makeyeva, director of Kindergarten No. 49 in Samarkand. "So during play we say to the children, 'You see, she's playing badly. *Nelzya* ["That's not allowed"].' The teacher plays the role of organizer so the children can then do it themselves." The objective is spelled out in the authoritative handbook for adult leaders of the Pioneers, the organization that includes virtually all Soviet children ages nine to fourteen. "What to do with a boy who doesn't yield to any influence?" asks the *Kniga Vozhatogo (The Book of the Pioneer Leader)*. "Every denunciation should come not from the leader," the manual instructs, "but from the collective of the boys, the section, the unit. This is the most effective way." Again, the children's collective is a good model for grown-up society, where the party committee enforces discipline on its members, and the factory brigade is rewarded or punished as a whole for its productivity or inefficiency.

The *Kniga Vozhatogo* assumes adherence to the collectivist ethic so completely that it finds little need to mention the word. At the end of the book, in a list of the most important terms and ideas for a Pioneer leader, "collective" is not even included. But the entire thrust of the manual presupposes the existence of the collective as the Bible does God. The handbook contains not a single reference to individual forms of work with children; all suggestions and ad-

vice are in the plural, all discussion is of units, sections, and forma-
tions of young people.

A certain continuity of authority patterns is reinforced by the
practice in Soviet schools of assigning the same teacher to follow
the same class through the first four years, so that a first-grade
teacher will teach the same class second grade the next year, third
grade the year after, and then fourth grade, in the fifth year moving
back to pick up a new class at the first-grade level. Because families
often move to new towns and teachers change jobs, the system is
not perfect, but in many cases it works to provide a comforting
familiarity and sense of permanence. The classroom collective can
also be warm and supportive, for both those who do well and those
who do not. In all grades youngsters having trouble are regularly
given help by abler pupils, who stay after school or go to their
homes to tutor them, a practice called *shefstvo.* A young Russian
mother in the Central Asian city of Ashkhabad remembered this
process fondly, recalling that in her school the children were expected to help kids, push kids, "but were encouraged to do it
nicely." Two of her classmates who got all 5's until fourth or fifth
grade, when they started to slip, were assigned a girl to help them,
"and they came back up," she said.

Furthermore, despite the rifts and cliques that naturally divide
any group of children, emphasis is often placed on formal expressions of goodwill in the name of the collective. "When a child has
a birthday," said a Moscow third grader, "the teacher stands with
her hand over their shoulder and says, 'I hope you do well in the
school year and have a nice long life,' and, you know, all sorts of
nice things. And everybody else who wants to says the same things,
all sorts of nice things, 'I hope you get fives, only fives and fours,'
and to people who aren't doing very well, 'I hope you do better,'
and all that."

Nor is the collective always such a fierce disciplinarian, as can be
seen by the bedlam that regularly erupts in hallways and classrooms
when the teacher's back is turned. In a Soviet school, as in an
American one, you take your life in your hands if you get caught
in a corridor when the bell rings and hundreds of youngsters are
released in torrents of shouting and shoving. And despite the effort
to shape peer pressure for control purposes, close conversations
with children reveal considerable readiness to follow bad examples

among classmates. A telling episode was described by a third-grade girl in Moscow. Her class was working with plastic triangles, using them to draw rectangles, when the teacher left the room for a moment. "A kid stood up and started tapping his triangle on his desk," the girl said, "and the other kids got up and were tapping them together. Then she [the teacher] came in and everybody sat down immediately—immediately." There seemed little doubt about where the authority lay.

But it would be wrong to suppose that the collective did not function at all. It operated as it seems to in many schools and often among adults: not strictly by the book, perhaps, but as a complement to power from above. When the teacher of these nine- and ten-year-olds was faced with a bad apple named Eric who was always getting into fistfights, she tried using the collective, though rather mildly and unsuccessfully. According to two of his classmates, the children were expected to set him a good example, and when they did, the teacher would point it out, saying, "Eric, look how well the other children behave. You behave that way." She tried seating him next to the best pupils, but when he just copied their work, she moved him to the other side of the room. She never went as far as to invite the class to criticize him, however. Her last resort was something out of Mark Twain, not Vladimir Lenin: she put him and others who misbehaved in the corner.

If the teacher, not the collective, was the ultimate dispenser of criticism and punishment, the class cooperated to a remarkable degree in fingering offenders. "Everybody informs," said one boy, an American who spent several years in the school. "Everybody is an informer. If somebody does something, then whoever saw it goes and tells the teacher. Like, if someone hits someone else, then whoever saw it will go and tell the teacher." In other words, the tattletale is a fine citizen. The other youngsters don't get mad about this, the boy said in wonder; it is accepted as routine. A girl in a different school told of her third-grade classmates having to check their own mistakes, report on themselves, and then be checked in turn by pupils sitting next to them, who were to report any mistakes that had gone unmentioned. The girl's mother, furious when she heard this, was calmed by her daughter, who said, "Don't worry, we know it's not good to inform, and if anybody informs, we teach him."

In another third-grade class I watched as the teacher established her own authority, handed some to the children, and then reemphasized her own, like a symphony whose theme shifts from the violins to the cellos to the violins again. "Hands on the desk," she said. "Sit straight. You will listen to Valera, and if Valera misses anything, you will add. Hands on the desks. Look at me. Sit straight."

Out of this mixed picture several patterns emerge. The sanctity of the collectivist idea remains intact, like motherhood, but its practice in the schools is shaded by the varied preferences of individual teachers, who may invoke the term "collective" like a talisman to bring good fortune to their educational efforts. Lidiya Agaryova, whom I asked about collectivism in her Moscow Kindergarten No. 104, pointed out a circle of small children practicing a folk dance for a holiday show and proclaimed happily, "There— a collective," though it was no more of a collective than any circle of small children anywhere. So as usual in Soviet society, the slippage between the textbook prescription and the reality is large. What begins as a good intention often survives mostly as a façade to impress superiors. In one Moscow elementary school a teacher began the year by dividing her thirty-nine pupils into six *zvenya* and illustrated the upcoming competition by an elaborate chart on the bulletin board with rockets racing to the moon. But that was it. She then seemed to forget about the grouping, a couple of the children said, and never returned to it.

Neglect of the methodology is also salted with an outright wariness of collective punishment, especially in the lower grades. After reading the teachers' manuals, I was startled to find so many teachers themselves with an aversion to using children as each other's critics. Fira Dobrovetskaya, the orphanage director, said that the usual punishment was "a strong and expressive stare" from the upbringer and that the most severe was "to deny the use of the favorite toy." When I asked about calling on classmates to reprimand, she answered unequivocally, "No. *Nelzya* ["That's not allowed"]. To annihilate the dignity of a child is to annihilate everything." The proper approach, she explained, was not to call attention to the negative actions of other children but to get the youngsters to analyze each other's performance, asking, "What's wrong with the drawing?" for example, or inviting them to watch how nicely two little ones were playing. Mrs. Agaryova at Kindergarten No. 104 shared this view, endorsing punishment by the teacher rather than the collective. "If a child misbehaves," she said, "you tell him, 'You don't have the right to play today. You sit on a chair and watch how the other children play.' " Some teachers were less categorical, but several responded to my question about using the collective to discipline with the word *ostorozhno,* which translates as "carefully" but is really an all-purpose word of extreme caution when uttered in the grave tone the teachers used, appropriate for warning a child who is about to cross a busy street.

The collective has even been portrayed by some recent, moralistic fiction as a dangerous, destructive force. In one searing film shown on Moscow television a class of teenagers, manipulated by a malevolent teacher, humiliated a wayward boy so viciously that they drove him more deeply into misbehavior. On the Moscow stage a popular play examining a teenager's drift into crime concluded that one cause lay in the torment he suffered at the hands of a hostile collective of classmates who teased him about a lisp. His teacher was entirely blind to his pain.

But the official media are also quick to dramatize successful collective pressure. The weekly *Literaturnaya Gazeta* published an article on a disciplinary court made up of inmates in a reform school for girls:

> The thirty girls, the former "courtyard queens," outcasts, and public terrors, are sitting in judgment. The thirty are the cream of the school, the Supreme Council. They are giving five "greenhorns" a thorough dressing down for bad behavior at the quarantine. The older four teamed up to whack the fifth, the smallest. The chairman of the session, Asya, drives home the point forcefully: "Remember, this is your last fight here. It's mean to beat up the smaller ones." Asya's dossier testifies that her mother works as a train conductor and brings home "friends." The last time she came to see her daughter, she abducted her and tried to lock her up in a hotel room with one of the "friends" for the night. Asya was not yet thirteen then.
>
> But the victim, the small Zina, is no piece of candy herself. Right upon emerging from quarantine—that is, this morning —she told one of the teachers where to go, and when a patrol chided her for that, she made a "shake-off" gesture—a rude way of showing how much she cares for unsought advice.
>
> The verdict is "guilty," and the sentence is unusual: All five

are forbidden to communicate with each other for a probation period. Each of the five is assigned a personal overseer, and the most difficult one, Oksana, whose record includes drunken fights, thefts, and sleeping in men's dormitories, got herself Valya [a fourteen-year-old who comes from a family of promiscuous alcoholics].

Unsuspectingly, these girls are demonstrating the finished product of the penitentiary: the normal, conventional, good children. Asya, Ira, Natasha, and others are trying to influence the new arrivals, and they find quite fresh and convincing words. And to one's mind come the other words, the words that are smoldering in their character references and dossiers: "Secretive, dishonest, unruly, thieving . . ." It is strange to think that totally opposite characteristics will coexist in the same folder after the girls are released. For the school is different from other, conventional ones in that it forgets all that has been said about the contingent outside its walls. It begins with a clean slate and discovers that the "secretive" and "dishonest" girls are kind, love to help the small ones, and are very clean.

This notion that the collective brings forth the finest qualities in people is highly important in the Soviet system of ethics. Even in the film and stage portrayals of the collective's destructive power, there is a sense that something noble has been perverted. Never does the idea itself come under attack; never does the Western value of individualism gain ascendancy. Whether or not the story is a happy one, its moral is always the same: The collective is a potent force that can bring great good if used correctly. The thesis plays to the Soviet penchant for varnishing reality with a veneer of officially polished optimism.

One of its corollaries is the principle that responsibility for a child's performance is widely shared among teachers and parents and that the successes and failures are exposed to public view. This holds even in classrooms where collective discipline and competition are not exploited with much enthusiasm. In one such musical literature class the teacher never even went through the motions of dividing the children into *zvenya* or asking for collective criticism. But she read all test scores aloud and made her own critique of each child in front of the entire class. Once, another teacher burst into her classroom, looking for a boy who had not been showing up for individual lessons on his instrument, although exams were approaching. Spotting him, his teacher laced into him. "It's going to be a catastrophe for you!" she shouted as his classmates stared. "A catastrophe!" His face turned red.

What she meant was that it would also be a catastrophe for her if he did poorly. Teachers are held accountable for their pupils' proficiency, and they get as nervous as the children themselves in the face of exams. In music schools, where youngsters must perform several times a year, both before panels of examining teachers and to auditoriums full of parents and siblings, the preceding weeks of private lessons see tension build to excruciating heights, sometimes to the point where the teacher gets mixed up about just who is being tested, child or adult. A violin student who wanted to play a duet with a friend in a recital was told by her teacher that he would not allow it unless she worked on it very hard. "I cannot do it badly," the teacher declared. And when exam time came and his students were taking their tests one by one, he was doing his own countdown. "Three done," he said one day. "I have six more." It was not *"You* cannot do it badly" or *"They* have six more," but *I.* And in the recitals, as each youngster was introduced by a faculty member and the piece to be played was named, the teacher's name was announced as well, as if to say that here, molded by the master's hands, stood the product of skillful labor and love. It had a nice quality, conveying a sense of communal caring, spreading both the credit and the blame.

The parallels in adult society are considerably less attractive. Medical students are rarely flunked out, doctors say, because their professors' prestige would suffer. Factory managers and heads of research institutes are held responsible for the political behavior of their subordinates. If a Jewish scientist decides to apply to emigrate to Israel, his act of disloyalty casts a shadow on the director of his institute; the man's career can suffer, especially if the phenomenon repeats itself with a number of his employees. I knew some would-be émigrés who were so fond of their bosses that they resigned their jobs before applying for visas, just to diminish the impact on their superiors, who would usually be forced to dismiss them after their applications anyway. Spreading the guilt this way has set up such corrosive dynamics that many institute directors refuse to hire Jews out of a fear that they may then try to emigrate; such refusals cleverly turn Jews against Jews as those who wish to stay nurture a venomous resentment toward those who "stir up trouble" by wanting to leave. The lines of authority and control grow tangled, forming a complex fabric of restraint.

In schools, parents are drawn explicitly into a close identification with their children's performance. It begins on the opening day in September, a grand event with children scrubbed raw and gleaming, parents and grandparents gathered proudly. Kevin Klose described to me the day he and his wife, Eliza, put their older son and daughter in a Moscow school. "This mass of kids all lined up," he said, "Class Two A and Two B and so on, and then the principal said, 'Our Politburo!' and these wonderfully large teachers all arrived at the front, and then she delivered this impassioned speech: the school year and what it means to society and how important it is. She really wasn't fooling around. It was very real to her. And the parents all listened very carefully."

Soviet classrooms are designed in the no-nonsense three R's fashion of the old brick schoolhouse: pairs of hard, worn desks and benches anchored to the floors in strict rows; walls hung sparely with austere slogans and portraits. Into these rooms five or six evenings a year, mothers and fathers come to sit like their children to hear the teacher upbraid or praise them for their youngsters' deportment and schoolwork. This institution of the open parent meeting sets Soviet and American society apart dramatically, for while some teachers may be more brutal than others in exposing a pupil's sins to the parents of all those in the class, never does one honor the privacy that is taken for granted in an American meeting of this sort. There is just no hiding. Irina McClellan, who has been on both sides as parent and teacher, said she disliked the system enormously. "The parents are afraid inside themselves," she said disgustedly. "They are afraid to go, and they feel like children."

Eliza and Kevin Klose were intrigued by the process. After reading off the names of children with various grades, the teacher turned on each parent to recite his youngster's ills. "One by one the parents of children who were having troubles got up and tried to explain," said Kevin, "and actually stood at their desks—we were actually crammed into these little desks just like the kids—and they sort of stood up and addressed the teacher as to what was wrong, why so-and-so wasn't doing well, 'I don't get home from work in time,' well this, well that, well, 'The *babushka* was sick,' what have you. And that surprised me, such open discussion of failings, to kind of confess errors or to talk of things that were on your mind. It was that sense of everybody's watching."

"It wasn't totally abject," said Eliza. "There were also parents who complained because one of the English teachers had been ill and they'd gotten some sub in who they thought was really second-rate, and they said, 'Who's gonna be the teacher? English is the main subject, and I want to see a better teacher in here!' and everybody'd say, 'Yes!' "

By and large, though, authority rests in the hands of the school. Children are funneled into activities and excursions on a compulsory basis, with or without parental consent, and parents often find themselves sitting nervously in the evenings helping their children with homework or in some cases, a few teachers told me, simply doing it themselves. "In a certain way," Irina McClellan observed, "the authorities at school are the authorities for the parents, too."

Yet it is common to hear that the school regards the parents as the last resort in discipline and academic problems. "If children respect their parents and are a little bit afraid of them, then it's easy for the school to deal with them," said Ona Uzelene, principal of School No. 40 in Vilnius, Lithuania. In Latvia I was told that if it seems inadequate for a student committee to investigate a wrong-doer and judge his behavior, the matter then goes to his parents and if that fails, to a parents' committee in the class.

The interlocking responsibilities are all part of the spirit of collectivism. But countercurrents also run against the strong instinct to identify with and defer to the larger group, and some of these opposing trends can be seen in the society's changing treatment of the family.

Anyone who reads Marx is bound to be astonished when he looks around the Soviet Union. The family, like the state, was to wither away. The repository of marital and parental oppression, the family appeared in the writings of both Marx and Engels as an expression of inequality and economic exploitation. Under communism it would give up its major functions, especially child rearing and property holding, to the society at large.

The idea proved difficult to transplant to Russian soil. Lenin and some of the other Bolsheviks who came to power in 1917 elaborated on the theme, translating it into specific programs for the development of communal children's houses, dining halls, and other institutions that would decrease the importance of the individual household. Often it was the goal of liberating women, which had its political objectives as well, that drove the early, idealistic Soviet theoreticians. "Women grow worn out in the petty, monstrous household work," Lenin wrote, "their strength and time dissipated and wasted, their minds growing narrow and stale, their hearts beating slowly, their will weakened. . . . The backwardness of women, their lack of understanding for the revolutionary ideals of the man, decrease his joy and determination in fighting. They are like little worms which, unseen, slowly but surely rot and corrode."*

Gripped by the disorder of civil war and infected by the still-fresh zeal of revolution, the country stumbled away from old precepts and grasped for the new in these early years. The doctrine of eliminating the traditional family matured among educators into the late 1920's, when the commissar of education, Anatoly Lunacharsky, wrote:

> Our problem now is to do away with the household and to free women from the care of children. It would be idiotic to separate children from their parents by force. But when, in our communal houses, we have well-organized quarters for children, connected by a heated gallery with the adults' quarters, to suit the requirements of the climate, there is no doubt the parents will, of their own free will, send their children to these quarters, where they will be supervised by trained pedagogical and medical personnel. There is no doubt that the terms "my parents," "our children," will gradually fall out of usage, being replaced by such conceptions as "old people," "adults," "children," and "infants."†

Some proponents of more radical revolution in everyday life saw the child as the property of the state, which therefore had the right to take him from unwilling parents. The doctrine of disrespect for reactionary fathers was urged upon young people, who were en-

*Klara Zetkin, *Reminiscences of Lenin* (London, 1929), quoted in H. Kent Geiger, *The Family in Soviet Russia* (Cambridge, Mass.: Harvard University Press, 1968), p. 46.
†Susan M. Kingsbury and Mildred Fairchild, *Factory, Family and Women in the Soviet Union* (New York: 1935), p. 205, quoted in Geiger, *op. cit.*, pp. 47–48.

couraged to criticize, expose, and reform parents possessing insufficient revolutionary ideals. The hero of the era was Pavlik Morozov, a twelve-year-old Young Pioneer who reported his own father, chairman of the village soviet, for selling false documents to exiled *kulaks*, private farmers who were resisting the brutal collectivization being imposed by Stalin and were allegedly withholding grain from the state. The father went to trial, where Pavlik testified against him. The boy was later murdered in a forest by *kulaks* and became a martyr of the party, which he remains today in songs and stories, although the celebration of his deed in schools and Pioneer groups has acquired a listless spirit of lip service. Under Gorbachev, newspaper articles have even attacked Pavlik as a false hero.

The efforts to communalize the family did not take, even in the twenties. In 1925 only 3 percent of city children were being sent to the public crèches; the remaining 97 percent included those kept home and those still homeless and roaming the streets.* Today only about 17 percent of the children under three years old are placed in daytime nurseries, and about 30 percent of all preschoolers go to nurseries and kindergartens. Moreover, the unnatural patina of antifamily doctrine has been scrubbed away almost without a trace. Mothers with ten or more children are ceremoniously made Heroines of Socialist Labor as the state tries, mostly in vain, to encourage large families to relieve the labor shortage. Party rhetoric increasingly emphasizes the central role of the family in shaping children's outlooks and personalities. The individual, separate apartment has become the premier objective of young married couples, who detest being thrown into a pair of crowded rooms with brothers and sisters and parents and in-laws. The "communal apartment" is no ideologically approved life-style, but a euphemism for the flats that still exist in the centers of the older cities, where the housing shortage has forced families to share accommodations, with each family assigned a room and everyone sharing the apartment's single kitchen and single bathroom. These are being emptied out as new, austere high-rises are put up in rings around the cities, and the term "communal apartment" has come to signify anachronism and poverty. And while the society's steady urbanization has brought the same decline in family stability as in other

*Geiger, *op cit.*, p. 58.

countries, with the divorce rate running at approximately one out of every three marriages at present, sociologists, educators, psychologists, criminologists, and others concerned with social problems are looking to the family unit for causes and answers as intensively as their Western counterparts.

The ideologist may argue that since the Soviet Union is still at its socialist stage, not yet having attained communism, it is premature to render the judgment that Marxism-Leninism has been perverted. But the fact remains that certain aspects of that creed do not sit comfortably on Russian culture, and the forecast of the disappearance of the individual household is one of them. All you have to do is watch Russians in train stations wrapping their children and spouses and parents and siblings in heavy hugs and tearful kisses as they come and go to understand that at least on this point, Marx is doomed to be proved wrong.

The tugs toward private life are strong. In film and literature they pull away from the monumental themes of patriots at war against the Nazis, of heroism in the steel mills, or bold performance in the flowing wheat fields. These are the obligatory themes, but increasingly the private individual looms large in Soviet writing. The most popular works are those neither of broad social criticism nor of the synthetic heroism that turns assembly lines and battlefields into poster art. Rather, they are the novels and short stories, the films and plays that reach into the intimate world of the family, that explore regions of personal anguish and grief and love, and do not always end happily. Some are serious works; some are melodramas; most make no gesture toward glorifying the achievements of socialism.

As I left Moscow, the rage in film was *Strange Woman*, a contorted chronicle of Yevgenia Mikhailovna Shevelyova's futile search for love, a search beyond the conventionally accepted attributes of happiness, one that took her away from her husband—well placed in the Foreign Trade Ministry, blessed with a handsome and comfortable apartment, strictly faithful, and admirably sober, all qualities antithetical to the gravest defects of Soviet men. She found a lover who was a bachelor with a neat, well-furnished flat, but with a conviction that he must remain unencumbered; he limited his affairs to brief flings of frivolity. "Devil take this love!" the husband declares, speaking for the official values of society. "People are busy with work, work—understand? Everybody is going crazy about this love as if nothing more important existed!" And Yevgenia, who believed that nothing more important existed, continued looking.

One of the most brutal examinations of tension and scheming within the family occurs in the late Yuri Trifonov's short story "The Exchange," in which grotesque characters are driven to monstrous behavior by social conditions. In apartment-short Moscow a greedy and hateful wife seizes on the news that her mother-in-law is dying and, after years of refusing to live with her, contrives to move into her pleasant one-room flat before she goes. This way, when the mother-in-law dies, her room plus the one they are now living in can be exchanged for a two-room apartment, an arrangement frequently agreed to by couples who want to separate but are forced by the absence of housing to stay together. Trifonov's pitiless writing about Soviet urban life earned him the contemptuous remark from one Russian that reading his works was like "looking through a keyhole at people." But everything he wrote was snapped up as soon as it appeared; each copy of any literary journal that carried his stories and novels was read by scores of people until the pages were limp and dog-eared. When a stage version of "The Exchange" opened in Moscow's avant-garde Taganka Theater, all tickets were obtainable only through intricate connections. Swarms of hopeful Muscovites packed the street in front of the theater and, as they do often at popular plays and concerts, accosted those on their way inside, asking if they had extra tickets to sell. By contrast, Debby and I once attended a modern dance performance based on Leonid Brezhnev's saccharine memoir of the war, *Malaya Zemlya,* a melodramatic pageant of battle and heroism with red banners and soldiers and stirring martial music. There were many empty seats in the auditorium, and outside, people who must have been given tickets at their factories and offices were trying to get rid of them at practically any price. It was the only time in Moscow, whose jammed theaters foster elaborate schemes of barter for seats, that I saw people trying to sell their tickets. And there were no takers.

The writers who engage Russians today are those who give relief from the pompous propaganda—science fiction writers, spy novelists, tellers of love stories—and those earning the most serious praise are those who take Russians into the small, fine foibles of individual human existence, the way you walk in from the titanic architecture of Moscow's Stalinesque sand-castle skyscrapers and its sweeping fourteen-lane boulevards and the thunderous steel and chrome statues of men with bulging biceps holding hammers and women with sickles, hair blown back in visionary poses of heroic optimism, through the cracked courtyards of apartment houses with their buckled pavements, into the narrow doorways and up the dingy stairways, until you get into the tiny apartments with their cheap, uncomfortable furniture and sit around the kitchen table, burning your tongue and fingers on glasses of steaming tea, *krepky,* strong, dark, sweetened with jam or sugar and plenty of talk. Talk. The best conversations in the world are around those Russian kitchen tables.

That is what the best writers are like nowadays. Valentin Rasputin, widely considered the most talented writer in the country, is known for the beauty and pain with which he captures life among the Russian peasantry and the withering of old values. Fyodor Abramov has produced some powerful stories of personal suffering in the countryside. Bulat Okudzhava, a balladeer and novelist, writes of a Russia that has passed and of private lives and private trials. Not only do they write, but they get published. Not widely or often, and not with unanimous enthusiasm in the echelons of power, but their work is seen; they remain members of the official Writers' Union. And the tolerance from on high—as thin as it sometimes is and as quickly as it has been removed from others, such as the brilliant satirist Vladimir Voinovich, who was forced to emigrate to the West—tells something about the slowly shifting values of the society, the extent to which the private individual has come to stand apart from the collective.

The ambivalence was expressed in a Moscow Young Pioneers organization where I was told that boys, after school, make model boats in two ways: individually, so that they have a sense of possession, and in groups, sometimes on an assembly-line basis, with each boy doing the same job over and over again. "We are the unlucky generation," said a Russian friend in his late thirties, "because we are torn between these two values." And another acquaintance of mine, a full-fledged and very active party member, assessed the strength of collectivism this way: "It is stronger than many in the West believe, but weaker than many here believe. There *is* a feeling of belonging to something larger, but as for the idea that the individual is nothing—no, that's no longer true."

TWO

The Willing Suspension of Disbelief

You know, we Russians now and then are such good-humored dreamers.

—Father Dmitri Dudko,
Moscow, 1978

Teaching Political Values

On the eleventh day of April no hint of spring had yet reached Moscow. Snow covered the ground, and the frosty cold kept the children heavily bundled as they walked up Yermolova Street to a school next to our apartment house. This school specialized in teaching English, and inside a third-grade class of nine-year-olds the teacher was writing a poem on the blackboard. When she had finished, she had the whole class read it aloud:

April, April, are you here?
Oh, how fresh the wind is blowing,
See, the sky is bright and clear.

They huddled over their desks, writing the lines in their copybooks. Along the walls were the usual red and white slogans and posters, except that they were in English, an English far too complicated for these youngsters to understand: "The Draft Constitution

94

of the USSR"; "A New Step on the Road of Communism"; and below, long texts headed "Brezhnev's Commentary"; "All Education Available"; "Nationwide Discussions"; "Internal Commentary." When they had finished copying the poem, the teacher began drilling them with questions.

"Is it spring or winter?" she asked, nodding through the windows at the snow.

"It is spring," said the child she had called on.

"Yes. All together."

"It . . . is . . . spring." No trace of irony.

The children had read the parable of the fox and the crane, and as the teacher held up a picture, she called on a girl to retell the story. It was Aesop's fable. The fox invites the crane to dinner, serves soup in a shallow dish, and thinks it very funny that the crane, with its long beak, cannot drink the soup. So the crane invites the fox in return, serves soup in a tall, narrow jar that the fox cannot get its snout into, and says to the fox, "I am so glad to be able to return your courtesy. I hope you enjoy your dinner every bit as much as I did mine when I visited you." The girl in class stood and stumbled haltingly through the tale while her deskmate prompted her in whispers that the teacher could not possibly have failed to hear. But the teacher made no effort to silence the deskmate, and when the girl had finished, she received a *khorosho* ("good") from the teacher, as if she had done it all without help.

"What is this?" the teacher asked, holding up a bugle tied with a red pennant.

"A Pioneer bugle," said the class in unison.

"And this?"

"A Pioneer drum," said the class. "A Pioneer flag."

Children whispered to one another, talked, drew funny pictures, and giggled. A boy played with a small mirror at his desk.

"All of you have Pioneer ties," the teacher continued, ignoring the misbehavior and pointing to the red neckerchiefs the children were wearing.

"Do you have a Pioneer tie, Andryusha?"

"Yes, I have a Pioneer tie," the boy replied.

"Are you a Pioneer?"

"Yes, I am."

"Is he a Pioneer, Peter?"

"Yes, he is."

Then she asked them to open their notebooks and write down new words. "Slogan," she said, translating it into the Russian, *lozung,* so they would understand. "Have you slogans in your class? How many slogans have you in your class?" The kids looked around the room and counted.

A girl rose to her feet. "We have eleven slogans in the class."

Then the teacher wrote on the board, "Long Live!"

"Write it, please. 'Long Live!' The translation is *Da Zdravstvuet!*" It may not come in very handy when these children are speaking English, but the expression in Russian is ubiquitous, strewn around the streets on banners and posters. "Long live our school!" she said, and had the children repeat. "Long live our Pioneer organization!"

A boy in the front row piped up irreverently, "Long live the fox!" Titters.

It seemed to me when I had finished sitting through this class that it contained most of the main ingredients of Soviet teaching. It was spring by the calendar, and the poem of the day talked of clear skies and a fresh breeze, and therefore, cold facts outside the window could be stared down with the supreme reality of the lesson, without so much as a smirk. It was a good metaphor for the political dimension of education, in which reality and truth are not investigated but constructed. A small girl could be praised for parroting the whispers of her classmate, a style of cheating widely ignored by Soviet teachers, who express and reinforce concern for the façade rather than the substance. Slogans obviously designed for older grades could be hung on walls to meet some superior's requirement, regardless of the children's inability to comprehend them. The trinkets and props of political orientation could be laced inextricably into the lessons; the only fresh wind that day was the small boy's sudden, spontaneous statement "Long live the fox!"

But the atmosphere in the classroom was warm despite the dull material, fairly disciplined despite the buzz of talking and wriggling in seats, and aimed at serious learning. Sincere praise came for quick students. "Bob got up early," said the teacher. "What does 'early' mean?"

"*Rano,*" said a little girl with the correct Russian word.

"*Umnitza!*" The teacher beamed. "Smart little one."

Americans who have gone to Catholic schools at home invariably see parallels between the political and religious instruction, between the inevitable portrait of Lenin and the painting of Jesus on the wall. "It's like parochial school, with catechism," said Kevin Klose. "The Young Pioneers in war are like the martyrs of the church."

His wife, Eliza, added, "You have your picture of Christ up there, and you say your prayers, but the important thing is that you do your work well and learn."

To live contentedly within the intricate construction of political attitude that schools build carefully for children, it is also important never to confront whatever disbelief may stir inside you, lest the spell be broken. This, I came to feel, was one of the earliest lessons of Soviet childhood, and it helps keep many, perhaps most, adults in a spirit of political comfort with their country and their system. To disbelieve is to destroy.

The academic levels of Soviet schools are uneven and inconsistent, somewhat less impressive in many cases than the formidable image invented by the American inferiority complex in the years after the first Soviet Sputnik beat us into space. The specter of ordinary Russian teenagers doodling brilliantly in mathematical formulas on the tablecloths of Leningrad cafés has faded now, partly as the society has opened slightly and the official press has displayed more candor. One discovers quickly that there are good schools and bad, just like everywhere else in the world, and that parents plot and scheme to get into the main cities and escape the dreadful rural schools. Well-educated men and women from Moscow and Kiev, working for a few years as engineers on railroad and oil-drilling projects in the Siberian wilderness, told me of their dissatisfaction with the local village schools and their decision to leave their children back home with grandparents for a decent education, much as American parents might sacrifice to send their youngsters off to fine boarding schools. A teachers' journal, *Uchitelskaya Gazeta,* reported in 1978 that such low-level high school graduates were being admitted to pedagogical institutes that these future teachers had to spend the first two semesters or more learning how to write grammatically.

Yet the basic three R's are the main stuff of the classroom, supplemented by what might be called the three P's—politics, party, and patriotism. The relationship between the two dimensions is complex, one intertwined with the other. In high school years the courses in chemistry, physics, languages, history, and the like are so demanding that teenagers who emigrate to Israel and the United States often find the load suddenly lighter—to their relief and their parents' dismay. But political orientation is an integral part of the diet as well, like bread with meals, and while it does not appear to detract from the seriousness of learning the lean scholastic skills, it makes an ample contribution to the stout convictions by which Russians view themselves and the world.

The nucleus of the creed is not Marx but Vladimir Ilyich Lenin, whose saintly wisdom and moral vision become the original intro-duction for all children to the blended reverence for communism and country that guides their growth. Lenin is portrayed as the embodiment of goodness, the avuncular figure of kindness who sits and talks with little boys and girls as Jesus tended His flock. Lenin's name is used today to inject righteousness into the most unlikely places. I once came across a flower show in Baku adorned with a huge banner proclaiming, "For a Leninist Attitude Toward Na-ture!"

Every class in every kindergarten has its portrait of Lenin, usually in a special corner of the room where drawings and picture books portray his life. In one kindergarten's holiday show a cute little girl with ribbons in her hair recited a small verse about "Dear Lenin, he taught us how to live in a friendly way." Parents and grandpar-ents chuckled warmly and burst into applause. In elementary and high schools the corner is often located in the room set aside for Pioneer and Komsomol meetings, and it is called the Red Corner, a term usurped from earlier tradition when Russian Orthodox fami-lies had, in their homes, a Red Corner for the icons and the oil lamps or candles, often backed by a swath of material the color *krasny* ("red"), of the same root as *krasivy* ("beautiful"). Indeed, *krasny* itself meant "beautiful" in antiquated usage, so Red Corner was Beautiful Corner and Red Square, Beautiful Square.

On page 310 of the reading book for the third grade, a section of poems and stories about Lenin is headed "Lenin Lived, Lenin Lives, Lenin Will Live." Quotations from Lenin are sprinkled gen-erously through textbooks on most subjects (if an author omits them, he is usually advised by his editor to insert a few, and college students quickly learn that a few lines from Lenin and the current party leader are prerequisites for a good grade). On the other hand, I came across a zoology textbook for sixth and seventh grades that contained not a single reference to Lenin. It fulfilled its obligation by opening with a dissertation on the sinister effects of religion in retarding zoological research. And many middle-aged Russians who grew up under Stalin discern some relaxation of the Lenin cult. "Children's propaganda about Lenin used to be crude and massive," said a loyal Soviet citizen in his forties. "Now I just don't see it anymore. He was portrayed like a saint, halo around his head. He could do no wrong. Once, the story went, he broke a pitcher. At first he lied about it, then two hours later was bothered by his conscience and declared that he had done it. It was nauseating, you know. And nobody believed it. Everybody laughed at it."

But not aloud. The most solemn place in all the vast reaches of the Soviet Union is the glazed brown-red granite mausoleum in front of the high brick Kremlin walls, where Lenin and Stalin once lay side by side and now Lenin lies alone, embalmed or waxed so that thousands upon thousands of pilgrims, who wait for hours in freezing long lines and are admonished by guards to stand erect and straighten their clothes, file silently into the darkened tomb and around its interior walkway to gaze upon the face of greatness. A friend said he once saw an old Russian woman cross herself as she came into view of the body.

Even the rich political humor by which Russians preserve their sanity rarely indicts Lenin himself. A joke that comes about the closest involves the famous artist commissioned to do a painting entitled "Lenin in Zurich." After weeks of work the painter lugs his huge work into the Kremlin, where the Politburo assembles for the unveiling. But when the cloth is pulled aside, there is a gasp of horror. There, lying in bed together, are Lenin's wife, Nadezhda Krupskaya, and Trotsky.

"Where's Lenin?" someone demands.

"Lenin's in Zurich," says the artist.

Then there's the one about Lenin coming back to life and showing up at a Thursday morning Politburo meeting. Andropov and his cohorts are fawning, obsequious, asking what they can do for him. Lenin says that all he wants is a room and a supply of all the issues of *Pravda* since his death. This is duly done, and he locks himself in for weeks of reading. As time passes, concern grows, and finally someone is dispatched to enter the room to see what has happened. All the *Pravdas* have obviously been thoroughly read, and the room is in disarray. But Lenin is gone. There, on his desk, is a note in his hand: "You have made a mess of it. I've gone back to Zurich to start again."

The famous joke about the train to communism exempts Lenin from its bitter wit. Stalin, Khrushchev, and Brezhnev are on the train when it stops. When it does not go again, Stalin orders the crew taken out and shot. That done, the train still does not go. So Khrushchev orders the crew rehabilitated posthumously. Still, the train doesn't move. So Stalin and Khrushchev turn to Brezhnev. He pulls down the shades and says, "Now let's pretend the train is moving." After Gorbachev came to power with his revitalized work ethic, the joke was updated. Gorbachev says, "Everybody get out and push."

Late one night in our office, at the end of a tedious day covering the Twenty-fifth Party Congress, my colleague Chris Wren began speaking whimsically to the ceiling, which we imagined to be crammed with microphones. "Think I'll go see Yuri Zhukov tomorrow," Chris said loudly. Zhukov was a crusty cold warrior and Central Committee member who wrote table-thumping polemics for *Pravda* and delivered anti-American diatribes on television, a thoroughly distasteful character to anyone with an open mind. "I like old Yuri," Chris continued. "The only trouble is those Lenin jokes he's always telling. They're really embarrassing. But I guess once you get to be on the Central Committee, you can get away with anything."

It was a delicious prank, and we both were doubled up in hysterics, but a couple of months later Chris began to have trouble with the authorities. He was among three American correspondents—including Alfred Friendly, Jr., of *Newsweek* and George Krimsky of the Associated Press—accused in the Soviet weekly *Literaturnaya Gazeta* (frequently a KGB outlet) of working for the CIA. Official interviews started getting a bit more difficult to line up, and trips outside the Moscow area, requiring Foreign Ministry approval, encountered obstacles. There was no hard evidence that his joke was the cause, but it was a possible contribution. Lenin remains surrounded with taboos.

When Ina Rubin and her husband, Vitaly, were granted permission to emigrate to Israel, she took boxes of books to the post office to mail to their new home. They were heavy and required lots of stamps, many of which bore Lenin's portrait. She was sticking them on quickly in great numbers, pasting them in whatever way they would fit best, when a woman clerk ran shrieking out from behind a counter. "What are you doing?" the clerk yelled. "What are you doing?"

"I'm pasting on stamps," Ina replied calmly.

"But—but you're putting our dear Lenin on *upside down!*" shouted the woman, out of control. She demanded that Ina remove the stamps and put them right side up. Ina refused, and so the clerk painstakingly did it herself. In Stalin's day this would have been cause for arrest; Ina, however, did not hesitate to tell me about the incident while she was still in Moscow, and it did not foil the Rubins' plans to leave.

Lenin's birthday is an occasion in schools for canceling lessons and holding pompous ceremonies and lectures at which the memory of the Bolshevik leader becomes as much a patriotic theme as an ideological vehicle. At a practice session in a kindergarten in the Central Asian city of Dushanbe a small boy in a sailor's costume held a bouquet of white carnations and sang:

> In many countries children live,
> And everywhere all children love Lenin.

The song went on for a while about Lenin. Then, as other children joined, the verses moved smoothly into adoration of the motherland:

> We children live better than anybody on earth,
> Our country is happy and lucky.

There was a song called "Beloved Motherland," exactly the same one I heard back in Moscow, where Debby, Laura, and I attended a show at Kindergarten No. 104 celebrating the anniversary of the Bolshevik Revolution. These were evidently centrally planned pageants. "We get the songs from books," one teacher said.

At 4:00 P.M. a few days before the holiday the Moscow kindergarten's music room began to fill up with mothers and grandmothers and a few grandfathers, one of whom was armed with a still camera and a jury-rigged light (he had no flash attachment) that he was fumbling with, trying to plug into a wall socket. At the lower right-hand corner of the Lenin portrait that dominated the front wall a puffy red ribbon had been tied in a fancy bow.

First the girls skipped in, wearing red skirts, red ribbons in their hair, holding a red flag in each hand. Then came the boys in olive drab helmets with big red stars on the fronts, reciting and singing songs about the Revolution, the "glorious holiday." Other children were dressed in blue and yellow, holding bunches of plastic autumn leaves, chanting, "Glory to our great motherland, let her future be stronger and redder." Then the whole group broke into song as a teacher played the piano:

> Our motherland guards the peace,
> Victorious Red Army,
> Our motherland is strong,
> She guards the peace.

"Long live the Great October!" shouted a teacher.
"Hoorah!" yelled the tiny voices.
"Long live our great motherland!" the teacher shouted.
"Hoorah!"

Boys in helmets and a girl in a nurse's outfit then marched with drawn swords to martial music, shouting, "Forward!" and "Hoorah!" Two contests were held. In the first, two boys sat on chairs. When a whistle was blown, they had to run to a rocking horse, put on a helmet, put on a sword, sit on the horse, and draw the sword into the air. Whoever did it first won. A teacher asked the children to give a critique of the loser, to tell what he had done wrong. They replied inexplicably that he had put the sword on first, when he should have started with the helmet. Then two girls tried, running to the rocking horse, putting on the helmet and the sword, drawing the sword. The second contest began with a recited verse by two girls and a boy about the harvest, followed by a song about growing things in a garden. Two youngsters then raced each other back and forth to pick up a cabbage, a handful of potatoes, and some carrots from two chairs and put them into a truck. The teacher let the other children judge the winner.

After the contests came a song about rain and wind and flowers. A boy, dressed up as rain, did a dance with girls carrying red and white parasols. Other children danced with tambourines. A couple of poems about nature were recited. Finally, a buxom teacher, dressed as a farm woman with a basket over her arm and a scarf tied around her head, announced greetings from the collective farm "where we live gaily and sing." She did a little dance with a handkerchief, then stood behind a big pot, singing about making soup from a potato, cabbage, carrot, peas, and beets. When she was finished, she dipped a spoon into the pot as if to ladle out soup—but the spoon came up heaped with candy, which she scooped into bowls and passed to the children. The program ended, and as people got up to leave, the director of the kindergarten sent two small boys over to present Laura, then six, with a little brown teddy bear.

The children's show represented fairly well the variety of themes that are woven together in these younger years: Lenin, the motherland, the military, nature, the virtue of work on the land. In a classroom for six-year-olds one bookshelf was devoted to a row of folders containing pictures, which the children would talk about to improve their diction. All but two of the nine folders had political or patriotic overtones: "Our Army," "Pioneers," "Collective Farm Labor," "Our Moscow," "V. I. Lenin," and so on. The only exceptions were "Times of the Year" and "Transport." The same was true of a middle school's library in Riga, the capital of Soviet Lativa. The shelves reserved for first and second graders learning to read contained the following sections: "Lenin," "The Great Patriotic War," "How Children Lived Before the Revolution," "Life of Children Abroad," "Our Motherland," "About the Lives of Noteworthy Communists," "About Plants," "About Animals," "About Cosmonauts in Space," "About Science and Technology," "I Want to Know Everything," "Being Strong, Brave, and Agile," "Cheerful Books," and "Children of the Soviet Land."

There is no escaping the political message. It pervades every dimension of education, becoming so ordinary that it seems as natural and unremarkable as chalk on a blackboard. Even in the apolitical subject of mathematics, textbook authors sprinkle exercises with word problems designed to remind pupils of the superiority of the Soviet state and to sensitize them to the fundamental mechanics of a socialist economy. In the third-grade math book, for example:

The first cosmonaut was a citizen of the Soviet Union, Communist Yuri Gagarin. He made a flight around the earth in 108 minutes. How many hours and how many minutes did the first flight around the earth last?

In our country the world's first atomic icebreaker, *Lenin,* was built. What is the length and width of this icebreaker if it is known that ⅛ of its length consists of 16 meters 75 centimeters, and ⅕ of its width is equal to 5 meters 52 centimeters?

A brigade of oil workers must drill 6 kilometers 650 meters per year. In the first half year it drilled 4 kilometers 900 meters, and in the second 1 kilometer 50 meters less. Did the brigade fulfill its annual plan? If it overfulfilled it, by how much?

A *sovkhoz* [state farm] pledged itself to give the state 3,350 tons of cotton. But it gave 4,200 tons, then added another ¹⁄₁₀ of this quantity. By how many tons did the *sovkhoz* overfulfill its obligation?

If the authors' political instincts lapse, there are always authorities to issue clear reminders. Roy Medvedev, the dissident historian who worked in a textbook publishing house during Khrushchev's era, told me of some amusing encounters with the censors that revealed principles he said were unchanged today. "The censor comes to us and says, 'Comrades, what is happening in your office? You have a Russian-language textbook, with exercises: "Write here, co——ism." And the children must put in the missing letters, "*commun*ism." Or "so——ism," and the children must put in the missing letters, "*social*ism." Or take "pa——y." The children must write, "*part*y." These sacred words, and you don't write them in full!' " Roy declared, imitating the censor's pompous tones.

"We say," Roy replied, quoting himself and his colleagues, " 'That is the method of teaching the Russian language. We must teach the children to write these words correctly. And what if they write "communism" with one *m* instead of two? And if they write "party" not with an *a* but an *o?* That will be worse. How are we going to teach children to write these words unless we teach them the same way we teach other words?'

" 'No, dear comrades,' the censor replies. 'You don't need to

mutilate these words. You may not mutilate such important words.'
So as a result of this dialogue, in all textbooks the words 'communism,' 'party,' 'socialism,' all words connected with ideology, are
written in full.

"Or," Roy continued, "they come to us and say, 'In Russian-
language textbooks, thirty percent of the text must be political text.'
It means that you must cite Khrushchev and Lenin—then it was
Khrushchev, now Brezhnev—and other political figures. We said,
'Dear comrades, we can't. The children will end up knowing the
Russian language more poorly because political figures speak
badly. Pushkin, after all, was better, and Lermontov, or Gogol,
or Tolstoy. That is why all the Russian-language textbooks were
made up of texts from the classics. We wrote dictations. Schoolchildren are not going to be interested in taking dictation on
excerpts from speeches by Khrushchev, right?'

" 'No,' they said to us. 'One-third of the text must be political
compositions. They don't have to be from Khrushchev, but about
politics. For example: "The Soviet economy is the best economy in
the world." ' We said, 'Let geography deal with that. Let history
deal with that. What does that have to do with Russian language
and literature?' They made us do it."

There were times when the wind blew in the opposite direction,
Roy said, and orders came down that Russian-language texts were
not to include so many political passages because children speaking
ungrammatically would make mistakes and pronounce stupidities.
But generally a high political content was required, and "security"
matters were examined with farcical scrutiny.

"Suddenly, a directive arrived: Change the precise measure-
ments, the lengths and widths, of the cities of the Soviet Union. But
we all know that Moscow has such and such a width and such and
such a length, and textbooks have published the dimensions for a
hundred years. Now we were supposed to change the widths and
lengths in textbooks that had published them for a hundred years.
We said that in regard to new cities, it was understandable. OK,
foreigners don't know about them. The censor said, 'In the textbooks you must move Moscow, Leningrad, Kiev one degree north
or one degree south.' And we had to obey that. Then an order came
to prohibit the mention in all textbooks of bridges. Because a
bridge is a strategic structure that could be used in an invasion by

adversaries, bridges must be secret. It is understood that new bridges can be secret. But they told us, 'Exclude photographs of all bridges.' In our textbooks we have pictures of the Krimsky Bridge, the Kamenny Bridge in Moscow, in Leningrad the bridge of the Winter Palace. This was funny. I took the censor some stamps, postage stamps. 'Look, please: bridges.' "

When Yuri Gagarin became the first human being to fly in space, Roy recalled, an order came to insert a page devoted to the flight in every textbook. "That was just," he said. "It was a particularly important event. But the country is large, textbooks are stable. The printing plants are all over the Soviet Union, and the time Gagarin flew in space was April, and printing had already started for the next year. The printers work all year. You can't print that many books in two days. It was impossible. They said to me, 'No. A decree has come down that Gagarin will be in all textbooks.' So what to do?" The mat with the Gagarin page was delivered to all printers in May, Roy said, but books printed previously didn't have it. "So there were perhaps twenty million books without Gagarin and three million books with Gagarin. The twenty million books we distributed in the provinces—Kazakhstan, Novosibirsk—and the three million we put in Moscow, the Moscow Oblast, Leningrad. And everybody was pleased. Nobody knew about it."

It is the inflated regard for country that stands as the centerpiece of all that can be called political in Soviet education. Lenin may be idolized to small children as a naïve combination of George Washington and Jesus Christ, and older students may be immersed in detailed studies of the history of the Communist Party, of the principles of class struggle and internationalism as seen through the ideological amalgam that the Russians call Marxism-Leninism. But ultimately the power of these ideas to move Soviet citizens lies in their patriotic content, in their association with the adoration of country. As a concept of righteousness, a vehicle of analysis, and a focus of loyalty, the nation rises above competing elements of Soviet doctrine and shapes the teaching of political values.

This is accomplished first by preposterous boasts, as in the kindergarten song, "We children live better than anybody on earth," then by a mixing of patriotic and communist symbols so that the difference between the Soviet Union as a country and communism as an ideology is blurred into near invisibility, and finally by mystical appeals to the sanctity of the motherland in bold contrast with the frightening, alien, hostile world outside. A synthetic history is an essential ingredient of the process.

The reading book for nine-year-olds, for example, opens with a passage declaring, "The world's first socialist country has become the world's first country for children's happiness. 'All the best for the children'—that has become law in our country." Page 105 of the book carries a color picture of a welder and a construction worker surrounded by a network of steel girders. "Soviet People Build a New Life" is the caption. It is followed by one poem extolling the motherland, another about the Soviet flag, and a passage on "the emblem of the Soviet land," the hammer and sickle. Further along is a reading entitled "Our Goal—Communism." The passage asks:

> Is it possible to find, already in our current life, the first examples of how communism begins? Look carefully and see: There is already in our life a considerable amount that the people receive by the rule and law of communist society. Under communism each will receive not according to his work, as under socialism, but according to his needs. Thus, for example, in our country today everyone can already receive as much free medical care as is needed. All children are taught free of charge—all equally, whether their parents earn much or little. That is also done according to communism. But the most important way in which communism is beginning is in the work of our people.

The paragraph continues on the theme of labor's high productivity.

Sometimes the tone is one of simple boosterism, chamber of commerce style, as in another textbook used in all schools to teach Russian to Russian children. A paragraph about "Our City" and how it grows each year, how "beautiful cars and buses go throughout the city" is full of italicized words that are to be put into the right number and case. Another paragraph reads: "Our scientists, engineers, and workers invent and manufacture ever more wonderful cars, machine tools, equipment. Electricity has long lit the gay lights of the cities and towns. Our people will build new rockets and spaceships. Cosmonauts will fly to other planets."

Here also, the deeper invocations to patriotism emerge. "Read the sentences. 1. We have a huge, beautiful, excellent motherland. 2. The most beautiful, the warmest and dearest name—motherland. 3. Motherland—this place, where we live, where we were born, where we grew up."

And some pages later: "An exercise on the word *zemlya* ["land"]. 1. On all sides spread the land of the *sovkhoz*. 2. There is no end to the expanse of this land. 3. There is no land richer than ours. 4. In the sky shines the sun, and on the land walks the wind. 5. Spring, summer, and fall the machine operators work the land. 6. They are pleased with the land; it gives a good harvest."

One exercise probes the root of the word for motherland—*rodina*, which has as its core the original building block for the verb "to be born," the nouns "parents" and "relatives," the adjective "native," and the concept of one's own, something integral to oneself. *Rodina-Mat* ("Motherland-Mother") the exercise is called, and it touches a point of fondest emotion in both children and adults. "We call our country *rodina* ["motherland"] because we were *rodilis* ["born"] in her, because in her our *rodnoi* ["native"] language is spoken, and everything in her is, for us, *rodnoye* ["our own"]." For any Russian, and certainly for those of nine, the sentence evokes strong feelings. "When we pronounce the word 'motherland,' " reads an exercise in another text, "before us opens endless open space—woods, fields, mountains, snow, sand, rivers, seas, islands."

For older children, there are attempts to resolve the obvious contradictions of the high-pitch nationalism that grips Soviet society with the internationalism that lies almost dormant in the ideology of Marxism. High school seniors—that is, those in the Soviet tenth grade, age sixteen—get a social studies course whose textbook of communist ethics and social morality includes the following section, under the heading "Social Duty":

Patriotism is the deep social feeling consolidated by centuries and millennia of the existence of isolated native lands. In it is found the expression of love for the country in which we were born and grew up, for its history, people, inseparably linked with what we feel ourselves part of. Patriotism concerns the best manifestations of human nature, motivating people toward active efforts in the name of their countrymen. Socialist patriotism is linked with the selfless devotion to progressive social construction, the business of communism, with the feeling of great pride in the Soviet people, which is building for all humanity a road to a bright future. More than once, poets and writers have described how a person, confronted with the face of death, remembers the motherland, his native house, the weeping willow or the birch. For the Soviet people, the motherland embodies not only the sweet picture of nature. We find her form in recollections of Pioneer meetings and Komsomol youth; she personifies for us a unique atmosphere of comradeship, which defines the life of the Soviet collective. The motherland and socialist construction merge in the consciousness of the Soviet man.

In other words, it is OK to be both a nationalist and a Communist; in fact, it is desirable because since the Soviet Union is at the vanguard of the Communist movement, devotion to the country becomes devotion to the cause. There is no suggestion that a true Marxist might ever question the behavior of the Soviet Union as a national entity or that the government's conduct in support of its state interests might not always coincide with communist ideals. The two forces are fused. This is more than just a curious and rather boring piece of pedantry in an obscure tract: This textbook is used by every graduating secondary school student in the country. It is the best distillation of the party's notions of how the emerging "Soviet man" is supposed to think. And although there is usually slippage between the printed word and the reality, in my experience of talking with young people I found general acceptance of the textbook view on the blurring of nationalism and communism. In fact, the issue is rarely examined, even by disaffected young adults in private conversation.

"Socialist patriotism" is presented as more mature than plain patriotism; students are warned away from "blind feeling" and are informed that "to Communists, so-called '*kvas* patriotism'—the unrestrained extolling of everything that we have—is deeply alien." *Kvas* is a malty, beerlike drink made from burned bread and served at curbside from dirty yellow rolling tanks into widely shared glass mugs. It can be good if you're really hot and parched, but otherwise its stale bitterness is an acquired taste, symbolic of the tough, earthy simplicity of the peasant in harmony with unthinking reflex. The textbook declares:

> The *kvasnoi patriot* is ready to brag even about the quantity of shortcomings. . . . Real love for the motherland is love with open eyes. We are rightly proud of our remarkable successes, but we uncover shortcomings boldly and apply all our strength to eliminate them. We are not ashamed of imitating the better achievements of other peoples, and can learn something from the capitalists as well. . . . To the Soviet people, national egotism and chauvinism are alien. . . . In the future Communist society, all peoples of the world will stand as one friendly family. And then patriotism and internationalism will dissolve into one great feeling of love for all humanity and for its cradle —the planet Earth.

Still, *kvas* patriotism is precisely what is taught in the lower grades, in those songs and stories that children feed on from their earliest days in kindergartens and that foster unquestioning love of country and denigration of others. Esteem for the military is an important concomitant, beginning with the themes of war that run through holiday pageantry; moving into the first reading books, which are sprinkled with drawings of heroic soldiers flanked by imposing missiles; ending in the high school social studies texts with their precise passages on the military obligations of every citizen. For the little ones, the soldier is portrayed melodramatically, with a sappy romanticism that would make most Westerners wince. He is the defender of all that is dear, protector of goodness and truth, and his exploits from war to war are mixed up into the present so that time and history dissolve into the moment. And children are heroes.

"Young drummer. The war was on," begins a passage in the third-grade reading text, accompanied by a color drawing of a drummer and men on horseback, riding with drawn swords beneath a red flag. "The enemy encircled the division. In the division there served a young drummer. At night he stood at his post. Suddenly a light shadow appeared. Enemy! But the fighters slept. The drummer with all his might beat on the drum. The fighters awoke, grabbed their rifles and beat off the attack."

In an eighth-grade civics book entitled *The Basis of the Soviet State and Rights,* the military section, called "Defense of the Fatherland —Sacred Duty of the Citizen of the USSR," is replete with religious terminology. "Our youth fervently love the Soviet Army and Navy," the chapter begins, "and preserve the holy memory of the wars, of those who perished for the freedom and independence of the motherland." A clear distinction is drawn between the Soviet armed forces and "the armies of bourgeois countries, which exist in the hands of the exploiters of violence with arms, terror with arms, imperialist aggression and war. The Soviet armed forces laid down a glorious path of battle from the first heroic victory over the hordes of counterrevolutionaries and interventionists in the years of the civil war to the full, utter defeat of German fascism and Japanese militarism in 1945. . . . Our army is a united, friendly family, a school of internationalism, a school for the teaching of brotherhood, solidarity, and mutual respect for all nations and peoples." And so forth.

Elementary school classrooms are visited regularly by military lecturers, usually retired career officers, who give chauvinistic pep-talks on the need for preparedness in an alien world. Civil defense drills include training with gas masks, usually primitive, homemade affairs of thick cotton and window glass for eyepieces; the effect is probably more psychological than practical. During the ninth and tenth grades, the last two years of high school, a compulsory military training course is given twice a week, and for several weeks the boys go to a military summer camp, where they learn many of the skills of boot camp. At fourteen they can join a repository of super-patriotism and infatuation with all things military, called the Voluntary Committee for Assistance to the Armed Forces, or DOSAAF by its Russian initials. In centers and clubhouses across the country, the youngsters and adults study military history and tactics, learn to shoot and to maintain truck engines and electrical equipment, and engage in other hobbies with military overtones. The theme continues into higher education. A friend in the prestigious Institute of Foreign Languages, whose graduates often go into diplomatic service, told me that all students were required to take a military course that met three times a week. "We study the American military," he said. "How many battalions, methods of defense. The whole institute is frighteningly militarized."

All this expresses and enhances the Russians' sense of isolation and adversity in relation to the world outside, a state of mind no more vividly conveyed and encouraged than in a third-grade book of readings. Beneath a drawing of a soldier in battle helmet, a caption says, "The soldier of the Soviet Army stands guarding peace, happiness, and freedom." There follows a short composition:

THE BORDER IS NEAR!

The soldier walked down the road. Along the dirt road of the border camp.

The soldier walked, not alone. He walked with his son. A big son—Pioneer, thirteen years old. He had come to his father on vacation.

A division of cavalrymen galloped by. A detail of frontier guards marched past; in the front, a great grey sheepdog.

"Our Rex," said the soldier. "Good boy! Twenty infiltrators to his credit!"

"We also train dogs for frontier duty!" exclaimed the son.

"A job will also be found for you youngsters."

But all around bloomed apple trees and cherry trees. Bees and butterflies circled above the blossoms. And birds in the orchards sang clearly.

"Good," said the son.

"The border is nearby," said the soldier.

On the soccer field off-duty frontier guards pursued a ball. They used a horizontal bar on wheels.

In the woods a magpie flew out, flitting to the side away from the soccer players and suddenly landing calmly on one of the wheels as if nothing were happening. The magpie felt like drinking. She lowered her beak to a puddle—and drank. Again she lowered her beak—and drank again. Then she spread her wings and flew back to the woods. And there, in the woods, stood tanks and armored cars. On the edge of the woods artillery was deployed. But the magpie was not afraid. Apparently she was used to it.

In the distance there were reeds, and beyond them a

river. Not wide, calm, the water shining in the sun. Along the river runs the border. This bank is ours, and the other—not ours, alien.

"Quiet," said the son.

"The border is nearby," repeated the father. "Well, it's time for me to go on duty! Till evening!"

The soldier left for his post. The post was nearby. Alongside the border.

On the bank of the river, the frontier guards stood stock-still in the bushes. The soldier stood still. He looked through binoculars at the reeds, on the nearby alien shore.

The border is near!

Learning Hypocrisy

Shura Sverdlova was nine years old when her teacher in Leningrad gave her class a thoroughly routine assignment. They were to read a story called "Vanya the War Hero," of a boy who spied against the Germans and helped attack rural villages that served as German bases. Vanya came through to Shura as a very tough, very bad, rather mean boy, not a pleasant character despite his heroic exploits. So when she and her classmates were told to write an essay entitled "Why Do You Like Vanya?" (not, of course, "Do You Like Vanya?"), Shura came home in great distress. Her mother, Mira, knew quite well what was expected: some high-blown platitudes on sacrifice and devotion to the motherland, on fearlessness in defense of the sacred soil. She herself was a teacher, and her field —college-level history of the "bourgeois countries"—required finely tuned political antennae. But Shura did not like the Vanya character and just could not write that she did. Her mother backed her up.

Even a decade later, after both mother and daughter had emigrated to Israel, Mira's recollections were full of the anxiety of that evening, remembering how her small, sensitive girl confronted the question of her own integrity and sat down and wrote honestly why she did not like the war hero Vanya. How would the teacher react? Would there be a low grade, a public condemnation before the entire class? Would Mira be called in? Would a report be made to her institute, casting a shadow on her reliability? These were the tense uncertainties that wound tightly through the evening and the next day, as Shura was sent off with her heretical little manuscript.

The teacher was a young woman, bright and perceptive, who responded in a fashion so unpredictable that Mira and Shura were both amazed. She gave the essay a 5, the top grade, read it to the entire class, and praised it for its honest reflection of Shura's real feelings. Then she asked how many pupils shared Shura's dislike of Vanya. Half the class raised their hands. All but Shura had written lies.

Truth telling is not the forte of Soviet education. In the structure of values the façade is more important than what stands behind it; a smooth, unbroken surface of acceptance comforts both teacher and pupil, political leader and citizen. To crack the veneer is to violate the basic ethic of hypocrisy and to embrace utter loneliness. There are few parents like Mira Sverdlova to lend support, and few teachers like Shura's.

Indeed, hypocrisy is taught as a virtue in effect. As children learn what to say regardless of what they think, they grow more responsive to outer form than to inner conviction. There is not always a difference between the two: The incessant saying and hearing of untruth have a numbing impact on thought. But many Russians with their wits about them also find that they must exist on disparate levels, keeping their common sense to themselves, nurturing a careful schizophrenia.

Shura Sverdlova learned this in kindergarten, after she had come home one day saying, "I'm lucky I was born in the Soviet Union."

"Why?" her mother asked.

"Because children are starving in America." Her mother explained that it wasn't so. And she then began to teach her four-year-old not to talk outside the house about what was discussed at home. A four-year-old boy had absorbed the caution so well that it carried over to Israel, where he warned his father one morning to stop telling a Bible story because they were getting close to the kindergarten and the teacher might hear.

Some teenagers master the slick technique of hypocrisy. "We had a boy who wanted to be a journalist," recalled Irina McClellan, the former high school teacher. "He started writing articles for some youth newspapers and magazines. He realized very quickly what would work in this society, what was permitted. In conversations he was open, but in writings he knew the formula. You see how they are corrupted so young. He was a careerist already, at the age of sixteen."

I saw a few such cases on a bulletin board in a school in Latvia, where tenth graders had been presented with questions to which they were expected to reply with firm expressions of disdain for material goods. This was a lot to ask of urban teenagers in a society that craves consumer items and whose most fad-conscious members will pay up to half the monthly wage of an average factory worker for a single pair of American jeans on the black market. But the kids performed as required. "Why do people try to surround themselves with things?" the questionnaire began. "Would you like to get an apartment, a dacha, many stylish clothes, and a car right after school, or would you prefer to earn them with your own labor?" The answers, hung there in a corridor for all to see, had a wonderful Sunday-school quality about them. Student after student renounced any desire for anything at all, condemning "thingism" as some malevolent disease foreign to their personal attitudes. "I, for example, hate things," wrote a boy named Igor Tarasov. "I think that in the next ten years, with the approach of the ideals of communism, the materialist mania—thingism—will pass." An inventive girl commented that she would, actually, like to have a car—but just so she wouldn't be a burden on her parents.

The honest statement is such a novelty that youngsters remember it for years. Mikhail, a lanky Moscow teenager, told me about a candid essay he once wrote in sixth grade, after a school celebration of a holiday devoted to "Young Antifascists." He had to write "about my general impressions of the day" and dealt with a story that had been told about a young Pioneer boy in wartime Estonia who had defied a fascist's command to take off his red neckerchief. Because he had refused, he had been killed. "I said the boy was foolish," Mikhail explained. "What did he accomplish? I didn't understand what was heroic about him. The teacher read the composition to the class, didn't say who wrote it, and asked for opinions. Somebody said that what was written was right. Somebody else said it wasn't right. You could feel that she wanted the class to denounce it, so a girl stood up and said it was all wrong." When the paper came back, however, it had been graded with a 5 for writing and a 4 for content. Mikhail judged her a good teacher because she had not been dictatorial but had merely nudged him gently in what she considered the proper direction. She had written on the composition, "Think about whether you're right."

Mira Sverdlova told me that she also tried, subtly, to nudge her classes on the history of "bourgeois countries," but in the opposite direction, "to put a positive accent, a nuance, to correct the official line," as she explained. "I thought there were informers in the class, so I had to be subtle, so much so that many students didn't understand." She drew a parallel between Nazi Germany and the Soviet Union, for example, by stressing that Germany had one party and that all newspapers said the same thing. "Some students saw it; you could tell by their eyes."

Few parents encourage political recalcitrance, however, preferring for their children the safer submissiveness to the line. "Parents say, 'Don't talk too much,'" explained a Russian in his twenties whose father is a ranking party member. "They say it to defend themselves and the child. They say, 'Quiet. Don't think about it.' They believe it is better to sit in a party meeting thinking about your lover, but with a serious face, raising your hand to vote at the right time—and everything is fine."

Russians often make fun of themselves on this score. There is a joke about the man who went to a clinic, looking for an eye and ear doctor. "We don't have an eye and ear doctor," said the receptionist, "only an eye doctor and an ear, nose, and throat doctor."

"I need an eye and ear doctor," the man insisted. "I keep hearing one thing and seeing another."

In Leningrad Debby and I saw an audience of mostly young adults go into excruciating laughter as a lanky pantomimist, Yuri Medvedev, impersonated a sleepy party member doing his duty at a "Mass Meeting," as the routine was entitled. The man sat in an imaginary audience (facing the real one), listening to an imaginary lecture. His eyes glazed over. With supreme effort, he propped them open. His eyelids fluttered, then closed. His head fell back as he slept. Suddenly, at the right moment, his hand popped up for a vote. He slept again, his head lolling to the side. Another vote, and his hand came up like a perfect machine. Again he slept, slumped forward, and so on through every conceivable sleeping position, broken by the obligatory votes. The crowd was in hysterics. Medvedev then perked up as an imaginary superior sat down next to him. Another superior sat on the other side, and one behind. Fawning obsequiously, he catered to one and then the other, trying to crouch and move so the official behind could see. Finally he made his neck rubbery and held his head so far over it seemed to sprout from his left shoulder, just so the bureaucrat behind would not have to lean even slightly. Then he began to try to figure out how he should react to what was being said in the meeting. He took his first cue from the imaginary superior on his left, glanced at the man, and laughed heartily until he glanced to his right, saw a different response, and abandoned his laugh for a glower. Back and forth he went, torn between the superiors flanking him, laughing and frowning, laughing and frowning until the meeting was over. At the end he stood and walked slowly offstage, his head and shoulders bowed in ignominy. In the audience the laughter ebbed into a long moment of silence, before the applause.

A bitter moral on the loss of integrity, a therapeutic release. But real life continues without the satire. In classrooms it does not often matter how a child gets the right answers, as long as he gets them. And because teachers are judged partly by the performance of their pupils, cheating is widely tolerated. "Yes, it's very popular," said Irina McClellan. "The year-end test is sent to the regional committee. Teachers are afraid the tests will be badly done, so they walk along the rows and help them. Sometimes they take them into the corridors and give them notes. It is also done in exit exams for the universities and institutes."

Cheating is so accepted and obvious that even visitors can't miss it, and Debby and I saw some ourselves. When a teacher walked out of a sixth-grade physics class during a test at Dushanbe's School No. 35, the students, as if on signal, turned to neighbors and whispered answers to each other. The teacher could not have avoided noticing when she returned, but she said nothing. In a corridor of a Moscow school, a class of youngsters about to go into an exam prepared by writing answers on their hands and folding crib sheets into accordion shapes for easy concealment. In two classes at different schools we watched as pupils were told one by one to close their books and stand to recite lessons, all the while glancing down at their deskmates' books, left open within easy view.

Teachers have varied responses to this. "If she doesn't like you, she won't let you get away with it," said Mikhail. "I went to a school for young workers. The teacher would walk in the aisle, helping kids. But in a strong school there is less cheating, and there are times when the teacher catches and scolds kids. Students also know that you won't get a two [a D]. You can say, 'I don't know that, I don't know that, I don't know that,' and she'll say, 'What do you know?' 'I know that,' and she'll give you a three."

Grades, as part of the façade, are constructed with considerable bargaining among teachers, according to Irina McClellan, and may have little to do with actual performance in some cases. "At the end of the semester teachers' meetings are held to sum up results," she told me. "The mathematics and literature teachers will say Ivanov is bad—'I'll give him a three if you give him a three'—and they do it, like in the market. They can't give bad marks because it's such a disgrace for the school. I had two students who did not want to learn English. I had to give them bad marks. At the teachers' meeting I said I couldn't give them threes—they didn't know a word. The director [principal] said, 'I order you to give them threes. Why do you care so much about your English? The main subjects are literature and mathematics. Why do you try to attract so much attention to yourself and your subject?' "

Pioneers and Komsomol

In the third year of elementary school, as children turn nine, bright red neckerchiefs suddenly flare against the somber brown and dark blue uniforms, signifying entry into the first formal, institutionalized commitment to a political idea. The children become Young Pioneers as naturally as they come of age. They are inducted, in the illusion of having been carefully selected, with fanfare and ceremony, with banners and solemn oaths. But this passage is virtually automatic and universal, like a puberty rite, a bar mitzvah, or a first communion. Nobody is not a Pioneer. To refuse the oath and to go without the neckerchief—that would be the lonely step into a wilderness.

The induction ceremony has a military tone. Adult commanders shout orders, and the children, scrubbed and neat, march in precisely.

"Halt!"

"About . . . face!"

"Units, atten-tion! Eyes . . . left! Shun! Group commanders, prepare to report! As you were!"

"Comrade Chief Pioneer Leader! The section of Pioneer leaders of Class Three A, named after Feliks Edmundovich Dzerzhinsky, is lined up for the ceremonial ritual formation! All ten members are present for the ceremony of presentation of the Pioneer scarf and badge."

Parents watch proudly. Children's eyes gleam as they take the oath. "I, Sulomsky, Aleksei, entering the ranks of the All-Union Pioneer Organization named after Vladimir Ilyich Lenin, solemnly promise before my comrades: to love my motherland fervently; to live, study, and fight as the great Lenin bequeathed us, as the Communist Party teaches. I promise always to observe the laws of the Pioneers of the Soviet Union."

The laws are as follows:

The Pioneer adheres to the motherland, the party, communism.

The Pioneer prepares to become a Komsomol member.

The Pioneer emulates the heroes of struggle and labor.

The Pioneer reveres the memory of the fallen fighters and prepares to become a defender of his motherland.

The Pioneer is persistent in studies, work, and sports.

The Pioneer is an honest and true comrade and always stands for the truth.

The Pioneer is a friend and leader of the Octobrists [members of a youth organization of younger children].

The Pioneer is a friend to other Pioneers and to the children of workers of all countries.

The adult commander concludes with a word of congratulation: "This day will be remembered throughout all your life. Ask your father, mother, or grandmother who was admitted to the Pioneers; they will always tell you about this because this is an unforgettable event. The Pioneer organization bears the name of Vladimir Ilyich Lenin from 1924, and according to our tradition, we always remember him on our brightest days and occasions. Atten-tion! A minute for Lenin's remembrance is announced! Place the wreaths!"

Valentin Vasiliev was nine, but he was not a Pioneer. He was a believer. Strictly speaking, in the cold irony of the Soviet lexicon, one cannot be both a believer and a Pioneer. The term "believer" *(veruyushchii)* is applied with official opprobrium to a believer in God, whose views are incompatible with the Pioneer's atheism. In practice, however, parents who are quietly religious rarely wish their sons and daughters friction in school and so encourage them to be overt Pioneers and secret believers. But Valentin Vasiliev came from a Pentacostalist family quite devout and fundamentalist in its conviction that there was only one God and that one should not worship Lenin.

The boy walked into School No. 36 in Vilnius, Lithuania , one morning, took off his coat, and put it on the counter for the old woman in the cloakroom. She reached for it in a weary gesture of habit, then stopped as her eye caught something strange. "Where is your Pioneer neckerchief ?" she said sharply. Valentin politely explained his remarkable failure to become a Pioneer. The flabbergasted woman sputtered, wagged her finger, and refused to hang up his coat, forcing it back into his arms. The two stood at an impasse in the lobby, children swirling into the building around them. The principal was summoned, a haughty woman who knew the case all too well and who told the boy sternly that of 2,000 eligible children in the school, he was the only one who was not a Pioneer. "You should wear a sign," she scolded, "saying that you are a believer."

More typically the neckerchief carries little political emotion for children but is worn as a badge of pride in having reached the appropriate age. The daughter of Jewish dissidents recalled blushingly how pleased she felt to be seen walking to and from school in her fresh neckerchief when she was nine and how uncomfortable it became as she approached fourteen, the age at which youngsters move from the Pioneers into the Young Communist League, Komsomol. The waning months in Pioneers seemed endless, she remembered, and the neckerchief such a garish advertisement of immaturity that she and her friends used to take theirs off on the way home from school, just to look older.

I once asked some young Western-oriented adults who were

mildly critical of the Soviet system what they saw as the most important quality in a good Pioneer. "Honesty," said Natasha. "To be devoted to your country," said Alyosha. "To defend the young, respect the old." These are the Boy Scout, Girl Scout ethics that occupy a large measure of the Pioneer organization's mission. A revisionist cartoon of "Little Red Riding Hood" on Soviet television, for example, had a Young Pioneer named Petya Ivanov as the hero. He tried to warn the girl in the woods, but she took no heed. "Haven't you ever read 'Little Red Riding Hood'?" he asked. "No," she said, "I myself am Little Red Riding Hood," and she went on her way. As the wolf schemed, the boy scared him into thinking the hunter was close at hand, pointed him toward a "short-cut" to Grandmother's house that was really a long way around, and took the shortcut himself, arriving there ahead of the wolf. He hid Grandmother in the closet, put a jug with a hat and glasses in bed, and tied his red scarf around his head to disguise himself as Little Red Riding Hood. The wolf arrived, ate the jug, and chased Petya around the house. But the boy was too quick for him and held him off until the hunter turned up. Little Red Riding Hood came along at the denouement, flapped her eyelashes at Petya, and declared, "You are a real, a most real Pioneer."

Near the Caspian Sea I saw the fruits of a project by Pioneers honoring the Soviet World War II spy Richard Sorge, who had warned Stalin from Tokyo that Hitler would attack the Soviet Union. The airy house where Sorge had lived until he was three had been turned into a small museum; photographs and documents collected and labeled by some Pioneers in the late 1960's told the story of the man who was executed by the Japanese in 1944 and, twenty years later, awarded the title Hero of the Soviet Union. Only one part of the story was missing: the fact that Sorge's warning, which contained precise information on the timing and strength of the upcoming attack, was ignored by Stalin.

The emphasis on political indoctrination through the Pioneers varies somewhat from one region of the country to another, but generally there seems to be more fun than politics in everyday Pioneer activities. Every city has its Pioneer Palace, usually an elaborate building fitted out with workshops and classrooms for after-school instruction in modelmaking, painting, sewing, weaving, folk dancing, drama, filmmaking, stamp collecting, woodworking, ceramics, astronomy, and other crafts and hobbies. The director of the Pioneer Palace in Kiev, Lyubov Petrovna Ivanyuk, told me that most children come every day after school and one or two days a week, for two hours each, study Marx and Lenin. Political content is lighter elsewhere, and in Moscow the central Pioneer Palace is a palace indeed, spreading across a spacious campus at the edge of Lenin Hills, overlooking the Moskva River. The sprawling complex, built in 1962, resounds with the Russian love of immensity: a total of 15,600 youngsters, up to 7,500 at any one time, come here to pursue any of 162 different activities in groups of 10 to 20 each under 650 adult instructors. The operating budget for this palace alone is $3 million a year, funded by the government; the children pay nothing.

The facilities are sumptuous, and the instruction is serious. As Debby and I were escorted through the maze of corridors and classrooms, we came across chemistry and physics labs better than in any school we had seen. In an astrophysics lab, equipped with spectographic and other sophisticated gadgets, thirteen children were studying Jupiter and Saturn. In a small planetarium, adjacent to a room with huge globes and models of the moon, Earth, and the solar system, eleven ten-year-olds were being told about the movements of the planets. The complex even has an observatory where older students do telescopic photography. Soviet cosmonauts have visited here to lecture.

Downstairs in a garage a group of boys hunched over the open hood of a car, learning about engines. In a huge kitchen paneled in dark wood, and an adjacent dining room outfitted with an attractive sideboard, a dining table, a tablecloth, and china, a cooking class for girls was going on. There was a weaving room with looms where girls were making sweaters and hangings, a sewing room where clothes were being produced, a set of large and well-lit studios for courses in sculpture and painting. In one workshop, boys were making model boats powered by electric motors and controlled by radio transmitters. In another, boys were coming several afternoons a week to make model airplanes from scratch out of balsa wood and paper—not from prefabricated kits—and learning the principles of aerodynamics en route. Then, equipping the models with little gasoline engines, they would take them outside to a circular arena built on the palace grounds especially for airplane competitions, where the youngsters would go up against each other periodically in acrobatics, dogfights, and races. I watched one of these on a Saturday afternoon, and as the planes buzzed around and around and leaped and looped to cut crepe streamers off the opponents' tails, I was struck by the intensity, the all-business and somewhat cheerless tone of it all, as if the boys had already learned to defer momentary joy for a longer-range, subdued satisfaction. There was no childlike laughter, no shout of happiness at a victory, just a professional polish and drive.

In its luxury, Moscow's central Pioneer Palace may be the most extravagant institution for children anywhere in the world. It is also the most difficult for Soviet youngsters to get into. Moscow itself is a "closed city," where only those with special permission may live. And 98.7 percent of the capital's 1.2 million Pioneers are enrolled not in the central palace but in thirty-two Pioneer "houses" located in various neighborhoods. The "best" Pioneers from the neighborhoods are recommended to the central palace in a selection process that gives considerable weight to parental position and pull, with the result that the youngsters enjoying the richness of the elaborately equipped activities are the cream of the elite.

It was in that central palace that Debby and I had a remarkable encounter with a group of politically minded Komsomol activists, teenagers who had graduated from the Pioneers at the age of fourteen into the Young Communist League and had chosen and been chosen to participate in after-school study groups, "circles," on the United States, Africa, Latin America, the Middle East, and so on. These youngsters were part of the well-placed stratum of Soviet society that requires strict political orthodoxy in exchange for privilege, the sons and daughters of professors and scientists and diplomats, who were likely to follow their parents into party membership and relative comfort.

Komsomol is a mass organization like the Pioneers; it envelops virtually all children when they turn fourteen. But since its members are of a thinking age, the tone is more heavily political, sometimes setting up silent conflicts in young minds that cannot help questioning. Most teenagers know—and if they don't, their parents will explain—that failure to belong to Komsomol jeopardizes acceptance into institutions of higher learning and threatens careers.

"If they don't get in, we push them a little," said the principal of a school in Vilnius, Lithuania. "We tell them it will be better for them if they join."

I came across one surprising exception in Estonia, whose cool Baltic population has resisted Russification since Soviet troops drove the Germans out in World War II and then stayed. A twenty-three-year-old woman named Rina, who had a sensitive job interpreting for foreign visitors, told me that she had never been a Komsomol member and had never been pressured to become one. "And that's allowed me to see more pluses in the system than if I had been put under pressure," she said candidly. She even made it into Tartu University without the Komsomol credentials, although she was asked by university officials why she had not joined. "I answered that I just didn't go for being in any organization. I'm not a joiner," she said.

For Estonian intellectuals who have tried not to join Russian culture, such a reply may be appreciated as a sardonic metaphor. But in most of the rest of the country it would probably disqualify the ablest student. The outer trappings of political participation are more than obligations; they are as integral to the society's mores as wearing clothes in public, no more easily shed than any mantle of decent behavior. So pervasive, so expected, so reflexive have these political gestures become that they have also been devalued. "To be a member of Komsomol is an empty formality," said a Russian woman with a penetrating eye. "It is like citizenship or age."

As a result, youngsters adopt varied levels of vigor or lassitude in their Komsomol activities, many showing up at meetings just to be warm bodies checked off on a list of names, others—often egged on by parents with ambitions for them—engaging more eagerly in the sorts of efforts that pass for political activism in the Soviet Union: circulating petitions for the release of Communists imprisoned in Latin America or holding rallies to support "national liberation movements" in the third world.

The group we met at the Pioneer Palace were activists of this latter breed, selected by officials in response to a request I had made several months earlier. I had asked for a round-table discussion with four or five Komsomol members in their teens, knowing that the most orthodox would be produced. I wanted a glimpse of what made loyal Soviet youngsters tick, how they saw their own world and ours, what they cared about, what moved them. It was easy enough to talk on these themes with the sons and daughters of writers, scientists, and artists who were dissidents or independently minded enough to welcome friendships with Americans; it was more difficult to get to the more conformist or zealous, who were wary of contact with foreigners.

My request evidently caused some consternation in the party apparatus that handles Komsomol. Nothing happened for a long time, despite my badgering officials with phone calls and letters. When they finally decided to set up the meeting, I was not even told but was simply taken on a tour of the Pioneer Palace (which I had requested separately) and, midway through the walk through corridors and classrooms, was deposited at the head of a long table in a room with about fifty fifteen- to seventeen-year-olds. They had obviously been well prepared; I had not.

I sat at the table, staring at those young, scrubbed, earnest faces, and was asked by one of the few adults in the room to begin. As we talked over the next hour and a half on a late Friday afternoon, more people kept coming in until there were about a dozen adults and many more teenagers. I heard later from semiofficial Russians that such a session was unprecedented; nobody could remember an American correspondent's ever having been permitted to sit with a group of Komsomol activists and talk about whatever he wished. The risk of contamination by alien ideas is usually considered too great, and youngsters of that age considered too impressionable. I thought that those few who spoke—most remained quiet and listened attentively—were pretty impervious to other viewpoints, and just to make sure they remained so, a middle-aged man at my left, the group's chief ideological chaperone and watchdog and head of the astrophysics department, punctuated the discussion repeatedly with tendentious remarks.

I asked them first how they thought their lives would be different if they lived in the United States. Nobody ventured a response. They were a bit shy, and the watchdog was watching. So I called on a girl who had introduced herself as being from the "circle" specializing in the U.S.A. She said that it would depend on whether or not she was from a well-off American family. If so, her life would be about the same as in the Soviet Union, she thought. I prodded them to address the issue on some dimension other than the material, the economic. There were no takers.

"What is wrong in the world that you want to set right?" I asked.

There was a moment of hesitation; then the answers began to spill out, one after another, traveling down the grooves well worn by the Soviet press. Dictatorship, the denial of most elementary rights, as in Chile, Rhodesia, said one boy. Discrimination, as against the Palestinian people who do not have their rights, said another. War, said a girl. If it breaks out, it will annihilate all humanity. The colossal amount of American weaponry that nobody needs, said another, while at the same time people are perishing from hunger. Unemployment, said a boy, meaning unemployment in the "capitalist countries." Racial discrimination. The growth of crime in the U.S.A.—murder, robbery—people ought to do more useful things, another boy declared. "Fascism grows in America and Western Europe, where democratic reforms are needed," said another.

I pointed out that they had listed problems only in the West, not in their own country. "Is there anything in your own country you want to set right?" Silence. I pushed a bit. "Nothing that you want to do to make your own society better?" I asked of this future governing elite. Finally one boy said, "To build communism." But nobody else had a thing to say. Even after several adults had prompted them, they were silent. Debby, sitting beside me, searched their faces and saw no flicker of impulse to speak.

I asked what they did in their study circles. A girl in the Latin American group said they tried to understand the world, particularly economics, more deeply. She kept talking about *solidarnost,* solidarity with Latin American Communists. What did she and others do to further this solidarity? Kids had been selling souvenirs to raise money for Communists in Latin America, she said. Gifts were sent to a Communist festival in Havana, a boy explained. There had been a "campaign of solidarity" for Dean Reed, an American folk singer who is a celebrity in the Communist world and completely unknown in the United States. A supporter of Chilean Communists, he lives in East Berlin and travels through Eastern Europe and the Soviet Union, giving concerts of revolutionary songs that have teenagers nearly swooning over him. Whenever he visits the United States and gets himself arrested in some peace demonstration, he becomes a *cause célèbre* in the pages of *Pravda,* further evidence of the American regime's oppression of dissenters. The singer had recently been jailed for several days on a trespassing charge in connection with a demonstration. "We collected ten thousand signatures for the freedom of Dean Reed," said one girl proudly. "We have a campaign of solidarity with Chilean Communists," she continued. "In February we phoned Chile and conveyed our solidarity, our support."

Debby whispered a suggested question to me, and I asked it: Did they ever disagree with their parents on political issues? No, all the heads shook. And with their friends? No, never. Do they discuss politics? Yes, they said, but never disagree. I asked for a show of hands: Who ever disagreed? Not one. I laughed and told them they must be the only teenagers in the world who never had a difference with their parents.

"Who are your heroes?" I asked. A long silence stretched into embarrassed tension. Finally a boy, the same one who had announced his desire "to build communism," offered a name. "Lenin," he said. More silence followed. I looked around the room. The adults were uncomfortable. "Che Guevara and Fidel Castro," said the girl from the Latin American circle. Silence. Silence. "No more heroes?" I asked. Silence.

I invited them to ask me questions. Somebody began with a vague one on the state of the world. I said I thought both superpowers were playing a dangerous game by selling arms and competing for influence in the third world, magnifying local conflicts and doing nobody, least of all the local people, any good. The reaction to this was shocked and indignant, utter disbelief that I was equating the United States and the Soviet Union. The United States was doing those things, several youngsters asserted, but not we Russians. A boy with a fuzzy, new-grown mustache lashed out: "The United States is an imperialist power that sucks the blood from smaller, weaker countries, taking their harvests and giving them nothing. The Soviet Union, by contrast, does what it does to help those countries. Look at the American-supported countries, how backward they are—South Korea, for example, and the Philippines, which is nothing more than an American colony." The watchdog on my left sneered a word of praise for the boy—*molodetz* ("good fellow"). I suggested that neither the Soviet Union nor the United States gave aid out of pure altruism. The boy countered that the Soviet Union got nothing in return for its help, except sometimes ingratitude. Look at Egypt, he said, which turned away and rejected the aid. He cited Cuba as a big expense. Perhaps the Soviet Union did get something in return from Cuba, I said. "Something?" the watchdog belched incredulously. Yes, I said. For example, a base where Soviet submarines can be repaired, air bases only ninety miles from the United States, and a source of troops for various operations in Africa.

My simple effort to maintain that neither of our countries always acted out of the noblest of motives ignited an astonishment and rage that swept the entire room, twisting the youngsters' faces into hurt and anger. Unwittingly I had challenged a most fundamental vision of a world divided neatly into good and bad, and the teenagers and adults were each struggling, fighting to regain that vision and keep it intact. It reminded me of the view from my teenage years in the 1950's, when the world was cut unambiguously by an iron curtain, and America still stood on the side of purity. Here was the mirror image of that naïve and comfortable time, staring back at me in complete incomprehension.

We went back and forth, back and forth. I gave an example of the opportunism of international relations: Some years ago the United States had backed Ethiopia; the Soviet Union, Somalia. Then Ethiopia switched sides, and the superpowers' clients were reversed, with Somalia—America's new "friend"—now using Soviet-made weapons to invade Ethiopia. Gasps of disbelief.

The youngsters were not just performing; they were jumping into the argument with hostile questions, declaratory statements, efforts to score debating points rather than to exchange information. The watchdog encouraged them, trying to exhort them to the most extreme, hateful, anti-American views. But they were clearly put off-balance somewhat by my readiness to criticize American as well as Soviet behavior; I did not seem to fit the standard mold of propagandist. And slowly, slowly the rancor ebbed, the interest grew, the questions shifted until they began to seek answers about American life, about crime, about narcotics, about young people, about American reactions to the end of the Vietnam war, about the Middle East, about arms control.

"What are the reasons for the high crime rate and narcotics addiction?" one boy asked. The watchdog tried to answer by saying that they were lower-class problems, born of poverty. I said there was something to that, but it did not explain the narcotics phenomenon among the comfortable middle class. The answers were unclear, I maintained, just as the causes of crime in the Soviet Union were not known definitively. Well, said the watchdog, we don't have much crime, and the loyal children agreed. I countered that I had done a bit of research on that and had found a considerable juvenile crime problem right here in Moscow. Hah, scoffed the kids. For example, I went on, I had had quite a lot of stuff stolen from me, and I began to talk about the three teenagers who had broken into the moving van in Brest. The watchdog quickly called on another youngster, who asserted that the Soviet crime rate was lower than in the United States. Quite possibly, I replied, but we don't really know, do we? The Soviet authorities do not release crime statistics. "Oh, you can find out the figures," said the boy in an enlightening statement of ignorance about his own society. No, I explained. I had tried and was told officially by the Ministry of Internal Affairs that crime statistics were considered a state secret. The boy looked surprised, and the subject was changed.

Debby watched the faces. They were interested, even fascinated, she said later, though none betrayed a hint of accord with me. A group that had to leave early to attend another session did so reluctantly, she observed. Yet the overall atmosphere was so hostile that Yuri Demin, a representative of the youth committee that had organized the meeting, felt compelled at the end to lecture the youngsters sternly.

I was a guest, he said, and therefore was entitled to courtesy and respect, even when they disagreed. Furthermore, when I asked them questions about problems in the Soviet Union, they should have answered honestly, he declared. How could they say there were no problems? Just the other day he had bought a pen, and it had already broken. There was a problem with quality, *kachestvo*— ah, *kachestvo,* they all repeated, recognizing the code word hammered out daily by the mass press in its criticisms of economic shortcomings. *Kachestvo,* that was a permitted word, the formula for summarizing the society's problems. Finally Demin scolded them for not being forthright about their disagreements with their parents. "Everybody has disagreements with parents," he said.

THREE
Fathers and Sons

Leaving home for the last time for the plenum of February–March 1937 (from which he never returned), my father said to my mother, "Don't become embittered: there are sad errors in history. I want my son to grow up as a Bolshevik."

—Yuri Larin Bukharin, son of
Nikolai Ivanovich Bukharin, 1978

Breaking Faith

Alyona Kirtsova led us into the dank foyer of an apartment house and up a darkened stairway. She used a key to open a door and ushered us inside. It was an apartment of some comfort, but not of luxury, reflecting a moderate level of privilege. Her mother drifted like a grey shadow at the edge of the living room, paying little attention as Alyona took us through the house to a small bedroom in the back. She closed the bedroom door, then locked it from the inside.

On the walls of the tiny room hung her paintings—landscapes and portraits and churches in blurry blues and soft pastels. This was her cloistered world, carefully closed off from the rest of the house and family, so confining that she had no room for an easel. Debby and I sat and looked at the canvases, admiring their lilting lightness and delicacy. And Alyona told us her story.

She was twenty-five, the daughter of a Soviet diplomat, the

granddaughter of a vice-president of the Council of Ministers of the Russian Federation, the great-granddaughter of a czarist governor in the Russian Empire's Far East, and the descendant of a line of Russian Orthodox priests. Both her mother and father were members of the Communist Party. But in Alyona the long chain of loyal attachment to Russia's nobility, czarist and Communist, had somehow broken. All she wanted was to leave the motherland forever and move to America.

When she tried to trace the beginnings of her disenchantment, she found her way back to her years as a little girl. She was six when her father was posted to the Soviet Embassy in Canada. There she spent four years, attending a special Soviet school for embassy children but living in an ordinary apartment house among Canadians. She did not get along well with her Russian classmates; her best friends were Canadians. She learned to speak a fluent, practically unaccented English. When she returned to Moscow at the age of ten, a corrosive homesickness for Canada began to grow within her. In the restricted life of the Soviet Union she felt alien. She and her mother drew rebukes on the street because of their Western clothes. She had troubles at school because her political antennae were not well tuned. "I said things I shouldn't have," she recalled. "After two months here I asked my mother when we were going home."

Time was no help, and Alyona just never adjusted as a good Soviet girl. "When I was taken into Pioneers, I didn't like the system. Something false. I felt there was something fictitious about the whole thing. I just didn't like it. I didn't want to join Komsomol, and didn't, and I had a lot of problems and almost got kicked out of school. At one meeting a geography teacher said, 'You have to think about your future.' I said, 'I don't believe it has any sense because it is all false.' "

The only thing that seemed true to her was art. She remembered first encountering the universe of colors and canvases as a child, on a class trip to the Pushkin Museum. "I got into the hall where the Impressionists were, a Matisse. I stood in front of that painting for two or three hours, and it was like magic. They lost me. The next day when I went to school it was awful, how the teacher yelled at me."

Gradually her art evolved into the antithesis of the formal political realm and into an alternative to the bonds and wishes of her family and country. Her parents pressed her to go to college, preferably in the sciences, but she had no taste or aptitude for chemistry or physics, no desire for an advanced degree. "I was strong enough to say no," she recalled proudly. Only painting spoke to her, touched her. When she began to draw portraits, her father, the diplomat and Communist, ridiculed them as products of an activity without seriousness.

Rifts within her family ran along the lines of her own attitudes. Her father drifted away from her and divorced her mother. "I didn't like my father personally. He wasn't very good to my mother. Kids usually don't forgive their fathers if they act that way." Ultimately he came to represent nothing that she valued.

She married at seventeen, divorced at twenty-one, and through the years moved into a silent separation from both her parents. She had not even seen her father for ten years when she asked him to sign the required permission paper for her to emigrate. He was appalled, and refused. Her mother also objected. "Why do you want to go?" she asked Alyona.

"I don't like the climate," Alyona replied.

In earlier years, "We had lots of debates about my political feelings," she said. "My mother believes in the whole thing—absolutely. I don't talk to my mother anymore about it. My grandmother had to completely forget about her relatives—priests and nobles—and it was very hard for her. She had to lie to herself, because she had to take the whole system. Now she says I was right."

One would have expected a tortured face, at least a hint of conflict in the eyes. But Alyona's face was serene, cherubic, framed by light brown hair like a Midwestern cheerleader child's. She talked and talked, about her politically orthodox sister, a scientist, "the daughter of her father and mother"; about her brother, a stagehand, who had also avoided Komsomol membership; about her painting, how long it took her to do each canvas, how she was burning inside to say something, how she had tried poetry without success. How much she wished to emigrate, she said, and how little chance she had, not only because the authorities required the parents' permission even if the child was fifty—a cynical way of placing the parents at risk for the child's act—but also because she was not

Jewish or Armenian, the two groups most easily able to get out.
Ethnic Russians are hardly ever allowed to leave.

I had met so many like her, those of Communist, believing par-
entage who had taken another path against great odds. How does
it happen? I asked. "I think it happens everywhere," Alyona said.
"In your country, for example, children of very rich people went
into the hippie movement. Children start realizing what's going on
in the world." Yes, I suggested, but there is something more here,
something much more complete and final. Alyona might have said
again what she had described when she stood in front of that
Matisse in the Pushkin: "They lost me."

Once mixed into a swirling brew of anger and alienation, the
ingredients of political attitude, personal values, and generational
friction cannot be separated. They play on each other like volatile
acids, introducing a strange chemistry into family relationships.
Because the Soviet Union aspires to totalitarianism (while not quite
achieving it), and because the system depends on the twin myths
of thorough political mobilization and unquestioned unanimity, the
family is rarely a reliable sanctuary for alienated young people.
Even in its intimacy, the family often magnifies the pain of deviation
from the society's political norms.

I was struck again and again by the disaffected from families with
solid Communist Party credentials, by the outspoken dissidents
whose parents remained enamored of official Soviet ideas, even as
their children suffered at the hands of the secret police. I was moved
by the intricate ambivalence in being both liberated and rejected,
freed from the stifling inability to speak the truth, yet cut from the
loving ties of parental warmth. There was always sadness in this,
mingled with the heady sense of righteousness.

Some attained a wary understanding with their parents. One
woman in her late twenties, who adopted the pseudonym Alissa to
conceal her identity on the phone (and because she felt a bit like
Alice in Wonderland), worked actively and covertly helping the
dissident human rights movement smuggle out documents on arrests and trials without running directly afoul of her father, although he was a party official of some rank. Her style of keeping
a low profile and never signing open letters or public petitions was
adopted out of deference to him, and he responded by suspending

rancor. "He understands me," she said.

Another friend, "Andrei," managed to maintain a dialogue with his father—a journalist and party member—through their shared political disaffection and a certain duplicity. I knew Andrei as a bitter young man with a passion for American rock. He never involved himself in dissident activities, but privately he was angrier than any dissident I ever met. He wore several faces. In his small apartment with the stereo turned up high, he used the most extreme terminology to describe the Soviet system. He played a proper role as a student in a foreign language institute whose graduates often entered the diplomatic corps. His close friends included party members with a liberal bent; once I noticed that he softened his complaints when Russian acquaintances were present, and later, during one of his harangues, I asked if he ever spoke so stridently to his non-American friends. He said no. I suspected that he measured his words with his father, too. Which was his true face, and which were masks, I was never sure. I wonder if even he knew.

He had tried to join the party himself, not for ideology but for career. He had been rejected because of a close friendship in his high school years with the son of an American who had been working temporarily in Moscow, a rejection that had driven both Andrei and his Communist father into venomous despair. "I wanted to go abroad, to get a higher post," he said of his party application. "Now I know I will be a simple man, that's all. My father said it was a good thing I didn't get accepted because I would have had to have lived a lie."

Boris Shcharansky's first reaction when his son Anatoly was arrested in March 1977 was fear. And the first reaction lasted a long time, for the elder Shcharansky was a good party member and loyal Soviet journalist whose son had become a prominent figure in the Jewish emigration movement, so prominent that Soviet authorities charged him with treason. Anatoly and his father had worked out a *modus vivendi:* his father, being an open-minded man, did not object on political grounds when Anatoly applied in 1973 to emigrate, figuring the decision was Anatoly's to make. And Anatoly kept his dissident activities completely separate from his family, to the extent that although I knew him well, I never met any of his relatives until after his imprisonment, when they rose to his defense.

"My father is scared," said Anatoly's brother, Leonid, after the arrest. "He is afraid of everything. He lives within the system. He has the attitude that we should not upset the investigators, that we should be loyal people." By the time of the trial in July 1978, however, Boris Shcharansky had changed, having been led step by step by his wife, Ida, who had become her son's chief supporter. "He knows his son is not a criminal, that he is an honest man," she explained to me as we stood outside the courthouse. But Anatoly never had a chance to see his father's shift firsthand. On January 20, 1980, while riding to a birthday party to be held for Anatoly *in absentia*, Boris Shcharansky died of a heart attack. Six years later, Anatoly was finally released. His mother followed him to Israel; his brother and sister-in-law settled in the United States.

Anatoly's wife, Natalia Stieglitz, had less understanding parents. Both were party members; her mother was a prosecutor of juvenile delinquents for a time, her father an army officer in the supply corps. In 1951, in one of the last spasms of Stalin's anti-Semitic paranoia, they were deported with thousands of other Jews to a stark existence on the banks of the Lena River in Siberia. There Natalia—who has since taken the Hebrew name Avital—and her older brother, Mikhail, suffered from severe strife in the family. At the age of fifteen Mikhail ran away from home, making his way alone to Moscow, where he then sent for his sister. In the early 1970's he gravitated to the dissident movement and sought to emigrate. When he refused to report to the army for induction, it was his mother, as a state prosecutor, who ordered him arrested and then tried to have him rearrested after he had been released. Once he and his sister had emigrated to Israel, their parents maintained little contact and did not acknowledge Mikhail's two sons or his wife, Anita, from whom he was later divorced. In one letter they wrote of Avital in the past tense, as if she were dead.

Lidiya Voronina's relation with her mother was the most hateful I encountered. Lidiya was an ethnic Russian, married to a Jewish mathematician named Anatoly Reznik. Together they wished to emigrate and ultimately did so to the United States. But in the process of applying for visas and moving into dissident circles, Lidiya entered a stormy region of profound anger and hurt. Her mother was a party member who held a high position in the Ministry of Justice. She was the author of the law on disconnecting dissidents' telephones, "and my telephone was cut off," Lidiya said with bitter appreciation of the irony. For years her mother blocked her emigration. "For her, it is nothing, a zero, that I am her daughter," Lidiya declared angrily, spitting the words. "She would sentence me to prison if it came to that."

Again, the political and personal divides ran along parallel lines, marking deep faults in the family's structure. Lidiya's grandmother had lived in exile under the czars, accompanying her brother, who had been sent to the Siberian town of Irkutsk for a political crime. Lidiya's mother's father had died of tuberculosis after exile, and the grandmother's second husband had been shot during Stalin's purges in 1937. Lidiya's father, who became a party member serving on a court-martial board, had run away from home and had worked shoveling coal on a ship that sailed around the world. Then he lived by choice in Siberia, and he saw his daughter only several times. She was raised mostly by her grandmother, though she spent ages eight to ten in an *internat,* a boarding school designed to remove children from their families for the ideological purpose of communal upbringing. Her mother became for her an amalgam of personal rejection and orthodox communism. "No love," Lidiya said of her mother. "Communist ideology means you stop being a human being, stop having human feelings. Very early I became independent from communism. No love."

In some measure, these are continuing generational struggles between the old order and the new, between the resolute parental embrace of once-true values and the iconoclastic assaults of youth. Russia, despite its great inertia and isolation, has never been immune to these grinding passions of discord. Thus did Turgenev portray the universal frictions in *Fathers and Sons,* leaving in the bitter rebellion of his character Bazarov a taste of joyfulness in the free play of irreverence against the musty, venerable canons of propriety. And even if the old order seems to triumph in Turgenev's tale, as Bazarov's nihilism dies with him, both Nicholas Petrovich Kirsanov and his son Arcady, and all the other characters who came into contact with the waspish brilliance of that young mind, are somehow better for it at the end.

In modern Russia, of course, the venerable old values have now become those of Marxism-Leninism, atheism, the party's autocracy. Parents, for instance, have long felt bound to name their children in accord with Russia's broader faith, thereby burdening each generation with the indelible brands of the old beliefs. Before the Revolution, choosing from an array of saints' names sanctioned by the Russian Orthodox Church was *de rigueur*. In the fervor of the postrevolutionary period names such as Vladlen (for Vladimir Lenin), Karm (Krasnaya Armiya ["Red Army"]), Dotnara (*doch trudnovogo naroda* ["daughter of the working people"]), and Kim (Kommunistichesky Internatsional Molodyozhi ["Communist International of Youth"]) were briefly popular.* Ina Rubin said she knew twins whose names were derived from *revolyutsiya* ("revolution"). He was Revo; she was Lyutsiya. Ina had a teacher named Plamenny ("flame") and knew a girl called Industriya ("industry"). The orthodox Communist father of the Medvedev twins, who both later became dissidents, named his boys Roi and Reis; *roi* is the imperative of "to dig," and *reis* means "a route"—in other words, to dig a path to communism. Reis later changed his name to Zhores.

The heritage represented by such names is as difficult to erase as a birthmark, removable only with pain. However continuous are the forces of national chauvinism, authoritarian politics, and religious-style devotion that connect Russian history on both sides of the turbulent revolutions of 1917, the relationships across the generations have been complicated, often embittered, by the political shifts, the cycles of oppression and relaxation, the demand for adherence to the empty shell of an idea. Mixed into the personal dynamics unique to each family, the political conflict becomes both petty and monumental.

Both the terror of Stalinism and the sudden, frightening release from that terror, when Khrushchev denounced Stalin's crimes in his "secret speech" to the Twentieth Party Congress in 1956, were catalysts in the relationships between fathers and sons, mothers and daughters, including families of the leading Bolsheviks. Permission was granted to disbelieve a little. Svetlana Alliluyeva, Stalin's daughter, became religious and defected. (Moscow charwomen sometimes asked me in half whispers if I could tell them the latest news of her life in the United States. Was it true, as they had heard, that she had had another child?) Yuri Larin grew into a young man

---

*For more on names, see Genevra Gerhart, *The Russian's World: Life and Language* (New York: Harcourt Brace Janovich, 1974).

before 1956 came and he learned who his father was: the Bolshevik Nikolai Bukharin, executed in the purges of 1938. Larin, who bore his mother's name, had not been told his own identity all those years. When he found out who he was, he finally added Bukharin to his name and later joined his mother in an unsuccessful effort to have his father rehabilitated posthumously by the party.

The phenomenon of open dissent, virtually unseen before the late 1960's, has colored the generational conflicts. As the limits of outspokenness have broadened and shrunk, broadened and shrunk again—whether in painting or theater, music or poetry, scholarship or dress, political protest or emigration—new choices have been opened, and new tensions introduced into families. Parents and children have been caught in the shifting ambiguities beyond the home, the uncertainties between permissiveness and rigidity. Sometimes whole families have moved together, but often the option to publish abroad, to leave the country, or to state a protest has opened irreconcilable gulfs. Rarely has the making of a dissident been entirely free of strong family emotion.

In his apartment on Red Army Street in Moscow, Vladimir Solovyov kept a small cardboard box containing his late father's most treasured medals: Hero of Socialist Labor; Order of Lenin; Tenth Anniversary of the Victory over Fascism. The red and gold ribbons and orders with hammers and sickles and profiles of Lenin must have made an impressive display on the chest of the old man, Isaak Yakovlevich Solovyov. He was a Communist Party member and an officer with the elite troops stationed on the Chinese and Finnish borders. He was so trusted that in the 1930's he was assigned to Stalin's personal guard, and in the small box with the medals lay the yellowing credentials bearing his picture and identifying him as a lieutenant colonel in the NKVD, the security service. He was close to the Politburo, so close he went hunting with its members, and years later discreetly told his son of one outing with Bukharin. Solovyov said to Bukharin, "We need to go to the right; that's where the bears are." And Bukharin replied: "No, I'm going left. I will not go to the right anymore. I'm afraid of Stalin."

In the pervasive terror of that time Lieutenant Colonel Solovyov kept hearing footsteps on the landing. In the kitchen, a suitcase full of food and clothing was kept ready to send with him in case of his arrest. "Mama always changed the food," Vladimir recalled. "She changed the bread every evening." But the precautions proved unnecessary. Years later Isaak Solovyov could point to himself as one of only two or three in a photograph of about thirty comrades in his military unit who remained free and alive. He died of natural causes in 1966.

His son, Vladimir, short and peppery, worked successfully in the ideologically sensitive area of film and literary criticism, writing frequently for the prestigious weekly *Literaturnaya Gazeta.* He married a placid girl with a turned-up nose and a ponytail, Yelena Klepikova, also a literary critic with a party official for a father. Vladimir attained membership in the elite Union of Writers, Yelena in the Union of Journalists, with accompanying access to special clubs, special bookstores, and special housing in cooperative apartments for writers. It was a life of material privilege but constant compromise. So much of what Yelena wrote was changed by editors that she barely recognized the published versions. They were loaded with paragraphs, not hers, quoting Brezhnev, hailing the five-year plan, extolling the working class; about 30 percent of her writing survived.

Slowly, slowly their lives began to fill with suffocating restriction; a kind of claustrophobia set in. Like many young intellectuals, they had allowed themselves to hope, especially in one brief period of the early 1960's, when the first refreshing breeze of cultural liberalism swept away some of the stale taboos. "I liked that time," Vladimir said. "It looked as if it promised something better. I didn't write badly, in my opinion. I was honest. I praised what I liked and criticized what I didn't like." As the sixties progressed, they watched the relaxation in Czechoslovakia with excitement, thinking that despite the tightening that had already come to Soviet literature, the experiment in Prague might affect the atmosphere in Moscow. If the Czechoslovaks were allowed to move toward a more open society, he and his friends thought, perhaps the Soviet Union could do so, too.

Vladimir was vacationing in Vilnius, Lithuania, with his wife and small son when Soviet troops went into Czechoslovakia in 1968. He heard the news from an old Lithuanian woman selling newspapers on the street. She took him for a Russian, although he is a Jew, and she spit her words: "You bastards. You've invaded Prague." He refused to believe it. He clung to some hope that it was just the hateful lie of a prattling old woman until a day or two later. Driving through Latvia, their small car was forced off the road at night by a huge convoy of trucks and tanks and armored vehicles, some with wheels taller than their automobile, all roaring toward the border, their angry searchlights piercing the darkness, their machine guns manned and ready. It was a fearful sight, an invasion of their dream. They wept.

"We hoped that it would be better and better, and we would be free," Vladimir said. "But it became worse and worse. Opportunities became narrower as my desires expanded. I was centrifugal, and they were centripetal."

The decision to leave the stifling but secure habit of obedience does not usually come in a moment of fiery rebellion in the throes of youthful impertinence, but gradually, almost subtly, accumulating over years of living in compromise like a slowly filling cup of quiet grief. Few Soviet dissidents are in their late teens or early twenties; most are well into middle age when they finally arrive at the line that marks the outer edge of permissible behavior and step across. Andrei Sakharov was forty-seven. General Pyotr Grigorenko was fifty-four. Yuri Orlov was fifty-one. Sergei Polikanov, a prominent nuclear physicist, party member, and full member of the Academy of Sciences, was fifty-one by the time the routine, standard restrictions on his and his family's work and travel abroad had rubbed and rubbed a smoldering resentment into flames, and he called a press conference to issue a denunciation.

Vladimir Solovyov and Yelena Klepikova were on the young side; still, they both were thirty-five, with a good fifteen years of the real world behind them, when they came to understand inside themselves that somehow they had to get out. "We were going to leave very quietly," Yelena said. Her father would not agree. Konstantin Klepikov, loyal Communist and narrow survivor of the purges, was afraid. In 1937 he had been dismissed as party chairman of Murmansk's port administration because of his vote ten years earlier to seat, at a party congress, a Leningrad delegation opposed to Stalin. He, too, heard footsteps in the hallway; he made a small hole in his apartment wall so he could peer out into the corridor to watch for the secret police. The knock at the door never came, and in 1956, after Khrushchev's "secret speech," Konstantin

Klepikov was readmitted to the party. Twenty-one years later, under KGB threats of a second expulsion and perhaps even imprisonment, he went against his daughter and refused to sign the permission papers.

Undaunted, Vladimir and Yelena, who is Russian, collected the other documents for themselves and their twelve-year-old son and presented them at the office for exit visas to Israel. The results contained all the ingredients of catastrophe. Soviet officials refused even to accept the papers, citing the missing parental permission. Their articles suddenly disappeared from magazines and newspapers. They were expelled from their professional unions, and a book of hers scheduled to appear was canceled by a state publishing house, which then brought suit to retrieve the advance royalty she had been paid.

The couple responded with a bold challenge to the authorities. They continued their professional work as journalists, but this time by distributing, to Western correspondents, typescript copies of reports they wrote on sides of Soviet life that officialdom preferred to keep invisible. They began by doing a story on the dismissal of two Leningrad literary editors for publishing a poem expressing compassion for Czarina Alexandra in the aftermath of the Bolshevik Revolution. Next came a report on Muscovites boycotting taxis after the doubling of fares; then a look at the censorship of feature films.

"It's not hard for us to guess in advance the reaction of the KGB to our decision," they said in a written statement announcing their plans. "Since the repertoire of this internationally known organization is extremely scanty, monotonous, and not very inventive, we can even foresee the measures that the KGB will take against us in the near future: threats, intimidation, telephone disconnection, search—right up to an arrest or a gangster attack."

These were daring words, and Vladimir and Yelena were clearly thrilled by their risky adventure. "Finally we have become people," he said. Suddenly they could speak, and the rapid flow of free ideas tumbled over each other faster than sentences could be formed. Conversation was a constant bombardment of literary allusions and intricate thoughts about Soviet complexities that interrupted each other in an exhausting, breathless fusillade. Where in all this was the fear? "Each person has his norm, his quota of fear, just as each person can sleep only so many hours, then wakes up," Vladimir explained. "I have had my quota of fear. I have used it all up."

Despite their expectations, Vladimir and Yelena were left like their fathers—waiting for the footsteps that never came. In an uncommon stroke of shrewdness, the KGB got rid of them not by arresting them and making them martyrs but by inviting them one day to submit their visa papers, even without the parental permission. The exit visas were issued immediately, and the couple were to leave in a few days with their son and Vladimir's mother for Vienna, the first stop in the bewildering outside world. Their destination, they had decided, was to be the United States, not Israel.

When I went to say good-bye, Vladimir went into a chest and pulled out the small box with his father's medals. He gave them all to me. I tried not to take them, but he insisted. Customs would not allow him to carry or send them out of the country, he explained, and besides, he wanted to be rid of them. He told me about each one in some detail and said he never wished to see them again.

A few months later he and his family were in New York, living in a seedy West Side hotel. I was there, too, by chance, and I stopped by to visit them, to welcome them to America. I asked if he wanted his father's medals back. He said no.

Two years after that, when I had left Moscow for good and was passing through New York, I called him. He and Yelena were struggling to write for émigré publications and were adjusting, with difficulty. I asked again whether I could give him back his father's medals. Again he said a firm no.

In 1978 Semyon Slepak was an aging, iron-minded Bolshevik, and his son, Vladimir, named after Lenin, was the rock of the Jewish emigration movement. For nearly a decade, since Vladimir had submitted his unsuccessful application for an exit visa to Israel, the old man had cut him off, refusing to see him or speak to him. Only on the occasions when the father's failing heart would put him into the hospital for a time, and his son would visit, did they look each other in the eye and talk, and even in the words they exchanged the gulf of silence remained. The first time, the son took the father some fruit, and from his bed the old man growled, "Thank you for your visit. And now go away and never come again."

Vladimir, known to everyone as Volodya, the Russian diminutive of his name, became a foundation of calm in the dissident community. From behind his great grey patriarchal beard, his deep voice rumbled in assuring tones of unyielding patience; his eyes rarely showed his profound fatigue. Toward his father he never betrayed any bitterness, although he had cause.

Semyon Slepak was born in 1893, the last of the four children of a pious Jewish family in Dubrovno, Byelorussia. His father, a teacher in the local yeshiva, was named Israel, and Israel named his son Solomon, fitting for an infant who, it was fervently hoped, would grow up to be a fine and respected rabbi. And so Semyon Slepak began his life as Solomon Israilevich—Solomon, the son of Israel.

When Solomon was still a boy, his father died, and Solomon eschewed piety, at least of Judaism's kind, running away from home on the eve of his bar mitzvah, before his thirteenth birthday. This was a time of dark, clandestine talk of revolution in Russia, magical and fascinating talk to a lonely boy, and Solomon found comradeship among these revolutionary circles, dangerous as they were in the corrupt and crumbling final chapter of czarism. At the age of twenty Solomon took the path of Lenin, Trotsky, and others who would make a revolution and sought safety in the West, moving to New York to settle with his sister, who had gone there five years before.

He painted houses, worked in a belt factory, and studied medicine before the distant revolution in the autumn of 1917 rekindled the embers that had been smoldering within him. After the Bolsheviks had made their move in Petrograd, he searched for a way back, journeying into Canada and across the continent to Vancouver to catch a ship to Vladivostok.

When Solomon Slepak arrived in the far eastern reaches of what had once been the czarist empire, the Bolsheviks had not yet extended their power beyond European Russia, 4,000 miles to the west. From the vast pine forests that stretched across Siberia to the Pacific coast, the old order held out against the new; a civil war had erupted, but Admiral Aleksandr Kolchak had erected a regime to stand against the Revolution. It did so for a while with help from the troops of the United States, Britain, and France, which also provided supplies to the anti-Bolshevik forces.

In the United States Slepak had come to know a man by the name of Grigory Voitinski, whom he now met again in Vladivostok. Voitinski was an active member of the underground Bolshevik organization in the Far East, and he eagerly recruited Slepak, putting him to work using his good English to head a propaganda unit aimed at the American soldiers. Kolchak's agents were busy, however, and in the end both Slepak and Voitinski were arrested, sentenced to death, and imprisoned to await execution. By the good fortune of which legends are made, Kolchak declared a partial amnesty on some holiday, commuting Slepak's sentence to life at hard labor in a camp on the island of Sakhalin. And when Kolchak's regime collapsed in the winter of 1919–20, marking the Bolsheviks' victory, all political prisoners, including Slepak, were released. He became chairman of the soviet, or governing council, of northern Sakhalin, which then came under attack by the Japanese, who occupied the southern part of the island, driving Slepak again into a struggle for survival. He organized partisan units to fight the Japanese, moving to the mainland and assuming the post of deputy in the military ministry of the Soviet Union's new far eastern republic. With the subsequent arrival of regular Soviet troops in the region, Slepak finished his military career, becoming chief editor of *Chitinskaya Pravda,* the party's newspaper in Chita, and then delegate to the First Congress of the Communist International in Moscow. There he was elected to the Presidium of the Comintern, as it was known, the international association of Communist parties whose duty was to further the worldwide revolution.

One of the targets of the Comintern was China, where a young revolutionary named Mao Zedong was leading the fledgling Communist Party. In 1922 came word that Slepak's old comrade Voitinski had been arrested while on a secret mission to make contact with the Chinese Communists. Solomon Slepak was sent to free him. He traveled on a fake American passport, posing as an American businessman, and managed somehow to pay the right bribes in the right places. He secured Voitinski's release and established connections with the Communists there.

Back in Moscow, Slepak went to work for the Soviet news agency, Tass (then called ROSTA, the acronym in Russian for its name, Rossiskoye Telegrafnoye Agenstvo), and he quickly drew another adventurous assignment. He was to go to Tokyo as a correspondent, the only Soviet citizen in Japan at a time when diplomatic relations had not even been established. Before departure, he received two pieces of advice, issued when he went to pick up his passport: one, to get married, presumably to reduce the opportunity for a compromising sexual liaison, and two, to change his name. The second suggestion came from Maksim Litvinov, then deputy foreign minister and later Stalin's foreign minister. Litvinov —some of whose children and grandchildren would also step into the ranks of the disaffected—was a Jew who had changed his family name from Vallakh. He told Slepak that people all over the world were saying that the Jews had taken power in the Soviet Union, and it would be better not to have a Jewish name. So Solomon Israilevich Slepak, Solomon, the son of Israel, became Semyon Ignatyevich Slepak. It seemed a final burial of the Jewish roots of the past. But it would have to be done again, later, more brutally.

In Japan Slepak filled whatever mixed role had been worked out for him as correspondent, intelligence agent, and diplomat. He participated in the early negotiations on setting up a Soviet embassy in Tokyo. And in 1924 his new wife gave birth to their first child, a girl. They named her Rosa, after Rosa Luxemburg, the Polish Jewish Communist who helped launch the Polish Social Democratic Party in 1892-3 and founded the German Communist Party after World War I. After Rosa came twins, who died at birth, and another infant who did not survive. Slepak believed the babies had been killed by Japanese doctors because of his previous activity against the Japanese in the Far East, so when his wife became pregnant again, this time with Volodya, they returned to Moscow for the birth. It was October 1927.

The new son, named after Vladimir Ilyich Lenin, was just two or three months old when the Slepak family left again for a foreign post, this time with Tass in China. They lived first in Peking, then in Manchuria during the Chinese-Japanese War there, then again in Peking, where Volodya began his studies in an American school and where he also contracted a dysentery so severe that his life was endangered. A German medical professor advised them to go home for treatment, and they did in 1934. Semyon continued with Tass in Moscow for another four years, rising to become deputy head of the foreign department.

Stalin's purges were upon the country. No one was safe. The higher the position, the more vulnerable, it seemed. In 1937 the head of Tass was warned by friends that he was to be arrested; he shot himself. Then the head of the foreign department, Semyon's immediate superior, was taken into custody and put before the firing squad, leaving Semyon in charge of the department for a short time. A new chief with whom Slepak did not get along was appointed, and Slepak moved to a publishing house to work as "control editor," or political watchdog and censor, overseeing works being published in foreign languages. He went through a series of responsible jobs, becoming deputy head of Comintern's press department in 1943; then, because of his linguistic abilities— he spoke English, French, and German fluently and Polish, Czech, Italian, Spanish, and Yiddish less so—he wrote summaries of the foreign press for the Politburo. In 1947 the Central Committee assigned him to the Jewish Anti-Fascist Committee, a propaganda organization sponsored by Lavrenti Beria, Stalin's sinister chief of the secret police. There Slepak served as head of the press department as, one by one, nearly all the committee members were arrested and shot. He then returned to the publishing house, where he worked until the anti-Semitic spasm of 1952. In that year he was called to the Central Committee by a friend and told secretly that all Jews, including him, would be dismissed in a month or two but that if he would quickly collect papers documenting his activity in the Far East during the civil war, his friend would send them to a higher authority and at least try to get him a pension. Slepak did as he was advised, lost his job, and won his pension.

As he learned long after the purges, he had had reason to be afraid. But his fear, if it existed, was never a subject of open discussion between him and his children. They could only surmise, and mostly in retrospect. "In '38, '37," Volodya recalled, "I sometimes saw my father at night standing near the window and looking out. Maybe he was waiting for arrest. I heard from my mother that he slept very badly."

One day in 1950 Volodya, then a new engineering graduate, answered a knock on the apartment door to find a bent old man leaning on a stick. He gave his name as Klimov, a good friend of Semyon's from the Far East, an expert on the economy of Mongolia. The Klimov the Slepaks remembered had been very tall and athletic, strong and strapping. This man was stooped and aged. Volodya called his mother.

Klimov had disappeared some years before, into the prison camps. He had emerged broken and sick. Solicitously he inquired after the family, asking Volodya's mother whether life was difficult. Yes, she said. But Volodya had begun work, and they had his father's pension.

"You get a pension?" Klimov asked incredulously. "Was your husband rehabilitated after death?"

"But he is alive," said Mrs. Slepak.

"He survived? Where is he?"

"He went to buy bread at the bakery."

"Impossible!" Klimov declared. "When was he released?"

"He wasn't arrested."

"I don't believe it!" said Klimov. "The main accusation against me was my connection with the Japanese spy Slepak. I was sure he was in the cell next to mine."

Several years later Semyon confronted his narrow escape himself, on a Moscow street. He was taking a stroll with his grandson, Volodya's son Aleksandr, along Tverskoi Boulevard, not far from Red Square, when he saw the faintly familiar figure of an older man walking stiffly from the other direction. As they approached each other, Slepak recognized him as the retired party secretary in Tass, from the thirties. The old man recognized Slepak, too, stopped short, stared at him in disbelief, and howled, "How! You are alive? It can't be!"

No more than a month after Slepak had resigned from Tass in 1938, this party secretary had received a secret order from the Central Committee instructing him to collect compromising material on a list of Tass employees. The first name on the list was Semyon Ignatyevich Slepak. The secretary called the Central Committee to report that Slepak and two others listed no longer worked there. He was told to make a note to that effect beside their names. He did so, assumed that Slepak would easily be found at his new job, assembled the damaging material on the others, and sent it in. All were arrested and shot. He had no reason to think that the relentless police mechanism would slip and fail to carry through with Slepak.

The close calls, the terror did nothing to shake Slepak's faith. When friends and colleagues were executed, he religiously inked out their faces on the old snapshots in his photo album. When Stalin died, he wept, the only time Volodya could recall him in tears. "I don't remember seeing him cry when my mother died," he said.

As Israel Slepak had wanted his son, Solomon, to enter the rabbinate, so Solomon—now Semyon—expected his son, Vladimir, to enter the Communist Party. The assumption that he would do so was an unquestioned feature of life in the Slepak household, and when it disintegrated suddenly on a wintry evening in 1952, the ruins it left were irreparable.

Volodya had married a young radiologist, Mariya, who worked in a Moscow hospital. She was well acquainted with some of the leading doctors, most of them Jewish, who were arrested in December 1952 and accused of engaging in a conspiracy to assassinate party leaders and commanders of the army. The Doctors' Plot it was called, and it became one of the final landmarks along Stalin's last road, a precursor of what would probably have been a new inundation of arrests and executions similar to the purges of the thirties, had it not been cut short by Stalin's death in 1953.

Mariya Slepak knew that the Doctors' Plot was fraudulent. She returned home in the evenings with tales of mass meetings at the hospital. "They put Jewish doctors on the platform," she said, "and made them say dirty words about Jews as traitors, Jews as spies, about anti-Soviet activities of Jewish organizations abroad." She asked Semyon Slepak, the old Bolshevik, what was happening. She knew many of the professors under arrest, she told him; she was sure they were honest people. She had no doubt.

"Maybe they are honest people," the old man replied, "but when you cut down trees, chips fly." It was a Russian proverb, adapted to the new task of building common good even at the risk of individual suffering. "It is better to prosecute one hundred innocent people," he declared, "than to let free one traitor."

And the silent conflict between father and son, festering for some time, burst into their first open argument. "Right after these words," Volodya said, "I told him, 'I'll never be in your party. There's too much blood on your hands.'"

Old Slepak let out a stunned shout. He roared in disbelief that his own son could tear at the core of what was so dear to him, that his own flesh could reject what he had spent his life fighting and nearly dying for. He finished the argument by taking drops for his heart. "I stopped understanding him," Volodya said. And from then on, little by little, Volodya and his wife moved intellectually away, out of the Soviet world and into an identification with their Jewishness.

"When we were in China, I didn't know we were Jews," Volodya recalled. "But when we came here, I understood immediately that I was an abnormal boy—in the yard, in the street. I asked my father what it meant. He said it remained from the czarist period, and very soon it would be over. I believed him. And I waited. Because I was brought up in a Communist family, I believed what he told me. And then after World War II a big wave of anti-Semitism began. I asked my father what was happening. He said, 'You see, it's an influence from the Germans, and very soon it will be finished.' But then I began—very slowly, very late—I began to understand."

In the early sixties he managed to get hold of a pamphlet by Vladimir Jabotinsky and a book by Theodore Herzl, and the influence of these two Zionist thinkers had a profound impact. "Then we began to understand that Israel is the only place for Jews," he explained. "Of course, we understand that every free country is better than here. But for Jews, the only place to live is Israel."

Exhilarated by the Israeli military prowess in the Six-Day War of 1967, "we felt proud for our people," he said, "and we understood the danger for this state of Israel if there were not enough people to defend it. We understood that if something bad happens to Israel, our fate would be very bad—that we, Soviet Jews, can be in safety if there can be a strong Israel." It was a widespread feeling among Soviet Jews, and it triggered the emigration movement.

In the autumn of 1968, by way of that vibrant circuit of underground news that keeps Soviet citizens well briefed on the unmentionable, the word circulated that forty Jewish families in Riga had been allowed to leave, and suddenly the impossible became a dream. Volodya and Mariya made their first, tentative move in December, asking, through the informal intermediaries who come and go as tourists to Moscow, that "relatives" be found in Israel who would send them the "invitations" required to make their case one of family reunification. This was the only ground on which Soviet officials would grant exit visas. Volodya did not tell his father of the decision that they had quietly taken.

The invitations came in March 1969. The following month Volodya lost his job as head of a laboratory trying to develop new television equipment, some with military applications. In 1970 he filed visa applications for himself, Mariya, and their two sons and told his father. And the old man made a final break: no more contact; no more visits; no more conversations by phone. He told Mariya's mother angrily that he would fight their departure, that he had connections in the KGB. Later he wrote Volodya a long letter of bitterness: "Here things will be worse for you. I have the impression that you will not be allowed to go anywhere, and you will rot here." It was said with satisfaction.

Volodya was never certain how much his father had to do with blocking his departure. There were other pretexts, too, apparently. He was once grabbed by KGB men in the street, shoved into an unmarked car, and delivered to an office where a man identifying himself as a KGB general told him, "If you didn't know state secrets, we would allow you to leave."

"What secrets are you speaking of ?" asked Volodya. "In that field of technology where I worked, we are behind the United States and other Western countries twelve to fourteen years."

"Ah," said the KGB man. "This is the main secret."

"Every child knows this," Volodya shot back.

"But you know it better."

Still, he could not shake the sense that his father's distinguished record and intimate friendships among the party's old guard had been an important factor. But with a determined devotion to family affection, Volodya never gave up on the old man. He tried again and again to see him, succeeding only when his father was hospitalized. On Volodya's fiftieth birthday, when his father took no notice, Volodya picked up the phone and dialed his father's number.

"Hello, who is speaking?" asked Semyon.

"Your son."

"I have no son."

"Then who am I?" Volodya said.

"An enemy of the people."

The only trace of softness was reserved for the grandsons, Volodya's two boys, Aleksandr and Leonid. Aleksandr married an American who worked in Moscow and on that basis was granted an exit visa. Before he left, his grandfather wished him well, without rancor. Leonid, several years younger, evaded the draft, living on the run, hiding with friends in various parts of the vast country. And the Soviet authorities, for whatever reason, chose not to arrest him but finally to let him leave with his wife for Israel, after they had had a baby boy. In his bitter letter Semyon expressed sorrow for Leonid, who he said was too young to understand what he was doing.

The strong wills of the Slepak sons through the generations held firm in these two young men. Both possessed the realization of their father's dream to live in Israel; both rejected it, each moving after a short time to the United States and settling there. Their parents remained in the Soviet Union.

In 1978 Volodya and Mariya hung a banner on the balcony of their Gorky Street apartment, just a few blocks from the Kremlin, declaring, "Let us out to our son in Israel." They were both arrested. Mariya received a suspended sentence, but Volodya was given a five-year term of exile in a small village in the far eastern wilds of Siberia, not far from the region where his father had gone underground to help make a revolution so many years before.

In August 1978 old Semyon Slepak died in Moscow. And in a curious gesture of compassion, perhaps more for the memory of an old Bolshevik than for the feelings of his dissident son, the authorities allowed Volodya to fly back from his remote exile to attend the funeral. Then, when his father had been reduced to ashes and the eulogy spoken by a party functionary over his grave, Volodya was placed on a plane back into the wilderness.*

Keeping Faith

The spirit of free inquiry dwells not in any broad expanse, but in small, hidden places of privacy, sheltered by the quiet bravery of a few restless minds. One of those rare places is a tiny book-lined study on the fifth floor of a walk-up at the northern edge of Moscow, a good forty-five-minute drive from the Kremlin. A massive desk, neatly kept, practically fills the small room. A page of manuscript arches gracefully out of a battered portable typewriter. In shelves and cabinets stand folders and folders of files so meticu-

---

*Vladimir Slepak's exile ended in December 1982, when he returned to Moscow. He and Mariya were finally allowed to emigrate to Israel in October 1987.

lously labeled and well ordered that even the secret police have been impressed during their occasional searches.

Roy Medvedev does not always greet visitors to his study with the traditional cup of steaming tea. He is cordial and reserved. His habits are spare, like his frugal conversation; words and minutes are meant to be utilized constructively, to delineate and analyze events and ideas with the fine focus of a mathematician on a problem. There is no taste here for the trivial, just a patient curiosity about the truth, in all its forms and complications. The search must be methodical; the telling, cool and lucid. In the bookcases stand his volumes, translated into many languages, some of the most significant contemporary work on Soviet society: *Let History Judge: The Origins and Consequences of Stalinism, On Socialist Democracy, A Question of Madness, Khrushchev: The Years in Power.* The last two he wrote with his twin brother, Zhores, the first two alone, and in a kind of loneliness integral to his carefully calibrated dissent as scrupulous historian and loyal reformer.

I went fairly often to see Roy. We would sit and talk on one theme or another, and he would sometimes turn a radio up or turn on two to different stations in the hope of jamming the ubiquitous microphones. His precautions would be exacting at one meeting, abandoned at the next; they seemed related less to the subject of conversation than to the ever-shifting atmosphere of oppression and relaxation, to which he was instinctively attuned. He was calm and kindly-faced; his silvering hair and soft, rounded chin made him look like a neighborhood druggist. But his eyes contained some elusive melancholy, and his mind was honed with a candor and openness uncommon in Moscow. He had a clearer vision and fewer prejudices than most men I have met in the free societies of the West.

In the early 1970's Roy's cautious dissent became part of a triangular debate about the ills and future of Russia. Unlike Aleksandr Solzhenitsyn, whose devout Russian Orthodoxy and Russian nationalism drove a burning moralism and nostalgia for an ecclesiastical Russian purity, and unlike Andrei Sakharov, whose open confrontation with the regime on behalf of political prisoners made him the elder statesman of the beleaguered human rights movement, Roy Medvedev imagined that the system could reform itself by returning to its true values. A party member from 1956 to 1969, he did not like being labeled a Marxist; but he found much to revere in Marx's thinking, and he embraced socialism as a desirable structure of human civilization in which, he believed, democracy could prosper. Indeed, he writes in his 1972 study *On Socialist Democracy* that no genuine socialism could exist without democracy as it is practiced in the West. "The democratic order of many Western countries constitutes their most important tradition, their most precious political heritage," he writes. "It is democracy of this kind that makes it possible for workers in capitalist countries not only to fight for an extension of their rights or for a higher standard of living under capitalism, but also to strive for the abolition of capitalism and its replacement by socialism." And in the Soviet Union, "although it is right to be proud of Soviet achievements with respect to social, economic and cultural rights, it must also be recognized that Soviet society is today still very backward when it comes to the whole complex of civil and political rights." Despite the progress since czarism and Stalinism, he writes, elitism, bureaucracy, a caste system, censorship, and elections that are empty formalities deny Soviet citizens "the freedoms our socialist society deserves: freedom of speech, opinion, of the press and of thought. There is still no freedom for artistic creativity and scientific research, particularly in the social sciences. Nor is there freedom of the individual or inviolability of the person. We still do not possess freedom of movement and choice of residence. There is no freedom to travel abroad, nor is there the right to leave one's country, as laid down in the International Covenant on Civil and Political Rights. We still do not have freedom of association and organization or the right to hold peaceful meetings and demonstrations, as befits a socialist society."*

Of course, these words could not be published inside the Soviet Union. This book and his others, including essays that he originally circulates in typescript among selected Russians and foreigners in Moscow, have appeared only in the West, where he has achieved a respected place among both non-Communist advocates of Soviet democratization and the leaders of Communist parties inclined toward unorthodoxy, such as those of Spain and Italy. Italian Communist Party publications have run some of his work, and party officials

*Roy Medvedev, *On Socialist Democracy* (New York: Alfred A. Knopf, 1975), pp. 32–38.

visit him when they are in Moscow, lending him a certain protection, perhaps, against severe action by Soviet authorities. His own careful conduct of his dissent has also been designed to minimize trouble. He rarely signs petitions or holds press conferences; his only overt move during the four years of my acquaintance with him came when he acceded to a dissident group's request to try to get him on the ballot in 1979 as a candidate for the Supreme Soviet, the rubber-stamp parliament. Being an advocate of democracy, he said smilingly, he could hardly decline the opportunity to offer the voters a choice beyond the usual single candidate. Predictably the elections commission refused to register him. He responded with silence.

"I have worked out several rules of political behavior," he explained. "One I call the rule of walking through a swamp. Movement through political ideas in our country, for writers or people like me, is like movement through a swamp. If I want to express opposition to the regime, I must consider it a swamp. And if I take direct steps, I'll immediately sink. Therefore, I must carefully check each step. You can walk through any swamp because in swamps there are dry hummocks, hard places on the surface, on which you can step. An inexperienced person will sink immediately; an experienced person places himself on the hummock, looks around to see where he can step further, and takes a further step. And if he sees that he can't go farther, he turns around and goes back, trying by another route. If he is an intelligent, experienced person, if he is not hurrying anywhere, if he does not act emotionally, he will get through that swamp."

After nearly four years of periodic conversations with Roy, I asked one day if he would trace the evolution of his dissent from the roots of his parents through the purges into the present, and as he did so, there emerged again the familiar blend of family and history, the personal mixed thoroughly into the larger groundswell of events. His father, Aleksandr Medvedev, was a political officer in the army, a stalwart party member, and teacher of the ideologically laden subjects of history and philosophy at the Tolmachev Military-Political Academy, which trained commissars for the army. But Roy did not rebel against him; he idolized him, and does today.

"My parents were people of their time," he began. "My father had an especially great influence on us, a moral influence, an influence of ideas. Our father was a participant in the civil war, he was a commissar of a brigade, and in the twenties and the beginning of the thirties, among all the young people then, there was a very strong romanticism about the civil war and the Revolution. What had happened in the past was seen with an idealized view, a view of man as especially heroic. And in this regard my father turned out to be an unusual man for us. He was very unusual: very kind, keenly intelligent, a man who was very brave, very decisive, very cheerful, loved to joke, loved to play with children. All his comrades loved him. I loved him very much. And when you love a person, it's natural that his views gradually become your own views."

The reminiscence, cascading forth in a clear, melodic Russian, must have had some sweet pain for Roy. He spoke for a long time into my tape recorder, slowly giving shape to the foundation of his remarkable role as loyal oppositionist. The anomaly of the critic who still held affection for the potential of the Revolution grew less difficult to grasp.

The father of the Medvedev twins was, by Roy's account, an impressive man of many talents as orator, poet, musician. He was a friend of the poet Vladimir Mayakovsky, who wrote in praise of the party and who visited the Medvedev home when Roy and Zhores were very small. Their father's affinity for the arts and his flair for ideological discourse combined to make a superb, moving speaker, Roy recalled. "Even today I remember two lectures I listened to," he said. "One he gave in my school. I remember my impressions. I was a schoolboy in third or fourth grade, and the lecture was for older pupils, and [I remember] the attention of about fifty or sixty pupils as they listened to my father, how they applauded him. He was in military uniform, with awards for excellence, a senior officer, and that created in me, then, a strong love for my father.

"We loved our father more than our mother. And our father, naturally, exerted an influence over us much more than our mother. Our mother was also devoted to our father, loved him madly. But she was a simple woman, a simple musician, and didn't play any sort of intellectual role or influence us. Father was a member of the party, a professor. He raised us from the beginning in the spirit of the party, the spirit of the ideas to which he was devoted. I remember once he called us into his room. We were boys of ten, we sat, and he began to read, especially expressively, a poem by Mayakovsky about Vladimir Ilyich Lenin, and this impressed us strongly. Often he took an interesting text of some revolutionary writer, short stories, and read them himself, read them as an artist reads them, with expression, read them for an audience of two, two listeners, for his two sons. And thus he raised us with a huge devotion to that regime and to that system and to that ideology in which he himself believed. I remember when Kirov was killed in 1934,* my father cried, and that impressed us tremendously, that a grown person would cry. He took us to the demonstration when they had the funeral of Kirov. I remember to this day the torchlight procession in the night at the funeral of Kirov. And to the very end, to the moment of his arrest, Father constantly exerted a very big influence on us. Although he was arrested when we were only twelve and a half, his influence was huge, much stronger than anything else. Not a single teacher, not the school, not the party, not the situation in the country had an influence on us like our father—his example, his views, his life, his tragic demise."

They came for Roy Medvedev's father in 1938. One moment he was the center of devotion and conviction and morality in the boy's world; the next he was branded an enemy of the people by the party and the system he loved and had taught his sons to love. He disappeared into the prison camps. He was interrogated and tortured. "They tried to force him to confess that he was an enemy of the people, that he headed a so-called counterrevolutionary organization in the military academy," Roy said. "He was one of many prisoners who didn't confess anything. He survived all the torture, frightening torture, and he didn't confess to anything." He was sentenced to eight years.

In 1939 the family began to receive letters from him. "The letters were full of kindness toward us. He wrote to us not to be disappointed in life, 'Don't be disappointed in socialism; an unexpected and temporary catastrophe has befallen us; I will soon return and help you with your education.' " They wrote back and through

*Sergei Mironovich Kirov, who joined the Bolsheviks in 1905 and became a Politburo member in 1930, was assassinated under mysterious circumstances. Some historians believe Stalin had him killed for allegedly leading a Central Committee faction opposing Stalin's personal autocracy. The murder provided Stalin with a pretext for making arrests within the party and set off the wave of persecutions that came to be known as the great purges.

his letters learned that during forced labor in the Kolyma mines of Siberia, he had been hurt in an accident that apparently led to some form of bone disease. He wrote from his hospital bed. Then, in March 1941, when the family cabled him some money, the post office returned the funds with the terse notation "Addressee deceased."

His father's military rank had entitled the family to an apartment in an army building with other officers, their wives and children, and when they lost the father and husband of the house, they lost that right as well. "But we didn't leave that apartment because we had no place to live," Roy said. "After several months we were warned. And then the custodian came with some volunteers, carried out the furniture, put it straight into the snow, and said, 'Children, you must leave!' In Moscow. A mother with two children. Her things were bought up right there. She sold them for almost nothing. She received a little money, and we went to live with some distant relatives, temporarily." His mother found work playing the cello in a Kalinin movie theater near Moscow, part of an orchestra that accompanied films without music.

His father had never explained what was happening in the country, what the meaning was of the articles in *Pravda* and other papers on the arrests and trials of some of the leading Bolsheviks. "Adults were silent," Roy said, and the boys were unprepared. "That my father was arrested was something frightening and completely incomprehensible and something completely out of accord with the ideas of Leninism or Marxism or socialism. So I understood that our lives had been visited by a great evil. The extent of that evil I could not then understand, but I wanted to investigate it, even then. I decided in my earliest years to busy myself with politics, with social science, to examine what was good and what was bad in our society. That explains why I took up philosophy. Even in the ninth grade I began to read Marx, Engels, to understand that world view. I was fifteen, sixteen then. I had a working hypothesis then. I could not change what my father believed in; that is, if my father was a Marxist, if my father believed in socialism, then I believed in it. But I created for myself this working conception: that in our country we changed something in Marxism. We changed something in socialism; somehow our state was moving away from these ideas, from these ideals. But moving away how? Already, doubts had been born in me then. I had doubts about everything. I began to write books. I wrote my first book in tenth grade, a book about philosophy. I wrote it for myself. I read Marx and all the books about the party congresses. I began to construct a model for political behavior.

"I understood the danger of free thought in our country; I understood that I could not, did not, have the right to rework everything in the Soviet Union because in the Soviet Union, after all, dictatorship exists. I saw how people were arrested. And so I selected a very simple method, picked it completely consciously: Study the history of the development, the history of the establishment of socialist countries in Eastern Europe and China. I wrote two books when I was a student. One was called *People's Democratic Revolution in Eastern Europe,* and the second was called *The Particulars and the History of People's Democratic Revolution in China.*" He concentrated on the countries he could criticize—Yugoslavia and China. "I wasn't accused of opportunism or Trotskyism. I could praise Gomulka, or criticize Tito, or praise Tito, or criticize Mao Zedong, or praise Mao Zedong, and it would never be a display of anti-Sovietism. So I wasn't inclined to reject Marxism, but to regard what had happened in the country as a rejection of the ideas of the Revolution. Already then I understood that I had to devote my whole life to an investigation of how, not my father, but my country had moved away from those ideals which I considered right, the ideals instilled in me by my father. So before me was a dilemma: my country or my father? I always chose my father, and not my country."

Sustenance in those early years after his father's arrest came from a coterie of classmates whose fathers had also vanished into the camps; there, within that circle of grief, free thought flourished. "We calmly discussed all these questions—who was arrested, what happened, what was known, what wasn't known, our ideas, opinions, doubts—so I didn't feel isolated. In my one class there were at least ten people whose fathers had been arrested. In my university course there were seven children of 'repressed' parents. Of my most important four friends, three had arrested fathers, and only one has a father living. One of my friends, his father was the first secretary of the Tbilisi City Party Committee and was arrested and shot. The second had a father arrested and shot. The third had a father arrested and shot. And only my fourth friend had a father alive and healthy. Therefore, we were all generally unhappy, and we discussed calmly, without fear, without risk, our doubts, sufferings, opinions." They are still his good friends: party members of a somewhat liberal bent, not powerful officials, but men occupying sufficiently prominent places in the society—one a philosophy professor; another a linguist at the Institute of Marxism-Leninism; another heading the faculty teaching Marxism-Leninism at a university; another a department head at an agricultural institute; others teaching at other institutes, heading sociology departments, exploring theory, writing books. "I wouldn't say that these books are especially interesting to me," Roy said, "but these friends are good people; they would come at any difficult moment, at night, to give help. They are liberal, but not oppositionists. They don't reject the society, but they understand me. They also see many shortcomings in our country, but they have no desire to become dissidents. They have no wish to act against the regime, even inside the system, inside Marxism. When we gather for holidays, our first toast is always to friendship, that thirty-five years have passed since we met, and we are nevertheless, first and foremost, friends—friends in childhood, friends in youth, friends for all our lives." Moreover, they treat him as if he were still a member of the party, Roy said, obviously touched.

As a young man he did not want to join the party because of what it had done to his father. "When they told me the party doesn't err, naturally I didn't believe it. But I was careful because I understood that to speak openly, to declare this openly, was for naught. I understood that this business needed a long future, long years of work, work, work and study. I did not enter the party. Since I was the son of an enemy of the people, when I finished the university, with excellent grades, I was not given any work. And the only hope was for me to go to the Ministry of Education in Moscow and ask them, 'Give me work as a teacher, any school.' And they gave me work as a teacher in Sverdlovsk Oblast. My friends became instructors in institutes, got into graduate school, and I ended up in a remote Ural village as a history teacher. But I saw that that was also very interesting because working as a teacher, you could understand people. The main thing for me was the ability to talk with people, to discuss things with them. I knew that in our country many of the facts would never be written down, many of them would never be deposited in documents, because our country is a country of oral conversations, a country of oral instructions, a country where the archives tell nothing. It is not possible for us to look at the archives and explain the history of the country. You have to know people; you have to listen to people talk. Then you will know the history of this country."

Roy did not make an effort to join the party until it had cleansed itself by renouncing the purges and officially rehabilitating his father. This came after Khrushchev's 1956 speech to the Twentieth Party Congress, where Stalin's crimes were denounced, leading to posthumous declarations of innocence bestowed on the memories of many of those who had been imprisoned and shot. When Roy received the document absolving his father, he became a Communist.

Even before joining the party, Roy worked as the principal of a school, then as an editor in a textbook publishing house, biding his time in planning his major work on Stalinism, *Let History Judge*. "It was still before the Twenty-second Party Congress [at which de-Stalinization was reinforced], people were still silent, and although I had the idea in my head to work on this book, there were not yet the conditions. Nobody had yet said anything, nobody had yet written anything, and nobody yet knew anything. If someone wrote memoirs, if somebody wrote something, thought about something, he hid it carefully. In 1961, when the Twenty-second Party Congress took place, when they began to publish memoirs, when books appeared, when recollections appeared, with the open denunciation of Stalin's cult of personality, I understood that the time had arrived for me to begin this work, the main work of my life. And then I left the publishing house, moved to a teaching job at an institute. I started to spend all my attention and all my time studying the history of the society, the history of Stalinism, the crimes of Stalin. I was quite young, thirty-five or thirty-six. I stayed up all night. We didn't have this apartment where we're sitting. We lived in a communal apartment. I went into the kitchen, worked from one to five A.M. to create this book. I wrote eleven different versions of this book—wrote one, gave it to somebody to read, then wrote it a second time.

"I didn't do anything secretly. I understood immediately that to behave properly, I must not make my work secret. Of course, you can hide some things, but it must be very little. The basic part of the work must be open. So what I was doing I told my friends: I showed my work, the first versions, to the Central Committee of the party, both under Khrushchev and after Khrushchev." Roy figured that since the KGB's main job was to know, he would have fewer problems if he worked openly. "If it knows that Roy Medvedev is writing such a book, then they are not worried. They don't have to arrest me, search me, summon me. Because they already know." He circulated his manuscript among selected people; one early reader was Yuri Andropov, then head of the Central Committee's department for international affairs, later head of the KGB, and finally secretary-general of the Communist Party.

His hope to have the monumental work published in the Soviet Union was erased by the hardening of the political climate after Khrushchev. In 1969, when the authoritative ideological journal *Kommunist* published an article defending Stalin, Roy protested in a letter to the editor that ended up appearing in West Germany. He was expelled from the party. The following year his twin brother, Zhores, a geneticist who had written an exposé of the fraudulent theories of Trofim Lysenko, was confined to a mental hospital; Roy conducted an international campaign to get him out, then collaborated with him in writing the story, published in the West as *A Question of Madness.* Later Zhores won permission to go as a biologist to England, where he was stripped of his Soviet citizenship and still lives. Roy, who published *Let History Judge* in the West in 1971, two years before Solzhenitsyn's *The Gulag Archipelago,* was harassed by the KGB but not arrested. And he continues to work, quietly but not secretly.

Self-control, discipline, the sublimation of personal animosity, the determination to work with equanimity mark Roy's approach. When we talked that long morning about his past, he told a revealing story and used it to illustrate his cultivated calm. "I don't have any personal enemies," he said. "I don't feel any personal unpleasantness toward anyone. I bear no evil to anyone, not to the leaders of our government, not to Western people, not to Eastern people, not to people who assail me. I answer those who criticize me, but I answer without malice, with a calm spirit and with a little humor. This helps me look at things more objectively. Solzhenitsyn's mistake is that he looks at everybody with frightening indignation. Often he has not a Russian but a Caucasian character. I study all activity as political activity. Therefore, I try to eliminate from myself any feelings of personal hostility toward people.

"I developed this in my youth," he continued. And then he told the remarkable story: "When I entered Leningrad University, there was a faculty member named Chaigin, a man who had denounced my father, and on the basis of the denunciation my father was arrested. I had no thought of killing him or beating him or committing any crime against him. I simply paid him no attention. I never went to his lectures. I couldn't bring myself to read a single one of his books. I never had any conversation with him. But I never tried to discredit him or punish him. I tried to expose the system of Stalinism, not a separate person. My view is that it is necessary to change the system that gives rise to such people. We must fight not against the separate people but against the entire system that trains such people."

FOUR

More Equal
Than Others

If you made it into graduate school—Fool!
Pack your thinnest suitcase,
Kiss your mama,
Hug your papa,
And get a ticket to Magadan.

—A bitter verse of self-pity,
Moscow to Siberia, 1979

The Distribution

In the spring of their final year of college the young men and
women who have been elevated into the upper educational ranks
of the Soviet system enter a grinding ritual of tension called *raspredeleniye* ("the distribution"), a process replete with bribery,
string pulling, anxiety, occasional ecstasy, and sometimes suicide.
It is the young people themselves who are to be distributed, raw
graduates parceled out across the breadth of the country to the
institutes and factories and laboratories and government bureaucracies that require an annual input of freshly trained citizens to feed
the voracious appetite of a blundering, stumbling, profligate economy. Those completing studies at institutes of food processing will
be assigned work in food plants as "engineers" in the Siberian cities
of Omsk, Tomsk, Magadan, or—if they are fortunate—Moscow.
Those from institutes for construction engineers will be given jobs
overseeing new housing going up in Siberia or the Ukraine or

Kazakhstan or any of a thousand cities or towns or villages where they are needed. New teachers will be told where they will be teaching; new physicists, where they will be doing their research or conducting their classes; new linguists, where they will be translating and interpreting. Failure to fulfill these assignments, which run for three years after graduation, means forfeiting the diploma. And while everyone is theoretically free to shop around for another job after the three-year term, the tightly structured system makes it virtually impossible to leave the narrow field of specialty, the *spetsialnost,* for which one has been trained, except by dropping down into the lower levels of menial work. Nor is it easy to get permission to move geographically from outlying areas toward the more desirable urban centers, where living standards are higher and residence permits are closely controlled by the authorities.

"The distribution" is merely the last of a series of educational crossroads that afflict young lives. The first comes at the end of the eighth grade (equivalent in age level to the American ninth), when teenagers divide into general and vocational tracks, the general being better positioned to continue into higher education, the vocational marching lockstep into the ranks of the "workers." Then, as general secondary school concludes in the tenth grade, those going on must select their *spetsialnosti* to determine their fields and apply appropriately to the respective professional institutes or university faculties. Here is where the individual makes his important choice; there is no liberal arts curriculum in the Soviet system through which a student can search at leisure for his own area of aptitude and interest. His course is set the moment he enrolls in college, and he ends his five years of studies in a university or technical institute by submitting to the *raspredeleniye.* It sucks the power from a person but soothes him with a balm of safe certainty and assuredness that the system will find him a place, watching over him as he yields childlike to its ultimate care. Many Russians like it. They are comforted by the security, relieved of any dread of joblessness.

No sixteen-year-old has a very realistic image of the world that lies before him. In America he is encouraged to see his future as if it were a broad sweep of unlimited opportunity to be shaped solely by his individual talents and hard work, a pristine field on which he will leave his own distinctive footprints. In the Soviet Union the cultural myth is something quite different, but no less appealing to the young: a future of multiple choices, each equally available, each a well-marked path of material security and comfort, each of equal value as a noble contribution to the building of a new society.

The Soviet sixteen-year-old finishing high school is forced by the tracked educational system to make some of these choices, and to make them almost irrevocably, long before he has come to know himself and his strengths or to discover the injustices of rank and hierarchy that exist in his country. It is clear for most Soviet young people by seventeen what careers or job levels they will be in for the rest of their lives, and whatever striving they are to do, whatever attempts they are to make to get ahead, to improve their living conditions, and to acquire the symbols of status must be undertaken within those limits.

This is a society uniquely equipped to maintain illusions about itself, so the failure of the Soviet dream cannot be expected to produce frustration as angry or bitterness as corrosive as has the failure of the American dream. The worst results can be seen in a complacency on jobs from which workers know they will probably neither advance nor be fired and in a numbing cynicism fostered by the importance of favoritism, political hypocrisy, and corruption in determining who succeeds. Still, far beneath a heavy mantle of acquiescence, there stirs the restlessness of rising expectations.

The mark of success in the Soviet Union today is a pair of jeans, or a decent piece of meat on the table, or the right to live in Moscow instead of in some dreary provincial town. Money is only incidental, for cash alone will not buy goods from barren shelves. Financial wealth cannot guarantee access to roomy apartments, good books, excellent schools, vital medicines, stylish clothes, automobiles, pleasant vacation resorts, or even red meat and fresh vegetables. These and other elements of comfort are made available by the state to employees of select factories, farms, scientific institutes, government ministries, and military commands; or they are obtained *nalevo* ("on the left") through friends and connections; or they are brought back from the West by those whose jobs authorize such travel; or they are accessible to people who have permission to live in cities that are favored with good stores, schools, and housing.

To the extent that success is measured in terms of a materially comfortable and cultured life, then, it means positioning oneself strategically rather than just accruing income. It is a game not of Monopoly but of chess, and those who play with cunning and alertness live well. Like money, the access to privilege can often be passed to heirs; unlike money, it can be taken away at the whim of the state.

The *raspredeleniye* descends grimly into students' moods before the thaw turns the snow grey. It looms as a fateful machine. Behind its glistening objectivity, within its intricate conception as a flawless matchmaker of skill and need, the process becomes satisfyingly corruptible. "It was the worst time of my life," said "Lena," a thin history teacher. She was sitting in a little restaurant near Mayakovsky Square, hunched over the table and sipping black coffee. "I can't think of anything worse. We called it the syndrome of the fifth year. Everyone waits for the *raspredeleniye*, and everyone is afraid."

Some wait passively. Others hustle. Still others have the hustling done for them by ambitious parents who learned years before where the system is flawless and objective and where it is not. For some, there is comfort in having such an important decision in their lives taken out of their hands. "There is a type who wants to have everything done for him," Lena observed caustically. "My husband never in his life could look for a job. He got a good one because his mother worked at the university and was on the party committee."

The routine works in various ways, but the pattern usually goes something like this: Every university faculty and technical institute employs a powerful middle-aged or elderly woman, a secretary who is the master sergeant of the place. She is the first to learn what jobs are opening up, and of course, she has her favorites among the students. For some reason she is a favorite of theirs, too, for they always seem to be showering her with gifts: a big box of chocolates; a pair of Levi's jeans (worth more than $200 on the black market). The students are so kind, and touched by their affection, she responds with what little she has to offer: the names and addresses of those agencies and factories and schools (in coveted Moscow, Leningrad, and other desirable cities) with openings. Students then rush to the prospective employers to persuade them to ask for their assignment there; those lucky enough to have parents with pull or well-placed friends, who can call a factory manager or a laboratory chief with the unstated promise of some favor in return, usually seem to turn out to be just what the particular employer is looking for, and he makes the request of the distribution board, whose representative from the college and from the responsible government ministry invariably find the assignment precisely right, a perfect match of skill and need. It is quite a wonderful system.

Debby and I were both struck by the cynicism it fostered, the extent to which young people were growing up assuming that nothing was done truly on merit. We had dinner one evening in the meager apartment of some newlyweds, both with ranking parents—his father a military man, hers a medical professor. The husband was already settled into a career in a government financial agency; she was graduating from a foreign language institute, so thoroughly fluent in English that her conversation and accent were barely distinguishable from an American's. She was extremely well read in English and American literature and could quote verse after verse of A. A. Milne, catching every nuance and inflection. Yet she had managed to irritate an old-maid professor by asking for a postponement of her oral final exam because it was scheduled for her wedding day. "Is that the only reason?" the professor snapped, and my friend suddenly remembered how some women students would take off their wedding rings before going in for the test, just to avoid stirring the woman's resentment. She knew then that she would not be given the top mark, a 5, so she didn't study. The professor, testing her orally, tried hard to flunk her, she felt, by calling her on a few shadings of meaning. When she translated a sentence as "He decided to take a risk," the professor insisted wrongly that it should have been "He decided to run a risk." She got a 4, the next best grade but not good enough to get her into an excellent position without pull. Her father knew somebody at Intourist, where she might have worked as a guide for foreign tourists—considered a good job, with access to the outside world—but her father saw it as beneath her. When I suggested that her interest in literature could be satisfied by translating at a publishing house, she brightened and said to her husband, "We'll have to see if we have anybody there."

Here was a sadness of contrast between the young bride—nervously giving her first dinner party, anxiously putting out her new crystal on the tiny, cheap table jammed into a corner of the living room, apologizing for the crowdedness and the awkwardness, flustered when the least thing went wrong, charming in the freshness of adulthood—and the seasoned, street-wise user of people. It was a time of life for pristine ideals, and here she was saying hopefully, "We'll have to see if we have anybody there." It left Debby and me in a spirit of melancholy as we made the long, late drive home through Moscow's broad boulevards.

Lena was sitting in the restaurant telling horror stories. In her years at Moscow State University she knew of five suicides by students of chemistry even before the *raspredeleniye.* Some just cannot take the pressure, the uncertainty. Some kill themselves after the assignments, in despair that they are to be sent to some remote Siberian town, thus losing their right to live in Moscow. One student with a five-year-old daughter was failed when he defended his dissertation and was told that he would have to work as a simple laborer; he went home, beat his daughter, and jumped out of a tenth-floor window. Lena herself had a bizarre confrontation with the head of her department, who would not recommend her for graduate school unless she slept with him. So she and some other women, who knew that his wife was a terror, decided as a practical joke to compose a love letter to him from Lena. They had an uproarious time, writing how much she adored him, how she wished to marry him. The perfumed missive was delivered to his home. "He was so frightened," she said, "that he signed all the papers and stopped coming to work for two days."

Students spend considerable effort trying to analyze the requirements for landing good assignments. A graduate receiving a "red diploma," signifying straight 5's, is technically entitled to choose his own place of employment. But short of such perfection, other factors seem to weigh heavily.

Conventional wisdom in student circles holds that while good grades are important, the distribution boards also look for a supplement of extracurricular, quasi-political activity known as *obshchestvennaya rabota* (literally "social work"). Without this well-rounded profile of Komsomol activism, petition-circulating on behalf of imprisoned freedom fighters in Latin America, expressions of *solidarnost* with oppressed Communists in odd corners of the capitalist world, without enthusiastic (or at least dutiful) participation in the annual autumn exodus to the potato fields around Moscow, or the cotton fields in Central Asia, to help with the harvest, the record doesn't look good. So the kids do it. Although the low level of mechanization makes the extra labor essential in peak seasons (even the army is deployed to help with the grain harvest), collective farmers often look upon the bungling city slickers as more trouble than help. But the farm work can be fun for the young, a time in the fresh air away from the crowded apartments and classrooms, living in barracks with plenty of vodka and sex. And if it provides a sense of participation in the good of the larger society, its real value lies in avoiding a black mark in the individual dossier. All else being equal, one candidate will clearly be chosen over another on the basis of this social activism. Sometimes even an inferior candidate will be chosen. Lena remembered a case of a young woman who lost out to an ex-army man for a slot in graduate studies. She was the excellent student; he, mediocre. But in the army he had become a crack shot and a party member. "She's a woman, she'll marry, have children," Lena quoted a party official at the university as explaining. She got a menial job for a year, then was accepted into graduate school on the second try.

Nor does the distribution always do well in its matchmaking task. A speaker of Swedish, one of five specialists in Swedish history graduated one year from the History Faculty of Moscow State University, was assigned back in her little village in the remote Tatar Republic, 600 miles east of Moscow. Another graduate was assigned to teach philosophy to students at an institute of fish production in Kaliningrad, but there was no place for him there, one of his friends said, so he ended up spending a long time looking for another job.*

Even officials complain publicly that assignments are often uncoordinated with requirements. There are too few accountants and too many geologists. People are frequently sent where they are not needed and not sent where they are. The Fourth State Ball Bearing Plant of Kuibyshev reported having 2,000 workers with engineers' degrees, and while "engineer" in the Soviet Union is a title representing considerably lower skills than in the West, the employment

---

*Although this now seems to result from inefficiency, in the past it has also been motivated politically. During anti-Semitic attacks on "cosmopolitanism" in the fifties, some Jewish students were given false *raspredeleniya* and sent deliberately to places without jobs.

of such technical specialists as workers means a waste of talent. The phenomenon has become so common that the factory has developed a coding system to designate each such underemployed worker—a red stripe is drawn across his personnel card. According to *Pravda,* at least 5 percent of all graduates are assigned where there is no need, and they often end up sitting at empty desks with nothing to do. From 1976 to 1978, *Pravda* said, 12,483 graduates had no places at all. They entered the ranks of the underemployed, filling slots in the labor-short, unskilled sectors. Shifting into a discipline where people were needed would not have been an option, however; an engineering student doesn't study literature, and a history student doesn't take math. Nor does the government give a student a stipend more than once, so to change fields means going to night school while working, to get a new diploma in a new specialty.

It is rare to find students who choose their specialties because they are interested. The reasons are usually more pragmatic, having to do with the access a certain field may provide to well-stocked stores, foreign travel, residence in Moscow, and other enviable aspects of privilege. And parents are often the ones to snuff out any spark of enthusiasm that seems impractical. I once witnessed an excruciating episode between a father—a journalist who had never joined the party and could therefore never get a regular, responsible post in that sensitive profession—and his sixteen-year-old son, a pimply and bright kid who wanted to be a journalist, too, and possibly study at an institute of foreign languages so he could report from abroad. The father scoffed, berated him for his naïveté, and crushed his son's desire under a weight of argument about connections and politics. He had no pull to get the boy into a decent position, he said. "The only job you'll get is on a factory newspaper that comes out twice a week in four pages," he lectured, "unless your father becomes a member of the Politburo!" As for the language idea: "While all your classmates are going off around the world, you'll be guiding Indonesian tourists around Moscow. Get a job, then apply for the Psychology Institute. You have to do what is possible." The boy looked at the floor and said nothing.

This young man did have one thing that millions of other Soviet youngsters did not: the right to live in Moscow. He possessed it simply because his parents lived there. It appeared in his internal passport as a dark blue visa stamp, a *propiska,* a most coveted authorization dispensed selectively by the police to control the size and quality of the capital's population. Usually denied to ex-convicts, beggars, cripples, peasants, Gypsies, certain political dissidents, and citizens without jobs or apartments there, the *propiska* keeps the showplace of Soviet achievement clean and orderly. Without it, staying in Moscow for more than three consecutive days is illegal. Like any attempt at such extensive control, the law is widely ignored; some Russians guess that hundreds of thousands of people live without *propiski* in the flats of friends and relatives scattered throughout the great city of 8 million. But it takes daring and inventiveness to survive, for the internal passport must be presented to any prospective employer and may be spot-checked by any policeman on the street or by any beefy woman *dezhurnaya* who sits imperiously over her tea in the entrance of an apartment house. The penalty for violating passport regulations is exile to some village in Siberia; most people prefer living less precariously.

Not only Moscow but Leningrad, Kiev, Tbilisi, and many provincial capitals are closed cities, barred to the surrounding sea of rural deprivation that stretches across the vast expanse of Soviet territory. Were the barriers suddenly lowered, the urban centers would certainly be inundated in a flood of migration. Indeed, it was famine in 1932 that led to the reintroduction of internal passports, which had been abolished after the Revolution.

Even so, the country people come to shop. They fill the weekend trains into the cities, where they lengthen the lines for buying red meat, aluminum pots, and heavy cloth coats for winter. In rough, padded vests and scuffed work shoes, they darken the queues like shadows among the bright parkas and slick boots of the Muscovites, who grumble at them for taking so much of their meat. In the evenings the railroad stations are a maze of bundles tied with coarse cloth or wrapped with newspaper and twine or stuffed into string bags. Cardboard valises litter the floors among the women's thick wool leggings, the men's dun trousers. They wait for their trains by stretching out on hard wooden benches or by staring silently into a patience as endless as the earth they till. They go home slowly to another world, stripped of the thin veneer of modern life, where the only convenience is thanks to Lenin's absurd dictum: "Communism equals Soviet power plus electrification of the whole country."

There is electricity. In the villages of wooden huts and log cabins, of outhouses and outdoor wells, of buckets slung on yokes across the sturdy backs of peasant women, of unpaved roads that turn to mud in spring, of towering woodpiles stacked against the deep cold of winter when only porcelain or iron stoves supply a heat that hisses and crackles and tries to fight the frost that forms inside the cabins' walls, from the steeply pitched roofs deep with snow, television aerials reach up to catch the sounds and images from a world away. The pictures of Moscow, always the most flattering the ambitious party journalists can find, nourish the seed of desire far from the capital. Soviet sociologists have begun to worry quietly about the curse of rising expectations transmitted by the screen that now flickers beside the remotest fire.

In Estonia, the most urbanized and most Westernized republic, nearly three times as much meat is consumed per person as in Azerbaijan, one of the country's most heavily rural and impoverished republics—161 pounds a year in Estonia, 57 pounds in Azerbaijan. Similar patterns hold for other products—926 pounds of milk in Estonia, 501 pounds in Azerbaijan; 531 pounds of eggs in Estonia, 198 pounds in Azerbaijan; 176 pounds of vegetables in Estonia, 104 pounds in Azerbaijan. The gap shows also in figures comparing industrial workers with collective farmers throughout the country—179 pounds of meat a year for each worker, 106 pounds for farmers; 216 pounds of vegetables for workers, 154 pounds for farmers; 106 pounds of fruit for workers, 75 pounds for farmers. Farmers exceed workers' consumption of eggs (642 pounds to 606), sugar (93 pounds to 79), and potatoes (441 pounds to 256), but this does little to offset the severe imbalance.* The figures, from 1970–71, are not believed to have changed significantly. Production of meat and butter, highly correlated with local consumption, showed about the same contrasts between Estonia and Azerbaijan in 1981 as a decade earlier.

The complete absence of meat, even *kolbasa,* a staple sausage like salami, is a permanent feature of many villages; a friend who lived in exile in Siberia told me that all she could get through an entire winter were strips of heavy pork fat—no lean of any kind. Some larger cities, such as Novosibirsk, have also suffered empty meat

*Viktor Perevedentsev, *Zhurnalist* (November 1975), pp. 79–80.

counters, so that many residents depend on packages sold to them at their factories—and only certain factories considered especially important in the economy, including those making weapons or those involved in high-priority civilian projects, are entitled to distribute packets of scarce commodities to their workers. "The whole country is covered with blast furnaces," one friend complained, "but I can't get a table knife."

Russians weather the hardship with humor and ingenuity. There is a joke about the man who goes into the fish store and asks for meat. "This is a fish store," says the saleswoman.

"I want meat," the man persists.

"Across the street," the clerk replies. "That's the place where there's no meat."

Another one has Capitalism, Socialism, and Communism sitting around talking. Socialism says he's got to do an errand and goes off. Three hours later he's back with a small package.

"What took you so long?" asks Capitalism.

"I had to buy some *kolbasa*, and there was a long line," Socialism explains.

"What's a line?" asks Capitalism.

And Communism inquires, "What's *kolbasa*?"

Collective and state farmers raise much of their own food, and enough extra to sell for profit, on small plots they are allowed to cultivate. Despite severe limits on the acreage and the number of livestock each family is permitted, the sales in the private farmers' markets, usually at exorbitant prices, provide an essential lubricant to the creaky, government-run economy. But the unequal, centralized distribution system, which stocks the cities better than the farms, and the most prestigious cities better than the outlying ones, still induces the country folk into tapping the urban market, one way or another.

Some sign up at their factory or farm for two- and three-day tours to Moscow to ease their way into the capital's tight hotel space, then slip away from the sight-seeing, abandoning Red Square and the Kremlin and the Lenin Mausoleum for the more practical routes through the department stores and food shops. Others wait at remote stations for the overnight passenger trains that move from Moscow outward through the countryside to distant cities.

The train from Moscow to Warsaw left in the early evening,

gliding through the outer neighborhoods of high-rise boxes that stand like sentries at the edges of the Soviet capital, picking up speed as darkness swallowed the final remnant of the city. Debby and I were in the swaying dining car, finishing some tasteless goulash, watching the night shadows of woods and fields slide past and the occasional fleeting glow of a cabin window.

We were several hours out of Moscow when the train slowed smoothly and pulled into the small station of the town of Vyazma. No sooner had we come to a halt than the forward door of the dining car burst open, letting in a billow of cold air and a dozen or more hefty peasant women dressed roughly, some carrying string bags of empty glass bottles. They divided quickly into two groups, one at each end of the car, and only then did we notice that the two waitresses in white smocks had been prepared for this, each positioning herself behind a table near each door. On the forward table were bottles filled with creamy *kumys,* fermented mare's milk; on the table toward the back were piles of oranges and apples, luxuries reserved for the cities' traveling public.

The peasant women and the waitresses conducted their transactions with a practiced swiftness grown obviously out of long experience. At the forward table the empty bottles were returned and replaced by full ones, money paid and change made with such dexterity that I had to watch steadily to see it all. A blink or a glance away would have been enough to miss it. At the other table the fruit was already bagged, the bags handed out hurriedly and the money flashing from hand to hand. The women, bulky in their heavy layers, pushed out of the car with their parcels, the last one stepping onto the platform just as the train began to move. We had been in the station no more than three minutes. Never was I to see such an efficient operation anywhere else in the Soviet Union.

When I told a Russian friend about it, certain that he would be as awed as I, he smiled knowingly and explained that it was common. All over the country the rural people living close enough to a railroad line pluck off what they can as the trains roll through. He remembered working one summer as a student on a collective farm in Kazakhstan, where there were infinite fields of wheat, but no fruit or meat. Once a week the farm's director would let the *kolkhozniki* take a truck to a fairly distant town where the Trans-Siberian trains pulled in, so they could buy fruit and meat, beer and vegetables from the dining car. Sometimes he would even give them money.

Housing, also a function of geography, is also a major source of grinding frustration and expanding desires, so much so that when a new constitution was being discussed in the late 1970's, housing occupied a large concern of citizens in their letters to newspapers and their discussions at meetings. During elections to the Supreme Soviet, local party committees, charged with getting as close to 100 percent of the vote out as possible, frequently encounter citizens who refuse to vote as their way of making a frail protest against housing conditions. Devious schemes and black-market payments characterize the maneuvers into better dwellings. One Muscovite in his thirties, married for eight years and still living with his mother and one child in a cramped flat, told me that he had had to get a place of his own or he and his wife would have gone crazy. But to qualify for a separate apartment, he had to produce a signed statement from his mother that she could not stand his wife, and a signed statement from his mother-in-law that she could not stand him—in short, affidavits that because of family friction, he and his wife had nowhere to go without splitting up. On this fictitious basis of uniting the family, he got on a list for a cooperative, waited four years, and finally heard from a friend about an apartment being vacated. Then he had to pay 2,500 rubles for each room, the equivalent of eight months' pay. Although he moved, he never officially changed his registered residence, for if he had done so, his seventy-year-old mother's place would have reverted to the state when she died. "Twenty years ago," he said, "the housing situation was worse. Probably nothing like it ever existed in America. Communal apartments were like a hotel corridor, twelve rooms opening out, four or five people living in each room, endless arguments about who would sweep the corridor today. You had to wait half an hour to urinate; you couldn't bathe; there were horrid smells, people washing, cooking all the time, no privacy. It wasn't so bad when everyone lived like that, but as soon as a friend got an apartment of his own and you went and saw him, you knew you had to have an apartment like that, and nothing would stop you. It's like compressed gas. As long as the tank is closed, it sits quietly. But once there is even the slightest indentation, the whole thing explodes, and the gas must then occupy a much larger space."

The discrepancies in living conditions and the restrictions on movement give city residence a mystique. Roy Medvedev writes of the official fear that free migration would bleed the countryside of essential labor, eroding agriculture, and "probably lead to a vast shift of population from the eastern regions of the country as well as from the Urals, Kazakhstan, and the far north to the more developed and 'warmer' areas: the central region, the Baltic states, the Ukraine, Moldavia, etc." But he argues that the restrictions cause "economic and cultural waste."

"Many people are not working where their abilities can best be utilized," he writes. "Not only are gifted individuals being prevented from moving to Moscow, where of course it is easier to develop specialized skills, get the best training, and obtain information, but it is also the case that a person living in Moscow or Leningrad, afraid of losing his residence permit and his apartment, often refuses to move to the provinces where his particular abilities could be used to best advantage."*

Furthermore, the burning drive to get to "the center," as Russians call Moscow, distorts personal values and priorities. On a long Moscow–Novosibirsk flight I once sat next to a lovely young woman named Natasha, who could have been the picture of a propaganda poster's ideal: a clean, level gaze of optimism; long auburn hair to soften the features of dedication. She had been born and raised and now studied in Novosibirsk, that remote city originally founded by Czar Alexander III as Novonikolayevsk in 1893, when a railway bridge was built across the Ob River, becoming under Soviet rule a burgeoning metropolis with a scientists' town in its suburbs—a monument to the Russians' pioneering push into their Siberian frontier. Natasha's parents were both railroad construction engineers, and she was following in their footsteps, studying at Novosibirsk's Institute of Railroad Construction Engineering. She would be graduated in the midst of the Hero Project of the last quarter of the twentieth century, a second trans-Siberian railroad line that was being laid through the hostile mountains and forests between Lake Baikal and the Pacific coast, the Baikal–Amur Mainline, or BAM, as everyone called it. The papers were full of accolades to the young Russians braving the fierce cold of the

*Medvedev, *On Socialist Democracy*, pp. 212–13.

winters and the swampy, mosquito-ridden summers to forge this new 2,000-mile iron link between wilderness and sea. At nineteen Natasha could have been imbued with a fierce devotion to this cause; she was no dissident, but a completely normal, loyal, relatively happy Soviet teenager who loved her country.

"I suppose you'll be working on BAM," I said enthusiastically.

"Probably." A sigh of resignation.

"You don't want to do that?"

She shot me a quick glance to see if I was kidding. "Of course not."

"I had the impression that this was a romantic project for idealists who wanted to build their motherland," I said. She looked at me in sardonic disbelief, wondering if she was being teased. "Why don't you want to work on this new railroad?" I asked.

"It's very cold," Natasha replied.

"So where do you want to go to work?"

Again she looked at me curiously, tolerantly, obviously intrigued by the idea that someone would not know the answer to that question. "To the center," she said quietly. "To Moscow."

"Why?"

"It is the center," she explained patiently. "All the students want to go there. Life is better there."

If all the students at the Novosibirsk Institute of Railroad Construction Engineering wanted to go west to Moscow instead of east to the Hero Project in Siberia, that was something. "And what work is there for a railroad construction engineer in Moscow?" I asked.

"They're extending the Metro," she said hopefully. And then she admitted that the chance of her or any of her classmates' getting there was slender indeed, unless they had parents living in the capital "or a husband there," she said with a smile.

So consuming is the passion for the *propiska* that many young people from the provinces who gain acceptance by a Moscow institute or university—and are inevitably destined to be "distributed" back to the provinces after graduation—work diligently during their student years to find a mate from the capital. Just as one marries into money in the West, one marries into the privilege of residence in Moscow, and the behavior is no less conniving. It is nice if you fall in love, but not essential. Marriages of convenience are arranged as friendly favors or for fees, especially just before or during the *raspredeleniye*. One student told me that friends had paid up to 2,000 rubles, about $3,000, to Muscovites willing to marry them; American exchange students at Moscow State University heard similar fees quoted. Sometimes the marriages remain fictitious, existing only on paper; the couples never live together and divorce after the out-of-towner obtains his or her *propiska*. Less explicitly businesslike unions often end sadly and bitterly.

"After the university," said Lena, the history teacher, "I got assigned to a small town in Siberia, so I quickly got married to a Muscovite, and they attached a paper to my diploma saying I could find my work in Moscow." Unfortunately, however, that was not the end of it, for the government bureaucracy reaches deeply into personal lives. To get her *propiska*, Lena also needed the approval of her in-laws, with whom she and her new husband would have to share an apartment because of the housing shortage. The young man's mother refused, and Lena was forced to leave the capital. Her husband, unwilling to sacrifice his Moscow residence, remained behind. "I got nothing from this marriage," Lena spit. She sneaked back into Moscow, took a job illegally with a foreign business office, and filed for a divorce. Her life was filled with constant tension; she chain-smoked nervously.

To hold some clear vision of honorable values is to tear yourself inside, to let the things you believe and the things you want gnaw at each other and open secret wounds. I saw this happening to "Igor," a graduate student in law in a small city thousands of miles from Moscow. He and two women students came to sit at my table in a restaurant one evening; we stayed long and late and talked about America and Russia. They had many searching questions, and so did I. They asked if we could meet again the next evening, and we did, though one of the women—the most orthodox and active in Komsomol, Igor said laughingly—didn't come, making an excuse about a dying grandmother. The three of us ate and then walked for hours through the streets, sat on a park bench, talked and talked. Igor relaxed slightly, revealing flashes of irreverence.

The third evening Igor came alone. We didn't bother eating then, just strolled and talked in a drizzling rain; he gradually let down his defenses and told me how unjust he felt it was that Russians could not travel freely to the West or even live where they wished inside their own country. He wanted Moscow. He wanted the theater, the music, the dance. He wanted the stores and the crowds and the sense of excitement of a real city. He felt caged here, he said. The claustrophobia was making him panicky. And he could get to Moscow, he knew, just by pulling a string. But he was revolted by what he would have to do.

His father, it seemed, was a military officer with a connection high in the Ministry of Internal Affairs; he could probably get a young lawyer a job with the police or the prosecutor's office in Moscow. But Igor saw it as an ugly position—"You have to kick people," he said. His ambition was to become something nobler, a defense attorney. But that would mean staying in his small provincial city. He did not know what he would finally decide to do, and I do not know what he finally did. I left him in his despair that rainy night, and if he came to visit Moscow as he said he planned, and if he telephoned me as he promised he would, even after my warnings that my phone was tapped, then we somehow missed each other. I never saw him again, and I wonder about him still.

Siberia: Exile and Frontier

The meaning of geography in a Russian's life is most vivid in the wilderness of Siberia, so remote and deeply isolated from urban existence that its simple villages are still considered fitting punishments for common criminals and political dissidents. But their gold mines and oil fields also exert a magic pull on the frontier spirit profoundly embedded in Russian history.

There are basically two ways to get to Siberia. One is voluntary. Iosif Begun went by the other. It was a journey of 5,000 miles and sixty-eight days, in ten trains and through nine prisons, into the dark reaches of suffering. Crammed like cattle into the cubicles of special railroad cars, the prisoners were twenty-five to a space meant for four. Each compartment had been fitted with two extra bunks, making two ranks of triple-deckers. But it made no difference; there was no room to lie down during the three to four days taken by each leg of the trip. The single window in each cubicle was barred and shuttered. The door out to the corridor was locked, opened only once a day, in the morning, so the men could be taken one by one to a toilet at the end of the car. Each was given half a loaf of sour black bread and a cup of water a day; each was also offered one or two tiny pieces of salted herring, spoiled. The prisoners were afraid to eat the fish, knowing that they would receive no more water and would be driven to wild thirst. Every few days the train disgorged the weakened men into crowded vans, and the vans trucked them to prisons, where one hundred of them were jammed into a cell built for twenty. Lice and other insects thrived in the dampness. There the convicts would spend a day, or two, or three, or four, or five, until herded onto the next train that made its slow way along the rails of the Trans-Siberian. Finally, as the exiles reached the remote wilderness, to be scattered out among the isolated villages of Siberia and the Soviet Far East, they were taken in smaller and smaller groups from the railroad junctions by bus or truck to the regional centers, then singly to the small clusters of log cabins or dingy dormitories at the state farms or mining towns that were to be their homes, their places of forced residence, for the next year or two, or three, or four, or five.

The journey into exile is known by the innocent word *etap,* which means "transport" or "a stage." *"Etap,"* said Iosif Begun, "was a frightening thing, completely inhuman. People lost their strength, became completely helpless." Tough criminals preyed on the young and the weak, stealing whatever warm clothes they wore and carried in bags packed hastily by wives and mothers. Iosif lost a suitcase full of things designed to get him through his first weeks in his new home. Vladimir Slepak contracted dysentery but could not inform his guards; his cellmates warned that they would kill him unless he kept his ailment secret, for the case would have quarantined them all for weeks and prolonged their misery. *Etap* is even worse than prison. And when it is over, the condemned is left in the vastness of fear and cold and the tranquility of solitude. He has nothing but his prison clothes, rarely enough to face the winter temperatures of 60 to 70 below. He has virtually no money for a meal or an overcoat. He has been stripped of all scraps of paper, so he must carry in his head the vital addresses and telephone numbers of friends and family, who are not told by the authorities which village has been chosen as the place of exile. Even the condemned himself is rarely told his destination until the journey has begun. So when it ends, relatives cannot know where to wire money or mail clothes until the prisoner, reaching the village, gets through by phone or telegram. This often makes the first few days desperate. Some have told of begging for bread, of camping in hotel entranceways until money arrives or local authorities provide housing.

The trip is occasionally made easier by an individual's being allowed to report on his own to his place of exile or by his being taken separately under guard. But for the masses of detainees transported in the fetid prison cars, the journey into exile remains today, as through Russia's history, one of the most difficult phases of the prisoners' experience. Until the Trans-Siberian Railroad was built around the turn of the century, long stretches of the trip were often made on foot, sometimes in chains. And through the sweep of centuries, no segment of the population escaped the lure and the dread of Siberia. In the seventeenth century the relatives of merchants who had left the country illegally were sent by the czars into Siberian exile. Under serfdom landlords could have serfs exiled by the authorities. In the 1800's waves of Russians condemned for common or political crimes were sent east into the vastness. Lenin, sentenced in 1897 to three years, managed to use connections to gain permission to choose his place of exile; he selected a village in a relatively mild southern region, where he befriended the local policeman, who let him maintain communications with the outside and continue his political work.

In 1977 Iosif Begun had no such connections. Because he had applied to emigrate to Israel, he had lost his job as an electrical engineer, and because he had no job, he was tried as a "parasite." His prison was the village of Burkandya, a gold-mining town of 3,000 located as far east as the easternmost edges of Japan, so distant that the sun rises eight hours earlier than in Moscow. Iosif had the relatively good fortune to be assigned a decent place to live and a nonstrenuous job. He was immediately given a bunk in a two-story brick dormitory with central heating and cold running water and was assigned 160-ruble-a-month work repairing electrical mining equipment. He found the villagers intrigued and wary, interested in him but constrained by strict local authorities to demonstrate ill will. Party officials were so anxious to isolate him from residents that they turned down his offer to set up an after-school

technical and hobby program for youngsters. And when he volun-
teered to repair the school's only tape recorder, broken for two
years, he was not allowed to do it in the schoolhouse. It was brought
to his dormitory. His only amicable acquaintances during his six
months there were among disgruntled villagers who wanted him to
convey their appeals against religious oppression to the authorities
when he returned to Moscow. He had no normal relationships, no
friends.*

Volodya Slepak also found himself in what his wife, Masha,
called "a full vacuum." He was exiled in Tsokto-Khangil, east of
Lake Baikal near the Chinese border, where the Buryat Mongol
population speaks a language foreign to him and knows little Russian. He was met by politeness, but no more.

Malva Landa, a geologist and dissident, found during her eight-
month exile in Vershino-Shakhtaminsky, a molybdenum-mining
town also near the border with China east of Lake Baikal, that the
villagers had no capacity to comprehend her transgression or her
ideals. A tense woman with darting eyes and short-cropped grey
hair, she had been sentenced as a member of the Moscow group
monitoring Soviet violations of the Helsinki accords. Most villagers
thought at first that she was a spy. When she explained her struggle
for the right to read and write books freely, they thought she had
been speculating in books on the black market. Only a few showed
her any kindness and friendship.

Pavel Litvinov's experience was different. The grandson of Maksim Litvinov, Stalin's foreign minister, Pavel was exiled after having
participated in a small demonstration in Red Square against the
1968 invasion of Czechoslovakia, and when he first arrived in
Siberia with his family, he was treated well. Some villagers looked
upon him as a kind of guest, a Moscow intellectual with a famous
name, deserving of hospitality. A storekeeper put aside flour for
him and his wife while other customers went without. Even party

---

*Iosif Begun's sentence was for one year, cut short by six months because of pretrial
time in prison, where every day is calculated as the equivalent of three days in exile.
However, once released from Burkandya, he was not permitted to live in Moscow with his
wife, Alla, and his repeated violations of this restriction—during which he once joined a
group of supporters outside a fellow dissident's trial in Moscow—brought him another
arrest, another trial, and another exile, this time for two years. In 1981 Alla was allowed
to leave for Israel, while Iosif was forced to stay behind. They were divorced. He was then
arrested a third time, on the more serious charge of anti-Soviet agitation, imprisoned until
February 1987, and permitted to emigrate to Israel in January 1988.

members came to his house (usually after dark on somebody else's motorcycle) for long evenings of vodka and good conversation. After warnings from the KGB, they grew more cautious.

Villagers are often puzzled by the presence of exiles. One man told Malva Landa quite definitely that there was no such thing as exile anymore. Andrei Tverdokhlebov, who spent nearly two years in Nyurbachan, a state farm producing meat and dairy products, found residents baffled and hurt that their town should be used as a prison of sorts. "They said, 'Why is our life, which we live all the time, considered a punishment?'"

For a man with soft hands, a biologist like Tverdokhlebov, the conditions were punishing indeed. He had been sentenced for serving as secretary of Amnesty International's Moscow chapter, and he had never seen anything like the world he endured in Nyurbachan. Whether by malicious design or cruel chance, the local officials devised a torment worthy of Dante. Tverdokhlebov was assigned a job shoveling coal into the furnace of a heating plant. But the plant was not connected to the wooden dormitory where he lived. There the only source of fragile warmth was a woodburning stove that never managed to hold sway against the deep winter. Inside, the walls were heavy with frost. Anything placed low, on the floor, would freeze; only close to the ceiling did the temperature rise to a barely comfortable level. There were no toilets, just unheated outhouses. There was no running water. The outdoor wells froze solid. Water had to be trucked in tankers from twelve miles away during the long months of winter.

Across the eastern steppes where the Slepaks lived, the wind never stopped. In winter it multiplied the pain of the cutting cold. In summer it whipped up scorching dust from the parched earth, deadening the town. "Not a bird, not a dog, nothing is heard," Masha told me on one of her frequent trips back to Moscow. She and Volodya occupied a one-room flat that had no stove, but an electric hot plate; no water, but a well 400 yards away. Yet this collective farm of Tsokto-Khangil did not strike her as impoverished. It was an odd mixture of hardship and comfort. A relatively new *kolkhoz,* built in the late 1940's, it represented a step up for many of its 1,700 residents—mostly Tatars and Russians and a few Buryats—who lived relatively well, raising their thousands of head of cattle, sheep, and pigs. Each family also kept several cows and sheep of its own. And the *kolkhoz* had a greenhouse where cucumbers and tomatoes were grown for the farmers' own consumption. There was a decent store carrying an adequate selection of clothing; influenced by television, the farmers and their families dressed rather fashionably, Masha observed, acquiring even a good deal of local mink for their fur hats and collars. Practically everyone owned a motorcycle, and many had Zhigulis, the small Soviet-made Fiats that have pervaded the cities. From a nearby mining area, which enjoys some priorities in consumer goods, the *kolkhozniki* could buy apples and cabbages, and their own grocery store usually had frozen fish, bread, sugar, cookies, candy, cognac, vodka, champagne, and wine. Meat was also distributed to *kolkhozniki*, and they had their own few head to keep them in stock. But Masha and Volodya depended for their meat in winter on parcels mailed frozen by relatives in Moscow; the packages stayed frozen all the way to Tsokto-Khangil. In warm weather Masha stood and waited for a couple of hours for the bus to Aginskoye, seventeen miles north, where meat was sometimes sold.

Siberia has no definite boundaries. It occupies no place in the governmental diagram of administrative divisions: There is no republic, oblast, or city named Siberia. Russians speak of it colloquially as a vast region beginning approximately at the Ural Mountains, running eastward through thousands of miles of deep forest, steppe, and tundra, and ending in an indeterminate area somewhere short of the Pacific coast. They call the final stretch to the sea the Far East. To the geographer, however, it is all Siberia, all the way to the Bering and the Okhotsk seas, covering an area one and one-third that of the forty-eight contiguous United States. And in this imprecision of dimension, Siberia fits somewhere in the Russian soul, an exile and a frontier, a place of dread and adventure, a sweep of misery and romance.

Since 1581, when Yermak the Cossack invaded the Siberian khanate of the Tatars, and Muscovy then annexed Western Siberia, Russian pioneers have gone east. Trappers, explorers, prospectors, the Russians built their log cabins and fought the fierce elements much as Americans did as they moved westward across their continent. By the 1630's, a decade after the *Mayflower* had landed at Plymouth, the Russians had made their way to the Siberian Pacific coast, and a long search into the natural riches of the wilderness had begun. Salmon, cod, herring, sable, ermine, fox, wolf, bear, mink, timber, coal, gold, diamonds, iron, cobalt, nickel, tungsten, molybdenum, tin, copper, zinc, lead, magnesium, antimony, barium, bauxite, beryllium, platinum, mercury, asbestos, mica, arsenic, salt, gas, and oil have been brought out of the frozen vastness in great hardship, at great cost, and with great satisfaction.

It has been done in a mixture of compulsion and voluntarism. Convict labor works the mines, hauls the lumber, builds the railroads. A joke circulating in Moscow had Brezhnev making a ceremonial visit to the new Baikal–Amur railway line, gazing out over the crowd of assembled workers and beginning his slurring speech that Russians made fun of before he died: "Dear comrade sailors . . ." An aide pulls on his coat. Brezhnev stops, waves the man brusquely away, and begins again: "Dear comrade sailors . . ." The aide interrupts again, and again Brezhnev waves him away. "Dear comrade sailors . . ." Finally the aide presses himself on the party chairman. "Comrade Brezhnev," he whispers, "those are not sailors. The stripes on their uniforms go up and down, not across."

Yet it would be wrong to think that all Siberia runs on impressed labor, for the state has gone to some lengths to construct a system of elaborate perquisites—bonuses, cars, free travel, extra vacations—to lure the skilled and unskilled into this hard land. In the small city of Yakutsk, first settled by Russians in 1632, the incentives are fairly typical for the entire region: a 40 percent salary increase immediately upon arrival, followed by an additional 10 percent after six months, then up to 80 percent within the first five years. After five years the pay can jump to 2.2 times the normal rate, with a maximum of about 1,000 rubles a month, exorbitant by Soviet standards. In the oil and gas fields of Western Siberia, where nearly one-half of the country's entire production originates, workers are given various bonuses depending on the hardship—usually the farther north, the larger the pay—and are allowed to keep their apartments in whatever hometown they come from, even Moscow, Leningrad, Kiev, and other closed cities. Siberian oil workers are put at the top of the list for private cars, so their waiting time is cut from several years to about six months. They get free plane tickets annually to anywhere they choose inside the country, and their summer vacations run for forty-two working days, more than eight weeks.

It has become a fad among some highly educated Muscovites to do manual labor for a short time in Siberia; one group of about ten physicists spent a month and a half of their leave building cow barns in Sakhalin, earning about 1,000 rubles apiece. But the labor shortage in Siberia is still severe. Officials told some of us visiting the oil fields that workers for rigs were being flown in by plane and helicopter from larger cities for shifts of twelve to twenty days. Even the more permanent laborers rarely stay more than three or four years.

It is cruel country, a great subarctic wasteland in the long winter months, a treacherous mosaic of swamps and lakes in the brief summer, when the crust of earth above the permafrost melts into muddy marshes that breed thick swarms of mosquitoes. Man is an interloper here, alien. From the air, the occasional roads, pipelines, and railroad tracks he has managed to construct are only the slightest scratches across the great expanse of snow. In the mornings I've seen men drink cognac for breakfast to wash down piles of kasha and plates of horse meat. The oilmen in Surgut board the bus out of town before there is any hint of dawn in the black Siberian sky. Bundled in rough, padded coats, they leave like fishermen setting out from a snug harbor into a sea of wind and wilderness. The winter daylight comes late and lingers for only a few hours, casting a melancholy greyness across the endless flatland. It is a manly life, a constant struggle against the adversities of the frontier, with all the romance and tough work of a Jack London novel. "When these guys go south," one Siberian journalist observed, "they're regarded as heroes, big men."

Jack London's tales of life in the Klondike are familiar reading to Russians, who like to see themselves as survivors against the elements. But the romance is stronger from a safe distance than close at hand; of all the various types I met in Siberia—railroad workers and oil drillers, party functionaries and music teachers, scientists and bus drivers—I found few starry-eyed over their daily lives, and more than a few yearned for "the center."

But the deepness of winter does hold the country in a spell of pleasure. Russians sniff the air, savoring the cold as a gourmet turns a taste of wine on his tongue. By November, when the snow is solid on the ground, weekending Muscovites forsake their overheated apartments for the forests of pine and birch that surround the capital, hiking briskly or gliding smoothly on cross-country skis through the calming woods. Men and boys appear as dark dots against the frozen Moskva River, chopping holes in the ice with hatchets and threading fishing lines into the murky water below. When a thaw provides an opening among the river's chunks of ice, a few hardy "walruses" jump into the drink for a bracing swim. Once, taking my kids sledding in Lenin Hills, I was startled by a woman in a bikini, bare feet and all, jogging merrily along among the drifting snowflakes.

But the Muscovites are just dilettantes compared to the Siberians. The day I arrived in Yakutsk with my colleague Peter Osnos of *The Washington Post,* it was 46 below. When our plane landed, the door was frozen solidly shut, and it took about half an hour for a powerful hot-air blower—standard equipment at Siberian airports—to break the icy seal. Stepping outside was like stepping onto another planet, for at those low temperatures nothing seems quite normal. The air burns. Sounds are brittle. Every breath hovers in a strange slow-motion cloud, adding to the mist of ice that pervades the city and blurs the sun. When the breath freezes into ice dust and falls almost silently to the ground, Siberians call it the whisper of stars. Frost as fine as sand sifts into crevices, clings to power lines, coats the scrubby trees along the main avenues until they look like misshapen sculptures. Every few minutes people on the streets put gloved hands over their mouths and noses to keep the flesh from freezing. The smallest children are wrapped in layer after layer so that little more than their eyes are exposed. Buildings have triple windows and triple doors. Private cars are put away for the winter. Taxis are kept in heated garages and are fitted with thick double panes of glass that look like portholes peering into a sea of frost. Trucks for lumbering and other work are kept running constantly through the six months of winter, for to let their engines cool would be to lose the ability to start them again until the spring. In this climate, where the low that year was 72 degrees below zero Fahrenheit, steel cranes can snap, photographic film can shatter like glass, rubber soles on boots can break cleanly in half (as one of Peter's did). Mercury freezes, so thermometers must be made with alcohol —"spirits," in the Siberians' word. "Of course, that's not all we use spirits for," said a local newspaperman with a warm grin.

He was Yuri Semyonov, whose grandfather had been exiled to Siberia under the czars. When he asked us what we wanted to do in Yakutia, an "autonomous republic" nearly the size of Western Europe, Peter and I had more wishes than our few days—or Soviet travel restrictions—would permit. There were gold mines and diamond mines and reindeer herders. There was one lake for every resident. But one requirement was a brief trip, at least, into the taiga, the virgin pine forest that blankets most of the wilderness.

The taiga is the wellspring of legend and adventure, containing the challenge of the cold that Siberians love. They go off to hunt, or fish through the open ice, or build a campfire and cook a sumptuous meal in the open, surrounded by the cleanest snow you ever saw. So Yuri and our other guide, Yelena Pankova, an English-language interpreter at the Permafrost Institute, were delighted by our interest. And when one day the weather showed the first sign of spring and the temperature rose to minus 20, five of us, including a driver, piled into a four-wheel-drive Gazik, a Soviet version of the Jeep, and headed along a narrow, unpaved road west from Yakutsk. We were going on a picnic.

About twenty-five miles out of town we turned onto a little-used track that led into the forest. The Gazik scrambled through axle-deep snow, wound for miles among the trees, and came to a stop at a flat expanse of pristine woods. The engine was left idling, but we walked up to our knees in snow, back, back into the deep forest where we could hear neither engine nor any other whisper of distant civilization. Within minutes the fluffy snow had been shoveled away from a chosen spot, dry wood had been gathered from dead branches, and a fire was going. A blackened teapot had been filled with snow and was hanging over the flames. A two-and-a-half-gallon bucket, also brimming with light snow, sat on the logs, the snow melting and sizzling and hurling steam into the icy air.

Yuri and Yelena had spent about 30 rubles on heaps of food: three kinds of local fish, the meat of half-wild colts, bread, apples, onions, salami, mineral water, and, of course, vodka. The vodka was our lily-livered substitute for the Siberians' preferred "spirits," or *spirt* in Russian, an innocent-looking clear liquid of 95 percent alcohol that's dangerous to drink while smoking. Since it does not freeze until close to minus 170 degrees Fahrenheit, the freezing point of pure ethyl alcohol, it can be lethal to drink in very cold weather unless it is kept relatively warm; anything of minus 50 degrees gulped down will freeze your insides, so Siberians are careful to carry their *spirt* among their layers of clothing to pick up body heat.

The best food in the region was local. Large herds of reindeer and wild horses, tended by the Yakuts, a Mongol people believed related to the Eskimos, produce meat that is cooked and processed in dozens of ways—grilled, boiled, smoked, ground into sausage. Reindeer and horse milk are used variously. Fish are abundant from the rivers and lakes, and their taste is fresh and clean. All the fish in our small feast were in the salmon family but are rarely found outside the area. Two were smoked—*omul,* a delicacy virtually unattainable in Moscow, and *ryapushka,* a larger variety. Yuri cleaned them and cut them latitudinally in broad chunks to be eaten by hand, the skins with scales to be thrown into the fire. By then almost everything was frozen, including two white-fleshed salmon called *muksun.* He held the first one over the fire to thaw it slightly, then cleaned it, cut it as he had the others, and put the chunks aside, to be tossed into a soup. The second *muksun* he skinned and be-headed, then balanced it on two logs to be softened slightly by the hot coals. The line between hot and cold was thin, and the differ-ence sudden. A step toward the fire and the heat was scorching; a step away was a step into deep cold. We could not find the right place for the bottles of mineral water; they were either frozen solid or boiling fiercely, and we kept moving them back and forth to keep them in transition from one state to another. A few bottles cracked. Yuri began working on the fish, so close to the fire that he shed first his sheepskin coat and then his fox fur hat as he stepped up the pace. He crouched, held the fish on end in front of him, and started to run a sharp knife down its body as if he were whittling. Fine, thin slices curled off the fish, the centerpiece of a dish called *stroganina,* from the verb *strogat* ("to plane or shave"), as a carpenter planes wood. When the slices filled a pan, Yelena added lots of salt and pepper (vinegar, mustard, and tomato are also common ingredi-ents) and passed the pan around. We ate the frozen slices raw with our fingers.

The first course was then spread out on a copy of *Pravda:* the *stroganina,* some sliced salami, smoked *omul* and *ryapushka,* black and brown bread cut into thick slices, and chunks of lightly smoked colt's meat, which was tender and tasted like a cross between ham and tongue. There were cups of steaming tea. The bread froze, and the apples turned to stone until they were brought close to the fire. Yuri had to keep waving his jackknife through the flames so he could pry it open. The vodka, poured into metal cups, had to be kept close to the heat; otherwise the metal cup would stick to your lips.

After the first course Yelena and Yuri turned to making a soup called *ukha.* The snow in the pail had melted down to about three quarts of boiling water. Into this went two pounds of peeled potatoes, six green laurel leaves, a dozen small balls of pepper and plenty of salt, two onions, and the big *muksun,* cut into chunks, including bone. The soup was done when the fish floated to the surface and the eyes turned white, Yelena said. And she spooned it out. It had a thick, wonderful flavor. And in the woods around the fire, dusk came slowly, turning the snow blue and moving the darkness closer until it pressed against the tight glow of the flames. By Yakut tradition, we left a little vodka in the bottoms of our cups to be thrown into the fire. As the flames flared for an instant, we said, *"Bai Ya Nai,"* Yakut for "God of the Taiga." It is an offering to bring the hunter luck. The night deepened; the talk fell to murmurs. From the vast taiga came the winter silence. The fire spit and crackled.

There were moments like this when I thought that if I had grown up a Russian lad, I would have gone for at least a few years to Siberia, to taste the challenge and the frontier, to escape the ambitious careerism of Moscow and flee into an elemental life where the party's political hypocrisies seem distant and diluted. I can understand why some who go into exile never want to return; many of today's Russian Siberians, like Yuri Semyonov, are descendants of those for whom this land, forced upon them, came to exert an unyielding hold. Even Malva Landa, although an older woman and alone, attained contentment in her exile and considered staying. For 250 rubles she bought a wooden cabin with one room and a kitchen, and although she had to chop wood and haul water, she was retired and on pension, so had no obligation to hold a job. As a geologist she had traveled widely in remote corners of the country and was used to a rugged life. "If I had wanted to live quietly, I would have stayed there," she told me after coming back to Moscow. "I had a house. I had a garden. Nearby was the forest. Why not? If I had thought only of my personal life, I would have stayed." But back in the capital dissidents were being arrested, and there was work to be done for human rights. She came back.

Some like it for the people. A professor in Central Asia, a Jew fired in 1949 from Kiev University during Stalin's attack on "cosmopolitanism," had stayed in the region because he felt that Central Asia and Siberia were generally more hospitable than the European parts of the Soviet Union to the society's outcasts. And since Soviet society rejects some of its most interesting members, there are a good many interesting people there. The professor gave as just one example an archaeologist who had been curator of a museum in Kalinin. As the Germans were attacking, he gave the valuable pieces to friends for safekeeping, saving the museum's treasures. He was later accused falsely in *Pravda* of giving pieces to the Germans; he lost his job and settled in Bukhara.

I met a woman in Siberia, however, who represented another side of the Soviet personality. It was during a trip to the area of Lake Baikal, where engineers and miners and a range of other specialists were tunneling and laying track for the 2,000-mile Baikal–Amur railroad. The countryside was wild and beautiful, not the flat expanse of Yakutia but mountains capped with pristine snow that caught the light of the sun, low on the horizon even at noon. The ice on the huge lake, covered with swirls and mottled webs of snow, was so thick that it became a winter highway for heavy trucks heading north from Irkutsk to remote camps and villages. The air was like crystal, sharp and clean. At the northern shore a trim settlement of neat log cabins called Nizhneangarsk was nestled beneath a rise of hills studded with rich pines. There Lidiya Bessolova of Moscow was living, and she did not like it. She was thirty-one and city-bred, unable to shed her need to feel the pulse of city life, her hunger for the theater, her desire for sophisticated friends. She struggled to screen out the wilderness, dressing as she would in Moscow, incongruously in a full-length fox coat, gold earrings, nail polish, lipstick, trying to keep the remoteness from sifting into her. "I'm nervous all the time," she confessed.

Mrs. Bessolova had followed her husband, Vladimir, a party member, who had been working on extensions to the Moscow subway system when he was invited to become chief engineer on the tunnel projects in Siberia. "We call ourselves Decembrists' wives," she said wryly, a reference to the women who followed their husbands into exile after their abortive uprising in December 1825. Behind the city-wise sardonic humor with which she repelled despair, Mrs. Bessolova had unhappy eyes. The enjoyable status of living in Moscow had been stripped from her. She longed for her eight-year-old daughter, whom she had left behind with her parents so the girl could continue in a special Moscow school where intensive English courses were given. She did not think much of the school in Nizhneangarsk. She did not think much of Nizhneangarsk or of the two-room cabin where she and Vladimir lived, a rudimentary shelter with "sort of a bath and toilet" and running water that was rarely hot. She sighed sadly at her husband's whims. "He's the kind of man who can't refuse a challenge," she said. "He's fond of it here. I can't understand it."

Class and Social Mobility

To move geographically is to move vertically. The horizontal path can also be an important path upward, one of several through this intricately stratified society, where advancement means rising from manual labor to skilled work, or from the farm to the factory, or from a secondary to a higher education, or from the rural to the urban, even where the "higher" position does not always pay more, or much more, than the "lower." Chronic shortages of material items distort the hierarchy of values to such an extent that even the job of salesclerk with access to a rare commodity often becomes more desirable than a scientist's post.

The paths upward are less open than they were during the first years following the Revolution, when the country was thrust into a frenetic period of rapid industrialization and social upheaval. The creation of vast new industry, the hunger for millions to fill the newly made skilled jobs, the burgeoning of a towering bureaucracy, the meteoric rise from factory worker to government minister within a single lifetime—all these heady features of change, which made the entire society upwardly mobile, have faded into a nostalgic past as the system has matured and stabilized and stagnated. Much of its fluidity is gone. Young men and women trying to move up today face both opportunities and severe obstacles; while many still manage to climb above their parents' levels in life, most do not. Even the officials who are supposed to uphold the legends admit that the system has congealed. "The times for soaring careers are past," said *Literaturnaya Gazeta* a few years ago.

The geographical component of upward mobility has been largely overlooked by Western scholars trying to assess the economic openness of the society. The data do not come easily, for even urbanization as a whole is a poor index; the country is strewn with small recently built and expanded industrial centers classified as "urban," but devoid of meat, decent clothing, good furniture, comfortable housing, and other privileges of Moscow, Leningrad, Kiev, and the like. The system of the discriminatory *propiska* is as decisive a determinant of a person's life-style as schooling is, and since big-city residence can be inherited from parents, married into, and obtained by pull, its exclusivity constitutes a drag on individual opportunity.

For decades after collectivization the peasants who worked the collective farms were held there as firmly as the serfs in czarist times by a simple device: They were not issued internal passports in which the *propiska,* or any police registration of urban residence, could be stamped. So those born on the farms, and their children and their children's children, were doomed to live humbly and in hardship. Exceptions were few, and even after a 1974 decree granting internal passports to all collective farmers, the freedom to move remained impaired. For one thing, the passports were slow in coming; five years after the decree I was told by farm directors that many had not yet been issued. And I once overheard a conversation on a train in the Ukraine, in which two women *kolkhozniki* were laughingly swapping stories about passport scandals; passports that had been issued were being held by the directors of their respective farms, who, one said, had to be paid off before releasing the document to its rightful owner. The other chuckled and chortled, "Such a life!"

Many prefer to stay in the countryside to keep the private agricultural plots and small numbers of livestock they are permitted as a more reliable source of food than the state stores. And many others never think to yearn for Moscow, so far out of reach. Those who crave a better life hardly ever seem to blame the system. Valentin

Turchin, a mathematician and human rights advocate who was forced to emigrate to the United States, explained this to me. "The basis of the social order is considered by the citizens as absolutely immutable, given for once and forever, absolutely unchangeable," he said. "They consider it as a given, as Newton's Law. When you fall down, you don't blame gravity. You blame your foot for slipping. So when a citizen has no food, he blames himself for not living in Moscow or some other center."

Education has also served as an important route upward; it, too, contains class biases, favoring those born into highly educated families over those born to parents on the farms or in the factories. The Soviet term "higher education" embraces such a broad range of institutions that it is not much more useful than the term "urban." Many "institutes," as they are called, would be regarded in the United States as little more than advanced vocational schools, training men and women in such narrow, technical specialties that many of those emigrating to the West are stunned to find their degrees as "engineers" useless and unrecognized. I once met a young man who described himself as an "electrical engineer" at Moscow's Sheremetyevo Airport. When I asked him what he did, he explained that when a light went out, he fixed the switch or changed the bulb.

It is to these narrowly specialized institutes that children of workers and peasants seem to come more easily than to the best universities and scientific institutes, such as those in Moscow and Leningrad. Youngsters from the farms, for example, sometimes go to agricultural institutes, then return to their home villages as technicians and future administrators. In the 1981–82 academic year, only 10.2 percent of those entering universities were rural residents, compared with 61.2 percent of those going into agricultural institutes, according to a survey in the Sverdlovsk area.* The upper crust of higher education appears considerably more accessible to children from professional families with the connections and money to arrange private tutoring before entrance exams—tutoring considered essential by many young people. Here, too, as in the United States, the motivation and the drive for learning picked up in the home are reflected in academic performance.

*Sotsiologicheskiye Issledovaniya, No. 3, 1982.

Statistics on upward mobility are sketchy; they are rarely published by Soviet authorities anxious to preserve the myth. But Western scholars and Soviet researchers have studied the question, and some of the unpublished Soviet data have been obtained by American experts.* The picture for youngsters who strive to exceed their parents' educational and job levels is mixed—a glass either half-full or half-empty. Most sons and daughters of workers stay workers, and most of those from families with higher education obtain that education as well. But the class structure can also be fairly permeable, and making it so is government policy.

The first selection of those destined to work with their hands occurs at the end of the eighth grade, when the educational system breaks into three branches: first, normal secondary school ending at tenth grade (eleventh grade in the Baltic republics of Latvia, Lithuania, and Estonia) and paving the way for entrance into a university or specialized institute of higher learning; second, the *tekhnikum,* a training school for middle-level technicians and foremen; third, the vocational school, known by its initials in Russian, PTU *(politekhnicheskoye uchilishche),* which produces skilled workers.

The lowest road, the PTU vocational school, is supposed to comprise students assigned by parents and school authorities on the basis of grades and aptitude, but youngsters told me that misbehavior is also often a factor. One vice-principal confided that the PTUs had become dumping grounds for what he called "problem pupils" and that their teachers were inferior. Political activism, called "social behavior," also comes into play. One girl's mother was told that her daughter would not get into ninth grade unless she became more active in Komsomol. The girl did as she was told and made it. I never found a single student who knew of a single child from a well-educated family who left secondary school to attend a PTU after eighth grade.

Surveys have bolstered the conclusion that grades alone do not

*The material here is drawn from several sources: Murray Yanowitch, *Social and Economic Inequality in the Soviet Union* (White Plains, N.Y.: M. E. Sharpe, Inc., 1977); Mervyn Matthews, *Privilege in the Soviet Union* (London: George Allen & Unwin, 1978); Murray Yanowitch and Wesley A. Fisher, eds., *Social Stratification & Mobility in the U.S.S.R.* (White Plains, N.Y.: Int'l. Arts and Sciences Press, 1973); Evelina Karlovna Vasileva, *The Young People of Leningrad* (White Plains, N.Y.: International Arts and Sciences Press, 1975; first published by the Leningrad University Press in 1973). Soviet sources are cited separately.

determine the student's track. Eighth graders with low marks have a much greater chance of avoiding vocational school and continuing through normal secondary school if their parents have higher education. Evelina Vasileva's study of Leningrad youth found that only 19 percent of workers' children with bad grades (below 3.5 on a 5-point scale) continued through regular secondary school, while 77 percent of educated families' children with bad grades did so.

A 1974 survey in Chelyabinsk showed that the upper track, the regular secondary school, was open to 94.3 percent of the eighth graders with highly educated parents and 77.2 percent of workers' children. In a 1968 Leningrad study the gaps were wider. It found 25 percent of unskilled and low-skilled workers' children attending secondary school, another 25 percent in *tekhnikumi;* by contrast, 86 percent of highly educated parents' children remained in the secondary schools. Similar patterns emerge from other studies through the 1970's. In a 1977-79 sample of nearly 6,000 students, 62.9 percent of those in PTU's and only 34.9 percent of those in regular high schools had fathers with fewer than ten years of education.*

A fourth track exists at the secondary school level, but it is open only to a tiny elite. A system of "special schools," running from first through tenth grades, concentrates instruction in particular subjects. There are schools for English, for French, for German, for physics, for mathematics, for ballet, for athletics, even for prospective circus performers. The best special schools provide a covert privilege for the children of ranking party officials and serve as the equivalent of the prestigious prep schools of the United States. Entrance is often by examination and pull.

Special afternoon and evening schools have also been established for instruction in many of these fields, and the most highly regarded are sought heatedly by ambitious parents. One young mother, a linguist, wanted so badly for her daughter to be accepted into the evening school of the Tchaikovsky Conservatory—to study piano —that when the school said she would have to study cello instead, the mother went along, rather than put the girl in a lesser school where piano was available. She weathered her daughter's anger and tears, and unceasing tension at home, just to have her in the "right" institution.

*Sotsiologicheskiye Issledovaniya, No. 2, 1981.

The next educational crossroad occurs at high school graduation; children of parents with higher degrees do better there as well. Their aspirations are higher, and they tend to apply more readily and to more advanced institutes and universities than do the children of workers. Since most entrance exams are given simultaneously, a student cannot compete for more than one institute or university department in his graduating year. So he usually applies to one he is sure of getting into; that is how a lifelong career choice is made at age sixteen or seventeen, under duress.

Workers' children often don't bother to apply at all. The Chelyabinsk study found only 34.4 percent of those questioned planned to seek higher education, compared with 71 percent from well-educated families. A similar question in the Leningrad region also revealed a gap between the aspirations of rural and urban youngsters. Of those in the city, 86.2 percent wanted to go to college, compared with only 56.9 percent of those in the countryside.

Workers' children have less success in their applications than those from well-educated families, the available research shows. A 1974 study in Ufa, about 700 miles east of Moscow, found that one-fourth to one-third of the peasants' and workers' children were upwardly mobile. Of a sample of those defined as intelligentsia, 72.5 percent had fathers in the intelligentsia, and just 14.6 percent had fathers who were workers. "Most *intelligentsia* parents are able to transmit their occupational status to their children," Yanowitch concluded, "while the majority of peasant and working-class parents—whatever their aspirations for their children—cannot reasonably expect to see them rise out of manual occupations."

Government policy has amounted to a rather cautious attempt to help workers' and farmers' sons and daughters upward. A modest affirmative action program gives some preference to university applicants from working and peasant backgrounds, but with limited success. It has been resisted by faculty members who see in it a weakening of standards.

The program was explained to me by Vasily A. Yudin, a deputy department head at the Ministry of Higher Education, who insisted on having all questions in writing well before our meeting. There were several methods used, he said. Government authorities could pick a certain number of workers' and peasants' children who have been accepted into institutes in their home provincial regions and send them to higher-quality institutions in Moscow or other centers. But the number was insignificant, he conceded. Sometimes peasant youth are accepted virtually without examinations into local institutes that train in professions that rural areas need badly. And special night preparatory schools, mostly for working youth, have been set up to create an additional path into higher education. But Yudin noted that no more than 20 percent of any institute's students may come from such schools. Finally, any youngster who has served in the military or worked for at least two years is given preference in admission over a tenth grader with the same examination scores. The aims of this program are being partly subverted, however, by children of highly educated families who, facing stiff competition for entrance, go to work for two years after tenth-grade graduation and then apply to universities and institutes. Thus they count as "workers" and get admissions preference. On the other hand, the universality of military service does encourage some mobility since the draft scoops up most young men, either at age eighteen or after their higher education.

Education has become such a symbol of success that many Russians now disparage manual labor, running strongly against the official values that glorify the worker as the heroic builder of the new society. In the cities of Novosibirsk, Leningrad, and Lvov and in Estonia, high school students questioned during the 1960's about occupations they saw as the most prestigious cited only those requiring higher education—physicist, mathematician, medical scientist, radio engineer, pilot, artist, schoolteacher—while the least desirable included sales personnel, cashier, farmer, construction worker, and bookkeeper. The system has catered to these ambitious attitudes by creating institutions of higher learning whose standards are fairly low but which operate under the same rubric as the more prestigious, and truly demanding, institutes and universities. But the result, in which the engineering diploma is seen less as a ticket to a bright future than as a shield against the stark alternative of physical work, has so alarmed officials that they have launched efforts in recent years to sell manual labor again. Secondary schools have filled up with even more propaganda posters; teachers have been told to push the assembly line as a desirable goal; and the PTUs, the vocational schools, have introduced some broader general education courses to make themselves more attractive to parents.

Party membership, available to about 6 percent of the population, has also been a conduit for the rise of talent from modest backgrounds into positions of leadership, though usually in combination with higher education. Rarely, nowadays, does one find a Politburo or Central Committee member without a higher degree, and even in the republic and oblast (county) party committees, where the party's function has as much to do with economic production as with political control, higher education is valued; often officials have technical training, as Brezhnev, for example, obtained a diploma as a metallurgical engineer before moving into full-time party work.

Party membership alone guarantees nothing, but a nonmember is usually blocked from holding certain positions in what is called the *nomenklatura,* referring to jobs under the party's jurisdiction and control. The party makes, or at least approves, assignments in such posts as school principal and factory manager. Full-time, paid party work, as opposed to membership that is incidental to a person's main job in a school or a factory, is usually a key to perquisites such as closed shops where imported food, clothing, and electronic equipment are sold; a top spot on the long list of those waiting to buy cars; access to slightly roomier, better-built apartments; and the chance to work or travel abroad. Leading party officials, those in the Council of Ministers, and some members of the Academy of Sciences are paid partly in "gold rubles" or "certificate rubles," coupons representing rubles exchanged for hard currency and usable in special stores selling imported goods or Soviet merchandise at reduced prices.

Party membership, acquired only upon the recommendation of Komsomol and other party officials and following a trial period, is often denied to those with some blemish in their records. The exclusivity adds luster. But nothing is categorical about the relationship between the party and the career; among successful scientists, for example, are both *partiiny* (members) and *bespartiiny* (nonmembers). Some who anticipate stepping into a garden of privilege find the fruits less succulent than imagined. This is especially so among those who remain simple card carriers, without becoming party professionals.

Sergei Polikanov, a party member, nuclear physicist, Lenin Prize winner, full member of the highly selective and elite Academy of

Sciences, and head of a nuclear research laboratory at Dubna, a scientists' village north of Moscow, could not get his daughter, Katya, into an institute of psychology because she simply scored too low on the entrance examination. I'm not sure how hard he tried to use whatever pull he had—he is a rather modest man, not given to throwing his weight around—but the fact was that Katya, a pretty blonde who looked like her mother, had to go to work for a year before trying the exams again. The incident was a nice illustration of the anomalies of the Soviet system, in which there often seem to be neither durable man-made rules nor constant natural laws, only the semblance of certainty papering over a turmoil of disorder. True, there are clear regulations governing every element of life, existing immutable procedures made like mazes, but with hidden apertures that slide mysteriously open to those armed with the proper rank or favor, and there are, indeed, rather reliable methods of evading the frustrating, winking one's way past the outrageous, even corrupting the just. But not always. Occasionally the rules stand like sturdy oaks, unyielding. It is an anxious game in which everyone is a violator, a lawbreaker; perhaps it goes partway toward explaining the Russians' desperate fear of *besporyadok* (literally "without order"), a word with the ring of immorality and threat. The Russians are afraid of *besporyadok,* disorder, and so they fear what they have created to get around the system, which they have also created and also fear.

When I asked Sergei Polikanov what privileges he got from being a party member, he couldn't think of any. In fact, his privileges—his pleasant, spacious apartment in the lovely Volga River town; his large automobile; his monthly stipend above his generous salary from the academy; his tickets to the Bolshoi; his freedom to mix with Western scientists who came regularly to his institute; his access to Western scientific publications and to sophisticated equipment for his research; his occasional working trips to Western Europe—all were results of his job, his position, and his scientific skill, not of his party membership. However, without the party card he could probably not have risen to such a job. Being in the party said to his superiors, "I'm safe, you're safe, don't worry about me."

When he gave up this coveted position in an elite by becoming an open dissident, he baffled many Russian friends. One thing the citizens of the classless society understand is class.

* * *

The polished black Chaika limousine glided slowly down the slight grade of narrow Yermolova Street until it came nose to nose with a battered old truck labeled "MILK" in half-rusted letters on its sides. There was no room for them to pass, yet neither would back down. Indeed, the milk truck could not, for it was towing a small broken-down sedan. The limousine would not, because although a driveway was there to slip into, its haughty chauffeur explained that his was an "official car." It had no passengers, but it was still an "official car," and its driver still a notch above the driver of a crummy old milk truck towing a sedan. For five or ten minutes they were at an impasse, the truck driver and several pedestrians shouting at the closed windows of the limousine until finally, having no choice except to sit there all day, the chauffeur indignantly backed into the driveway and let the truck pass.

This scene unfolded outside my office window like some updated Gogol satire, magnifying the fine layers of stratification that Russians define with easy expertise. In our apartment house the head superintendent—the "Commandant," who always wore a coat and tie and never dirtied his hands—stalked off in anger after a maid had complained mildly about his buzzing the doorbell repeatedly when the baby was sleeping. When the American tenant later questioned his behavior, the superintendent said, "If it had been you, sir, I would have said, 'Excuse me.' But she is only a maid. How dare she speak to me so disrespectfully!"

In many ways the Russians have achieved at least a superficial reduction of social distance. Custom requires a passenger in a taxi, for example, to ride up front with the driver, and even most officials who rate chauffeurs sit next to them, not behind them. Those who adopt the bourgeois practice of relaxing in the back, leaving the driver alone in the front as if he were pulling a rickshaw, are sneeringly regarded as putting on airs—unless they're in the Politburo. I learned this too slowly. Some weeks after arriving in Moscow, I was pulled aside gently by a couple of my colleagues who had seen me ride off in the back seat while our office driver was at the wheel. They explained that I was insulting him. I felt terrible and quietly began to ride up front, without apologizing to him for my faux pas. Much later the driver got up the courage to ask me why I had sat in the back at first. He seemed to have taken it as a serious slap. I explained, only half-jokingly, that I had still been acting on habits from the vestigial colonialism of my last post—Saigon.

This effort at an egalitarian façade has its effect. Taxi drivers have read as much Pushkin in school as their physicist passengers; the old women who sweep the snow from sidewalks with bundles of sticks can love Chekhov as fondly as the hurrying crowds of journalists and bureaucrats. The doctor and the nurse do not make dramatically different wages, and their apartments are usually of similar shoddiness and discomfort. Although apartment blocks are built by factories, universities, and professional trade unions for their employees and members, thereby creating some buildings with homogeneous populations, Soviet cities also enjoy considerable integration, and it is often difficult to put a class label on a neighborhood, where scientists and construction workers may be mixed together in housing that is all pretty much the same.

But the outer garment does not change the inner soul. The intelligentsia is gripped by a powerful contempt for the workers and the peasantry; the peasantry and the workers look back sardonically. A laborer in Zhukovka once delivered a dry comment on this. Zhukovka is a deeply wooded settlement near Moscow comprising an ordinary rural village and two secluded, fenced, and walled enclaves of dachas for government ministers and leading scientists. The workingman lived in the ordinary village in the ordinary house without running water. "What, you don't have water?" asked a startled American visitor.

The worker waved a calloused hand toward the unseen dachas of the elite. "The servants of the people have water," he said. "We, the people themselves, do not."

The man who works with his hands is silently despised by the man who does not. Manual work is called by the derogatory term "black work"; it is as if the loud posters and slogans glorifying the heroic worker were crying to be heard above the tacit truth. The word "shoemaker" has even insinuated itself into slang as an insult, some echo of a distant, ancient distaste for men who work with leather, a residue of untouchability. The shoemaker is considered an inferior species, likely to be drunken, and if a movie projectionist errs, for instance, breaking a film or mixing up reels, the crowd shouts derisively, *"Sapozhnik!"* ["Shoemaker!"]."

My colleague Chris Wren, at a dinner for a group of foreign correspondents on a government-sponsored tour, once followed a string of toasts to peace and friendship by standing and raising his glass to the waiters and cooks who had been doing all the hard work. The Soviet officials reacted in stony silence. Afterwards, a Foreign Ministry man told Chris that his toast had insulted his hosts. "Have you ever worked in a restaurant?" Chris asked.

"No," the Soviet diplomat replied.

"Well, I have," said Chris, "and it's hard work."

So great is the gap between worker and intellectual that a scientist or writer who once worked himself, or lived among workers and came to know their culture, is viewed with a curious admiration, as if he were an explorer who had crossed for a time into another hemisphere, an anthropologist who had been among the savages. I remember that Yuri Orlov, a combative and toughly built dissident physicist who headed the initial committee to monitor Soviet violations of the Helsinki accords until he was imprisoned, was seen by other dissidents—all with higher education—as possessed by some mysterious insight into the Russian character simply because he had at one time done manual labor and lived in remote areas of the country. This helped give him a certain charisma. Simultaneously, the distaste for the vast sea of *narod*, the common people of Russia, has blocked most dissidents who have been exiled to Siberian villages from using the opportunity to probe provincial life and write about it. Andrei Amalrik was an exception in his *Involuntary Journey to Siberia*, but he did not write with much respect; the *narod* earned mostly a disparaging tone. And in conversations with a few exiles who returned to Moscow, I was never able to elicit anything very perceptive about the people of those rural spots; the well-schooled political offenders were just not very interested.

The snobbery cuts away at any prospective Soviet alliance, along Polish lines, of workers and intellectuals who might struggle jointly to improve job conditions and political liberties simultaneously. It always struck me as unlikely that issues with mass appeal, such as the autocratic boss, the empty meat shelf, and the crumbling apartment, could be absorbed into the mechanism of Soviet political dissent as they were in Poland.

In at least one instance, dissidents of the educated Soviet elite rebuffed workers' efforts to gain support in forming a free trade union. The protagonist was Vladimir Klebanov, a disgruntled mining foreman from the coal region of Donbass who had been fired and locked in an insane asylum because he had complained too persistently about coal miners' being pushed into long hours and dangerous fatigue to fulfill unrealistic plans of production. In twelve-hour shifts instead of six, accidents were occurring, killing 12 to 15 men a year and injuring 600 to 700 in Klebanov's mine alone. When he got no hearing locally, he started writing letters to higher authority. The results were immediate: Since no sane Soviet citizen would dare make such protest, Klebanov obviously needed treatment, and he got it, for four and a half years, painfully with monstrous drugs. When he got out, he went back to his task, traveling to Moscow to the reception rooms of the Supreme Soviet, the Central Committee, and the prosecutor's office, three places of final appeal for crackpots, misfits, and fools who believe in justice. Dissidents say a special detail of secret policemen operates in these waiting rooms, hauling the particularly bothersome straight to mental institutions. Others are subjected to "conversations" with psychiatrists and ten- to fifteen-day jail sentences for "hooliganism." Those who escape such fates get to mix with their fellow complainants, who number 100 or more each day, and find they have a lot in common. In these reception rooms Klebanov met a few other workers who had also lost their jobs because they had stood up. They were people with an unusually clear view of right and wrong and an unusual anger.

Nadezhda Kurakina was a plain middle-aged woman with a white kerchief tied around her head. She had worked for twenty-five years in the Restaurant Volgograd, a closed dining room for the local party committee of Volgograd. "Fidel Castro was in our restaurant," she said. "Comrade Brezhnev, Kosygin—I served all of them." None of that did her any good when she discovered inconveniently that the restaurant administrators were stealing crockery, reporting it broken, and docking the salaries of waitresses they accused of breaking it. It is the sort of story often told in the columns of Soviet newspapers as part of the incessant anticorruption crusade. Therefore, Mrs. Kurakina had reason to think that she would be something of a heroine for blowing the whistle. She wrote some letters to officials and newspapers. No reply. She raised the issue in an open meeting of restaurant workers. Instant reaction.

She was fired, and so was her husband from his job elsewhere. The party secretary of the Volgograd Oblast, whom she had served for twenty years, would not even receive her. Higher officials in Moscow were not interested in her complaint. She lost her pension and her ability to find other work, for her dismissal was recorded in her "work booklet," a passportlike document, listing all places of employment, which must be shown when applying for another job. No agency, factory, office, or store would hire anyone fired on such grounds, except occasionally in part-time work. "They kill a person's morale," she said, "that's the most important thing."

Anatoly Poznyakov, a thin, bespectacled epileptic, worked as a locksmith for 75 rubles a month at Moscow's Institute of Biochemistry. His troubles began when he asked for a raise. "They insulted me crudely," he said. When he appealed to the local party committee, he was told that he had apparently forgotten that his "destiny in life was to eat from a pig's trough," in the words of one official. When he continued his protests, he was dismissed from his job and received just 21 rubles a month for his partial disability. When he asked for help from the Academy of Sciences, which oversees the Institute of Biochemistry, an official told him simply, "If you can, live. If you can't, go croak."

Valentin Poplavsky worked for a factory in Klimovsk, near Moscow, supervising maintenance of workers' housing. When a woman employee complained that officials were using factory funds to finance drunken parties, he was ordered to write a false criticism of her in her record. He refused, the factory's party organization admonished him, the oblast prosecutor warned him that if his accusations couldn't be proved, "we'll take the strongest possible measures against you," and he was finally fired from his job. Because of the entry in his work booklet, he could not find another.

Aleksandr Barchugov, a man of forty-eight who looked fifteen years older, worked in Leningrad's Izursky metal factory until August 1976, when he was hurt in an accident. But because factories get bonuses for being accident-free, the management tried to cover it up. To keep it off the books, they refused to pay him compensation to make up the difference between what he had been earning in his heavy work and what he made in the light work to which he was restricted by his injury, although regulations made such payments mandatory. He pressed, and was rewarded by being grabbed in the factory dining room one day, accused of being drunk, slammed into a sobering-up station, and then fired. He had done factory work for twenty-six years, sixteen of them there, and complained angrily that "not a single place of industry will take me."

Shagen Oganesyan, a thirty-seven-year-old Armenian with a thick black droopy mustache, worked as an engineer in an agency in Yerevan that repaired and renovated big electrical power plants. Elected to the People's Control Commission to guard against corruption, he took his job a bit too seriously, actually checking to see that work paid for had been done. He discovered that about half of it had not; the money had simply disappeared. His insistence in reporting the irregularities earned him a rejection of an application to go to Poland on a temporary job. And then he was downgraded, transferred to a lesser post. He quit in protest.

Vinera Kashapova, a young woman who tried to look stylish in an orange sweater, blue skirt, and gold earrings, had a bizarre story. She worked as a nurse in the First Railroad Hospital of Ufa, just west of the Urals; her mother worked at a school, and together they lived in an apartment provided by the school. When her mother died, Vinera lost her right to the apartment. "The director of the school threw me out on the street," she said. She asked for help in getting a new flat from the hospital where she worked, and in the face of no response, she made a pest of herself. She wrote letters; she sought appointments; she got scolded and threatened by her superiors, who told her, "We have power; we won't let you work anywhere." She applied in person to the Central Committee, where a bureaucrat laughed at her for coming all the way to Moscow without the necessary documents. She wrote a letter to *Pravda.* She wrote a letter to *Literaturnaya Gazeta,* which sent a reporter, who advised her to go see the oblast party secretary. In one of the many offices to which she appealed, a middle-aged official suggested that since she slept in railroad stations and didn't have a work permit, "Be a prostitute."

As Vinera told this story in a small apartment on the southern edge of Moscow, Tamara Manakova, a somewhat older woman with a gold front tooth, sat in disbelief and quiet tears. She had gone through a rough time herself. She had been the head bookkeeper of a sanitarium and vacation center in Sudak, the Crimea, and had had the bad judgment to object to the systematic pilferage of crockery and the ordering of large quantities of coffee, caviar, blankets, and sheets that never quite made it into the sanitarium but always seemed to end up in the administrators' homes. As a popular place on the Black Sea, the center was in such demand that the director's wife developed a lucrative little business selling *putyovki,* passes for stays there. The *putyovki* are normally issued free or for nominal fees by factories and institutions to their employees. These, however, were being sold under the table, *nalevo,* at 85 rubles for eighteen days, an exorbitant price by Soviet standards. "The money sat in their pockets," Tamara Manakova said with disgust. She apparently looked the other way for a good long time—"looked through her fingers," in the Russian idiom—until she was directed to sign a document certifying that 400 rubles' worth of crockery had been broken. She just couldn't do it. The rest of the tale was familiar: dismissal; harassment; threats of psychiatric hospitals.

Klebanov, the mining foreman, collected as many such sad people as were brave enough to escalate the fight and went to Andrei Sakharov, the Nobel Peace Prize laureate, participant in the development of the Soviet Union's atomic bomb, prophet and elder and guiding conscience of the human rights movement. Sakharov refused to get involved. He would not lend his name to the effort to publicize and organize on behalf of such obvious injustice, nor would he give advice. He simply wanted to have nothing to do with the entire business. Other lesser-known dissidents took the same position, although Yuri Orlov gave them suggestions on forming their "free trade union." Klebanov's bitter conclusion was that Sakharov and most of the others were snobs who did not think workers' mundane problems were worthy of their attention. "He knows very little about how average people live," Klebanov said scornfully.

I asked Sakharov about his refusal but received only a muddy explanation, making me suspect that Klebanov was at least partially right about class bias. Sakharov displayed a patronizing prejudice against the people in the group, asserting that such simple workers as those Klebanov had signed up could not possibly have any idea what risk they were taking by trying to organize. He seemed to think that for their own safety, these backward folk should drop such unimportant matters.

The dispute turned nasty, exposing an unattractive feature of Soviet society in which debate, so alien, rapidly becomes vicious, in which even good people cannot merely disagree but must try to destroy each other. I was stunned by what happened. Sakharov's wife, Yelena Bonner, a sharp-tongued *apparatchik* on behalf of human rights, said, "Klebanov is not entirely healthy."

"What?" I couldn't believe this.

"He's a little unhealthy," Sakharov echoed, rocking his hand back and forth next to his head.

"So," I asked, "you mean the KGB was right to put him in a mental hospital?"

"Well," said Bonner, "we're not psychiatrists, but . . ."

I asked for evidence to back up the charge, some incidents of odd behavior, irrationality. It was all very vague, just impressions.

"He's not a solid man," said Sakharov. "Be careful of him."

It was all done so thoughtfully, first to protect the naïve workers, then the naïve correspondents, that I was left wondering about the hidden antagonisms that must have developed deeply enough to drive Sakharov to such a ruthless assault, all the more poisonous in a closed society that feeds on innuendo and deceit.

He was correct about the risk these workers took, of course. The movement quickly evaporated as its key members, including Klebanov, swiftly disappeared into prisons and psychiatric hospitals. Some of them had certainly understood the dangers; perhaps others were more optimistic than was warranted. While political dissidents had generally abandoned faith in the system long ago, these were people who still seemed startled by the emptiness of the high rhetoric they had been hearing from the country's leaders.

"Our unions don't defend our rights," said Klebanov.

"Our unions aren't like Western unions," said Poznyakov, the locksmith.

"Our unions have no power," said Kurakina of the party restaurant.

"They are like second administrations," said Klebanov.

"I saw very outrageous things," said Kurakina. "But they don't investigate our criticisms."

In all these voices there ran the lilt of amazement.

The Archipelago of Privilege

Soviet society is not only stratified but also arranged in a series of enclaves, each as insular and impenetrable as a walled city. Every individual's profession places him in a circle of privilege and deprivation, providing him special access to what is within his borders and often denying him what is without.

An athlete can get a ticket to a crucial game, but a dancer cannot. The dancer can get a seat at the Bolshoi, but the athlete cannot. A writer can get a volume of Dostoyevsky or a translation of Kurt Vonnegut, but a doctor cannot. The doctor can sometimes get imported drugs, but the writer rarely can. A clerk in a vegetable store may get fresh tomatoes, and a clerk in a stationery store may get typewriter ribbons before the goods even reach the counter, but neither has easy access to the other, except through the system of mutual favors called *blat.*

Blat is the trading of privilege across these enclaves, the bartering of hard-to-get goods and services and ideas, the pull it takes to get something or somewhere. It oils the creaky wheels and makes friendships utilitarian. It means using people. At the box office, for instance, the lines of class and circle intersect in such a bewildering tangle that for ballet, opera, theater, and music in great demand, the quaint notion of first come, first served disappears under a fierce and intricate pecking order. To get tickets to the Bolshoi, whether opera or ballet, we had to write a letter on *New York Times* stationery, then wait until the day before the performance to see whether, once all the requests had been received and arranged hierarchically, we ranked high enough to be included. A tiny number of tickets was sold openly about three times a month to Russians who had the patience and persistence to stand in line and haggle. One friend got in often by befriending a woman in the box office with candy and flattery. But most seats were allocated to the Central Committee, the Council of Ministers, the diplomatic corps, luminaries in the theater world, and Intourist for Western tourists paying hard currency. During Supreme Soviet sessions, delegates from throughout the country were given the tickets, and the Bolshoi became an exclusive club for the party functionaries.

The system of controlled allocations also restricted access to Western and avant-garde stage productions. The Taganka Theater, whose director, Yuri Lyubimov, did some adventurous performances (the first theater version of Bulgakov's long-banned novel *The Master and Margarita,* for example, and acerbic social commentaries by Yuri Trifonov, including *The Exchange* and *House on the Embankment*), had such a small seating capacity that few Russians outside the well-connected got in. American orchestras, theater troupes, and others who performed in Moscow under cultural exchanges found most seats taken up by dour, orthodox, grey-suited party officials and foreigners, while crowds of ordinary Russians swarmed and pushed outside as if they were trying to get into a rock concert. The American Embassy always received some tickets to distribute, handing them to Soviet musicians, actors, directors, and writers who embassy officials knew would gain professionally from exposure to Western art. On its tour at the height of détente the New York Philharmonic even bought a good many seats to give away free to conservatory students and others who had the interest but not the pull. Debby and I handed a few of the leftover tickets to young, earnest Russians standing hopefully outside the Tchaikovsky Conservatory before the orchestra's final concert; they lit up as if a fairy godmother had just waved a wand over them. They tried to pay and couldn't believe the tickets were being handed out free. One woman was so excited she dashed across the street without looking and nearly got hit by a car.

Soviet authorities took extraordinary measures to isolate a 1979 embassy-sponsored festival of Academy Award-winning films, selling no tickets at all to the public but distributing them only through the State Committee of Cinematography, Goskino. This was in keeping with the treatment of film as one of the most rarefied privileges of the Soviet elite. The Soviet Union hardly ever buys American and Western European films, but Russians in the business told me that whenever an American or European producer sends a film to Moscow or to an Eastern European capital, offering it for sale or entering it in a festival, the state committee secretly copies it before returning the print. The copies, usually in black and white or poor-quality color and dubbed into Russian by a flatly read translation in one voice, are stored in a vast underground archive at the northern edge of Moscow, from which they can be lent to the closed clubs or the dachas of the powerful, whose country homes are often equipped with projectors.

In the evenings, at seven-thirty or eight, a highly restricted audience is admitted to a theater on the fourth floor of the state committee's office building at 7 Maly Gnezdnikovsky Lane to see first-run American and Western European films whose violence, explicit sex, and social themes are deemed inappropriate for viewing by ordinary, unprivileged Russians. Those inside the hall are carefully selected, holding passes supposedly given because of their professional interest. But just as Stalin loved American westerns, the Soviet elite today covets its access to the taboos from the outside world; touching some facet of the West is a mark of status and a source of craving and thus a valuable coin of affluence, spent carefully. The passes seep out of the magic circle, always to some purpose, favors for those who do favors in return. A film critic who has been to closed showings many times described the audiences: "Cinematographers and their families, and girlfriends, and heads of departments of meat stores and coffee stores, and hairdressers, and manicure girls. This is a tremendously high stimulus when you give your doctor a ticket," the critic said. In turn, the doctor provides special treatment and attention, access to the better hospitals and sometimes Western medicines. Other halls take other slices of the elite. A fourth-floor theater in the Goskino building is reserved for special groups—from party committees, the Defense Ministry, military industries such as aviation and electronics, and the like. A thirty-seat theater is located next to the study of the Goskino chairman, for his personal guests.

Films are shown in lesser circles of privilege as well. At 1:15 P.M. every Thursday a select crowd of several hundred, holding special tickets, files into the Illuzion movie theater on the left bank of the Moskva River for a closed showing of an old American or British film, usually Late Late Show material from the thirties or early forties, much of it captured by Soviet troops from Hitler's archives at the end of World War II. Those entitled to enter are supposed to need the English practice for their jobs. In cinema clubs scattered here and there, restricted Soviet-made films, and an occasional Western feature, are screened. Those Soviet-made are classified on a scale of one to four, to control distribution and access. Grades one and two may be televised. Grade one may be shown widely and must be reviewed favorably. Grade two gets only short runs in a small number of theaters and may be reviewed negatively, though not at all in the central newspapers, such as *Pravda* and *Izvestia*. Grade three films are for closed screenings, much as American films are, in writers' and actors' clubs, in special halls for ranking party members and the like and are not advertised, reviewed, or mentioned in the press. Grade four films are not to be shown at all.

Books, too, are exciting. Moreover, they are precious. Never anywhere have I seen books cherished as in the Soviet Union. I have never seen anyone hold them, almost fondle them, as Russians do. Those of us bathed in free thought have only the shallowest appreciation of literature, only a casual respect for the written word; we do not value so deeply what we can obtain so easily. Ina Rubin, a librarian and dissident, stayed up all one night in Moscow reading, devouring, a smuggled copy of Solzhenitsyn's *The Gulag Archipelago,* volume one, to finish it before it had to be handed on to someone else in the morning. By the time volume three was out she had emigrated and was living in Jerusalem, where she could have gone to a bookstore and bought a copy. She didn't bother, she admitted sheepishly. The taboo was gone.

The first time I went to meet Lev Kopelev and his wife, Raissa Orlova, both scholars and writers, I carried bundles of gifts from an American correspondent who had returned home after his Moscow assignment. He had sent them treasures of America: jeans and hand cream and good-quality clothing, all things that would have delighted people of lesser taste. They were touched but not ecstatic, and Raya almost cried in despair when she reached the bottom of the bags. "No books?" she wailed. "No books! David, you must never come to us without bringing books."

The enormous two-story bookstore on Kalinin Prospekt has shelves of engineering and mathematics texts; display cases groan under piles of unbought treatises by Lenin and Brezhnev. But ask one of the pudgy young women behind a counter for Chekhov or Gogol or Pushkin or Dostoyevsky, not to mention one of the permitted and often-translated Americans such as Jack London, Ernest Hemingway, or Tennessee Williams, and she will smile sadly and cluck in disbelief. She and her colleagues put the small quantities of such volumes aside for their friends and acquaintances who can return the favor; the few copies that reach the shelves are snapped up in a flash. Most ordinary people can get the Russian classics only by subscribing to entire sets in advance, receiving one volume after another as they are published, and even these editions are limited. Members of the Writers' Union, as the Kopelevs were before they were expelled and then left for West Germany, are entitled to buy in a special bookstore that is fairly well stocked and are given priority in signing up for new editions. "But it is necessary to telephone every day and to know someone," Raya said. Restricted subscriptions to literary magazines, in which works of the most significant officially approved poets and novelists usually appear before coming out in book form, are also more easily available to Writers' Union members than to outsiders. But books from the West—paperback thrillers, fine literature, works of Soviet writers too critical or unorthodox to be published at home—come in through diplomats and other foreigners who are befriended by daring and hungry Russians. An odd twist on this order of privilege was accomplished when some poetry in official disfavor, notably that of Boris Pasternak and Anna Akhmatova, suddenly turned up in a state-run hard-currency store in Moscow, in Russian-language editions printed at an official Leningrad publishing house but never sold openly to the Soviet public. Only foreigners with dollars, marks, francs, pounds, and other convertible cash could buy them. But predictably the volumes quickly reached the clandestine circuits of distribution among Russian friends and friends of friends, going from hand to hand just as the Western books and small-circulation literary magazines do, until their pages are limp and dog-eared.

Even the lowliest connection is exploitable. I knew a middle-aged newspaper deliverer named Igor, a happy alcoholic, divorced and living alone in a tiny, fetid room of a communal apartment, who had worked out a way to satisfy his passion—detective stories. These Soviet paperbacks sell out fast, so he struck a deal with a newsstand operator. The papers Igor delivered came off the presses not as separate copies but folded together, one inside another; the men and women at the newsstands had to separate them before putting them out on the counter. It was a lot of extra work, especially during the morning rush, so Igor would do the job for one newsstand, presenting the operator with neat stacks of ready-to-sell papers. In exchange, the operator put choice paperbacks under his counter for Igor, who paid more than the regular price—usually a ruble instead of 40 kopecks ($1.50 instead of 60 cents)—but was content.

The distribution of privilege can be capricious enough to entertain the sort of wry, irreverent humor that Russians find indispensable to sanity. The Jewish dissident Anatoly Shcharansky, who managed a laugh in the most desperate circumstances, recounted a stay in jail for "hooliganism" (i.e., participating in a proemigration demonstration) that turned unexpectedly profitable. His cellmates during the ten days or so were drunkards, wife beaters, and other genuine hooligans, whom he charmed with his wit and verve. One worked in a fruit and vegetable store and became such pals with Tolya that he invited him to stop by the store after his release. For weeks afterwards, the community of Moscow dissidents was blessed with oranges, apples, cucumbers, tomatoes, lettuce, and other hard-to-get delicacies, delighting everyone who enjoyed a good joke on the system.

Igor, the lowly and inventive newspaper deliverer, also managed to penetrate the protected rings of the elite and gain access to one of the most closely held commodities: information. This is a choice delicacy in the Soviet Union, where the press is so opaque that even public events are shrouded in ignorance and susceptible to rumor. And rumor itself is highly stratified, becoming more and more intimate about the country's leadership as one approaches the inner sanctum. I had an acquaintance with smoky Foreign Ministry ties (and, I suspected, KGB connections) who got a kick out of hearing and spreading infatuating tales of Politburo ribaldry and political perversion. He professed to know the makes and models of all dozen or so luxury foreign cars driven by Brezhnev, the messy details of a Politburo member's alleged suicide by shotgun (while drunk in the throes of a power struggle), what the head of the KGB said at a party about Jewish dissidents to the editor of *Literaturnaya Gazeta*, and so on. At a position more removed, though also somewhat well connected, Roy Medvedev would hear reports on political attitudes and upcoming Politburo shifts, not all of which proved accurate. But his friends in the party certainly provided him with more insight than the average Russian could possibly have attained.

One body of information closely guarded is what the Western press is reporting on the Soviet Union and the rest of the world. Articles from abroad are treated like classified documents, accessible only to those with an absolute need to know. Daily these are translated into Russian by Tass bureaus throughout the world, wired back to Moscow, and distributed in folders of more than 100 pages a day to carefully selected party leaders, government officials, and Soviet editors, who are supposed to treat them confidentially. The service, called White Tass, contains unpublished reports on domestic events as well—plane crashes, labor disruptions, political disorders—and even its existence is unknown to most Russians. But Igor, in the lower end of the newspaper business, so to speak, knew a great deal more about it than his superiors would have liked. When I first met him, he launched immediately into an intricate discussion of various aspects of world affairs, pleased to find an American newsman at his table. This was a man who had spent time in psychiatric hospitals during vain attempts to cure his severe alcoholism. His single room was stacked with dusty old newspapers. His linoleum-topped table was caked with flecks of dried tomato sauce, which he poured from a stained, half-rusted can over bits of pork fat fried in an eternally greasy pan on a hot plate. His material life was humble, impoverished; his mind, however, was stimulated by a fiery interest in what was going on around him. I was amazed at how well informed he was, and I asked him if he spent all his time listening to the Voice of America and BBC, then unjammed. No, he said, he just read White Tass. How? Well, he explained with a grin, when the editors upstairs are finished with it, they throw it away, and it comes down from trash baskets into big garbage bins in the basement, and he takes it out to read and hand around to friends. He loved the irony of this and poured another vodka. So much for security.

Information moves discreetly, selectively, even within professions such as medicine. It oozes reluctantly down through the layers of status and out through the barriers that shelter one cloistered medical elite from the next, rarely reaching the hard-pressed practicing physicians in the polyclinics and ambulances and rural hospitals. These working doctors are often unaware of the latest developments in drugs and therapy; they may never have heard that a certain institute in Moscow or Leningrad has equipment and specialists to treat a baffling eye problem or heart defect. They may not know the institute exists at all. The void of knowledge is extensive. A biomedical scientist from the United States doing research on an exchange program found ranking Soviet doctors and scientists in Leningrad pumping his American delegation for word of developments among their Soviet colleagues in Moscow, where the delegation had just been. "They're not aware of what's going on in their own country, much less what's going on in America," the visitor said in amazement. An American obstetrician serving for a while at the United States Embassy discovered how incompletely information travels when he had a foreign woman patient admitted to Botkin Hospital, one of Moscow's best, after a miscarriage. She had Rh-negative blood and needed the drug RhoGAM, which had been developed seven or eight years earlier to block the formation of antibodies that would destroy the red blood cells of an Rh-positive infant from a future pregnancy. The American doctor knew that at the Institute of Obstetrics and Gynecology in Moscow, the country's foremost teaching and research facility in the field, "one of the professors was conversant with the whole history of RhoGAM, was up on the latest developments, and even had it available." But across town, at the prestigious Botkin Hospital, there was no RhoGAM, "and the consulting physicians were not even aware of its existence." The American went to the professor, who had participated in researching the drug's effects in Western Europe, obtained some, drove to Botkin, and administered it to his patient.

The system of medical care expresses the full range of strengths and weaknesses of Soviet society; it is a model of the country's hierarchy, reflecting the instincts of authoritarianism, conservatism, and elitism that pervade all areas of life. It testifies to the acute contrasts Russians face as their centralized bureaucracy mobilizes immense power both to distribute vital services into remote hinterlands and to stifle initiative, creativity, and scientific advancement. Soviet medicine can be excellent and incompetent simultaneously, available in mediocrity to all and accessible in high quality only to the chosen or the canny or to those blessed by chance.

Free medical care is one of a group of economic rights guaranteed under the Soviet Constitution, along with housing, education, jobs, and other benefits that form the centerpiece of the Soviet definition of human rights. But despite the extensive network of hospitals, polyclinics, and neighborhood doctors (who even make free house calls), a Russian's access to good hospital treatment, knowledgeable specialists, and essential drugs is erratic and often unpredictable. One does not simply walk into the finest cardiac institute and arrange an appointment with the best surgeon; the way must be paved with references, connections, *blat,* and often bribery. Strictly professional referrals take place on the occasions when a doctor at the clinic level happens to know of the existence of a specialized institute and happens to know somebody working there. This was the lucky situation of the middle-aged sister of an acquaintance of mine. She lived in a country town about 100 miles from Moscow; her local polyclinic and hospital had treated her for heart problems that gave her little hope of survival without radical surgery, and the clinic staff managed to get her into the country's best cardiac institute, where one of the most skilled heart surgeons implanted an artificial valve. It was an eight-hour operation whose cost to the state was the equivalent of nearly $15,000. My friend's sister paid nothing.

Another friend knew a woman who had not fallen into a good connection, however, and during labor ended up at an ordinary maternity hospital. Her pelvis was too narrow for a normal delivery, and her chart called for a Caesarean section. But the lone, harassed nurse responsible for the entire floor had no time to read charts. The woman's labor went on and on. Now and then the nurse came to check the fetal heartbeat. The labor continued. Finally the fetal heartbeat disappeared. The baby was dead.

"They're really out to lunch in some areas," said an American neurologist after several months watching brain surgery in one of the top institutes. "They're back in the 1950's. Septic measures are very carelessly handled. Although they say they have antiseptic agents for cleaning up, I saw the old ladies you've seen in a hotel, they walk into the operating room between cases with a mop and a bucket, and they wash the floors. It's a 1930's operation generally. There is frequent visitation of people coming in and out of the operating room, people opening the door to ask questions. The surgeon scrubs much less than an American surgeon." The neurologist saw one routine spinal tap in which the equipment had not been prepared in advance, the correct fittings were not ready, and the tap went all night while the nurses tried to fit one stopcock and valve into another. "It was all bits and pieces, with tape. It was really like a high school chemistry class."

There is a widespread conviction among Russians that medical care you don't pay for is just about worthless. *"Lechitsya darom, darom lechitsya"* goes a sardonic little play on words that translates roughly: "Treatment for free is treatment in vain." The authorities have even tried to satisfy this urge to pay by establishing, in Moscow and other cities, small networks of fee-charging polyclinics that

Russians think are less crowded and of higher quality. Otherwise doctors who take money or gifts usually break the law. But the average doctor's wage is only about two-thirds of the average factory worker's, a symbol of the low prestige that has made the profession unattractive to most men; 70 percent of all physicians are women. So the need to oil the system is accepted, and Health Ministry officials say that no doctor in their memory has ever been prosecuted for taking bribes (although the law has been used occasionally against those in political disfavor). One Moscow woman gave her heart surgeon some lovely antique silver. A man gave his physician some of those coveted tickets to a closed film showing. A butcher in the Riga collective farmers' market let Dr. Herman Shapiro's wife take meat from his stall up to three times a week without paying, in return for regular treatment of a chronic endocrinological problem. "There is no meat in the stores," Dr. Shapiro explained simply, "so he comes to me for treatment, and my wife goes to him for meat."

Barter fits nicely into the tradition of incessant gift giving; it has a smoothness that eases the crassness of outright cash payment. Bottles of vodka are a common currency. One doctor declared proudly that he and his colleagues were above bribery. "At a low level of surgery we didn't ask, and as a rule we didn't receive money," he said. "We received cognac, wine." Dr. Shapiro once received a precious opportunity to buy typewriter ribbons. For two months he had been looking for ribbons in Riga, trying one stationery store after another until finally, when yet another saleswoman told him she didn't have any, he lost all hope. "I told her, 'I am a physician, and maybe sometime I can help you,'" he said. She brightened. She needed help urgently. She was eighteen years old and eleven weeks pregnant, with just one week to go before reaching the twelve-week legal limit for abortions. She did not want her mother to know, so she could not go into her neighborhood hospital, where her sister-in-law worked as a nurse. She had tried for weeks to get in somewhere else, and no place would take her. She reached under the counter and pulled out—two typewriter ribbons! "She was almost too late," Dr. Shapiro said, "so I bought two ribbons, and I called my friend in another hospital, and he did it for ten rubles."

Payment is a safety valve that relieves the system's inefficiencies, and for many, as for the saleswoman, it meets the drive to have a choice, to gain some sense of control over the care received, to manipulate the bureaucracy instead of the other way around. "In the hospital," said Dr. Iosif Ahs of Moscow, "patients try to choose their surgeon. They ask for the head surgeon of the department; they try to get a professor. My uncle paid two hundred rubles to a professor for a gallbladder operation on my aunt. She died."

Dr. Shapiro once tried to avoid paying for his father and wound up doing so just to avoid maltreatment. "My father had a benign tumor of the prostate," he said. "One doctor told him it was cancer. A second told him it was too late to operate. A third said he must be castrated. I had to bring him from Riga to Moscow to find two or three doctors I could trust. I finally had to pay a hundred fifty rubles to a surgeon to perform the operation excellently." He doubted that payment ever induced a physician to do his crucial work better. "Paying gets you the choice of a surgeon," he explained. "But I don't think a surgeon will ever operate worse than he can. The difference is that if he is paid, he will see the patient five to ten times afterwards and get the newest imported drugs. The doctor gave my father a French catheter, not a Soviet one."

Decent nursing care in hospitals is also sometimes for sale. "I sent my mother to the hospital with a bunch of one-ruble bills," said Irina Brailovsky, a mathematician. "After her operation, there was bleeding; she wanted the sheets changed at least every two days. Without one ruble a day she would have had new sheets only once a week. For the bedpan you wait an hour or pay one-fifty." And woe to you if you don't know the system. An American tourist who broke her hip in Moscow, not realizing that she had to bribe, "spent four days lying in her own excrement, grossly mistreated and abused," the embassy doctor said.

But there are enclaves of civility. My mother, who had a minor stroke while visiting us in Moscow, was accepted into Botkin Hospital's special wing for resident foreigners, where she was cooed and clucked over by ample nurses and maternal orderlies in such warmth and affection that the nightmare was softened and the experience tempered with fondness. One enormous woman garbed in white would swirl hot water around in the bedpan to take the cold edge off; another would gently scold and prod in motherly concern if a meal was left unfinished. The doctor was a woman with a bedside manner of kindness and competence, conveying a professionalism mixed with a touching personal interest. None of the mechanical detachment of an American hospital was present, and although it was a long stay—thirty days instead of the five or six she would have spent hospitalized in the United States—the attention and thoughtfulness of the staff never diminished. The wing is closed to Russians, of course. They need rank or *blat* to work their ways into the fine institutions where such good care exists. I was sent suddenly from the protected environment of the special wing into the rough-and-tumble real world when my mother was discharged and her doctor wrote three prescriptions I would have to fill at a pharmacy. The line was long, and the woman behind the counter cranky. She knew instantly which drugs were in stock and which were not; the customer had only to slide the paper toward her so she could give it a glance. She seemed satisfied when she could snap, *"Nyetu"* and flick the prescription back; she appeared put out on the infrequent occasions when she had the requested medicine and had to go pull it off a shelf. Most customers were turned down; when one man asked timidly when a certain drug might be received, she glared and bellowed, "How am I supposed to know?" He crept away. One of my three prescriptions was filled there, but inaccurately. The salesclerk gave me a bottle of anticoagulant in capsules one-third more potent than prescribed, but she made no mention of it, gave me no warning. I noticed and questioned her; she shrugged and said that was all she had. It was a dangerous oversight, given the precision with which anticoagulant dosages are usually administered, and I went back to my mother's doctor for an explanation of how to break up the tiny pills. The other two drugs were hard to find. I got a second one after trying several other pharmacies (the Russians do not honor the American practice of one store's calling another to locate a needed medicine), but after going to six or seven altogether, I could not find the third. I had the embassy clinic as a possible last resort, and in any case my mother was flying home the next morning. If I had been a Russian without alternatives, I would have felt a rising panic. Finally I went back to my office to ask a translator to call around to drugstores to save time. Instead, he called the Moscow city administration that runs all the pharmacies, told them who I was, and was quickly given the name of a nearby drugstore where I could get the medicine.

When I appeared in the normal line and handed in the prescription, the clerk scowled, snapped *"Nyetu!"* and motioned me away. I said that we had called. A flicker of recognition, and she waved me upstairs. There I was pointed into the office of the manager, who, upon hearing my name, reached into his desk drawer and pulled out the correct bottle of pills. Rank.

Doctors also require connections to get what they need, and the inadequacies are acute. "Diabetic patients sometimes die because of a lack of insulin," Dr. Shapiro said. "When I go to a patient with high blood pressure and I have no drugs to lower the blood pressure, I don't know what to do." Sometimes, there is a shortage of bandages, thermometers, or cotton. One desperate hospital took artificial snow made of cotton off a New Year's display. Another reused bandages. Dr. Ahs, who rode an ambulance in Moscow until emigrating to Israel, carried his own supply of scarce drugs, beyond those officially issued, in a tin box marked "Benson's English Toffee." Lined with plastic foam, the box contained ampules of medicines that were often needed urgently, but hard to get, such as potassium for regulating the rhythm of the heart. Dr. Ahs and his colleagues on ambulances obtained the drugs through medical friends in strategic positions, in Dr. Ahs's case a doctor from the Fourth Department of the Health Ministry, which runs exclusive institutions, including the Kremlin Clinic.

This well-equipped and well-stocked treatment center for the highest party and government officials is one of a series of special facilities serving military personnel, policemen, prominent scientists, athletes, dancers, and so forth. But the Kremlin Clinic is also known among many doctors as so security-conscious, politically stodgy, medically conservative, and ethnically prejudiced that professional quality has been sacrificed. At one conference where doctors were being assigned, the Kremlin Clinic representative was heard to say, "We need good doctors, but don't offer me 'shteins' and 'shvilis.'" The reference was to common endings of Jewish and Soviet Georgian names. A couplet to describe the clinic goes: *Poli parketniye, / Vrachi anketniye.* Literally it means, "The floors are parquet, and the doctors have been investigated" or, more briskly, "The floors are parquet, the doctors OK." One result, a surgeon explained, is that some party brass don't have much faith in the Kremlin Clinic and go elsewhere, to lesser institutions whose medicine is less rigid and more advanced. A friend who was once inside said the patients wore varied pajamas—stripes, no stripes, etc.—to delineate rank.

The authoritarian structure of the political hierarchy finds duplication in smaller agencies and bureaucracies throughout science, where individual promotion and approval for research is dependent on rank and connections. A leading eye surgeon told me candidly that he got too much money and equipment, and young researchers too little. And he deplored the conservatism of established professors who, he felt, stifled innovation.

Young physicians eager to advance through specialized training often find their ways blocked by the unquestioned authority of jealous or hidebound superiors. Advanced courses, which contain about 70 to 75 percent medicine and 25 to 30 percent Marxism-Leninism and Communist Party history, are, again, most accessible to those with *blat* and active Komsomol leadership. "It's very difficult to get such a place," Dr. Shapiro said. "He must be on good terms with his chief and must be an activist. Relations mean more than real knowledge. Without political activity, it's very rare that he can do well. He would have to be brilliant and have private relations with the chief of his department in an institute. If he has no such connections, no one would be interested in promoting him."

The intricacies of privilege extend into every region of existence, including those far beyond the view of the ordinary, mortal Russian. One such area is the upper level of the military, where unseen luxuries are enjoyed in abundance. A glimpse of these have been provided in *Tatiana,* a book by Edward Lozansky,* a scientist now living in the United States, who married the daughter of a much-decorated general. Lozansky once visited a special farm where fruits and vegetables were grown for the elite; he watched in amazement, he wrote, as women in white smocks took one tomato at a time from a basket, inspected it scrupulously, measured it with a ruler, and then put it in one or another box. The farm director explained proudly that the perfect ones went to the highest generals' families, the others to other officers, censors, the chief prosecutor, and so on. The stratification was so refined that a colonel general had a five-

*For Tatiana, by Edward Lozansky, published in 1986 by Henry Holt, New York.

room apartment and a lieutenant general, Lozansky's father-in-law, had a four-room apartment; the colonel general a stone dacha on a huge plot, the lieutenant general a wooden dacha on a smaller plot; the colonel general an eight-room house on a lake in a closed zone, the lieutenant general a six-room house on the lake; the colonel general a two-story villa on the Black Sea, the lieutenant general a one-story villa.

Lozansky watched once as a shift in rank brought a shift in privilege, right on the spot. He and his wife and daughter were vacationing in a small resort near Yalta for the families of the military elite; the daughter of the commander of the Kiev military district was also there with her husband, in the largest room because of her father's position, a room with a refrigerator, a color television set, and a telephone. "Our room and refrigerator were smaller," Lozansky wrote, "the television was black and white, and the telephone, although there, did not work." They came back from the beach one day to find all their things gone. The manager rushed in to explain: The commander of the Kiev district had been removed; there were rumors that Lozansky's father-in-law would be getting the position, so the management had moved their belongings into the largest room and had kicked out the commander's daughter and her husband altogether. Lozansky protested and tried to stay in his original room, but the manager was unyielding. "That is impossible," he said. "I do not want to lose my job."

Crime and Social Conscience

In the scramble for advancement and comfort, in the bending of unreasonable rules and the ignoring of impossible laws, an easy drift is attained, a state of moral weightlessness where there is no up or down, right or wrong. It is illegal, but is it wrong for private speculators to bring essential drugs for sale to cardiac patients in the Kaunas Hospital in Lithuania? It is illegal, but is it wrong for a pediatrician in Tbilisi who is faced with no antibiotics and an epidemic of bacterial infections to advise mothers how to buy streptomycin and penicillin on the black market? "We say directly to them to go to the speculators," explained one woman doctor in Georgia.

"We direct them there: 'Go buy it on the black market and bring it here, and we'll administer it.' "

Knowing that much of decent living depends on illegality, Russians move always in a diffuse mist of vague guilt and vulnerability, understanding that they have done many things on the dark side of the law for which they can be arrested at any moment. Even if the probability of arrest is obviously low, the sense of perpetual sin is very strong, casting a shadow of uneasiness over all striving. A friend who was no dissident, and as upstanding a citizen as they come, told me of the chills he felt in reading a short story on settling accounts. The hero of the story receives a summons to court, a slip of paper bearing only a case number, no details. He searches his mind frantically, wondering which transgression he has finally been called to answer for, which small infraction in his young adulthood has caught him. My friend also searched his own past while reading, turning out scores upon scores of his illicit acts, examining them in cold tension. Finally the court date ends up as an innocent need for the man's testimony in some benign civil case. But my friend was haunted by the story, for it spoke to some profound and universal fears.

From the viewpoint of political control, it must be convenient for the authorities to have most Soviet citizens in a constant state of illegality, always arrestable on apolitical grounds. Tangled in webs of indebtedness, the individual feels frail against the massive righteousness of the state and party. Corroded by his own transgressions, the citizen does not blame the system for failing to provide meat, but as Val Turchin observed, blames himself for not living in Moscow, where it is available. And as he schemes and deals and bribes and embezzles, and invents cute idioms such as *blat* and *nalevo* to mask his wrongdoing, he also keeps his head down, melts in, complies, and bends.

And often he loses his equilibrium. Because "speculation," as the private trading of goods is branded, is almost universally outlawed and almost universally tolerated, black-marketeering becomes normal and regular, taking on the illusion of legitimacy. Every Saturday, beginning in the late morning, some fifty or more young men carrying bulky leather briefcases would congregate in the Central Army Park near our apartment on Sadovo-Samotechnaya Street. From a distance they presented an odd scene. They neither strolled along the park's paths nor sat on the benches. They simply stood in small clusters, milling around, bundled up in tan and grey coats, as if holding a strange sort of cocktail party without cocktails. They all seemed very serious, and they spoke so softly they hardly seemed to be speaking at all. If you walked innocently among them, they would stare at you curiously, in a mixture of hopefulness and suspicion, and if you watched carefully for a long time, you would see how one or another moved from group to group, opening a briefcase so the others could peer inside. With unwavering attention you could spot the quick flash of a transaction: a Beatles or Elvis Presley record from one briefcase to another, a handshake in which 50 to 75 rubles were concealed. Neither the nearby traffic policemen nor the KGB agents who frequently followed us through this park as we met and walked and talked with Soviet dissidents ever seemed to take notice of this weekly session of *fartsovshchiki,* black marketeers, who spent other days hanging around outside tourist hotels asking foreigners if they had records, tapes, books, jeans to sell.

A book market materialized on Sundays across Dzerzhinsky Square from Lubyanka, the KGB headquarters. There you could find the scarce Dostoyevsky, the rare Pasternak, the bootlegged Bible, and even, at times, the banned Solzhenitsyn—all for prices between $50 and $100 apiece. Hemingway, Dickens, Tolstoy, Chekhov, and others raising no political objections went for $20 to $40 a volume, as much as a week's wage for a doctor or a teacher. Baby clothes were sold on a street near the American Embassy; one American friend gave his kids' outgrown clothes to a Russian and got icons in exchange. Automobile parts were available early on certain mornings near a northern exit off the outer ring road encircling Moscow; a Russian friend, a car nut, used to go there often. "This is an uninhabited island in the automotive sense," he told me. "There are fruits in the trees, but you have to learn how to pick them." He once replaced a broken spring in the distributor with six razor-blade halves. Shortages in services have also promoted extensive black markets populated by moonlighting government chauffeurs, carpenters, plumbers, electricians, and others whose skills are abundant and essential.

The penalties for black-marketeering involve long prison sentences, and even capital punishment in cases of embezzlement of state-owned goods, a frequent crime by imaginative entrepreneurs who set up underground factories, producing clothing from stolen textiles, shoes from stolen leather, and the like.

But because so much of ordinary life is enveloped in vast areas of illegality and because "speculation" is vilified in the official press as bourgeois, nearly anti-Soviet, this synthetic crime of private buying and selling becomes both serious and light, grave and ubiquitous. It stirs both revulsion and a sly, winking envy. And the concept of crime thus becomes blurred, disorienting, until synthetic crime and genuine crime fade in and out of one another, melting into a vague mash of disreputable acceptability.

A winter evening in Moscow. In the lobby of a small theater on Sadovskikh Lane, the audience gathered after the play—high school students, parents, teachers, all standing together in a crowd, the buttons of their heavy cloth overcoats undone, their hats of muskrat and rabbit fur held down at their sides. They faced a woman at the end of the lobby, an administrator of the theater, who was introducing a few members of the cast. Then she invited the audience to discuss what they had just seen, to debate openly. They treaded gingerly onto this unfamiliar ground of free give-and-take. "What do you want us to say?" asked one mother. Anything you like, answered the administrator. The mother looked uncomfortable. Another offered some courteous thanks to the cast, as if she were proposing a toast at a formal banquet. Only gradually did the layers of caution give way to discussion, disagreement, argument about the performance and its subject: juvenile crime.

The play was based on a true story investigated by a Soviet journalist, Valery Agranovsky, about a fifteen-year-old boy who mugged and robbed a middle-aged woman on the street. In real life, a friend familiar with the case told me, the boy murdered her with a knife; onstage he simply waved the blade in her face and tore her purse from her hands. *Stop Malakhov!* the play was called, and as it explored the roots of Andrei Malakhov's crime, it portrayed every element of society in the harshest terms: police and party, school and family, peers, parents and role models among adults. "Who is guilty?" the journalist, as narrator, asked time and again. "Who is guilty?"

"I, you, everybody," said the actor who played Malakhov in the discussion that followed. On this essential question of balancing responsibility between individual and society, the adults were sharply divided. The teenagers, from two Moscow schools, were silent.

Andrei Malakhov was judged a normal boy by the psychologist who examined him in prison—"He's as normal as the kids outside." His first theft occurred in kindergarten: He took a spade, and the recollection brought a gleeful smile to his face. His parents, fine and undistinguished, well adjusted and successful, were divorced, like many others in Moscow. A normal family. His mother considered herself "a cultured person."

"I read newspapers, magazines," she said. "I have a large library, modern furniture. I have a television set, a refrigerator."

And whom did Malakhov admire? He named a pop singer, a hockey player.

"We're not guilty!" thundered the father. "Ask them, in school. He's in school every day except Sunday. Why is my son a criminal? Why is my son a criminal?" He shouted at the school principal, who yelled that the parents were to blame. The parents yelled back.

"Why," the boy asked, "are you shouting at each other?"

"You must think I have ten people in my class!" shrieked Andrei's teacher, a hard woman. "But there are forty! What more can I do? What more? We are powerless, absolutely powerless. Malakhov had an alien ideology. Psychologists he doesn't need. He needs the police. I don't work in a police station, but in a school!"

The psychologist's son was in a reformatory. The journalist's son was drifting away, unable to talk to his father.

"Who is guilty?" asked the narrator.

"Parents!" shouted the principal.

"School!" shouted the parents.

In Agranovsky's book *Down the Staircase,* the boy remembered terrible stories about his father. On his fifteenth birthday his father gave him 15 rubles, but immediately borrowed it back until payday. One, two, three paydays passed without any mention of the money. And when the boy asked for it, the father claimed not to know what he was talking about. Andrei could scarcely breathe, he was in such a rage. The father said sternly, "At your age I had money that I earned playing marbles. And you want to live on windfalls!"

Another memory: On a Sunday the mother asked cheerfully

whether the family should go to a theater or to a friend's house. His father burst into hysterical laughter at the notion that there should be a choice. If you go to the theater, you have to pay for the tickets. But the friends will feed you for free.

And another: His grandmother went against his father's advice and sent an antique medallion out for repair. It came back with a copper clip substituted for the gold one, and his father was gleefully vindicated. He quoted a couplet that the boy then committed to memory:

> Don't believe your friends—they lie.
> Don't you pluck the flowers—they die.

Onstage young Malakhov had fallen in with a gang of thugs led by a street-wise boss who was something else by day: an auxiliary policeman and a model factory worker whose picture was up there on the bulletin board as a *peredovik,* a star laborer. He and the gang had taught the boy threateningly how to steal coins from public phones.

"Who is guilty?" asked a slovenly cop in an ill-fitting uniform. "Unfortunately they come to us too late. Who is guilty? Family, street, school, I don't know. I don't want to know. We're not guilty."

Finally the journalist-narrator arranged to have Malakhov released on parole. But the boy was unsure about wanting to leave prison. "If they let you out," the journalist wanted to know, "would you change your life?"

The boy could not answer. Were the stealing, the corruption still going on outside? he asked. "Out there, is it like it was before?" And on that raw question the play ended.

In the lobby, a woman who headed one school's parents' committee was observing with sorrow and frustration that neither the students nor the parents who needed this play and this discussion had attended, nor did such parents ever appear at committee meetings where delinquency was discussed. A teacher from Middle School No. 521 chided the play's producer, who was also up front, for muting the issue of personal responsibility. "It would seem everyone's to blame except Malakhov," she complained.

Another woman supported her. "I also objected on the personal responsibility issue. You are making Malakhov an orphan. He can take responsibility for his actions. Our young people who see this are taught to think that anyone but they themselves is to blame for their actions. The theater must teach some personal responsibility." The producer replied with the results of an interesting survey. After seeing the play, most adults believed that teenagers would think Malakhov innocent; in fact, however, 90 percent of the teenagers saw him as guilty.

The debate lurched on. A girl suggested that there was "insufficient communication between teachers and parents." A teacher contended that children were presented with too easy a version of life, before they entered it. A well-dressed man who seemed accustomed to prosperous authority—perhaps a party official—argued that some parents cared for their children only physically, buying them clothes and feeding them, with "no spiritual upbringing."

"Our teenagers don't encounter any harsh sides of life," he declared, going on at some length in the manner of a man who was used to being listened to. He criticized the play for presenting teenagers so negatively. "Malakhovs are statistically isolated cases in our society," he said, and here the crowd erupted into hoots of derisive laughter. People looked at him with disgust for spoiling the precious candor of the evening.

Another well-dressed man tried to pick up the theme. "It is an anomalous case in our society." But a group of mothers from a parents' committee overwhelmed him with shouts.

"It only seems so to you," a woman yelled, as if to say that he was too far above reality to see it.

"You don't understand anything at all," another declared.

And finally, as the talk moved into a search for the causes of such troubles, a young woman spoke up emotionally. "Just look around in trolleys and buses," she said. "We have become indifferent to each other."

So after the initial inhibitions, the topic of crime touched nerves of defensiveness and concern, dividing Muscovites approximately as it would have divided New Yorkers on the appropriate remedies and the apportionment of blame. The play was not easy to stage, for teachers and party officials objected strongly to its implication for young people that responsibility for juvenile crime lay less with the criminals than with the adult world. Nor was the ideological background conducive to its production, for in Marxist-Leninist doctrine the social causes of crime—namely, poverty and exploitation—will have been removed as society progresses toward communism. Here a conflict emerges between collectivism—in which an individual's behavior is somehow everyone's pride and everyone's fault—and the conservatism of Soviet rule, which parallels American conservatism in its tendency to hold the criminal responsible outside the context of societal defects. In the official Soviet lexicon, crime is an alien disease not at all integral to the system's failures, but the residue of "bourgeois culture," the perverse act of those infected by the feverish lust for material gain. Of course, those involved in trying to understand the growing incidence of Soviet juvenile delinquency see far beneath that placard logic and grapple in anguish and bewilderment amid the complexities. The play *Stop Malakhov!* won the support of the police and the Komsomol; the Ministry of Internal Affairs, which oversees the police, arranged the surveys of sample audiences that revealed 90 percent of the teenagers judging Malakhov guilty, and that carried the issue with the party.

That such a production could be staged at the Young Spectator's Theater, followed by such open discussions after each performance, testified to the rising worry among officials and ordinary citizens. Crime statistics are a state secret, I was informed by the Ministry of Internal Affairs after weeks of unsuccessful attempts to get an interview there. News items on violent crime are kept off television. General-circulation newspapers never report crimes when they occur, only selected cases after they have been solved, when some moral point or sociological analysis can be made. When *Izvestia* learned about the rape of a teenage girl by ten boys, a journalist there told me, the information was not published but was turned over to the party and the police for investigation. The instinct is to protect the society's image, and the rationale is to avoid publicity that could make the violence contagious. Similarly, film is usually purged of criminal violence; only the noble violence of war is acceptable. "Television and film are the most powerful means of influencing wide audiences," I was told by Aleksei Kapler, secretary of the Union of Cinematographers, "and therefore, it would be impossible to show endlessly violent films on television and not expect that they would influence, especially a youthful audience. The human being has good and evil, and depending on what the human being is taught, what this human being is shown on the screen, the evil aspects in him can be diminished and destroyed—or raised."

The man from *Izvestia* had another angle of insight. "If we wrote about crime in Moscow every day," he said, "there would be as much fear as there is in New York." And perhaps justifiably, for after months of conversations and interviews with many, varied Russians, and after culling law journals, teachers' magazines, and other specialized publications, I assembled a pretty gruesome picture of murders, rapes, beatings, muggings, burglaries, and other crime, much of it the work of boys and girls from fourteen to eighteen. Many are school dropouts with jobs and with nothing to do in the evenings except drink heavily and roam in packs that are sometimes led by older youths with prior convictions. Others attend school and lead outwardly normal lives; their crimes shock teachers, parents, and friends.

New York may suffer from exaggerated fear, but Moscow's ill is a sense of security so false that it can be dangerous. When a boy of fourteen, walking alone down a Moscow street, was approached by four or five youths his own age asking for money, he thought they were joking. In his innocence he smiled and tried to walk past, one of his friends told me. Suddenly a youth wearing homemade brass knuckles attacked, beating him so badly around the head that he was out of school for a month. Similarly, a young woman student, alone in Moscow's large, wooded Sokolniki Park, naïvely approached a man for directions to the subway. It was late afternoon, and the park was practically deserted. The man attacked her, tried to rape her, and beat her severely.

As in other aspects of Soviet life, information about crime is usually gained firsthand and passed by word of mouth, generating rumors and lore about safe and unsafe districts and practices. Well-educated Muscovites regard working-class neighborhoods, such as Taganka and Chertanovo on the city's south side, as dangerous because of heavy drinking that leads to violence. How much of this is an accurate assessment and how much class prejudice is difficult to discern. On the north of Moscow the Marina Roshcha district is called the bandits' nest, and nearby Timiryazev Park is known as an ideal place for getting beaten up and robbed; after dark, it is as forbidding and as empty as Central Park at night. A teenage girl told me that she avoided one neighborhood where illegal gambling houses are operated. "If you walk through there, you could get killed," she said. In Kiev a visiting American was advised by his Soviet guide to stay out of a major park because a woman had recently been murdered there. A policeman who was asked about the report said that the woman was still alive.

Many Russians take precautions. A young Muscovite, once followed into her apartment house by a tough in his twenties, who cornered her in a corridor and stole her bracelet, now takes off all visible jewelry when riding the bus at night, just to avoid attracting attention. With considerable anxiety one evening, she advised her teenage sister to make sure anyone taking her home saw her all the way into the building's elevator before leaving. Since Debby and I were about to give her a ride, we were given the lecture as well, and the big sister's final, worried farewell to us was: "Don't forget to take her into the elevator!" Another woman, with a husband and a small daughter, chose to live in a cramped three-room apartment upstairs rather than a more spacious four-room flat on the ground floor because she feared vandalism and burglary by young construction workers, ethnic Kazakhs from Central Asia, housed in a nearby dormitory. A third woman, who worked for the police, expressed amazement when moving into a ground-floor apartment that the windows had no bars.

The sketchy statistical picture available suggests a strong correlation between violence and socioeconomic level. The higher the vocational skills, the lower the incidence of crime, a leading sociological journal reported, citing the example of construction workers, whose crime rate was ten times that of technicians in the machine-building industry.* A deputy prosecutor general, Sergei Gusev, wrote that children of parents with a secondary or higher education were only half as likely to break the law as those whose parents had dropped out after elementary school. About 70 to 80 percent of juvenile offenders came from problem homes, he said, and although parental difficulties cut across socioeconomic lines, he argued that they were exacerbated in families with low educational levels. School dropouts, who tended to come from families in the lower strata, had a crime rate twenty-four times the incidence of

*Sotsiologicheskiye Issledovaniya, No. 3 (1977).

those still in school, Gusev reported.* An official of a juvenile punitive colony confirmed this with his impression, conveyed to a Soviet interviewer, that many of his wards had been dropouts without jobs.

Schools contribute to the syndrome by encouraging difficult, misbehaving youngsters to leave after eighth grade. The effect is to throw them onto the street, for in these early teenage years they happen to encounter a gap in Soviet society's structure and supervision. Those under sixteen may hold only part-time, not full-time jobs, according to the child labor laws. Both parents usually work, and increased divorce, urbanization, and geographical mobility have whittled away the extended family, raising the likelihood that no grandparents or other adult relatives are present during the working day. The elaborate Pioneer palaces and hobby centers cater mainly to younger children; most adolescents, especially those who do not fit into the matrix of model scholarship and political activity, find little attraction there. So at least in the evenings, and often during daytime as well, many teenagers have long, idle hours to hang around corridors and courtyards and street corners.

Some of them coalesce into groups and packs and gangs that roam outside their neighborhoods and prey on people alone, harassing women, frightening the elderly, beating, stealing, sometimes murdering. There is little gun problem in the Soviet Union; the laws are strict. No pistols or rifles are sold. Only shotguns can be purchased, and for this one needs to be a member of a hunting club and to have explicit permission from the Minister of Internal Affairs to buy the weapon. To hunt, permission from the local authorities is needed each time, for each location. So the gangs manufacture long knives and zip guns.

They operate in a milieu of drug addiction and heavy drinking, the former a youthful innovation, the latter learned from the adult world, where drunkenness is a socially approved method of entertainment and escape. Narcotics is an elusive ill, more deeply buried than in the West. An addict, twenty-three, once told Dr. Iosif Ahs that he had been injecting himself with morphine and another opium-based drug for four or five years and that he personally knew about 500 similar users in Moscow. He estimated Moscow's total

*Literaturnaya Gazeta (July 13, 1977).

number of addicts at 20,000, though there was no way to check his guess. Dr. Ahs accepted it as reasonable; he remembered some years earlier being approached in a hospital by two teenagers trying to buy tincture of opium. They showed him a syringe in a dirty rag and indicated that their regular sources were unscrupulous doctors and other hospital and pharmacy personnel. An émigré to Israel contended that vast acres of opium poppies were grown on state farms in Byelorussia, the southern Ukraine, and the Caucasus for medicinal purposes, but that much of the yield went to the black market. Young "tourists" camped in the fields during harvest time each year and made off with large quantities of the sap.

There is nothing surreptitious about drinking, however. Alcohol is the national indulgence, despite the relatively high price the state charges. The best vodka runs the equivalent of over $15 a liter, which is more than a day's work at the average industrial wage. Cognac is higher, and wine not much cheaper. Yet no Russian table, at home or in a restaurant, looks like fun unless it is littered with bottles and awash in alcoholic conviviality. The normal American is no match for this, and if we were in a drinking bout with the Russians instead of an arms race, we'd have run up the white flag long ago.

Alone one evening in Murmansk, I found a seat at a crowded table in a fish place called the Gifts of the Sea Restaurant, where a loud band was pounding away and the small dance floor was filled with seamen from freighters and trawlers, jammed awkwardly against graceless, stout women of indeterminate age. I had intended to eat and go to a dull movie to practice my Russian, but I hadn't even had a glance at the menu when a good shot of cognac appeared in my glass, poured deftly from a bottle wielded by a cheery fellow at the end of the table. There were two other men and three women, and they all raised their glasses in a toast of welcome. They gulped. I sipped daintily. They looked disappointed. We got talking—shouting, over the music—and the men introduced themselves as seamen, the women as wives of friends who were at sea. "To those at sea," declared the chief pourer, a ship's navigator, raising his glass and gazing off in a manner of distant seriousness. The laughter died away. He threw the raspy cognac down his gullet. I sipped again. "David," the navigator admonished. "On such a toast, to those at sea, you must drink to the bottom." He seemed a bit hurt. I certainly didn't want to be rude. I tipped the glass and swallowed it all, burning. And instantly the glass was full again. There were a good many toasts "to those at sea" that evening as the men had a good time with their friends' wives and grew progressively blurry, both in my vision and in their behavior. They bumped around from table to table, filling each other's glasses and shouting jokes over the music. I tried to work my way gradually through a glass of cognac and then, while it was empty, make a break for it—not to insult—but the glass never quite seemed to get empty. The chief pourer was always pouring. By the time the band packed up and the waitresses started to boot us all out, the navigator had thrown up all over the floor ("It happens," one of the women said apologetically) and my hands, feet, and lips were numb. I made it back to my hotel, not my movie.

Further testimony to American inadequacy came when a group of correspondents, finding ourselves with a few hours' layover in the Siberian airport of Tyumen, ordered some food and drink from the hefty Aeroflot women, who were intrigued by suddenly having a bunch of fifteen Americans in such a remote spot. "How many bottles of vodka?" one asked. We consulted and decided that two would be fine. Two? The women were immobile with disbelief. "Only two bottles for fifteen men?" one crowed. And they went off clucking and chuckling and shaking their heads in laughter.

I once accompanied a large contingent of American businessmen on a visit to the giant Kamaz truck plant, about 700 miles east of Moscow, built mostly by Western and Japanese technology. After the grand tour Soviet officials had the group to a large banquet replete with the usual toasts to peace, friendship, and good trade relations. (This was well before the invasion of Afghanistan and the discovery that the plant had, predictably, turned to making army trucks and tank engines.) A thin man from the United States Commerce Department, sitting across from me, had served for some years in Bulgaria and knew the drinking customs well. So dutifully emptied his glass on each toast, then turned it upside down on the back of his hand to see if any moisture was left. There always was, of course, in which case he felt himself obliged to down another shot. By the time his turn for a toast came he had performed the ritual so often that he stood in a rosy glow of graciousness, lifted his glass, and slurred loudly to his Soviet hosts: "As the senior representative of the Commerce Department [snicker], and the only one [chortle], I would like to drink to improved trade relations [pause for effect] between the United States [pause for more effect] and Bulgaria." He sat down, pleased with himself. The wave of guffaws and whoops of laughter, all from the American contingent, hit him like ice water, and a most bewildered look came over the poor man's face. The Soviet officials at the head table, who got an accurate simultaneous translation, did not know how they were supposed to react to this warm wish for American trade with Bulgaria, so they just sat there blankly.

Alcohol is a release, an escape, and its popularity is usually attributed by reflective Russians to the hardships of daily life. Certainly Soviet cities undergo a transformation between day and night. By late afternoon the steady grey geometry of movement along the sidewalks has begun to decay into the curves and slants of men weaving out of bars, red-nosed, friendly, and rude, staggering and muttering onto buses and trolley cars. By darkness there are stiff and crumpled figures in parks and doorways. The restaurants are packed and jolly. In one near the Bolshoi Theater, a tableful of merrymakers was drinking and singing with such abandon that one young man finally jumped up and did perfect cartwheels across the dance floor. The whole place cheered. In the working-class Siberian city of Ulan-Ude, near Lake Baikal, rough drinking brought intensive police patrols out at night; detachments of policemen were stationed outside bars.

In the medium of alcohol, violent crime flourishes. Legally anyone sixteen or older can buy vodka, cognac, champagne, wine, and the like, and in the packs of youths who congregate in idle hours, the liquor is often shared by the sixteen-year-olds with those of fifteen, fourteen, and thirteen. At the age of fourteen Aleksandr Mikhailov dropped out of school and began to hang around the streets and staircases of his neighborhood in Gorky, 250 miles east of Moscow. He had no job and practically no relationship with his parents. They receded into the background of his world. The most important figure for him became another boy who taught him how to burglarize kiosks and streetcar coin boxes and stores. The money went for liquor, according to the Soviet paper that described his case. In a Moscow movie theater, I once saw a short documentary on child abuse that opened with a shot of ragged, dirty kids vandalizing railroad cars, then shifted to a small girl who, the narrator explained, had run away from home and asked the police for protection against her mother. "She drinks vodka," said the girl. Officials contend that about 80 percent of all murders are committed in the midst of drunkenness and usually against relatives, friends, or neighbors. One American visitor to a juvenile reformatory near Moscow met a boy of fifteen who said that he and some other boys had beaten his mother to death while they were drunk because she had refused to give them money. The magazine *Ogonyok* reported a sordid murder of a drunken father by a son, fourteen. The father, Viktor Fedotov of the town of Uglovka, was an alcoholic and an ex-convict who beat his wife to the point where the boy, Igor, and his mother sometimes had to spend the night in the hall or with a neighbor. Once Igor came home to find his father at the table drinking vodka again, and the boy stabbed the man in the chest.

Rapid urbanization across the country has brought a breakdown of family and social ties, Soviet criminologists believe, magnifying the impact of peer pressure on young people. As industrial towns have mushroomed into cities, and cities have spread outward in forests of prefabricated high-rises, urban life has corroded the old values and the traditional, stabilizing relationships of the village. Divorce rates are high; family control is weak. Newly arrived urban dwellers, termed "migrants" by one law journal, are regarded as more vulnerable than native residents to the anonymity and disorientation of city life. "Deformed or altogether disintegrated family and kinship ties are much more common among migrants than among people who have always lived in the city," said the journal, *Sovietskoye Gosudarstvo i Pravo.* "A special kind of 'vacuum' forms around such individuals and is often filled by people whose influence is very harmful." A sample of lawbreakers showed that twice as many new arrivals as longtime residents spent their free time with ex-convicts, and that the percentage of offenders was higher among new residents than among old. The journal said:

> As a rule, the cultural level of these people is low, their needs are primitive, and their interests are restricted to their immediate environment. Only 15 percent of all urban couples with children live with any of their parents. Since in nuclear families the parents both work, as a rule, and there are no other

adult relatives in the family, teenagers and young people often spend a good part of the day on their own. This is a contributing factor in the higher level of juvenile crime in cities as compared to rural localities.

Family disruption, and the severe alienation between children and parents, have become a focus of immense concern for Soviet psychologists and sociologists. A study of students at Tartu University in Estonia found 75 percent feeling that they had unsatisfactory relationships with their fathers, and 60 percent with their mothers. Only 10 percent said they felt they had real emotional contact with their parents. The family's influence on crime patterns has been extensively documented. "Ten times the number of juvenile delinquents come from an atmosphere of vulgarity or heavy drinking as from a normal environment," one criminologist said. As an example, *Izvestia* cited the case of Sergei Shubnikov, a schoolboy with an alcoholic mother, who was sentenced to two years in a reformatory for hooliganism and brawling, was released in an amnesty three months later, then started drinking and finally led a band of teenagers in an assault on a nineteen-year-old stranger, who died.

Izvestia used the incident to argue for sterner punishment, part of a debate that parallels the American dispute between those who favor social remedies and those "law and order" advocates who push for stiffer prison sentences as deterrents. Professional journals for teachers, jurists, and sociologists are full of the various points of view, and the mass-circulation newspapers are quick to publish hard-liners' horror stories. In Nizhnekamsk, for instance, the police did nothing but warn two boys, fifteen and sixteen, who beat a classmate. A few days later the same youths murdered him. No action was taken when two eighth-grade boys repeatedly threatened a ninth-grade girl. Finally the girl's body was found, hacked and mutilated. In Petrozavodsk a twenty-two-year-old with four previous convictions committed a rape and murder, for which he received only a fifteen-year sentence. "Humaneness toward criminals," a Leningrad man wrote indignantly, "leads to cruelty toward their victims."

One law professor told a visiting American lawyer that about 3 percent of those eligible for the death penalty were actually executed. Public examples are usually made of them, as in the instance of a Moscow factory worker who was put before the firing squad for the rape and murder of a twelve-year-old girl. One case that received no publicity, however, involved ten policemen who operated a ring of car thieves. According to a psychiatrist who examined the officers before trial and who then told the story to a Western diplomat, the policemen would pull cars over on the outskirts of Moscow, murder the drivers, and steal the vehicles. In the summer of 1977, twenty-eight cars disappeared between the capital and Sheremetyevo International Airport. Some of the policemen were executed; others received long prison sentences.

Imprisoning young people exacerbates problems, some specialists believe; one wrote of prisons as "universities of crime." Recidivism accounts for a high proportion of crime—one source put it at 23 percent, but other estimates are higher—and criminologists have written of the damage imprisonment does to the structure of family and other relationships that can offer support once a prisoner is released. Furthermore, in the judicial system, where rules of evidence are lax and police and prosecutor powerful, "there are many mistakes," said a woman attorney who defends juveniles. An accusation of rape, she explained, easily gets a conviction, "even if a girl is known as loose and even if she admits taking off her clothes," the lawyer said. "If she claims she didn't want intercourse, then the boy is guilty." The sentence is eight to ten years if the convicted is under eighteen, and fifteen years for adults. "By and large, victims want heavy sentences and often get them," she said, adding that some improvement in the system's accuracy had been brought by allowing the accused, if he is a minor, to consult a lawyer before the police investigation has ended. For adults, there is no defense attorney until the police have extracted all confessions, compiled all evidence, and are ready to go to court.

It was in court, during the trial of those three teenagers who had stolen some things of ours, that I saw how inadequate the elaborate organization of Soviet society had been in monitoring and controlling the activities of its young people. The boys, sixteen, seventeen, and eighteen, had pleaded guilty to four burglaries: They had stolen the car of the local soccer coach in Brest, on the border with Poland. They had taken the radio out of a truck in the fleet of a state cargo agency, Sovtransavto. They had broken into a Soviet army warehouse on a firing range and had stolen some electronic equipment associated with targeting. And they had taken about $1,000 worth of our possessions from a moving van passing through Brest. It seemed an illness with these boys, for they stole, fiddled with the stereos and radios and other electronic stuff, then grew afraid of having the equipment and burned some of it or dumped it in the river. Their guilty pleas notwithstanding, the trial was held to search for the causes of their delinquency and to determine sentence.

The proceeding was open and free-flowing, not bound at all by the rules of evidence, the jousting between prosecution and defense, that grow out of the protection of individual rights in American courts. This People's Court, with a judge and two lay jurors sitting in high-backed black leather chairs beneath a stark drawing of a severe Lenin, provided defendants, parents, and victims the opportunity to raise objections and question witnesses, and it heard from a variety of teachers, employers, and others who knew the boys and could, presumably, have given some insight into their problems.

"Can you explain why you did it?" the judge asked the seventeen-year-old, Viktor Serguts, a thin boy with a hangdog look. "Maybe you are fond of radio and television equipment? You used some part of it?"

"No," said the boy sullenly.

"Why did you take it?"

"I don't know."

"Why did you have to take it if you just destroyed it and burned it?"

"I don't know."

His defense attorney, a slender, stylish, and sharp-eyed woman, took over the questioning. "Were you going to use it for yourself or not?"

"No."

"Then why did you take it?"

"Just because of curiosity and stupidity. I'm not going to do anything of the kind again." He looked at the floor.

"What is your hobby?"

"Helping my mother. Looking after my mother." There were a few smirks from some of his friends, sitting in the back rows.

The eighteen-year-old, Vladimir Poplavsky, was subjected to a series of rhetorical questions from the judge. "I was just interested in radio receivers," the young man said.

"Did you ask your father for money to buy one?"

"No."

"Why did you take to stealing? Why didn't you ask your parents for funds? Did your father teach you how to steal things from trucks? Why did you have to bring them here to blush before all the people? You are the oldest among them—why didn't you stop them? Why?"

"I don't know."

"Did they teach you in school to deny your conscience? Did your parents teach you that? Where did you hide your conscience? You, as a grown-up person, should have a conscience and obey it. You have your whole life before you, but first of all you must be honest before society."

The parents were astonished, ashamed, and fairly unenlightening. Aleksandr Fomin, forty-three but looking like an old man, a worker at the Brest power station, had the watery eyes of a drinker. His son, Anatoly, was the sixteen-year-old. "I was very surprised," said the father. "I never thought my son would dare to do such unseemly things." His friends were nice boys, it seemed, he had pulled his grades up in school, had helped around the house, had bought a camera and photographic paper and radio parts with money his father had given him. Occasionally he would come home late at night, after his father was asleep. The next day he would get "his due, morally and physically," for the lateness, the father said. But the man was truly bewildered. "I don't even know what he was lacking. He had enough clothes. We bought him what he needed. It turns out now that he was going around with bad boys, and he himself turned into a bad one. I realize now that he was lying, deceiving me."

When Nadezhda Serguts, a stout postwoman with glasses, took the stand to answer for her son Viktor, the judge asked her how she explained his behavior. "He must be just a fool," she said, "because he has everything—a camera, a bicycle, his own horse. One cannot say he lacks anything. Now he is studying fairly well at evening school. When he returned late at night, he usually said he had additional lessons or exams."

This was the theme: no material deficiencies to explain the crimes; no craving for unobtainable gadgets. The trial was a kind of pageant in which society reassured itself that its Marxist-Leninist ideals had not been forsaken. But its multiple institutions had also failed to spot these wayward youngsters. Tatyana Krukova, a hefty blonde in a blue sweater who served as secretary of the local commission on juvenile delinquency, testified that the boys had never come to the commission's attention before these incidents. The commission, under the city party committee, comprises schoolteachers, trade union officials, and other upstanding citizens. It hears cases and can send minors to reformatories without trials. The police division on youth, known as the juvenile room or juvenile department, did not have them registered, although it is supposed to watch out for potential delinquents. This is a general difficulty. T. Firsova, head of the juvenile division of the Moscow prosecutor's office, wrote that only one-third of all teenage criminals were on the books before their crimes, that police agencies made only perfunctory inquiries into the causes of crime, that communications between the police and prosecutor's office and among police precincts were poor, that health agencies failed to notify the police about teenage alcoholism or drug addiction, and that some vocational boarding schools tolerate frequent class cutting and lax supervision, leaving teenagers on their own.

Those who should be alert are usually shocked. Inessa Aksyonovich, a tall, motherly Russian literature teacher in School No. 4, was crushed. She had taught Anatoly Fomin since fourth grade and knew him as a good Pioneer leader. "Now he doesn't write very grammatically," she conceded, "but as for bad discipline, one could never see this in his behavior. This was more painful for me than even for Anatoly himself. I could never say anything bad about him." The boys in his Komsomol unit, who had apparently never noticed that he was going astray, took the appropriately righteous attitude, denounced him for his crimes, and expelled him from Komsomol. "At the same time," the teacher explained, "they asked me during a recent Komsomol meeting at school to ask the court to take into account that he repented fully. The whole class asked to take him as custodian."

The prosecutor questioned her closely about the sincerity of his repentance. She replied that he had asked whether he would ever become a member of Komsomol again. She speculated that he had been too afraid of her and of his parents to talk openly about his problems.

"Maybe you were too strict with him," said the prosecutor.

"It is necessary sometimes to be strict," she answered.

"But you also have to be humane," the prosecutor declared. "Please tell the collective that you cannot solve every problem by strictness alone."

And so it went. The court accepted a certain sort of plea bargaining. The judge and prosecutor heard the boys testify, apparently under instruction, that they had broken the padlock on the back of the moving van with their bare hands, just twisting it slightly until it came off. This absurd story was left unchallenged, and the prosecutor later explained to me quietly that the use of tools for a break-in constituted a violation of a more serious article of the criminal code, carrying heavier punishment. He accepted the fiction to avoid the more serious charge. The boys received suspended sentences.

Higher authorities probably do not know the full extent of juvenile crime. As a society that thrives on good news, the Soviet Union is organized to discourage negative reporting, even within official ranks. The entire civilian hierarchy works on the same instincts as every army, where no subordinate is anxious to tell his superiors about problems. The result is a pacific ignorance at upper levels.

Among those who conceal data to avoid bringing criticism on themselves are schoolteachers and principals. In Irkutsk, after two boys had raped a girl, the high school's principal and teachers tried to hush up the crime, a teachers' journal reported, dismissing it as a "childish prank" and pleading with the victim and her parents to drop charges. In Moscow, a special task force on juvenile crime in the Chertanovo neighborhood—a district of new high-rises on the south side—found that whereas a school's administrators had records of fifteen to twenty problem students, who had committed acts of violence, theft, prostitution, and the like, the juvenile section of the 130th Police Precinct had only five to eight registered. It turned out that principals avoided reporting all crimes so that their schools would not be listed as performing poorly. Local police commanders also suppressed statistics, the task force found. "If I were to send in to the city militia headquarters the genuine figures about juvenile crime in my district," the commander of the 130th was quoted as saying, "I would not last a day in my job. This is what they all do; I am not the only one. Juvenile crime is a scourge in Moscow and in other cities as well." Even the head of the Central Committee's schools department, S. P. Trapeznikov, said he couldn't get crime figures.

The work of the task force was revealed by one of its members, a party functionary who later emigrated to Israel and gave details to a Tel Aviv organization, the Research Center for Prisons, Psychoprisons, and Forced Labor Concentration Camps of the USSR. The report then found its way into my hands through a Western embassy in Moscow. The task force, created by the district party committee with the approval of the Central Committee, toured apartments and questioned parents, young couples, and other residents, compiling a list of bizarre crimes, both concealed and recorded, that were related to parent-child incest, extreme and hidden poverty, and other social ills never openly discussed.

While one thirteen-year-old girl's mother was in prison, the girl had an affair with her stepfather and became furiously jealous when she learned that he had taken up with her girlfriend. She tried to slash her stepfather's throat. Word of the attack was suppressed by the principal of School No. 857, identified as Tatyana Fedorovna Ilina, "who wanted to keep down the figures of problem children in her school," the report said. "The girl's stepfather agreed to keep quiet about the matter since he, for his part, did not want to be tried for statutory rape." Another concealed crime involved a boy, thirteen, from a poor family. Both parents were invalids, who received an inadequate pension of 60 rubles a month. The boy was hungry. When he saw an old woman sprinkling pieces of bread around for birds, "he shooed the birds off and started gathering up the pieces of the loaf. The neighbor rushed at him with a stick, which he tore from her; he started beating her savagely, causing her severe injuries."

The task force also reported a few sadistic crimes that did bring in the police. One gang of boys, fourteen and fifteen, had sharpened umbrella points into long stilettos. "At night they would systematically attack lone passersby in the street. Shouting and yelling, they would rush on the totally unsuspecting pedestrian, and the whole group would thrust their stilettos at him and immediately pull them back, run away, and leave the murdered or badly injured victim unconscious on the ground. When they were arrested and charged with murder, these schoolchildren had no explanation for their savagery and could only say that they had nothing to do at home in the evenings." In another case that begins to defy credibility, a seventeen-year-old got into a struggle with his mother, a party member, who was fighting his infatuation with Western fashions, especially jeans and long hair. When the boy was asleep one night, the mother cut his hair short. In the morning they argued angrily as the son went off to school. "That evening he arrived home with a group of friends, and they asked the mother to make tea for them. When the water was boiling, the son and his friends tied up the mother and poured the whole teapot of boiling water down her throat. She died." The youths were charged with murder.

Sexual promiscuity and prostitution were also documented by the task force, which found girls from twelve to fifteen laughing at others who were inexperienced. "They gather in homes where all the children dance naked and then copulate indiscriminately. In their later teens, girls out of school get jobs at the Central Post Office, which turns into a red-light district at quitting time, as they linger coming out of work, picked up by men who pay them with cash and scarce goods. 'Boredom' was the reason one part-time prostitute gave for her activity. 'And on my pay I can't afford the theater and especially restaurants, and of course there is no money for new clothes, for stockings, for shoes. The men who invite us give us perfume, imported stockings, or take us to restaurants where we can have a good time.' "

According to the task force member, the group's findings were not welcomed at higher levels. Trapeznikov, head of the Central Committee's schools department, called the picture exaggerated, rejected any relationship between crime and poverty, and branded the report "anti-Soviet." Its recommendations, which included additional educators to supervise children after school hours, revised educational methods to emphasize moral and spiritual upbringing as well as physical, the transfer of children from alcoholic homes to boarding schools, and more material aid for the poor, were impossible to implement, he said, without such increases in the Education Ministry's budget as to impair the nation's defenses.

* * *

Here, at the junction of suffering and indifference, exists the great vacuum of Soviet society. Where social conscience should stand, a void; where outrage should run, a drifting insensitivity. The notion of social injustice is so contrived and politicized—the exploitation of the proletariat by the bourgeoisie (in capitalist countries only), the persecution of Communists in Latin America and the United States, the oppression of blacks in America, the neocolonialization of the poor countries by the latter-day imperialists, the massive spending on arms (again, only in the West)—that it dazzles and blinds to the more tangible wrongs at home. Those Komsomol kids at Moscow's Central Pioneer Palace, who were so fluent in their denunciations of my society and so oblivious to the ills of their own, seemed honestly unaware of what surrounded them close at hand. At least, in their faces, I could discern no yearning to speak out, no tension between candor and caution. Their vision seemed truly impaired.

Once, in the pedestrian underpass that runs beneath Marx Prospekt and Gorky Street near Red Square, a man sat begging. He was missing a leg. A policeman was trying to get him to move along. Among the crisscrossing currents of passersby was a young American woman, an exchange student, who paused, took a 50-kopeck piece from her purse, and placed it next to him on the floor. But before he could pick it up, the policeman stepped on the coin with a heavy boot, then kicked it away. As the beggar scrambled for it along the concrete passageway, the policeman kicked him, too, trying to get him up on his one good leg.

In a meat line, a Russian friend noted how little sympathy there was for the hard-driven collective farmers who came from the country villages to stand also, to buy a week's provisions for their large families. A well-fed woman, a Muscovite, muttered crossly when a weathered farmer bought forty or fifty pounds of meat, cursing him for feeding off Moscow's supplies. If they'd work harder, she snarled, they'd have meat of their own.

Speaking of Russians' general reactions to social injustice, a Moscow pediatrician quipped, "I never saw a case of outrage." The virtue of acquiescence has even worked its way into slang: to demand your rights is to *kachat prava,* to swing your rights around, to flaunt them, to rock the boat. It is regarded as naïve, foolish, and a guarantee of a worse fate. The Chertanovo neighborhood's task force on crime uncovered a good deal of hidden poverty on its tours of apartments. Pensioners with large families received monthly stipends so small they did not cover the cost of food. Parents spent their wages on vodka, leaving vagrant children, who were beaten at home and "preferred to sleep under the stairways of houses, settling down by the central heating pipes." But the task force found no concern among most of the neighbors. The party secretary of a copper-smelting works, Valentin Yakovlevich Terekhin, "did not react at all to the fact that next door to his well-fed and provisioned family were huddled a blind mother and her three children who often went without eating," according to the émigré's report. "There was no furniture except an old garden bench, and the whole family slept on old clothes on the floor." Terekhin's reaction to all this was: "But how can I personally do anything about it?"

Since charity was unnecessary in the Soviet Union, it was not permitted until Gorbachev. Before he began to allow it, no church could give alms to the poor; no private groups of concerned citizens could organize to dispense aid. The only incidence of charity I encountered was a fund for families of prisoners—both political and common criminals—that Aleksandr Ginzburg operated clandestinely with Solzhenitsyn's royalties and Sakharov's Nobel Peace Prize. He helped relatives pay for plane and train tickets to Siberian labor camps for visits; he helped them buy winter clothes and packages of food for their husbands, sons, brothers, fathers in the camps. For this he was arrested and imprisoned, then released from jail and expelled from the Soviet Union during a prisoner exchange in 1979. Yelena Bonner and others took over administering the fund. Ordinary Russians had a vague sense that there was something wrong in this, that Ginzburg deserved to be prosecuted, that charity was somehow a statement of the state's inadequacy, the system's inability to provide.

The vacuum of social consciousness is part of a broader emptiness. Those Russians who think with penetration about what is happening to their country and are old enough to remember when communism was a vital idea, holding hope, see at the foundations of the nation's ills a deep disillusionment. The sense of motion is gone; the future is blank. Belief has waned into melancholy. Classroom hypocrisy has become a hallmark of stability. And the crime that rules some lives, they feel, springs from this emptiness. "You have it because of abundance," a writer said to me, "we because of scarcity. The whole society steals because of scarcity." He did not mean only the scarcity of goods. An American professor, teaching for a semester in Moscow, contrasted American students of the sixties to Soviet students of the seventies. In California, he recalled, "They were angry, passionate, out to change the world." At Moscow State University, he said, "I feel like I'm at a divinity school of the holy order."

How thoroughly external values evaporate under pressures by peers was apparent in the case of a gang of eighth-grade girls who beat Larisa Panteleyeva so severely she had to be hospitalized. About twenty boys stood by watching, cheering. "Kick her! Kick her!" one boy yelled. And the girls kicked her. The weekly *Literaturnaya Gazeta,* which examined the crime in a lengthy two-part series called "The Lesson," concealed the motive: According to a professional familiar with the case, Larisa was attacked because she had wanted to drop out of group sex that had been taking place, and the girls were afraid she would tell on them. The reader gets no hint of this. But the message, the lesson, is there in a scene after the beating. Everyone left the spot where it occurred, then decided to come back for one more look. Larisa was gone. "They stood in silence, feeling lost and empty," the paper wrote. A girl addressed the boys reproachfully: "What a bunch, you! Watched us just like in a zoo."

"We watched because you were beating," explained a boy.

"And we were beating," replied a girl, "because you were watching."

My friend who blamed scarcity had a further observation, one that struck a chord in many Russians. "There are no heroes," he said. "Who is your hero?" he asked his son, fourteen. The boy shrugged in silence. "You see? No heroes, just as in the West."

FIVE

Hammers, Sickles, Icons, and Flags

Nobody believes in anything.

—Katya Polikanov, seventeen
Moscow, 1978

Communism

The hammer and sickle are everywhere, emblazoned on coins and policemen's caps, worked into the decor of railroad cars and concert halls. For an American new to Moscow, the emblem stirs a secret dread planted long ago; each encounter is a pulse of tension. For a Russian longing to believe, it stirs a warming pride rooted in the future; the symbol blends the greatness of the nation and the movement.

If it were not everywhere, the emblem of the hammer and sickle would not numb with familiarity as it does. The crowds on Gorky Street and Kalinin Prospekt would notice it jingling in their pockets and looming over them from posters. They would feel something more than they do when they gaze absently at a streetlight or a phone booth. The symbol is part of them, yet the emotion no longer comes with spontaneity; it requires a measure of concentration to evoke the exhilarating vision of a new order.

In the soft, lingering summer dusks of Moscow, strollers amble through Red Square, past the lighted Kremlin walls, enveloped in the gentleness of relaxed conversations. The sharp, martial edges are blurred. The images of cold threat and comfortable casualness overlap, screening out each other, mixing in curious disharmony. Red Square. Lovers walking hand in hand.

Toward the hour, people drift to the austere red-granite Lenin Mausoleum to watch the changing of the guard. Three soldiers goose-step silently down a long walkway. They make a crisp left face in front of the tomb. Discordant, melancholy bells begin to chime in the clock tower high above the square. The new guards are in place; the old goose-step away into the evening. The murmur of soft conversations is heard again as the strollers move off across the cobblestones.

Twice a year, on November 7 and May 1, Red Square is cordoned off. The parades on the anniversary of the "Great October Revolution" (October under the old Russian calendar) and on May Day are pageants of military might and worker solidarity, done in the name of the common man, but not open to him. Admission is by ticket only, a ticket carefully provided to those deemed worthy. The streets in central Moscow are closed to unauthorized vehicles and pedestrians; from my apartment just over a quarter of a mile away, I had to pass thirteen checkpoints to the November 7 parade —five in my car, with the proper document, then eight more on foot.

In the vast square before the rust brick of the Kremlin walls, the troops are massed in grey and gold; red banners ripple in the icy breeze. The Politburo climbs the steps, faltering in age, waving stiffly to the diplomatic corps, the crowd, ascending to the mausoleum's balcony to stand and survey royally the spectacle below. Two open limousines race across the square; a man stands in each as would a charioteer. One, the minister of defense, the other, the commander of the Moscow district, salute and review the troops in greatcoats, greeting them and hearing their replies, thundering chants in military cadence rolling through the heart of power: "Oooooo-RAH! Oooooo-RAH!" Then the soldiers march in perfect ranks; then the tanks and missiles move, sweeping into view, filling the square with clatter and blue exhaust, followed then by card shows and precision drills like football half times. Then the workers come, carrying banners, pushing floats adorned with slogans: "We Put the Decisions of the 25th Party Congress into Reality"; "All Power to the Soviets"; "We Are the First on Earth to Create Developed Socialist Society. We Are the First to Build Communism." As Kevin Ruane of the BBC once quipped to me: "We Are Really Nice People!"

Does anybody read these slogans? Do they speak to the people? Do they have meaning? As you stand there in the cold, first your feet get numb, then your mind. You stop thinking. Everything is OK. There is order and virtue; the slogans tell us so. The May Day parade is on color television; the commentator is a woman with a beaming face, as if she were doing the Easter Parade down Fifth Avenue.

"May Day is a bright spring festival," she is saying, "and there are lots of children in the streets. Children are in the columns; they sit in the rows; they float over the square on the shoulders of their fathers. Happy, smiling, and excited, they of course feel tremendous joy over participation in the same celebrations. Children perceive everything much fresher than we adults. That is why all they will see and hear today—the mausoleum, Red Square, the Kremlin clocks chiming, the joyous music and the eyes, eyes happy and proud of those adults who surround them here today—all this will remain in their memories for the rest of their lives. The years will pass, and they will come to Red Square once again to greet the hundredth Soviet May Day. But they will come as the real managers and owners of the country. And they will come with their own children, of course, and then with their grandchildren, and this beautiful succession of the working generations and their heroic deeds and achievements will continue forever. Just as forever is this great column that marches along Red Square under the red banners of the Revolution.

"We continue to interview our foreign guests. Here, beside me, are a poet from India, a trade unionist from Nigeria, workers from San Marino, Italy, Great Britain, Scotland." Switching to English, she points her microphone at a man. "So what are your impressions?"

"First of all," he replies in English, "greetings on behalf of the trade union delegation from Britain. We are very impressed with the demonstration, with the theme of peace, because our own trade union congress is committed to detente and peace, and we all wish the working and the—"

"Thank you," the commentator interrupts, and translates into Russian: "Our guest from Great Britain says: 'The main mood of our May Day celebration is peace, is a tremendous movement for peace.' You know, today the new six winners of the Lenin Peace Prize have been named. Four of them are women"—shifting again to English—"You are men. What is your impression that women were given the prize?"

"Warm congratulations," one says in English. "I think it's right for women to be honored. It's wonderful."

"He says," she explains in Russian, "that all men of the world are proud that women occupy such a leading position in the fight for peace."

This is a special sort of Soviet fantasy, a synthetic world created by the sentences that flow endlessly from newspaper columns and radios, from toasts and speeches, from the banners and signs that deface streets and factories like some state-subsidized graffiti. All carry a unanimous, heroic, self-congratulatory message that all is well and getting better. "The Source of Mass Heroism," *Pravda* announces in a bold headline. "The working class of mankind has come to know by historical experience the selfless revolutionary heroism of the Soviet people who are blazing the trail to a bright communist future. In their difficult but glorious path, they have displayed unheard-of dedication in peaceful constructive labor and unbending fortitude in the time of ordeals." The product is a communist surrealism. No wonder Russian intellectuals like realistic theater; it is an escape.

In this milieu the mark of a mature citizen is his ability to know the real truth from the synthetic truth, to slice himself neatly in half and to keep his divided personality properly split. Thus a Jew, quietly a Zionist, can fulfill his obligation at his scientific institute to give an occasional political lecture denouncing Israel. I once met such a man; in this period well after Stalinism nobody minded what he believed privately, as long as what he believed publicly fit the party's line. It took him until his mid-forties before he filled with shame, applied to emigrate to Israel, lost his job, and no longer had to give lectures of any kind. Or a journalist can tell his private joke ("Communism is just over the horizon. But the horizon is an imaginary line, and as you approach it, it recedes'') as long as he writes openly about the inexorable advance toward the utopia. An author, writing a book on American film, can feel disgust when he receives instructions to insert a page and a half of quotes from Brezhnev, but he does it, and hates himself only a little.

Adults make their compromises as their children are taught to do. A violinist attends political lectures every other week, knitting and reading while the lecturers drone on, to get the required check mark by her name so she can go on the orchestra's upcoming tour to Western Europe. Nobody cares that she knits and reads or that others do the same. Her physical presence is the crucial thing, as if breathing the same air as the lecturer will build up her antibodies against the infections of alien ideas. A linguist wrinkles his nose as he describes the zeal of the party committee in his Moscow district, which organizes two weeks of daily indoctrination lectures every year or so for residents of the neighborhood. The lectures, every evening, tend to duplicate what has been in the Soviet press, driving that peculiar view of the world into heads that may not have quite absorbed it the first time. The linguist finds the exercise tedious, but he goes, and sits reading science fiction. To skip the sessions is to invite the party committee to report you to your place of employment as politically unreliable. "Then it's a quagmire," he laments. "It's easier just to go and be done with it." The Tchaikovsky Conservatory, the Soviet Union's premier institution of music and probably one of the finest in the world, requires each week that its students attend three hours of lectures on the history of the Communist Party, one and a half hours on military affairs, including civil defense, and one and a half hours on contemporary and highly politicized issues such as international affairs or economics. Irregularly, students are expected to prepare reports on political themes, to attend Komsomol meetings, and to be present at additional one-hour lectures on various propaganda topics. Music occupies seven hours a week of formal instruction.

The Russians are ingenious, however, at stopping just short of asphyxiation. As soon as you think you can no longer breathe, you're rescued by a fresh breeze of irreverence. On a collective farm in Kazakhstan one summer, where the local party newspaper is used for toilet paper, a cocky reporter from that paper arrived in a rakish Stetson hat, wandered around taking ostentatious notes, and then gathered a group of university students working there for the summer to ask, disingenuously, for suggestions on how the newspaper could be improved. "Use lighter ink," one student said.

"What?"

"Use lighter ink." The crowd began to titter.

"Why?" asked the reporter.

"Because we all have black asses."

As the students whooped with laughter, the Komsomol head stood up and cut off the mirth, pointing at the student and demanding, "What's your name?"

"He was hauled into the Komsomol committee and reprimanded," said a friend of mine who was there. "They were going to kick him out of Komsomol, but we defended him."

Casual remarks of skepticism and derision that would be commonplace in the West seem in the Soviet context like delicious tastes of independent thought. I remember a young man, one of the few genuine Marxists I encountered, watching a television news clip of Soviet leaders and comparing their astrakhan hats and collars to "the ermine of the czars." I was startled. Another loyal nondissident, commenting on the bragging in the official press, declared, "It is repugnant to us. It just undermines the faith and credibility of other important things they say. It indicates an inferiority complex, hints at some inner feeling of deficiency. It is like Stokely Carmichael—black is beautiful. For fifty years it has been said how great it is to be a Soviet citizen. I agree. But why that?" And he waved his hand contemptuously at that day's *Pravda*. A middle-aged Muscovite, after watching a televised Brezhnev speech: "It's better than an anti-insomnia pill—no side effects, just doze off and wake up refreshed." A party member scoffed at the lavish praise for Brezhnev during the Twenty-fifth Party Congress in 1976: "I got inoculated against all this in 1956," he said, a sardonic reference to Khrushchev's "secret speech" that year denouncing Stalin's crimes and setting the de-Stalinization process in motion. "After sixty years of Soviet power," a Moscow woman remarked during a television film critical of a fictitious factory's party committee, "it's high time we began thinking. Stalin did terrible things to us."

These were the voices not of dissidents but of well-integrated and personally happy and patriotic Russians, none with the urge to leave their country or the need to speak openly. They talked to me with candor only after we had come to know each other enough to trust each other, and they accepted the duality of their existence, the dichotomy between private and public thought, as if it were as natural as day and night. But the forced hypocrisy also seemed to corrode belief or make it fragile so that any blow could bring it crashing down. One evening in a drab apartment not far from ours, among a few young people discussing life, there were two young women: Suzanna, nineteen, pudgy, Jewish, a second-year student in an engineering institute specializing in the control of air pollution, and Maria, the slender, sinewy daughter of an exiled Spanish Communist. Both were born in Moscow, Maria because her father had taken refuge there in 1949. She had been brought up a Soviet girl, and now that she was in her late twenties, her eyes flashed with rebelliousness behind her tinted glasses. She worked in a 100-ruble-a-month job at the Institute of the Working Class on a seven-member team studying Trotsky and writing analyses of Trotskyite parties in the West. But never had she been allowed to read a word of Trotsky other than some of his letters. The Trotsky collection in the institute's library was off limits to her and her colleagues on the team; they did not have the clearance to read anything significant that the man had written. They were restricted to the Trotskyite parties' proclamations and newspapers, which they were to analyze appropriately, always delineating the incorrectness of the parties' positions. Maria found herself agreeing with some of what the parties said. But she wrote what her boss wanted, not what she believed. "I sell my soul for a hundred rubles," she said.

By contrast, Suzanna seemed to require delicate handling. She took the issues rather seriously. When she tried to remember the three questions intrinsic to studying ideology—"First, the distance between quantity and quality, or when does quantity become quality?"—the others in the room, including her cousin Yuri, cut her off with laughter, and she was hurt. So when I asked Maria if she considered herself a Communist, like her father, she cast a glance at Suzanna before answering. "If I had lived in Spain," Maria said slowly, "maybe I would have been a Communist. But not here—excuse me." She smiled wryly, bowing in sarcastic apology toward Suzanna. I had the feeling for a moment that Suzanna's crystal world was close to shattering. She reminded me of a well-bred churchgoer, flushed with a naïve fervor that couldn't stand the simple question "How do you know there is a God?" It was the shallowness of her convictions that were striking, yet how desperately she clung to them. When pressed, she could not say honestly whether or not she was a Marxist; perhaps she was, though she could not be sure because, she confessed, she had no clear grasp of what Marxism was. She could recite definitions but had decided that she would have to be older to understand them thoroughly. While this may have had a ring of humility and tolerance, her views were quite otherwise. She would not entertain the notion of competing structures of ideology, and she fell into a sharp disagreement with her more liberal cousin Yuri, who studied at a teachers' college. To his complaints about the absence of open discussion in classes, she replied in a scolding tone, saying that it was as it should be. Teachers must know clearly what to teach, she explained pedantically, because students are too young to think for themselves. If you don't have a firm system of ideas to teach, then young people might end up having a variety of ideas, which would be terrible, she said with distaste. She grew quite agitated at the thought of competing ideas flying wildly around the classrooms. As she explained herself further, I began to see that it was not the nature of the idea that appealed to her, but its singularity. Her allegiance was to conformity; she valued the common direction of her peers and figures of authority, and her displeasure with Yuri was not at all ideological. It was social. She seemed to believe in nothing but good behavior.

Here was a pressure point of the new society; the pulse could be felt beneath the surface like a fluttering, elusive truth. Here was what it all had added up to, all the blood and suffering, all the fierce hope and the angry dreams of the distant Revolution, now blurred in a misty past. Drained of passion, empty of desire, the Revolution now stood motionless.

We had been traveling for days in the subarctic wasteland of Western Siberia, a group of American journalists, pressing, probing, torturing government officials in charge of oil production with our relentless questions on the capacity and future yield of the country's most plentiful oil region. The questions had become crucial to knowing where the Soviet Union was headed, for the United States Central Intelligence Agency had just issued a report predicting a decline in production that would ultimately throw the Russians onto the world market as buyers, no longer exporters, with all the political and military ramifications of that dramatic shift in roles. Officials in Moscow had arranged our trip partly to counteract the CIA's projection, yet all the local administrators we had interviewed were too jittery to speak candidly. Nervously, evasively, they parried our insistent questioning, beads of sweat standing out on their foreheads like men in the dock. Our notebooks gradually filled with numbers that added up to confusion and left gaping holes where essential information was needed.

These men were all government officials, not party officials. Virtually all of them were in the party, to be sure, but their salaried jobs were as executives in various branches of governmental operation, including oil production. Despite their rank, they displayed a striking anxiety, an opaque style of practiced blandness that became all the more pronounced in retrospect, when we finally encountered our one and only party official and felt the contrast. We were on our way home to Moscow, frustrated, between planes at the Tyumen airport. A neat man in a dark suit, white shirt, and conservative tie emerged from a black Volga sedan and entered the VIP lounge in the small terminal. One of our local guides, a Soviet newsman, recognized him as Sergei D. Velikopolsky, first secretary of the party committee of the city of Nizhnevartovsk, the administrative capital of the Samotlor oil region, one of the most important in the country. He was catching a plane for some remote point in the region, and we doubted that he would grant our request for a few minutes of his time. But we tried him, and to our surprise, he seemed rather pleased to find a herd of American reporters in this unlikely spot; he stood in our midst for a long time while we peppered him with questions, and he responded with calm candor, revealing the statistics that had been so elusive, discussing future production curves and shortcomings with the open confidence of a man clearly in charge. (The Samotlor yield would peak in the next year, he predicted, then hold steady for seven to eight years before declining sharply and putting a burden on development of new fields.) He was only forty-one, yet he wore authority with an impressive ease, the crown prince of a remote and vital place.

This was the characteristic of party officials—those paid to conduct party affairs—as opposed to those workers, teachers, scientists, and farmers who were also members of the party, as in the West they might also have been members of a church. The professionals were very different from the rank and file: well groomed and well spoken, urbane and expert, comfortable with power. They were more difficult to meet than government officials, and more rewarding, for in my experience they were generally men with whom one could have an intelligent conversation and a genuine exchange of views, an impression I found shared by diplomats and other journalists. Their counterparts in Western societies occupy the boardrooms of corporations; they are the conservative elite dedicated to the smooth functioning of the existing system and to their own careers.

The party, the supposed agent of history, has evolved into an unrevolutionary political watchdog and, perhaps more important, into a management and efficiency board. Its local committees—at every factory and hotel, on every farm and faculty—are charged with making things run properly, a job so consuming (and futile, evidently) that it overwhelms most ideological activity. "Our first task is to see that things work better," said a young woman party member and Intourist guide in Tallin, Estonia. You could almost hear the bones rattle as Marx and Engels spun in their graves. She gave an example: When foreign tourists complained repeatedly about poor service in a new Tallin hotel, the party secretary at Intourist's Tallin office assigned her and another member to investigate and write up a report on the problems. They prepared a scathing indictment of the management and presented it at the monthly closed meeting of all the party members on the hotel staff. The Intourist party committee then ordered corrective measures. Everyone felt rather virtuous in having addressed the shortcomings frankly, but the results were just about invisible. Although the incident occurred between two of my visits to the hotel, the mediocre service before and the mediocre service after looked about the same to me.

This focus on work performance lends a strangely apolitical cast to party affairs, especially at lower echelons, where soporific lectures and empty slogans make political activity into a stylized ritual. As politics permeates all spheres of life, it grows mundane and unimportant, like background music in a restaurant. One party member in Tbilisi, a factory engineer, blushed with embarrassment when asked to name the thirteen members of the Politburo at the time; he couldn't get beyond six. "Brezhnev, Kosygin, Suslov," he began confidently. He paused and cleared his throat. "Gromyko." His eyes searched among the distant tables of the restaurant where we were sitting. He scanned the ceiling. "Andropov," he said, naming the then KGB head. An expression of uncomfortable irony crossed his face. He was stuck.

We coached him. "The same name as the czars'," my colleague prompted.

"Ah, Romanov!" He beamed.

But that was it. The other seven had to come from us. With a pained smile he ordered another bottle of wine and lifted his glass in some bravely cheerful toast.

I once asked a musician with the Bolshoi to what extent his party membership involved him in things political. "Political?" He laughed. "Ha. There's no politics at all. What do I do as a party member? Be a good example at work. And at party meetings discuss work discipline, especially of members."

What is not discussed is the performance of high officials or the incompetence of high policy; even in closed meetings the party leadership is always "correct" in the most important matters of foreign affairs, budgetary priorities, military decisions, arms sales abroad, and the like. The abortive SALT II treaty with the United States on limiting nuclear weapons was never a subject of debate, for instance. "We don't have any information, so we can't discuss it," one woman party member complained. "Even party lecturers don't know, for example, how much aid is given to the Arabs. We know how much the U.S. spends on the military, but we don't know how much we spend. I think we should be more open, yes."

In the absence of privileged information, and in the expectation that every member will "be a good example," as the musician explained, the party seems to have lost some of its luster for certain young people. Its members, especially its professional *apparatchiki*, are subjected to close and continuing scrutiny, and not only on the job. I once met two college students who were bright, curious, and active in Komsomol but had no desire to join the party. "The standard of behavior is stricter," one girl said. "A party member is not thought of highly if he goes out often to a restaurant or dancing. I want a little bit of private life and don't want to be scrutinized all the time from all sides." A boy added, "To become a member, you have to consider yourself better than others, and I don't think I'm any better than anyone else." Sergei Polikanov, the physicist, also regarded party membership as something of an annoyance, for members had to spend their free time in meetings and organizational activities. And they were supposed to be models of perfect behavior.

Even in this divorce-ridden society, a divorce can wreck a high party official's career, a Soviet journalist observed. Central Committee members are pressed by their colleagues to weather marital crises lest they risk their positions in the hierarchy, he said; the exemplary Communist is one whose marriage is in order, or at least appears to be. "We are the Puritans," said a party member, trying to explain to an American.

The party's social conservatism extends its deadening hand into many spheres. A friend who designed a new literature curriculum for secondary schools had it quickly squashed by party functionaries because he could find no eminent figure to defend it. He had been warned of the inevitable by Mikhail Alekseyevich Lavrentyev, a prominent mathematician who founded the scientific town of Akademgorodok, outside Novosibirsk. Lavrentyev discouraged him with his own story of pushing through a radical new mathematics curriculum. "A party man, also a mathematician, had come to question and oppose the proposal," my friend recalled, "and Lavrentyev, with all his honors and degrees, had simply glared him down. The sheer weight of his prestige and accomplishments had wilted the guy. But then Lavrentyev asked me, 'Who is going to do that with literature?' Nobody, of course, and the curriculum was dropped." Lavrentyev's stature had made him a competing center of power in effect. "He wouldn't even talk to the party secretary in Novosibirsk," said my friend, a former resident of Akademgorodok. "They were like two archbishops—they would talk to each other only through Moscow. Now that has changed. The old men with academic rank are gone, and the scientific community is more susceptible to party control. A local party official says to the director, 'Come to my office,' and he does so."

A well-known writer told me that he wished he could quit the party, which he had joined in his youthful, more idealistic days. "Membership holds me back," he said, referring to his work, his creativity. "They put pressure on me. But you're not allowed to resign. Once I asked an old Communist what kind of party it was if you couldn't get out of it. The old man said, 'Oh, you can leave a party, but you can't leave a gang of bandits.' " The writer gave a bitter laugh.

I heard his scorn in many voices. "The party is just a police force," sneered a young woman studying to be a teacher. Her brother belonged, but not out of any conviction. He had been enticed into joining by superiors in the courthouse where he worked, who told him if he did so, he could go with a group of tourists for a few weeks in Western Europe. A woman scholar was advised to join the party if she wanted to become a full professor. Yakov Alpert, a physicist, was invited by his superior in his lab to join the party and declined. "I said, 'I love science and nothing else,' and he said, 'Oh, that's not good.' "

It rarely has to be put so bluntly that the good jobs, the state prizes, the trips abroad, the key promotions—and with them the access to better housing and closed shops—tend to flow to those who are supposed to be the best and the brightest, the Communists. A young Muscovite looked at me quizzically when I asked why he wanted to join, as if I had asked why the sun comes up each morning. "For my career," he said simply. It reminded me of a leaden joke: Any Soviet citizen may choose from three characteristics—honesty, cleverness, and membership in the Communist Party—but he can have only two of those qualities at a time. A musician made his own whimsical comedy of the whole process, telling how he came to party membership. He had told his five-year-old son to stop doing something, and the boy had replied with a withering remark: "Uncle lets me, and he's more important."

"Why is he more important?" the father asked sternly.

"He's a Communist," the boy declared.

"So I decided I wanted to be important, too"—the musician grinned—"and I became a Communist."

It is an article of conviction among Soviet intellectuals today, a fact embellished by nostalgia, that the Bolsheviks who made the Revolution were men of ideas, creative thinkers whose vision did, indeed, possess their fellow Russians and inspire the country with a sense of forward movement. Lenin, Trotsky, Plekhanov, Bukharin were more than skillful activists; they were theoreticians for whom ideology lived, grew, developed, matured, and ripened within an evolving reality. Their mission was pure, holding a promised future guaranteed by inevitable history: feudalism to capitalism to socialism to communism, the inexorable progress of mankind. The exciting sensation of momentum lasted for Russians long after the ideal was crushed for most adherents in the West, dashed by the oppressive example of the Russians themselves.

Today in those engaging discussions and debates around Moscow kitchen tables, the bloom of faith is still recalled with a painful pleasure. Socialism, with its state control of the economy, was to be but an intermediate stage between the downfall of capitalism—the abolition of "bourgeois property"—and the advent of communism. As the proletariat took the reins of productive power in Marx's utopia, the class antagonisms that had determined the course of history would disappear, the state would wither away, and the abundance of material goods would allow a breakdown in the relationship between a person's work and his wage. The socialist dictum "From each according to his abilities, to each according to his work" would be replaced by the communist principle "From each according to his abilities, to each according to his needs."

This was not a rigid, unyielding dogma but a simplified model on which adaptable theory could be based, and it was subject to such varied interpretation from the outset that Marx himself once denied being a Marxist, his way of denouncing those who, he felt, misunderstood his ideas. Even the Bolshevik Revolution defied Marxist principles by occurring in a society that had not yet achieved the capitalist conditions supposedly prerequisite to proletarian revolution. Some scholars have written that Marx, more interested in revolution than in theory, regarded the Russia of the late nineteenth century as a unique exception to his model—"a backward country with a primitive peasant economy, the rudiments of modern industry and a mere embryo of a proletariat," as it was put by Tibor Szamuely, a former history professor at Budapest University. Marx thought Russia could skip the capitalist stage and move directly to socialism.

The ideology today inherits something from Marx's capacity to revise and qualify his own theory in the light of real events. Contrary to a frequent view from the West, Soviet ideology does not require inflexible or impractical behavior; it is highly pragmatic, a trait derived especially from Lenin. Soviet Communists rarely speak simply of Marxism, but rather of Marxism-Leninism, an amalgam of the original classics of Marx and Engels, plus a layer of action-oriented concepts contributed by Lenin before and after he led the Revolution. "Ideology," in Zbigniew Brzezinski's definition, "is essentially an action program derived from certain philosophical assumptions and doctrinal postulates about the nature of reality." Assertions about the inadequacy of the past or present state of societal affairs "include an explicit guide to action outlining methods of changing the situation, with some general, idealized notions about the eventual state of affairs." As such, ideology can be seen to comprise three layers. The underlying philosophical assumptions —dialectical materialism, the existence of matter independent of human consciousness—tend to be rather rigid and unchanging. The layer of doctrinal postulates—the inevitable collapse of capitalism, the inevitability of war, the withering away of the state, the Communist Party as an agent of history—are changeable, and their alterations have been responsible for some of the deep schisms during the relatively brief history of the communist movement. The layer of utmost fluidity is the action program, whereby strategic and tactical considerations allow the Soviet Union to buy grain and machinery from the capitalist West without flinching; the goal is to improve the material production of the socialist economy, a necessary step before the final stage of communism can be reached.*

Many Russians can remember when they believed in this, when they genuinely foresaw the advance of their society toward the flowering of communism. The recollection of the hope puts a bitter edge on today's despair. Something has died. The ideology still shapes perceptions of events, but the vital sense of forward motion is gone. The country feels aground, stuck in the phase of gigantic socialism, "state capitalism," as it is termed disdainfully. No party leader, straight-faced, could now make Khrushchev's 1961 prediction that the communist era would be reached in twenty years. The official position has shifted into the notion that no quick change can be expected, that socialism "encompasses a prolonged historical period," in the words of the party's late theoretician Mikhail Suslov, who was known before his death as the Grey Cardinal.

"The building of communism," lamented Roy Medvedev, "is

*Zbigniew Brzezinski, lecture, Columbia University, March 4, 1975.

still everywhere in slogans, repeated and repeated. But the statement twenty years ago that our generation would live under communism, those placards have all been taken down. Now nobody talks about a specific period of time; it is all in the future. In general, people don't think about it. Nobody knows what communism is. There is a lot of discussion about socialism, but what is communism? Nobody examines that question. There are dozens of books on 'the development of socialist society,' but you don't see anything about communist society, except a last chapter called 'From Socialism to Communism.' "

The ideology, once active, has grown passive. It no longer shapes the direction of change inside the country but merely molds analysis of the outside world, especially of the Western world. A constant presence in classrooms and newspapers, the doctrine's assumptions about reality have become automatic reflexes for many Russians, who are conditioned to see class conflict and economic exploitation at the center of all developments in the West. The ideology has atrophied into a convenient cant, a set of symbols, often used to camouflage anti-Marxist practices and to elicit stereotyped interpretations of events at home and abroad. "We have no more ideals of revolution, Marxism, Leninism," said Lev Kopelev, who held his faith through nearly a decade in Stalin's labor camps. "They are lost in this system of bureaucracy and falsehood—a crisis of ideology."

The crisis comes in part from the stagnation of debate, the dogmatism that has afflicted dialogue. The ideological heritage has passed from the thinkers and theoreticians to the textile engineers and metallurgists, the Brezhnevs, Andropovs, and Chernenkos whose interests in the everyday business of economic management have naturally prevailed over the more intellectual activity of enriching ideological thought. Brzezinski put it brutally and well: "Mr. Brezhnev has not suffered, even for five minutes, on behalf of his ideology. On the contrary, ideology for Mr. Brezhnev was a framework for his personal advancement and success. His ideological contribution has been meager." The same can be said of Brezhnev's successors, for no one in the upper ranks has an intellectual background. To this criticism, Khrushchev provided a down-to-earth answer of sorts in his memoirs: "Mao said we should reject material incentives and motivate our people with revolutionary ideas, but you can't make soup out of an idea."

Consequently, Soviet Communists are really socialists dedicated to the maintenance and improvement of the existing system of elaborate state ownership. They have become conservatives as their party has evolved from an agent of historical change into a guardian of the status quo. It is hardly a unique development, for as Stephen F. Cohen observes, the excessive nature of revolutions has often brought social conservatism in their wakes; "conservative aftermaths of great revolutions may even be something approaching a general law," he wrote.* The Bolshevik Nikolai Bukharin spoke of the phenomenon with prescience before he was executed by Stalin in 1938. "History is full of examples of the transformation of parties of revolution into parties of order," he said. "Sometimes the only mementos of a revolutionary party are the watchwords which it has inscribed on public buildings."

The loss of faith leaves a hollow mood in Russia. A hunger gnaws. A yearning stirs. A search begins. But the striving is not forward into a truer Marxist vision of the future. There is no leftist dissent, no surreptitious protest for the advance of the real revolution. "The most dangerous thing here would be Marxism," said Lev Kopelev, "not just propaganda, not just slogans, but Marxism as a system of historical analysis. A true Marxist couldn't make a revolution in Russia. If you tried to analyze, as a Marxist, what has happened in Russia in the last twenty years, it would be very dangerous, much more dangerous than to write about how good the czars were." To a purely Marxist attack, the regime would react with untold ferocity.

The yearning is not a lurch forward but a reaching back, back into the suffering and glory of World War II to nourish national honor and heroism, back into the tight authoritarianism of Stalinist times, back into the ethnic purity and nobility of what was "Russian," back into the simplicity and mythical honesty of Russia's village life, back into the church.

Christianity

The dark-haired girl of sixteen was a Komsomol activist and the daughter of two Communist Party members. In the middle of an

---

*Stephen F. Cohen, *Reformism and Conservatism in the Soviet Union, 1953–1978.* Paper at Midwest Slavic Conference, Indiana University, April 1978.

afternoon, at the end of the school day, she walked gracefully from the hard grey streets of Baku into the gold and candlelight of a church. Dusky icons hung framed in gilt, dim images suggesting mystery beyond the dancing gold reflections of the tiny flames. A trace of incense hung in the placid air, soothing. She crossed herself, lit a candle, and bowed her head in a brief prayer.

It was a frequent after-school routine, kept secret from her mother and father. The church calmed her, gave her delicate sensations of faith, warmed her as nothing had outside. But these important feelings were held closely, the magic of her double life. I asked how she could reconcile her Communist affiliation with her religious faith. "It's easy," she said brightly. "At the Komsomol committee, when they ask if I believe in God, I say no."

Thus do communism and Christianity coexist, intertwining through the layers of belief and disbelief, binding conviction with hypocrisy. Party members sometimes even have their children baptized, clandestinely; the KGB puts agents in the clergy. Nothing is ever as it seems. There are priests who do not believe in God, and Communists who do.

I once had dinner at the home of an Armenian athlete and party member in Yerevan. Before the meal, with his lovely children scrubbed and neat around the table, he invited my colleague from *The Christian Science Monitor* to say grace. The children placed the palms of their hands together in prayer, as they had evidently done many times before. The father said a grace of his own, in Armenian. Then he poured the wine and stood, lifting the glass and saying, "I am a Communist. But I believe that the only thing that keeps us from becoming barbarians is Christianity." We drank, wondering at the clash and overlap of values and forces tearing at this country.

The Armenian Church is a special case, containing the intensive quality of Armenian identity, the expression of ethnic and national pride; as such, the church embraces all Armenians by virtue of their being Armenians. When I asked a monk at the cliffside monastery of Gegard whether party members often came to have their babies baptized, he declared through wispy whiskers, "Yes! All of them! We say if you're not christened, you're not Armenian. If you're not christened, we say you're a Turk—an enemy!" Not every church in the Soviet Union taps quite that cultural reflex; even where other national minorities cling to their churches as symbols of their apartness and specialness—the Georgians their Orthodoxy, for instance, or the Lithuanians their Catholicism—the question of Christian identity is not something automatic, as in Armenia, but a question of choice and risk. For many, it is a deliberate decision to regard the church as a repository of minority culture and ethnic heritage that sets the group off from the dominant Russians. And the Russian Orthodox Church serves something of the same function for the Russians themselves, distinguishing them from the larger, diverse Soviet population, reaffirming their Russianness. This need springs largely from disappointment.

"Because of false politics," said a Moscow woman, Jewish, who finds herself drawn to church and sometimes to synagogue. "So much in our newspapers is false, and everybody knows it. In church there is something mystical, spiritual." Her teenage daughter "goes sometimes to watch and listen and be quiet a little." Her son does watercolors of onion domes and crosses. Another boy, the son of a scientist, believes in "pieces from Marxism, pieces from religion." A Jewish man, groping for some form of faith, has converted to Christianity because Christian literature, the underground leaflets and typescript circulated surreptitiously, was all he could obtain. Now he is sorry, for Jewish literature is available, smuggled in by American and West European Jewish tourists. More and more I saw tiny gold crosses on thin chains around the necks of young Russian women.

The longer I lived in the Soviet Union, the less amazed I was by the drawing power of the Russian Orthodox Church. It began to seem natural for Russians to search for belief, to look beyond the barren ritual of the state, to seek a connection with their own history, to find beauty. "Communism is like paganism," one friend told me. "It is full of idols. Fifteen years ago we believed in some new idealistic basis of living. People believed that something new could flourish from socialist ideas. Now there is no longer hope. It's all in the past, nothing in the future." Yet he also saw Christianity as a link with a deeper past, one intrinsic to the Russian people, one cast into grey oblivion by the empty ceremony of Soviet power. "We have no history," this man said sadly. "Every man who has no historical tradition feels himself weak, like a man in a country he does not know. He believes in ghosts—they may not be fairy-tale ghosts, but KGB ghosts—and he is afraid. So Christianity is the search for his connection with the history of his country. To be compared with Christianity, you have to do something as beautiful as the Christian life. It is necessary to have a person equal to Jesus Christ—it is an answer to all questions."

As an answer to all questions, Christianity can exert a special hold on Russians yearning for an enveloping truth, on those once inclined, in earlier, fervent years, to give themselves to communism as a full system of explanation and belief. As mechanisms of thought, both communism and Christianity satisfy a need for a structured intellectual life; both provide an anchor against a swirling sea of terrifying ambiguity and doubt; both can soothe the spiritual hunger for awe and reverence, once filled by czars and saints and then by the figures of Lenin and Stalin as more than earthly beings. And so in the drifting vacuum left by failing communism, the church holds potential power—not institutionally but spiritually—that Soviet authority watches warily and seeks to contain.

Not all attraction to the church is profound or complete. Some, merely aesthetic, turns on a taste for richer ceremony than that provided in the state's austere wedding halls and crematoria. Communist authorities have worked hard to create "new socialist ritualism," as *Pravda* called it. In the Krasnodar region on the Black Sea, a ceremonial registration of newborn babies was introduced in an effort to supplant baptism. The Ukraine formed a committee to manufacture new rituals, with appropriate costumes and pageantry to "help put bright and colorful finishing touches on ceremonies connected with various events in people's lives," *Pravda* said. The paper recommended blending the old and the new, the traditional customs with modern socialist themes. One such attempt is the Red Corner in schools and Pioneer centers, with a Lenin portrait and Lenin's works instead of an icon and a Bible. But the effort does not quite work, at least not for everyone.

A young friend of ours was so ashamed of her state wedding ceremony that she didn't invite us, fearing that as Americans used to church weddings, we would find hers plain and boring, worthy only of mockery. It was precisely the same as many other weddings that she had attended and that we had also seen: Presiding was a woman civil servant seated before the Soviet emblem with its hammer and sickle, reading a dry text in the unfeeling tones of having done it many times. Once the rings were exchanged, attendants hurried the party out to make room for the next couple on the assembly line. "It was awful," said our friend. "I hated it."

She and her new husband skipped the usual custom for newly-weds, which is to go in taxis draped with crepe paper straight from the proceedings at the "wedding palace" to the Lenin Mausoleum, where the bride's wedding gown is like a pass that gets the couple immediately to the front of the line. In other Soviet cities, and often in Moscow as well, they appear at the Tomb of the Unknown Soldier to lay a small wreath. Or in Moscow they ride up to a lookout point on Lenin Hills, where they can see over the capital and have their pictures taken.

Some find this mingling of privacy and nation uplifting; others find it sterile, and church weddings have become quite a fashion as an alternative of candlelight and vestments and gold, chanting and incense and organ music. The state does not recognize the religious ceremonies (on the ground that the Soviet Constitution provides for strict separation of church and state!), so the couple must still have a state ceremony or at least register their marriage with state authorities. Most try to keep their church weddings secret to avoid damage to career. The phenomenon thus becomes unmeasurable, taking on the appearance of a vast, partly hidden celebration, contributing to an impression of religious renaissance. "It is faster in the church," said one old woman, "and stronger. It will last longer."

Sometimes the church attracts the way a fad does, in a thin, fleeting whim of pleasure and naughtiness. Icons and compositions of liturgical music are admired as art and are also collected and played and heard for their overtones of mystical defiance. The infatuation is a teasing dance with authority, for officialdom also values the icon, even to the point of enforcing strict prohibitions against its export. The treasures of the Russian heritage are precious, needing preservation; the churches of the Kremlin, although museums now, are fussed over, scrubbed and painted and gilded again with gleaming gold leaf so that they shine among the taller towers bearing the ruby-red stars and the red flags fluttering. The icon and the golden domes are symbols with multiple meanings, connecting the intricate lines of what is Russian and what is Soviet, bringing the great Russian past into some strange harmony with the powerful Soviet present.

A thirty-three-year-old woman who said she knew nothing about

God wrote to the official atheist magazine, *Science and Religion*, that she wore a cross "as a symbol of the invincibility of the Russian people. Our people went at their enemies with the cross, and won. A mother would see her son off to a war and bless him with a cross . . . I see it as a powerful force which can repel any evil. In the cross lies the history of the Russian people." The magazine's editorial board replied irritably that the cross, also worn by Teuton knights on their armor and featured by the Nazis in the highest military medals, was "used by would-be enslavers of your own motherland." The editors concluded: "The cross is not exclusively a Russian symbol and therefore is not a national, but a purely religious one." But her argument must have touched many Russians, for otherwise the atheist magazine would not have felt compelled to publish and rebut it.

And so the creations of the church hover among intersecting beliefs, admired from this angle and that, raised as images of one faith or another, revealing and masking motives in a complex game. I remember in 1979 when Handel's *Messiah* was performed in Moscow for the first time since the Revolution. It was done on Good Friday in the Great Hall of the Tchaikovsky Conservatory. As with all performances, this was authorized by the Ministry of Culture. Moscow was buzzing. Some chords of sympathy in the hierarchy? Some safety valve to release the people's yearning, to make the church less of a taboo and thus less lustrous?

The authorities' ambivalence has made casual affiliation with the church a relatively safe form of fairly private protest. "In many cases it's an act of dissent, not an act of faith," said a nonreligious mathematician. "By this step, they deny the official ideology." They possess something of their own, quietly, something apart from the flat surface of Communist conviction. "Official religion," said the mathematician, "is the only permissible outlook other than Marxism-Leninism." Lev Kopelev explained it through the term *sobor,* which in Russian has two overlapping meanings. It is the word for "temple" or "cathedral," and the root of words meaning "to gather," "to collect," "meeting," "gathering." "The people have a need to bring themselves together," Lev said. "The party is also a *sobor,* but it makes demands. The church is the meekest one. The church does not oblige or press so much. It *is* an opiate. Soothing."

Marx's famous "opium of the people" epithet is actually part of a fuller, more compassionate passage written in a tone of pity.

"Religion is the sigh of the oppressed creature," he wrote, "the heart of a heartless world, the spirit of soulless stagnation. It is the opium of the people."*

Lenin was harsher: "Every religious idea, every idea of God, even flirting with the idea of God, is unutterable vileness, . . . vileness of the most dangerous kind, 'contagion' of the most abominable kind. Millions of filthy deeds, acts of violence and physical contagions are far less dangerous than the subtle, spiritual idea of a God decked out in the smartest 'ideological' costumes."†

Basic Soviet theory has envisioned the natural withering away of the church as the aged men and women raised in its traditions die, and the younger breed of "Soviet man" rises into adulthood in a society that has no need of the archaic, the unscientific. This may be why the elderly are usually left to worship openly, mostly old women hunched and bundled in heavy coats, muttering prayers, kneeling on stone floors, carrying candles in trembling hands—images of a supposedly dying rite. The young and middle-aged are the focus of officialdom's concern. To lure the young away from midnight Easter services, state movie houses usually run American and West European films that can never be seen any other time; the only showings are at midnight. For good measure, Komsomol activists and plainclothesmen ring the churches, letting through the old and screening out the young. Names are taken, and there are repercussions at schools and places of employment for those caught trying to enter. The severity depends on the period and the prevailing atmosphere, which shifts from year to year, from generation to generation. One linguist friend of mine, now middle-aged, remembers his grandfather as a church elder in Zagorsk, the residence of the patriarch and the site of the Trinity St. Sergius Monastery dating from the fourteenth century. But the old man's son—my friend's father—was a strident Komsomol leader in Stalin's time who tore down icons and blocked church doors. Now the linguist finds himself attracted to the art and music of the church, though not to its faith.

The original Soviet Constitution of 1918 permitted "freedom of religious and antireligious propaganda." If this reflected a certainty

*Marx and Engels, *Works*, vol. 1, p. 385, 1st ed. (Moscow: Marx-Engels-Lenin Institute, 1938–48), cited in Robert Conquest, ed., *Religion in the U.S.S.R.* (New York: Praeger, 1968).

†Lenin, *Works*, vol. 35, pp. 89–90, 93, 4th ed. (Moscow: Marx-Engels-Lenin Institute, 1941–50).

that the antireligious would prevail, the confidence soon ebbed, and the passage was amended in 1929 to "freedom of religious worship and antireligious propaganda." Thus deprived of its right to make "propaganda," the church lost the ability to transmit its creed and values formally: no group study, no Sunday schools, no evangelism. The party, meanwhile, was free, even obligated, to preach atheism. The Constitution adopted under Stalin in 1936 contained Article 124 on state-church relations, the provisions of which were retained in the revised Constitution of 1978, Article 52, guaranteeing citizens' "freedom of conscience," by declaring that "the church in the USSR is separate from the state, and the school from the church." To an American ear attuned to the value of the separation of church and state, this may sound surprisingly liberal. But in a society where the state is all-embracing, it means that there is little room left for the church. Mischievously I once asked a proper Soviet guide why there were no Christmas cards in her country, despite the purported freedom to celebrate religious holidays. She explained logically that since all printing was done by state printers and since the Constitution provided for the separation of church and state, state printers could not print religious greeting cards.

The principle of separation is observed only at the convenience of the authorities, however. Organized religion is, in fact, utterly dependent on the state: The church has no property but receives its candle wax, Bibles, vestments, buildings, and land from the state. Whether Christian, Jewish, Moslem, or Buddhist, no congregation may be organized, no worship service held, no religious publication issued, no charity undertaken without permission of the state. The Council on Religious Affairs, whose chairman and four deputy chairmen are all party members (and not the baby-baptizing kind either), acts on behalf of the state to register congregations, issue Bibles in severely limited and overpriced editions, and otherwise regulate and restrict religious activity. I interviewed one of the council's deputy chairmen, Viktor Titov, and found him predictably contemptuous of the church. He dismissed the growing interest in religion among young people as a bizarre manifestation of nonconformity. "It's the same thing as in New York, on a hot summer day, people in fur coats and bare feet," he said with a smirk. "We see with our own eyes how such fads disappear. This is a temporary and passing phenomenon, like the flu, which comes and goes." He laughed.

The ridiculing of religion occurs both in official texts and in the authentic attitudes of many Soviet citizens. I knew a Muscovite in his late thirties who was overcome by a visceral revulsion whenever the subject of the church arose; he genuinely despised the spectacle of men and women chanting and genuflecting and lighting candles, deriding it as ignorant witchcraft.

The message of atheism is everywhere, from biology textbooks to nightclub acts. The *Basic Biology* text for ninth and tenth grades is laced with antireligious references describing belief in God as antiquated, antiscientific, and incompatible with the theory of evolution and other modern thought. Noting that early science was mostly superstition, the book declares: "That was the time of blossoming religion. For a believer the issue of the appearance of life is solved easily: it is the result of divine creation, or, in other words, a miracle. Simultaneously with religion, false 'sciences' enjoyed considerable development; these were alchemy, astrology, black magic." The social and political evils of religion are spelled out in a chapter on the origin of man:

> The appearance and spread of religion gave birth to the teaching that man was created by god and that he consists of two components: body and soul. He is a temporary guest on earth and therefore must develop in himself patience, humility, and neglect of the earthly joys, for the sake of future life in a better world. It is easy to see who profits by such morality: it is directed at the justification of social inequality and the blunting of class self-realization.

Antireligious themes are reinforced in many spheres outside the classroom. A newspaper in Soviet Georgia printed a satirical poem portraying priests as drunken and dishonest. In a nightclub in Tallin's Viru Hotel, Debby and I watched as a group of chorus girls, dressed as nuns, suddenly tore off their habits to reveal multicolored tights, in which they ground and writhed as a singer did a rock version of a hymn full of "glory, glory, hallelujahs." Films often show the church as an eerie, frightening place. In a spy movie on Moscow television a church funeral was the scene for a cat-and-mouse game played by silent antagonists stalking each other. The faces in the church were sinister or vacant. The priest stared menacingly as he approached the camera, swinging a vessel of incense. Another television film, Soviet-made, was set in Spain during the Inquisition. A bride, after a weird wedding ceremony, was seized by church officials. Nuns kicked her, whipped her while she was still in her bridal gown in an attempt to get her to sign a confession about banned books her new husband was printing. Shots of the crucifix were accompanied by evil, sinister, frightening music.

Against this onslaught some Russians hold fast to their belief in the divine, the supernatural. They love to tell the story of the Church of Christ the Saviour, one of Moscow's most ornate, which stood on the bank of the Moskva River until Stalin had it dynamited in the 1930's to make way for a towering Palace of Congresses in sand-castle, gingerbread style, to be topped by a colossal statue of Lenin. But when construction began, the earth that had been beneath the church suddenly turned wet and mushy, and the building kept sinking. Revenge from the heavens? Many like to think so. The authorities had to abandon the project, finally settling for a huge round municipal swimming pool.

There is a delicious postscript to the tale, unknown to most Russians. The swimming pool, which is outdoors and heated in winter, has become the site of clandestine baptisms by underground Baptists who are part of an extensive network of believers. They worship and congregate secretly in each other's apartments and publish leaflets and thin periodicals in a hidden printing shop somewhere in the country. One who allowed his name to be used, Leonid N. Polivanov, was a round-faced man in his fifties, with merry eyes and a grey Hemingway beard. He said he was baptized in the pool in the early 1970's by an American Baptist sight-seeing in Moscow. "There were only two of us," he said. "We prayed and dunked." None of the other swimmers seemed to notice. In winter, as clouds of steam rise from the pool, he and his teenage daughter Iya would baptize many Russians and foreigners, foreigners whom they approached in Red Square as fervently as evangelists ply their trade in Times Square. The Polivanovs' apartment was strewn with snapshots of foreign friends and foreign-made religious trinkets. Spread on the couch was a blue T-shirt with a picture of Jesus on the front.

These fundamentalist Protestants, including Baptists, Pentacostalists, and Seventh-day Adventists, are usually treated more roughly than Russian Orthodox observers. Repeated, heavy fines are levied against those who hold unregistered worship services in their apartments. Religious leaders, such as the Baptist Georgi Vins, are sentenced to long terms in prison and Siberian exile. In rural areas particularly, the authorities have removed children from their parents' custody, under the guise of protecting the health and welfare of the young ones, when their families forbid dancing, television, and Pioneer or Komsomol membership.

Russian Orthodox activists have had sporadic trouble. In 1979–80 two prominent priests were arrested: Gleb Yakunin, who had organized a small committee to press for religious rights and to publicize harassment and imprisonment, and Dmitri Dudko, whose popular, outspoken sermons had packed his Moscow church in the early 1970's. Father Dmitri was a short, balding, stocky elf of a man with a grey beard and penetrating eyes; I sat with him for a long time in his apartment on the northern outskirts of the capital. We spoke at some length on a broad range of ecclesiastical and social topics. His dissertations were rather metaphorical and Aesopian and often hard to follow. He had been wounded and was being somewhat careful. In 1974 he had conducted Sunday evening question-and-answer sessions at the richly adorned Church of St. Nicholas, speaking openly about the state of Christianity in the Soviet Union, about moral living in an officially atheist society. The authorities moved in and forced the patriarch to deprive him of his church and to reassign him to a rural parish just outside the city. He gave his sermons there, too, boldly.

"Yes, many members of the party baptize their children," he said. "And moreover, there are many party members who have themselves baptized. Here the other day I christened a party member, his wife, and three of his grown children. This phenomenon signified, I would say, a paradox: that they are real believers and real Communists. If a Communist is for justice, then how can he deny the truth that all human existence seeks immortality? The church in our country will always exist because our country, by its Christian nature, has the richest soil just now for Christianity. Here are suffering and persecution. It is not those wallowing in luxury who clutch at a straw. I look upon this optimistically: We and the Communists must find a common language, and this common language is the language not of nonbelief but of belief. You know you will not build any communism on nonbelief. And our common language is such that we all—both believers and Communists, creatures of God—carry His image and must understand that we are brothers and have had enough hammering on each other."

The hammering between the church and the temporal authority of Russia has been part of the land's history since the influence of Byzantium brought Christianity to Kiev in the tenth century. Russians have a legend about their conversion from paganism to Christianity, explaining that they spurned Judaism because its people were defeated and stateless and rejected Islam because it barred alcohol, and "drink is the joy of the Russian."* The unruly church was frequently in conflict with the czars. The hierarchy harbored many of Peter the Great's opponents in the seventeenth and eighteenth centuries until Peter abolished the patriarchate, turning the church first into an official agency and later into an instrument of the police. In the 1920's and 1930's Stalin made three distinct attempts to eliminate religion by persecution, each followed by a period of relative softness. In the strife of World War II and the hardship of the postwar years, religion gained an increased following, and new churches were opened. Khrushchev then presided over a strident antireligious campaign in the early 1960's, followed again by a softening, which showed tentative signs of ending in the early 1980's.

Father Dmitri saw the historical threads running into the present. He judged the church too timid, too anxious, too compliant. "Believers avoid priests," he told me. "Priests run from believers or betray the interests of believers. This is our misfortune. They are afraid of each other." Sermons are not supposed to deal with the real world, so they and the rites become spiritually empty, he said. "Outwardly, splendor. Inwardly, emasculation."

Two years after our talk, and apparently because his sermons continued to excite interest among young Russians, Father Dmitri was arrested. But an even sadder event occurred five months later, when he appeared on Soviet television reading a statement of confession and apology. "I have seen that I yielded to those propaganda voices that are directed at undermining our system," the

*Nicholas V. Riasanovsky, *A History of Russia*, 2nd ed. (New York: Oxford University Press, 1969), p. 38.

priest read. "I repudiate what I have done and assess my so-called struggle against godlessness as a struggle against the Soviet power." He rejected "foreign press reports" that he had been falsely accused. "This is not true," he said. "I have been made answerable on lawful grounds for the crimes I have committed." He said some of his books and articles "referred to the Soviet system from anti-Soviet, slanderous positions." When they were published abroad, he declared, foreign radio stations broadcast excerpts in "a stream of lies and slander" against the Soviet Union. I was already in Jerusalem at the time, but when I saw the news reports of his confession, I felt how acutely his parishioners must have been weeping for him.

Patriotism

I wish I could remember her name. She was a woman in her fifties, I suppose, solid and grey-haired, her face proud and firm and slightly flushed with a glow of fervor and reverence. She worked for Tass, the Soviet news agency, and we fell into brief conversation as we walked in Volgograd, once called Stalingrad, behind a delegation of Soviet and American astronauts who had linked their spacecraft together in the joint Apollo-Soyuz mission. It was 1975, that fleeting moment of détente.

She suddenly stopped walking and pulled out a plastic jewelry box, held it toward me, and removed the lid. Inside, cushioned on a bed of cotton, lay several rusted, corroded shell casings—special, she said, from the Battle of Stalingrad. She took one out as gingerly as if it had been a precious gem, wrapped it carefully in a piece of paper, and presented it to me, beaming, a gift of honor and friendship. It stands now in a bookcase behind my desk, an archaeological find from the ruins of heroism.

The delegation walked to the eternal flame that burns in memory of those who perished during the ferocious Battle of Stalingrad from August 1942 to the end of January 1943, when every narrow street and house was fought for, often hand to hand, until the Germans finally learned defeat. The Russians rebuilt in equally ferocious pride, bestowing on their renamed Stalingrad the title

Hero City and enshrining their worship of country in a myriad of symbols that now keep alive the pain and triumph of what they call the Great Patriotic War. The eternal flame, the Tass woman told me, was lit in 1967 by the first spark from a new hydroelectric plant outside the city; she took pleasure in this sickly-sweet conjunction of tributes to the nation, past and future.

The monuments in Volgograd are steeped in religious solemnity. Mamayev Hill, site of the principal memorial to the Battle of Stalingrad, begins near its base with two large concrete bas-reliefs covered with the anguished faces and battle cries of the men who defended the city. "Every house is a fortress!" one cry reads. "Not one step backward!" calls another. The rough reliefs are cut by niches where mourners, pilgrims, have placed small bouquets of flowers, as on small altars. Through loudspeakers, choral music plays; it is not martial, but hymnal. Up the hill stands a sculpture of a kerchiefed woman cradling a dying soldier across her knees— so like a pietà that it would not seem out of place in a cathedral. At the very top towers a massive, heroic statue 282 feet high—a woman, Mother Russia, a broadsword raised high with muscular arm, her robes and hair whipped by an unfelt wind. Below, along the stairway, the inscription on the wall begins, "The iron wind was in their faces . . ." Something in the sacred, epic proportions of this place compels silence. The Tass woman is brushing away tears of sorrow and pride, as if it has all been yesterday.

Of all the ideas and beliefs and forces of allegiance that crisscross through Soviet society, patriotism is the most pervasive and the most powerful. More thoroughly than communism or Christianity, the passion for the homeland binds the diverse citizenry, commanding devotion across the contrasts of more than 100 ethnic cultures and languages in the vast Soviet empire. It serves as the common denominator, capable of blending into both the communism and the Christianity of the Russians. In these amalgams of belief, patriotism is often the dominant factor, and this is due in some measure to its reliance on the legacy of World War II, the Great Patriotic War.

No Soviet city is without a war memorial, no matter how many thousands of miles it was from the front. Even in places annexed after the war, the ingenious Soviet leadership has found obscure partisans and dogged Communists to honor with monuments. Any visitor who puts himself in the hands of an Intourist guide will be treated to dissertations on the small bands' heroic resistance to the German onslaught, and will be encouraged to photograph the plaques and statues.

The Soviet version of the pulp paperback is the war story, often maudlin and widely appealing; movie theaters and television broadcasts are full of melodramatic films about the war, both fiction and documentary, the sort of thing that long ago passed out of fashion in the United States. One on Stalingrad, with stirring music and booming narration, showed scenes of residents building fortifications, children manning factories, Hitler with his generals ("Hitler congratulates his generals too soon," the announcer gloated), and soldiers battling the Germans as the city was reduced to rubble around them. The narrator declared, "Their raging, burning hatred of the enemy proved stronger than death."

Many Russians were offended by Brezhnev's exploitation of the war and of his own role in it, for those years of trial are something sacred to them. As he enhanced his power within the Politburo in the last half of the 1970's, he became the focus of heightened adulation, receiving orders and medals, attaining the rank of marshal, and posing for pictures in military uniform. Although he had apparently been only a noncombatant political officer, he was made to seem like a battlefield hero, leading one Russian dissident to make up a joke about him: Brezhnev dies, and the Politburo meets to decide where to bury him. At first they consider the Lenin Mausoleum, but that seems too grand. Then they think of the Kremlin wall, but that seems not grand enough. Finally they decide on the Tomb of the Unknown Soldier. Why? Because it's unknown whether or not he was a soldier.

The memory of the war is fresh, both because it is kept that way by a leadership seeking to bolster national pride and cohesiveness, and because it was a genuine trauma that left scarcely a family untouched. At least 7 million died, the government reported in 1946, and foreign scholars have estimated up to 20 million. Material losses were immense. Mines were flooded, railroad tracks blown up, collective farms destroyed, livestock massacred, towns and cities wrecked. The Soviet authorities put the devastation at about half what all of Europe suffered.* Civilians lost family, went hungry, moved eastward out of European Russia into Siberia and

*Riasanovsky, *op. cit.*, p. 585.

Central Asia as the Germans pressed forward to encircle Leningrad, to advance within miles of Moscow and to occupy territory west of a long front extending from Leningrad into the Caucasus. Today the tales of suffering remain raw, and any hint of hunger stirs an old panic as mothers stuff their children with potatoes and cabbage and keep the cupboards full. The war is still cited by many ordinary Russians as the cause of current hardship, the reason that agriculture falters and industry fails to meet the needs. "So much was destroyed in the war," people say, believing the excuse.

Even though the war years are now remembered as a time of unparalleled comradeship, there are also bitter stories of Russian cheating Russian. A friend recalls his mother's trading her jewelry for a tub of butter in starving Leningrad and arriving home to find that the butter formed just the surface of the tub's contents. Beneath a two-inch layer was nothing but sand. She dashed back to the market, but the man who had sold it was gone. She screamed for the police. People tried to calm her. *"Byvaet, byvaet,"* they soothed. "It happens, it happens." Sometimes, my friend remembers, the stew sent by the United States was drained from its cans by Russian black marketeers, who replaced it with sawdust and stones.

However, the memories for most are filled with a nostalgic devotion to country and countrymen. It was a time when everyone stood together, blocking out the inner suspicions and terrors that had run during the purges of the thirties. The recollections now stir authentic patriotic emotions, truer than the placard declarations of fidelity that hang across city streets.

I walked into my office one evening to find our telex operator, a kind woman of middle age, sitting in front of the television set, tears running silently down her cheeks. On the screen was a program much like the old *This Is Your Life,* where people are confronted by surprise reunions on camera with long-lost friends, teachers, relatives. The Soviet version was reuniting those who had helped each other and suffered together in the war. A paunchy man had just been presented with a round, jolly woman who, it turned out, had nursed him back to health in a farmhouse after he had been severely wounded. Then came another man, a fellow soldier who had shared the trenches with him. They hadn't seen each other for more than thirty years. Everybody in the studio was weeping, along with untold millions watching across the land.

The war legitimized Soviet patriotism as an acceptable set of feelings, breaking the ideological contempt in which the early Communists had held any exaltation of the nation. For the true Marxists, the proletariat was united across national frontiers; it was a class transcending state borders and regional identities. "The word *rodina* and the concept of a patriotic motherland were never employed by Lenin," wrote Harrison Salisbury. "In his day, the word was the property of the pre-fascist 'Black Hundreds,' the anti-Semitic, xenophobic Slav organization sponsored by the Czar's secret police. Lenin believed with Karl Marx that 'the workers have no fatherland.' "* Trotsky declared, "Let patriotism be damned."

These were unnatural inhibitions in Russia, and when Stalin and the war released the country from its ideological constraints, the people hurtled into chauvinistic zeal. Stalin was the mad demagogue, but he had willing followers into fanaticism throughout the population. The country allowed itself to be infected with a collective psychosis, even to the point of imprisoning its own soldiers who had survived or escaped from German prisoner-of-war camps; Soviet authorities acted against them in the demented conviction that they must have collaborated to have lived. For nearly a decade after the war the labor camps of Siberia were populated with the unfortunate heroes, branded antiheroes. The only sure way to remain heroic was to die.

The war is still used today to explain the surrounding world, to make of the Russians a special people unique in their suffering and in their need for vigilance. "We do not want to bring our children up as pacifists," a woman elementary school principal told a European. "They must be ready to fight." And my fleeting acquaintance "Furtsev," from the Central Committee staff, saw a great continuity of history imposing strife on the Russian nation. "My great-great-grandfather was killed in the Turkish-Bulgarian War," he said. "My great-grandfather was killed in the Russo-Japanese War. My grandfather was killed in the First World War. And my father was killed in the Second World War. He was the oldest of them all. He was thirty-nine. You cannot understand us because you have not suffered and survived what we have. You have not been under the

The New York Times Magazine, February 1, 1981.

Tatar yoke, you have not lived under a Stalin—and God keep you from ever having to—and so you cannot understand. You are from a different world. You are like Martians to us. And I suppose we are like Martians to you."

The abiding fear of encirclement and invasion and warfare reaches back into the earliest moments of Russian history, when internal strife among squabbling princes weakened resistance to assaults by the Polovtsy, or Cumans, Turkic tribesmen from Asia, and later to conquest by the Tatars. The lesson—solidarity in the face of foreigners—is caught in the thunderous lines of "The Lay of Igor's Campaign," the twelfth-century epic poem on the Polovtsy attacks. The poem is one of the earliest preserved works of Russian literature, and it taps an unending mood:

> The war of the princes against the infidels has ceased, for brother said to brother, "This is mine, and that is mine, too." And the princes began to say of little things, "This is a great matter," and to forge strife each against the other. And from all sides the victorious infidels invaded the land of Russia. . . . And Kiev, brothers, groaned with sorrow, and Chernigov with affliction. Anguish flowed over the land of Russia, sorrow in abundance spread across the Russian land. And the princes forged strife each against the other, while the infidels, victoriously invading the land of Russia, took tribute of a squirrel-skin from every homestead.*

Approximately 900 years later the basic message of unanimity and vigilance was being preached in lectures to Muscovites who were bracing for an invasion of foreigners for the 1980 Olympics. Anthony Austin of *The New York Times* reported:

> The trolley bus pulled up at a stop and a middle-aged woman with a threadbare shopping bag got on. "So, comrades," she addressed the world from her seat, "the spies and diversionists have already begun." The others on the bus pretended not to hear. From the cloth bags of the women and the bulging briefcases of the men, it was clear that their minds were on the hurried shopping for provisions done on their lunch breaks.

*From *The Penguin Book of Russian Verse,* Dimitri Obolensky, ed. (Middlesex, England: Penguin Books, 1965).

"What, you don't know?" insisted the woman who had just gotten on. She recounted one of the warnings given in the lectures by Soviet security experts at all Moscow offices and factories in the weeks before the Games. This one had it that C.I.A. agents among the foreign tourists would order soft drinks in public cafes and cafeterias and leave the bottles half empty—after pouring in powdered poison. "I've found one of those half-empty bottles already," the woman said triumphantly. "I took it at once to the militia."

Even those who do not share this sort of xenophobia, even those who deride the system and its leadership embrace the values of patriotism. To Americans whose sense of virtue has been strained by Vietnam and racial injustice and other failings of their society, Soviet patriotism often seems old-fashioned and naïve, the stuff of self-deluding mythology, a false and melodramatic self-righteousness. But its grip on people is tight, and it does not let go easily. I first encountered the long grasp of the motherland before I went to Moscow, while I was studying Russian in New York. One of my teachers was a recent émigré, formerly an art historian at Moscow State University who had taken the risk with her husband and daughter and had sought to join the flow of Jews going to the West. They had lost their jobs but eventually received their exit visas; she had nothing good to say about the system, the party, or the government. During one of her tales of official imperiousness and dishonesty I remarked that the Soviet Union sounded like "a strange country." She suddenly bristled with offense, lectured me sternly on the beauty and fineness of her native land, and left me gasping. It was not a strange country at all. I had failed to discern the difference between the system and the *rodina,* the motherland. Similarly, Vera Chalidze, who had been stripped of her Soviet citizenship while she and her husband, Valery, a founder of the Human Rights Committee, had been let out for a supposed "visit" to America, told me longingly of her yearning for Russia, her need again for the nourishment of being in Moscow instead of New York, of strolling in her Russian forests of birches, of feeling the flow of the Russian language all about her. She could not stand not going back. In Israel, too, I met a former Soviet radio and documentary film narrator, Reuven Vygodsky, who relished his ability to pick up Syrian television broadcasts with a high antenna and catch the frequent Soviet programs. "They often have the Bolshoi!" his wife said delightedly.

Many who have suffered imprisonment for speaking and writing against injustices are still so emotionally bound to their country that they struggle to stay. When the state seeks to uproot them and exile them to the West, they resist, wrestling with their own fears for their safety, fighting inside themselves to overcome the terror and remain on their native soil. They know that the West can be an exile spiritually more trying for them than the physical hardship of exile in Siberia, for what is a writer cut off from his source of understanding? What is a thinker divorced from the fluency of his language and his people? Men and women who were towering and defiant intellects in the adversity of Moscow have withered in the West. Their departure from Russia has seen the beginning of a dull ache, never to be relieved. And Soviet officialdom sees the banishment as the ultimate punishment, the fitting torture of those who are deemed to have stepped away from the closed and loyal circle of the family. So it has been with Aleksandr Solzhenitsyn, who was forcibly deported in 1974; the late Andrei Amalrik, harassed relentlessly and threatened by the KGB until he unwillingly emigrated in 1976 and later died in an automobile accident; and Lev Kopelev, who left reluctantly in 1980 for a year in West Germany, hoping to return and knowing somehow that he never would. After his departure on a Soviet passport the Supreme Soviet issued a decree stripping him and his wife, Raissa Orlova, of their Soviet citizenship.

Lev Kopelev was a great oak of a man, six feet tall and barrel-chested, a bulwark of stubborn patriotism. He wore a thick white beard and moved stiffly with a gnarled walking stick, but his manner was disarmingly gentle, his mind finely analytical and sensitive to the undercurrents of Russia. As a young major in the Red Army's Political Administration, fluent in German and responsible for propagandizing the enemy as the Russians swept westward toward the war's end, Lev saw and reported and tried to stop his fellow soldiers' burning and raping and looting as they rolled through Poland and Germany. He was accused of harboring suspicious sympathies for the Germans, of criticizing his country's army, of "propaganda of bourgeois humanism and of pity for the enemy." The party expelled him, the courts tried him, and he spent nine years in Stalin's prison camps, a victim of the paranoia that then gripped the land.

Lev believed in Stalin and the party. His sturdy faith so struck Solzhenitsyn, whom he met when they both were prisoners, that Lev became a model for Solzhenitsyn's character Lev Rubin, the brilliant linguist in *The First Circle* who continues to support Stalin and the system even as they persecute him. Kopelev's beliefs took many years to crumble, and after they had fallen away, there remained, still, a passionate love of country. Through the 1970's, as he wrote of his wartime and prison experiences for publication in the West,* as his and Raya's apartment on Red Army Street in Moscow became a vibrant crossroads of foreigners and Soviet intellectuals of many streams, as Solzhenitsyn was banished west to America and Sakharov east to Gorky, Lev grew increasingly exposed and vulnerable. Derided in the official press as a "Judas" and a "traitor," he was given to understand that he would probably have to choose between going east and going west, east into exile or prison, west into exile and freedom and rootlessness. He turned over and over the thought of taking a year's sabbatical in West Germany to be with his friend Heinrich Böll, to pursue his studies of German literature. Raya resisted, knowing that if they went, it would be not for a year, but forever. She was quietly relieved when some official obstacle arose to securing the proper documentation, and it seemed as if they would not be able to leave. But finally the pressure on Lev grew, and the barriers to departure relaxed, and they took the fateful step.

Tony Austin of *The New York Times* wrote movingly of their departure on a 10:00 A.M. Aeroflot flight to Frankfurt on November 12, 1980. They arrived at Sheremetyevo Airport hours early, all they needed for a year packed into three suitcases, Lev using his walking stick, which he had ripped from a tree in the Crimea in 1957 during his years of recuperation from the camps. About fifty people had gathered near the customs counters to say good-bye, including some of the country's finest and most independent writers, Raya's two daughters by a former marriage, and some grandchildren.

"We go only to return," said Lev.

"We'll be back, we'll be back," cried Raya tearfully.

---

*To Be Preserved Forever (New York: J. B. Lippincott Company, 1977).

"Good luck, come back soon," some of the friends and relatives called from behind the railing. And everyone knew.

Six customs inspectors spent an hour examining their belongings. Selected items were put aside for confiscation: an old, slender book of Pushkin's poems published in 1874, a cardboard folder of papers, containing Raya's articles on Mark Twain and on Martin Luther King, Lev's notes for a lecture on Goethe's popularity in Russia, and a catalogue of the rich collection of books he had left behind, stacked and crammed into his apartment; two address books containing names and phone numbers of friends throughout the world. An inspector took a small plastic box in his hands and opened it. Inside, Lev had placed a handful of Russian earth. It was confiscated.

This was the fate that Andrei Sakharov dreaded when he contemplated asking to go to Oslo to receive the Nobel Peace Prize he had been awarded in 1975. He told me that he would attend the presentation ceremony only if he received assurances from Soviet authorities, before leaving, that they would allow him to return. He did not want to be stranded abroad, separated from his homeland. But his conversations with officials never reached that point, for they told him immediately that he would not be permitted to leave the country at all; as a key physicist in the development of the Soviet atomic bomb, he knew secrets, they said, and he might divulge them in the West. Sakharov was bitterly insulted by the suggestion that he would ever betray his motherland. His patriotism transcended his active campaign for human rights; his love of country was, in a sense, a motivation for his strenuous and courageous efforts to make his society better. When he appealed to Western governments to press Soviet authorities to free prisoners and end persecution and honor the standards of decency, he felt he was doing so for the benefit of his own country. But to officials jealous of their righteous authority, and to Russians nurtured through their history on chauvinism and xenophobia, the act of invoking foreign pressure against your native land is at first bewildering, then infuriating, nauseating. It is like spitting on your own soul.*

Many Russians see the principle as universal, applying not only

---

*Only in 1988, after Sakharov was accepted back into the official community, quoted in the official press, and even elected to the Presidium of the Academy of Sciences, was he allowed to visit the United States, where he was received by President Reagan in the White House. In 1989 he won a legislative seat in the first competitive elections.

to them but to every man who has a country. When Solzhenitsyn was being assailed in the official press shortly before his deportation, the American Marxist and folk singer Dean Reed wrote an open letter, which was published in several Soviet magazines and newspapers, joining the official assault on Solzhenitsyn and spelling out the defects of the so-called free society in America. However, Reed's letter disgusted many politically orthodox Russians who also detested Solzhenitsyn. Not that they minded an attack on Solzhenitsyn, but they minded it coming from a foreigner, who had no business meddling in Soviet affairs. Nor did they mind an attack on America, but they minded it coming from an American, who had no business smearing his homeland. "Reed is naïve and politically helpless," scoffed one such Russian.

Another remarked, "I dislike people who are pouring dirt on their own country. Maybe it does deserve it, but why do it publicly?"

In Russians' perceptions there is no more serious divide than that between the Soviet Union and the outside world. Even in this intricately partitioned society, no delineation of class, ethnicity, or family, no lines of domestic geography, party activism, or professional life compare with the profound gulf between the *rodina,* the motherland, and the world beyond, *za granitsei* ("beyond the frontier"). Here it is hard but home, the source, the balm; there it is exciting, thrilling, frightening, alien. Here the devotion must be unconditional, as the love by a mother for her child, a love that can never be shattered by any transgression. No matter what the country does, you must love it. But if you do the country wrong, it will stop loving you and will cast you out. It is an Old Testament God of anger and retribution, this motherland. I have heard Russians say that any Jews who want to emigrate should be allowed to leave but that their abandonment should be punished by the most searing condemnation: that they never be allowed to return. A linguist who pronounced this sentence smiled with cold satisfaction that he had found the key to inflicting ultimate pain.

Thus does the official propaganda, which sounds so stilted and unpersuasive to Western ears, have resonance for Russians. Hear this appeal, published in the newspaper *Sotsialisticheskaya Industriya,* pulling the strings of primeval attachment to place, and sounding the deep chords of a people's suffering:

The autumn wind tears down the crimson copper of the maples and throws it into half-open windows. It is warm and light inside. Around me are the voices, which lower to whispers or rise to a loud murmur, and the faces of old women looking down meekly. The silk of the women's parti-colored kerchiefs glitters like a rainbow; men's temples gleam with silver. Now comes the end of the prayer, and a dark-haired man of about forty-five comes up to a dais.

His sermon is on God's will, mercy, and justice, on love for neighbor. The preacher's words take us to his remote childhood, revive in memory the dreadful years of the war: "When the enemy's soldiers and tanks were approaching our house, when it seemed that death was inevitable, and parents and we children fell on our knees, lifting our arms to the sky and begging the Most High for help. And suddenly, as if directed by an invisible hand, the enemy would turn in the opposite direction, swing around our house and retreat."

My own childhood sails in front of me. It was barefooted, weather-beaten, rain-washed. I see curly birch trees in the field and dark blue forest on the horizon, flavored snow and pink clouds of blossoming cherries and apple trees in May, ruffling rye and groaning cranes.

I see another village: burned in the fire of war, with grey mounds. Over the mounds are modest five-pointed stars and hastily written last names—names, years of birth. Russian, Ukrainian, Georgian, Lithuanian, Uzbek last names. Under these mounds sleep those who, with their might and main, defended our life, our towns, your village and mine, with a nameless little river flowing past a little bathhouse sunk to one side, with a warm fire and the comfort of home, with a child's smile and the wisdom of old age. They have defended everything which was near and dear to the heart, which is personified by the idea of the motherland. It was not the Almighty's hand which turned the enemy back. Next to a grey-haired master sergeant stood a young soldier who just left school. The damp earth opened its embraces to a young nurse who did not have a chance to dress her first wounded. "Remember us, our dear, remember our tireless thirst for life, work, creation; be happy, keep our memory, and never forget that there is nothing dearer than the native land, there is no more sacred word than the word 'motherland,' " pale daisies whisper and green fir trees moan sadly over the graves.

Does Yuri Maryanovich Romansky, a driver in the Vilnius trolley administration, hear this whisper? Perhaps his father was killed defending a nameless hill, and the son does not even know where his grave is. The father laid down his life for the motherland, and what about the son? Having joined the sectarians, Yuri Romansky wrote a statement wishing to emigrate to . . . the U.S.A. He wrote it, yielding to the persuasions of the preacher, and now does not know what to do. What awaits him in the strange land? Who needs him? "I'll work like here," he tries to explain, with diffidence and the fear of uncertainty in his eyes. He cannot but know that millions of people in the capitalist countries are looking for work, but do not find it. There is no work for the local people, and what awaits the newcomer who does not know the language and habits of the strange land? Think, Yuri Maryanovich, make the judgment well. Think now and during your regular annual vacation, which you are going to spend in the south with a trade union accommodation pass.

Belongingness is more than physical presence. One can be in the country and still be considered alien. Membership in the family must be upheld by demonstrative behavior. One reason that would-be émigrés lose their jobs after applying for exit visas is the official interpretation that they have declared their apartness; they have withdrawn and no longer truly belong. Those who publish or criticize abroad are not penalized for wrongdoing; they are rejected by the national family, the collective, as an organism rejects a piece of foreign matter. The punishments spring from a far deeper source of revulsion and outrage than in the case, for example, of burglary.

In 1976 Igor Melchuk, a senior research fellow at the Institute of Linguistics, sent a letter that was published in *The New York Times* defending Sakharov, condemning Soviet scientists for their silence, and pleading with Western intellectuals to speak out more vigorously. "As for the West," he wrote, "I cannot understand the attitude of your scientists and scholars. Perhaps they do not fully realize that a powerful nation of 250 million, guided by the unscrupulous and having at its disposal first-class brains with no hearts and souls, may prove highly dangerous." His institute convened a meeting to denounce him and dismiss him from its ranks. "Ten people took the floor," he said. "Nobody defended me. Everybody accused me of waging war, besmirching my country, struggling against the Soviet way of life." He caught their words by hiding a tape recorder in his briefcase during the meeting; he played the tape for me.

"The letter," stated the institute's director, Viktoria Yartseva, "besmirches our country and covers every researcher with shame. It is quite inadmissible, not only in a scientific collective such as our institute but also in the collective of the whole Soviet people."

"Slandering our country," said Professor Mira Gukhman, "Melchuk does serious harm, not only to the USSR but to the whole of progressive mankind as well. I'm sure that this hostile act makes the future presence of Melchuk in the Institute of Linguistics absolutely impossible."

Soviet citizenship means being treated like a child and being childlike in response. Sergei Polikanov, respected nuclear physicist, full member of the Academy of Sciences, finally had enough. Once, during an earlier East-West thaw, he and his wife and daughter had lived in Denmark during a research project of his. Years later, when I met him, he was due to go to Geneva to continue work on a line of investigation that had consumed most of his life. But the authorities were not going to let his wife and daughter accompany him for the year; they would have to stay behind, as hostages, his wife believed, to ensure that Sergei would return and not defect. He was insulted, ashamed for himself and his country. So were many of his colleagues, who had gone through the same humiliation themselves but whose chance at a brief time in the West was too precious to ruin by making a fuss. For Sergei, this was the final indignity added to all he had endured from youth into adulthood, and it tipped the balance. He called a press conference for foreign correspondents at the home of Vladimir Voinovich, the satirist who was later forced to emigrate to Western Europe.

Sergei denounced the travel restrictions and called on all Soviet scientists to speak out against their absurdity. He had stepped across the line.

The reaction was not immediate. He and his wife lost friends and gained some in the close quarters of their ingrown scientific community at Dubna, on the Volga north of Moscow. Debby and I strolled with them one Sunday afternoon and saw how some snubbed them and others nodded discreet greetings. His superiors tried quietly for weeks to "save" him, to woo him back into the fold, to induce him to move back onto the right side by condemning Western journalists' "sensational" exploitation of his criticism. He refused all such invitations. And so he found himself accused in a party meeting at his research laboratory.

"Before the party meeting," he said, "a document was prepared about me. It was written that I had been provided with good conditions for scientific pursuits but that I had started to be somewhat separate from the party. This separateness led to my meeting with Western correspondents. They recalled some old things that had happened two years ago, which now, seen from today's perspective, showed how I had become separate from the party. There were a hundred forty people at the meeting. The document was read by the secretary of the laboratory party organization—the Nuclear Problems Laboratory. I was asked to explain my position. I said that it was necessary for our scientists to have better contacts with Western scientists and that now contacts should be made easier. Barriers should be lowered, but they are being raised. I said that it had not been so easy for me to come to Western correspondents but that sometimes in our lives it comes to that. I mentioned Klebanov and workers [Vladimir Klebanov, who went to foreign correspondents with workers' grievances after encountering indifference from Soviet officials and editors] and said I guessed it was not so easy for them. I said it was easier to fight for the freedom of Angela Davis than for our own freedom. I read the text of a letter I gave to you [correspondents]. Some tried to stop me, but I continued. Then there was a discussion about me. Three people spoke. One scientist said: 'Bourgeois ideology is trying to make a hole in our wall. They succeeded this time, but it will be the last time.' He quoted something from Brezhnev. One worker said I had been fed, clothed, educated, and I should be grateful. The director of the laboratory, Professor Venedikt Dzhelepov, said that there are some people who sacrifice, people who serve on icebreakers, and so forth, and I wouldn't make even a small sacrifice. Then I was given another chance to speak. I answered Dzhelepov. I said that his understanding of sacrifice was too small. I mentioned Yuri Orlov [who formed the Helsinki Watch Committee and drew a long prison sentence], devoted to science, but he lost his chance to work in science by fighting for human rights. Some people told me later that my talk made it clear that I didn't want to be in the party. All voted to expel. I did not ask to stay in the party. The second thing concerned my work in the institute. The party organization recommended that the institute expel me. They voted to do that at the same meeting. The next day one worker said, 'Why expel you from the institute? You are a scientist.' I said, 'Why didn't you say that yesterday?' "

But Sergei's "separateness" from the party was something genuinely felt by those in charge and by him, too; what it really meant was a separateness from the nation, from the clannish loyalty that the nation demands. He was ultimately stripped of his medals, his honors, his place in the Academy of Sciences, and finally—in a remarkable gesture of clemency by the Soviet authorities—he was allowed to take his separateness to its full conclusion by emigrating with his wife and daughter to Denmark. He did so apparently without the deep pangs that afflict many other departing Russians. But I knew another man, "Sasha," whose contradictory senses of separateness and belonging struggled within him, pulling him this way and that, driving him nearer and then away, and then nearer again to political orthodoxy.

He was Jewish by background, but not by conviction or identity. The only time he gave way to his Jewishness was when his father died, and he fulfilled the old man's wish by assembling a *minyan* for the funeral. He knew people in the Foreign Ministry, the Central Committee, and the small subculture of dissident writers and acerbic critics who lived on the edge of official tolerance. He fraternized with American diplomats and a few correspondents. In moving among these various worlds, he did not know quite where he belonged or what he believed. One month I would hear him dissect his society with a cruel perception and wit; the next I'd find him restrained and careful, his shifting moods usually the function of his rising and falling fortunes in the system.

Sasha was a journalist in his forties, specializing in American film and literature, but because he was not a member of the party, his opportunities within that ideological discipline were limited. He made his living by free-lancing, an uncommon practice in the Soviet Union, and although he managed to get articles published in some of the major papers and magazines (always yielding to editors' demands for abundant quotes from Brezhnev and Lenin), it was a stressful and uncertain existence. So he set out to find a steady job. His English was fluent, acquired during his student days in an English-language school abroad, where his father had been posted. But when he presented himself at a language institute for a teaching position, he was made to feel immediately that his Jewishness and his upbringing outside the country had somehow placed him outside the circle of loyalty. A party committee, not a faculty committee, interviewed him; he was asked in ominous tones whether he had ever sought to change his citizenship, a euphemism for applying to emigrate to Israel. He took the question as an insulting slap. Sasha did not feel Jewish and had no interest in Israel, no desire to leave his country. He was angry. He told them sharply that the question was entirely inappropriate to the purpose of the interview. He did not get the job.

Sasha then tried to pull some strings. Through a friend he arranged an appointment at the Central Committee, where he was bounced from official to official until he arrived at the office of a ranking *apparatchik* involved in overseeing newspapers and magazines. Sasha wanted a full-time staff job on a paper, preferably in his field of literary and film criticism. The *apparatchik* had briefed himself on Sasha's dossier, and with an air of arrogant remoteness he flicked aside my friend's appeal. Sasha was not in the party, the *apparatchik* began. He had once resisted helping the "organs" (the KGB) with some investigation. He had spent all those years studying abroad. You are not really "ours," the official said with a thin smile, not "one of us." The matter was closed. He had been judged an alien entity, un-Soviet. Stunned and hurt, Sasha rose to go. He was headed out the door when the man flung the final curse at him. "I suppose," said the official, "that now you'll emigrate?"

Sasha spun around in fury. So that was it. "People like me," he spit at the *apparatchik*, "will be here in this country long after your kind are gone." And he slammed out of the office.

Sasha told me all this in anguish as we walked beyond microphone range, we hoped, in a small park near a Moscow puppet theater. He was in such despair. Perhaps he could work for me, he suggested, translating and reporting for *The Times*'s bureau? It was a ridiculous idea, he knew: I had no openings then, translation was far beneath his skills, and in any case no Russian could work for a foreign firm without approval and assignment by UPDK, the state agency set up for that purpose. He was grasping wildly for something to stabilize his life.

Some months later he tried again to gain favor as a trusted member of the national family. He saw another, higher Central Committee official, who held out some hope for him, provided he proved himself by writing a small propaganda book on some theme of Western society. Sasha described it to me as a dirty job, but he did it. Apparently he did it well enough, for soon thereafter he was given a steady position in an agency associated with book publishing.

The question of belonging figured in another telling exchange. It was at a reception held by *Literaturnaya Gazeta,* the weekly of the Writers' Union, whose pages are also often used by the KGB to assail dissidents. The editor, Aleksandr Chakovsky, was complaining sardonically to Yuri Andropov, then head of the KGB, that the hand had been badly dealt to loyal citizens. Dissidents, with their foreign friends and hard-currency book royalties from the West, had access to the well-stocked Beryozka stores that accept only dollars, marks, and other convertible Western currencies, Chakovsky griped, while simple, honest Soviet writers and artists had no such entrée. According to a friend of mine who was present, Andropov looked up over his glasses at the portly editor. He paused patiently. Dissidents, the KGB man replied, were not really Soviet citizens. Honest Soviet citizens should suffer like anybody else. He delivered the pungent remark, then moved away.

In all these episodes, intensive patriotism became the vehicle for political intolerance, ethnocentrism, and a corrosive anxiety about the outside world's designs on Soviet territory and morale. The scientist in Dubna touched the essence of it when he said, "Bourgeois ideology is trying to make a hole in our wall." Our wall. As if this walled society could defend itself by sheer force against the onslaught of hostile ideas from beyond the gates. Hal Piper of the *Baltimore Sun* once asked a literature professor why writers like Solzhenitsyn couldn't be tolerated in Soviet society, why criticism of that kind was banned. The professor gave the following remarkable answer: During the war, his unit was surrounded by Germans. Weary, confused, hurt, the soldiers suddenly saw a Lithuanian appear on a balcony. "Moscow has fallen," the Lithuanian cried. "Lay down your arms!" The unit's officer replied by shooting the Lithuanian. And that was just what he should have done, the professor insisted, "because if the Lithuanian had been allowed to go on, we would have put down our arms. We didn't know." And that was why critical voices must not be heard today.

This is a society under a siege of its own making. The war becomes a metaphor. The clash of ideas assumes the gravity of a battle. The word is like a bullet, piercing armor, inflicting wounds, altering lives. Enhanced by all the taboos, the word has a power unknown in a West of plentiful debate and easy honesty. We do not treasure and fear fragments of truth the way the Russians do. We are not exhilarated by poets. We do not make our theaters electric with tension, poised over every nuance of irreverence onstage. We are bathed in information until we no longer feel its force. A Catholic priest in Lithuania told me that he had once visited America and was shocked. In New York subways people read and read the huge, great newspaper *The New York Times,* and then threw it away. *Threw it away!* All that precious information, just scattered in the subways, left on seats, dumped in trash barrels. If just one copy got into the Soviet Union, he said, it would be passed through hundreds of hands until it had disintegrated. The word is a bullet.

In the context of the facility Russians have for *vranyo* and other forms of mendacity, this regard for the power of the word achieves a certain mind-set in which whatever is spoken or written becomes more real than reality itself. Everyone knows that Trotsky was one of the Bolsheviks, but obliterating his name makes him go away, in a sense. Bringing him back into mention would shake a good many ideological and political assumptions, just as violently as bringing him back to life. The principle operates in many less momentous spheres, as Russians conduct esoteric debates in their newspapers and journals and watch for Aesopian allusions. One canny newspaper reader explained to me that when you see *Pravda* reporting that shock workers, like shock troops, are redoubling their heroic labor to bring the harvest in quickly, with a minimum of loss and spoilage, you know that the lazy bums are goofing off while the grain rots in the fields or spills out of poorly loaded trucks as they trundle lackadaisically along the bumpy country roads. And *Pravda* is worried.

The sensation of manipulating reality by controlling what is said about it has been helpful in creating patriotic zeal, fostering a pleasant simplicity in Russians' views of their country and their world. The Soviet Union is virtuous, struggling for peace and worldwide prosperity, ever ready to aid the victims of oppression. Its people live more comfortably than those elsewhere, and in greater harmony with their government. *"U nas luchshe* ["We have it better"]" is a declaration made often to foreign visitors. It is spoken sometimes out of real ignorance, sometimes in the willing suspension of disbelief, frequently in an effort to overcome a historic sense of inferiority against the technology and sophistication of the West. Or, most commonly, it is said as a mixture of all these, the ignorance and the inferiority and the struggle to believe blending together in a childlike approach to their country's blessings. It can be startling to attend a political meeting of adults—a party congress or a Lenin birthday celebration, for example—and discover suddenly that their flag-draped pageantry and elevated rhetoric are precisely what you've seen in kindergartens.

History plays a key role in this adoration of the motherland, for the Russians, through their own experience and in their basic Marxism, have come to feel the swells of history more instinctively than Americans. Indeed, history is so important to the Russians that they must falsify it. They cannot merely deny its power, as we tend to do. As in all other things, they must somehow control it, shape it, fashion it to their liking, and thereby conquer it. "What is the definition of a Soviet historian?" the Moscow joke asks. "A man who can predict the past."

The synthetic history of the Soviet Union, as offered today, is distinguished mostly by what it omits, rather than what it fabricates. The Stalinist propensity to credit Russians with inventing everything from the light bulb to the telephone has mostly passed. The tactic now is more often silence: silence about the early debates and dissent within the fledgling Communist Party, silence about the hardships and cruelties of forced collectivization, silence about the purges and executions of party leaders and the best Red Army officers before the war, silence about Stalin's mad imprisonment and slaughter of perhaps 20 million innocent citizens of his own land, silence about the dictator's 1939 nonaggression pact with Nazi Germany and its attendant psychology of excessive trust in Hitler, silence on the Soviet Union's unpreparedness for the German attack, silence on the $15 billion in American and British food and military equipment transported at great risk by convoy to Murmansk and Arkhangelsk through the submarine-infested North Atlantic.

If any of this is mentioned at all, it is played down and addressed so obliquely that it loses significance. Soviet versions of the war give little credit to the United States, which is remembered mostly for waiting more than two years after Hitler's invasion of the Soviet Union before entering the battle and opening a second front, as the Russians called it, on the west. America's idea of a second front was to send canned stew, Russians say. Even today similar canned stew is known contemptuously as "second front." Russians who know that trucks and tanks were also sent by the United States often believe the equipment was inferior—just leftovers, they complain.

The war in the Pacific is scarcely mentioned. Instead, on the thirtieth anniversary of the war's end, Soviet papers and journals exclaimed at the Japanese surrender days after the Soviet declaration of war against Japan. The grueling American-Japanese naval battles, the marine landings are virtually ignored. When the American atomic bombs on Hiroshima and Nagasaki are discussed, it is with moral outrage, and no connection is made between the bombings and the Japanese surrender. Against Germany, the Soviet Union alone is portrayed heroically. If Americans grow up learning that the Allied invasion of Normandy was the turning point, Russians grow up learning that the Battle of Stalingrad marked the beginning of Hitler's end. Few Russians are aware of the extent to which Americans and Britons, too, fought and died.

Despite our own biases, we in the West can know more about the Soviet Union, past and present, than Russians themselves. Many of the most elementary features of their history and their contemporary society are kept from them, creating large blanks in their knowledge. After a catastrophic harvest in 1975 the Soviet press reported nothing of the substantial American grain sales to the USSR, and although the Voice of America carried the news, my strong impression was that Russians generally disbelieved the reports and dismissed them as propaganda. A Moscow taxi driver got into a shouting match with one of his passengers, a dissident, that nearly led to blows, with the cabby screaming that the Soviet Union was feeding the whole world. Anatoly Shcharansky's father, a party member, attended a party meeting at which a speech was made about the lies on the Voice of America, an example being the reports of American sales of grain to the Soviet Union. Boris Shcharansky was sure that he was the only one in the room who knew that the grain sale reports were true.

The exclusivity of information is a hallmark of Soviet life, so much so that it is elevated into an ethical principle. Chris Catlin of Reuters and I were standing in line trying to get into a discotheque in Tallin one raw, drizzly night and making little headway as people with some kind of pull went right to the front. A well-dressed man in his thirties was waiting with us and in front of us; one might have expected a sense of camaraderie as we shared the same miserable conditions. But when the door opened, and the man had a quick conversation with the doorman about how long it might be before the line would move, and Chris walked up to find out what the doorman had said, the well-dressed man snapped something that made Chris come back looking as if cold water had been splashed in his face.

"What did he say?" I asked.

"He said, 'You don't have to know everything.' "

Not having to know everything is precisely where Soviet citizenship places you. I was startled again and again to find myself better informed than Russians about a whole range of issues, some so basic or close to home that they would have been major items of discussion and news reporting in the West. In Turkmenistan, near the border of Afghanistan, I was taken by an Intourist guide, a bright, articulate woman in her mid-twenties, to a collective farm I had asked to visit. The farm director and I talked for a long while about the slow process of issuing internal passports to collective farmers. He explained that his people had them, but other farms farther from cities had yet to make them available. On the drive back into Ashkhabad the guide said she was amazed to hear that some collective farmers didn't have internal passports; she had assumed that everyone always had them. She knew nothing of one of her country's most long-standing and fundamental tools of control over population movement. I visited a big dam project in Tadzhikistan, where the burgeoning reservoir created by the huge dam was causing small earthquakes as it filled with tons of water. A seismological institute in nearby Dushanbe was studying the phenomenon, had placed monitoring stations throughout the area, and had briefed me fully on the problems. But two guides in Nurek, a small town at the base of the dam, had heard nothing of this. They were surprised, and a bit distressed, when I breezed into their office asking for interviews and chattering about the seismological impact of the gargantuan reservoir and dam towering above them. "Oh," one said, "I thought we'd felt some tremors lately."

The nationalism that results from such carefully cultivated ignorance can hardly be very solid. A few dissenting Russians make jokes about it, often involving the Soviet phobia of the Chinese, a throwback to the historical specter of the Mongol hordes invading once again to seize Russia by the throat. One crack has Soviet schools teaching two foreign languages, Hebrew for those who leave and Chinese for those who stay. A news item from the year 2000: All is quiet on the Finnish-Chinese border. A popular one from President Carter's day had Brezhnev calling Carter and saying, "Jimmy, I had a dream last night. I saw Washington all in red —the Capitol, the White House, everything in red, with red flags and red banners fluttering in the streets."

"Well, Lyonya," Carter replies, "I had a dream last night, too. I saw Moscow all in red, with red flags and slogans flying over the Kremlin."

"What's so strange about that?" Brezhnev snorts. "What did the slogans say?"

"I don't know," says Carter. "I can't read Chinese."

Russians can laugh only because their regard for country is so central to them. But the seriousness with which they usually take their patriotism also masks the inadequacy of the nationalist attitude as a system of belief. For all its power, it is not sufficiently comprehensive, not thorough or enveloping enough to satisfy the Russians' need for some Truth, some abiding faith, to guide their lives. Imagine how fragile a faith must be when it is based on silence. The poet Yevgeny Yevtushenko, writing an open letter defending Solzhenitsyn in 1974, told of a confrontation with the absence of history, the disappearance of the past:

Last year around a campfire in Siberia, one good young girl, a student about eighteen years old, raised a toast to Stalin. I was shaken. "Why?" I asked.

"Because then all the people believed in Stalin, and with this belief, they were victorious," she answered.

"And do you know how many people were arrested during the years of Stalin's rule?" I asked.

"Well, say, twenty or thirty people," she answered.

Other students sat around the fire, and they were about her age. I started asking them the same question, too.

"About two hundred," said one lad.

"Maybe two thousand," said another girl.

Only one student out of fifteen or twenty said, "It seems to me about ten thousand."

When I told them that the figure is reckoned not in thousands but in millions, they did not believe me.

"Did you read my poem, 'The Heirs of Stalin'?" I asked.

"And did you really have such a poem?" asked the first girl. "Where was it published?"

"In *Pravda,* in 1963," I answered.

"But then I was only eight years old," she answered, somewhat at a loss.

And then I suddenly understood as never before that the younger generation really does not have any sources nowadays for learning the tragic truth about that time because they cannot read about it in books or in textbooks. Even when articles are published in newspapers about heroes of our Revolution who died in the time of the Stalinist repressions, then the papers fall silent about the cause of their deaths. In a volume of [Osip] Mandelshtam, which has been published just now, there is not a single mention of how he died—from tortures in a camp. The truth is replaced by silence, and silence is a lie.

And so the search for a Truth goes on.

SIX

Order and Truth

> *Russia is authoritarian. Let it remain so, and let us
> no longer try to change that. But the authoritarian
> system must be based on genuine concern and love on
> the part of the rulers, not only for themselves and
> those around them, but also for all their people, and
> all their neighboring peoples, too.*

— Aleksandr Solzhenitsyn, 1973

The Myths of Stalin

Leonid Borodin spoke a Russian as clear and melodic as the Siberian streams that tumble out of the mountains on the rim of Lake Baikal. It was an enchanting Russian, learned in his boyhood fishing village on the forested shore of the vast lake. He was thirty-eight now, a history teacher, a religious man, a former political prisoner with six years in a labor camp behind him. But none of the revelations and hardships of his life had tarnished the pristine Russian of his childhood or diminished his clean blond handsomeness, his level gaze of openness and certainty. We sat over tea in his small Moscow living room, a corner filled with icons, a bookcase's glass doors taped with snapshots of family and friends. Among the pictures hung a black-and-white photograph of his mentor, Solzhenitsyn, the great chronicler of Stalin's crimes.

Stalin ruled when Leonid Borodin was a boy, and the boy worshiped the dictator, as all good Russian boys were taught to do.

"When Stalin died, I cried sincerely," he said in serene confession, wistful explanation. "Toward Stalin I had complete monarchist feelings. My love was very clean, real. It was a good monarchist feeling based on the fact that one man embodied the goal of the nation, her ideas, her plans, dreams. And I'm not sorry now that I felt that way."

By the time I sat and talked with Borodin I had been in Moscow several years, and his contradictions no longer bewildered me. That a man could extol Solzhenitsyn and feel no shame for having also revered Stalin, that he could have taught his history students details of the purges and the unpreparedness for war and still describe his earlier love for the tyrant in such uplifting terms no longer seemed contradictory at all. For by then I understood the Russian yearning for a *vozhd,* a supreme leader, and the need for a solid structure of allegiance in which to order and explain reality. And I smelled the fear when the structure seemed weak. Borodin was no Stalinist. But he was a Russian nationalist who embraced the church and the land as the twin pillars of a new return to an old order of tradition and authority and faith. Now, as under Stalin, the unquestioning devotion to a leader and an idea provided a pleasant sensation of warmth and comfort. "For Russians," he explained, "it is generally impossible not to believe in something." And so his line of desire remained as unbroken from his childhood as the melody of his Russian speech.

I was also a boy when Stalin died, just a couple of years younger than Borodin. Through the hazy images that I absorbed in the safety of America, my recollection of that moment is brief and sharply focused: a news bulletin on television; the voice of the announcer; sudden relief; joy in the demise of a monster. I was entirely unprepared, when I arrived in Moscow, for the Russians' frightened recollections of that day in March 1953. For them the moment held no relief, just sudden emptiness, stirring up a terror as deep as had been felt while Stalin was alive. "What is going to happen to us? What will become of us?" These were the questions that haunted a Russia that had followed him too thoroughly, believed in him too absolutely to imagine itself without him. My Russian friends remember thinking that his death would be the end of them, the collapse of the country he had brought firmly through the war. Some joined the crowds of millions who pressed into central Moscow, trying to catch a glimpse of the body as it lay in state. Hysterical, frenzied mobs pushed and wailed; one friend was nearly shoved through a plate glass window as the throngs surged against the stores that lined the downtown streets. Hundreds were trampled and crushed to death by the weeping mourners. This I could not understand until I had been in Russia for a time.

Follow the threads of today's fear and anger, of submissiveness and defiance, of political attitude and philosophical conviction, and they tend inevitably to wind their way back, back to the adoration of Stalin and to the abrupt rejection of Stalin brought by Khrushchev's "secret speech" to the Twentieth Party Congress in 1956. These two events—the tyranny of the beloved Stalin and then the sudden smashing of the idol—set in motion broad currents that run today beneath the surface of Soviet life. The society is still possessed by his legacy and by the destruction of his flawless image, still unresolved in its judgment of his brutal regime, still infected by a profound ambivalence about his rule. The terms "Stalin" and "Stalinism" are hardly ever pronounced in public, are not at all the tools of open debate, but they exist in an underworld of political moods and instincts. For the many Russians who feel more comfortable under iron rule, his name evokes a passion for order and efficiency and political orthodoxy, which they miss desperately today; for others it triggers a dread of the oppressive reflexes that are part of the Soviet heritage. "Stalin isn't dead," said Lev Kopelev. "Stalin today is less dead than he was twenty years ago."

Look closely at the novelists, the poets, the painters, the dissidents who bring cultural and political variety to the country, and you are likely to find Stalin in their backgrounds, wrenching them from their fathers or from their beliefs. Yuri Trifonov, the late author who wrote brutally about contemporary urban life and the Stalinist era, set his candid 1978 novel *Starik,* about the oppression and terror of the first years after the Revolution, partly in his own family dacha at Serebryanyi Bor, from which his father, who had served as a commissar under the Special Don Cossack Expeditionary Corps during the civil war, was arrested on the night of June 21, 1937, never to be seen by his family again.

Vasily Aksyonov, who writes disturbing allegories about Soviet youth and party officials, was four when three men came to his house, put his mother and father, both party members, into a black car, and took him to a home for "children of enemies of the people." Twelve years later, at sixteen, he was permitted to join his mother in exile in Magadan. "It was the first time I saw the camps there, and the guards and the dogs," he told a *Times* reporter after he had emigrated to the United States, "and I was surprised. 'What is it, Mother?' I asked, but, of course, she was one of them—she, too, was a prisoner. What I saw there, this unbelievable suffering, was something I could not forget. It was maybe the most important influence for me, for my inner world." By 1979 he had become a prime mover in a onetime unauthorized collection of banned works, *Metropol*, put out by twenty-three writers who were frustrated by the official controls. When two young members of the group were expelled from the Writers' Union, thereby denying them the right to be published at all, Aksyonov resigned from the union in protest, then acquiesced to official pressure to leave the country.

"Vanya," a poet and balladeer well known for his sardonic irreverence, had written fiction about Stalin's persecution of the army officers' corps; he told me of his parents' underground work for the prerevolutionary Bolsheviks, their party activism after 1917, and then their arrest under Stalin in 1937. His mother was finally released, but his father disappeared. "My father was arrested for ten years 'without rights of correspondence,' which usually meant execution," Vanya said. "In 1956 an assistant prosecutor called me in, shook my hand, said my father had been 'physically annihilated' and was now 'posthumously rehabilitated.' He gave me a piece of paper. I had guessed, but I had hoped he might still be alive." Vanya had never thought to question the righteousness of the authorities under Stalin. "My father was a 'German-Japanese spy,' " he said. "When they asked me if my father was guilty, I believed he was. I was very sorry he was a spy, and I believed it. In those years I had nothing but a thin raincoat in forty below, but every morning I got up and on the wall were cheerful portraits of Dolores Ibárruri [the Spanish Communist leader] and other foreign Communists. I genuflected before them. Not literally, of course, but they were my gods." And his two sons, raised after the turning point of 1956? "For them my biography is deep history. They don't feel it, and they don't know very much. They are very ironic, and I think that is good. They understand everything. In our generation we were very clean, pure people, and very blind. But they understand, and keep silent."

The iconoclastic campaign that began in 1956 against the venerated memory of Stalin shook loose an elaborate structure of unconditional beliefs. It destroyed not only the legacy of Stalin's authority but the very notion of belief itself, trust in the permanence of an idea. Russians, schooled in the perfection of Stalin and in the complete identity of the man, the party, and the country, were now being told by the same thunderous voice of the party to scratch out his name, blacken his picture, erase him from history. The earlier devotion had been a lie, a false passion generated by a demented "cult of personality." And nobody who learns that his entire faith has been a fabrication can ever think the same way again; the upheaval changed the political and emotional landscape of Russia. "We were all born in 1956, in a sense," said Leonid Borodin.

The impact was most telling on those who were teenagers at the time. Irina Brailovsky, a mathematician, remembers her unquestioning phraseology in school: It was never merely "Comrade Stalin" when she wrote a composition, but "Great Stalin." When the terminology and the adoration were swept away, and all the feverish emotions were discredited, so was the entire foundation of conviction. The view of world and country, so carefully constructed out of flimsy untruths, collapsed like a house of cards. And there was no replacing it. "I realized that everything was a lie," she said. This was Irina's turning point, setting her and many others on a path of skepticism and freer thought, leading her ultimately to an effort, so far frustrated, to emigrate to Israel with her husband, Viktor, who was exiled to Kazakhstan for his dissident activities.

Mikhail Stieglitz, who did make it to Israel, recalled his classes during the process of de-Stalinization: "The teacher comes to the classroom and says, 'Now all of you take this history textbook, open it to page such and such, and mark out this picture that you see.' Then comes another textbook, and the next class, and you have to mark these words out. Then new books come, and you change all these old books, and just after several months you mark out this and that. It was the period of marking out and blacking out pictures, and this was the system of education. We were marking out Stalin; we were marking out Beria. Then later we were marking out Khrushchev, some years later. For us, for people of our generation, we grew up with this confusion. It developed a whole spectrum, from cynicism to complete disregard for the existing system."

In some, especially among those who were full adults and had lived and fought through the war, the denunciations of Stalin left a terrible void, one they have been trying ever since to fill. As Borodin observed, "For Russians, it is generally impossible not to believe in something," and the crushing of belief in Stalin had none of the liberating sensations in much of the population that it had for Irina Brailovsky. "There are people who even now cannot forgive Khrushchev for what he did in '56," said a woman university student one evening as we sat in the apartment of a young friend and talked and talked with a group of students.

"Even people who agreed with Khrushchev were angry at him," said a young man. Other students objected, and an intense argument exploded in the small living room. These young people were all fairly close, but their attitudes on crucial political values had never come to the surface before Debby and I began to probe and press. The resulting debate seemed to stretch their friendship; it was angry and distressed, for they did not like what they discovered about each other. One student turned out to hold Stalin in too high regard, and the argument became a tug-of-war between his nostalgia for Stalin's firm hand and all the others' revulsion at the massive imprisonments and executions, the fear, the paranoia. At the end of the evening, as the hard-liner was putting on his coat to go, one of the others nodded toward him and said to a friend, "I thought I knew him before. But I didn't."

The motives behind Khrushchev's "secret speech" to a special closed session of the Twentieth Party Congress in February 1956 are somewhat cloudy. In his memoirs Khrushchev portrays himself as practically alone against the fearful counsel of the other Presidium members who worried that their own complicity in Stalin's crimes, or at least their positions in the party leadership at the time, would make them equally culpable. "What's the matter with you?" he quotes Kliment Voroshilov as arguing. "How do you think it will reflect on the prestige of our Party and our country? You won't be able to keep what you say secret. Word will get out about what happened under Stalin, and then the finger will be pointed straight at us. What will we be able to say about our own roles under Stalin?" Lazar Kaganovich joined the opposition, Khrushchev writes, "arguing against me out of a selfish fear for his own hide." And so it went, with Khrushchev demanding an honest accounting. He quotes himself as saying:

It's impossible to cover everything up. Sooner or later people will be coming out of the prisons and the camps, and they'll return to the cities. They'll tell their relatives, friends, comrades, and everyone back home what happened. The whole country and the whole Party will find out that people have spent ten to fifteen years in prison—and all for what? For nothing! . . . I ask you to think about something else, comrades: we are conducting the first Congress after Stalin's death, and therefore we're obliged to make a clean breast to the delegates about the conduct of the Party leadership during the years in question.*

Western scholars have seen less principled political concerns at work, however. Writing before the publication of the memoirs, Michel Tatu observed that while Khrushchev's "idealism should not be discarded outright," there existed also a "close link in Khrushchev's mind between destalinization and his fight with his personal opponents among the post-Stalin collective leadership." This theme became even clearer as the campaign was brought more resolutely into the open at the Twenty-second Party Congress in 1961, when Khrushchev named the Presidium members who had opposed his 1956 speech.† Edward Crankshaw, in notes to the Khrushchev memoirs, points out the self-serving nature of Khrushchev's account; earlier in the congress, before the "secret speech," Anastas Mikoyan had criticized Stalin, other speakers had denounced the undefined "cult of personality," and Khrushchev himself, in his formal opening report, "had gone out of his way to praise Stalin for his determined smashing of the 'enemies of the people'—although eleven days later he was, in his Secret Speech, to denounce the use of this term," Crankshaw writes. He speculates that Khrushchev, working to consolidate his power and his image as a leader, was pressed by his colleagues, some of whom wanted

*Khrushchev Remembers, vol. I (Boston: Little, Brown, 1970), pp. 347–48.
†Michel Tatu, Power in the Kremlin (New York: Viking Press, 1970), pp. 141–43.

to remind the party that Stalin's successors were in solid command, others of whom hoped that by making the speech, Khrushchev would expose himself to attack. In Crankshaw's view, Khrushchev decided midway through the congress to seize the initiative.*

Whatever the motivations for the speech, it packed a wallop. About 20,000 words long, it was based on a detailed investigation of Stalin's rule undertaken by a special commission headed by Pyotr Pospelov (whose real name was Feigelson), an ideologist, former editor of *Pravda*, former director of the Marx-Engels-Lenin-Stalin Institute, and then a secretary in the Central Committee. Khrushchev writes in his memoirs:

> The evidence gathered by Pospelov's commission came as a complete surprise to some of us. I'm speaking about myself, Bulganin, Pervukhin, Saburov, and some others. I think Molotov and Voroshilov were the best informed about the true dimensions and causes of the Stalinist repressions, and therefore they had the least reason to be surprised by the commission's findings. Mikoyan was also more prepared than most of us to believe the facts that were brought to light. I can't be certain that he knew everything, but nevertheless he had been very close to Stalin. Many people who worked with Mikoyan and whom he trusted had been eliminated.

Khrushchev urged that Pospelov make the speech but writes that his comrades, once having reluctantly gone along with his argument that someone should do it, insisted that it be done by Khrushchev himself. He writes:

> We arranged for a special closed session of the Congress, and I delivered my speech. The delegates listened in absolute silence. It was so quiet in the huge hall you could hear a fly buzzing. You must try to imagine how shocked people were by the revelations of the atrocities to which Party members—Old Bolsheviks and up-and-coming young men alike—had been subjected. This was the first that most of them had heard of the tragedy which our Party had undergone—a tragedy stemming from the sickness in Stalin's character which Lenin had warned us against in his Testament and which Stalin him-

Khrushchev Remembers, vol. I, pp. 341–42, 347.

self had confirmed in his confession to Mikoyan and me—"I trust no one, not even myself."

Lenin's Testament, his 1922 letter condemning Stalin, formed the takeoff point of Khrushchev's indictment of the dictator. Cleverly, skillfully, Khrushchev held Lenin up as a paradigm of wisdom and virtue, then carefully sliced Stalin away from the Leninist tradition, documenting Lenin's dislike for Stalin in Lenin's own words. He had Lenin's letter distributed to the delegates, and included a portion in his speech. Lenin writes:

> Stalin is excessively rude, and this defect, which can be freely tolerated in our midst and in contacts among us Communists, becomes a defect which cannot be tolerated in one holding the position of the Secretary General. Because of this, I propose that the comrades consider the method by which Stalin would be removed from this position and by which another man would be selected for it, a man, who above all, would differ from Stalin in only one quality, namely, greater tolerance, greater loyalty, greater kindness and more considerate attitude toward the comrades, a less capricious temper, etc.

Khrushchev also quoted from an angry Lenin letter to Stalin of December 23, 1922, complaining of Stalin's rude behavior toward Nadezhda Krupskaya, Lenin's wife. "I have no intention to forget so easily that which is being done against me," Lenin writes, "and I need not stress here that I consider as directed against me that which is being done against my wife. I ask you, therefore, that you weigh carefully whether you are agreeable to retracting your words and apologizing or whether you prefer the severance of relations between us."

Khrushchev's attack on Stalin was heavy on rhetoric and also on detailed evidence. It began by denouncing as "foreign to the spirit of Marxism-Leninism" the attempt to transform one person "into a superman possessing supernatural characteristics akin to those of a god. Such a man supposedly knows everything, sees everything, thinks for everyone, can do anything, is infallible in his behavior. Such a belief about a man, and specifically about Stalin, was cultivated among us for many years." He criticized the "grave abuse of power by Stalin, which caused untold harm to our Party." He said that Stalin "practiced brutal violence, not only toward everything which opposed him, but also toward that which seemed to his capricious and despotic character, contrary to his concepts." He gave statistics. Of 139 members and candidates of the Central Committee elected at the Seventeenth Party Congress in 1934, 98 persons, or 70 percent, were arrested and shot. Of 1,966 delegates to the congress, 1,108 were arrested on charges of antirevolutionary crimes. He accused Stalin of using "mass terror against the Party cadres," of having "elevated himself above the Party and above the nation," of ordering "mass acts of abuse against socialist legality," of "fabricated court cases," of forcing false confessions from a prisoner by the "application of physical methods of pressuring him, tortures, bringing him to a state of unconsciousness, deprivation of his judgment, taking away of his human dignity." He read from court statements by party officials renouncing their confessions as having been made under torture; the officials had then been executed. He strongly suggested that Stalin and the security organs were responsible for the assassination of Sergei Kirov, the Leningrad party head, whose murder in 1934 became a pretext for the great purges. "It is an unusually suspicious circumstance that when the Chekist assigned to protect Kirov was being brought for an interrogation, on December 2, 1934, he was killed in a car 'accident' in which no other occupants of the car were harmed," Khrushchev told the congress. "After the murder of Kirov, top functionaries of the Leningrad NKVD were given very light sentences, but in 1937 they were shot. We can assume that they were shot in order to cover the traces of the organizers of Kirov's killing." He confirmed that the Doctors' Plot had been fabricated. He said that there had been no nationalistic organization in Georgia to justify the mass arrests there.

Khrushchev gave the delegates intricate details of Stalin's blind refusal to believe the intelligence he was getting about an imminent German attack in 1941; he read from cables sent by Soviet military attachés in Berlin, by the Soviet Embassy in London, and he punctured the myth of Stalin as great wartime leader, providing examples from his own experience of Stalin's refusal to act on the basis of reality, refusal to make the necessary preparations or to send the required arms to the battlefield. Khrushchev told the congress delegates:

Stalin was very far from an understanding of the real situation which was developing at the front. This was natural because during the whole Patriotic War he never visited any section of the front or any liberated city except for one short ride on the Mozhaisk Highway during a stabilized situation at the front. To this incident were dedicated many literary works full of fantasies of all sorts and so many paintings. Simultaneously, Stalin was interfering with operations and issuing orders which did not take into consideration the real situation at a given section of the front and which could not help but result in huge personnel losses.

Stalin planned operations not on a map but on a globe, he said, and he described one futile effort to get Stalin to change an operation in the Kharkov region to avoid encirclement. "Let everything remain as it is!" Stalin replied. "And what was the result of this?" Khrushchev asked. "The worst that we had expected. The Germans surrounded our army concentrations and consequently we lost hundreds of thousands of our soldiers. This is Stalin's military 'genius'; this is what it cost us."

Khrushchev's speech also detailed for the first time the mass deportations that Stalin had ordered of various ethnic minorities, mentioning the Karachai, the Chechen, and the Ingush peoples and the population of the Kalmyk Autonomous Republic, all uprooted from their lands and forced into areas of Siberia and Central Asia. "No man of common sense," Khrushchev declared, "can grasp how it is possible to make whole nations responsible for inimical activity, including women, children, old people, Communists and Komsomols, to use mass repression against them, and to expose them to misery and suffering for the hostile acts of individual persons or groups of persons."

Khrushchev told the congress: "You see to what Stalin's mania for greatness led. He had completely lost consciousness of reality; he demonstrated his suspicion and haughtiness not only in relations to individuals in the U.S.S.R., but in relation to whole parties and nations."

It was a powerful speech, shattering to the cult. And the party immediately began working to limit its impact. Khrushchev himself had withheld important information. In concentrating on the party officials who had been purged, he failed to report that millions of ordinary citizens had also been sent to their deaths in the throes of Stalin's madness. And he did not seek to rehabilitate the party officials who had been tried in public, such as Bukharin, Zinoviev, Rykov, and others, because, as Khrushchev explains in his memoirs, representatives of foreign Communist parties had attended the trials and "had then gone home and testified in their own countries to the justice of the sentences. We didn't want to discredit the fraternal Party representatives." Nor did he condemn Stalin's brutal collectivization of agriculture, from which the country still suffers.

Not until 1989 was the speech published in the Soviet Union, and its contents were thoroughly inadmissible in any Soviet forum between Khrushchev and Gorbachev. In 1956 it was read in closed party meetings at factories, scientific institutes, and collective farms. Summaries, without many of the specific details, were given to university and secondary school students. I have many friends who remember the experience vividly in party meetings and classrooms. Copies were provided to the Eastern European parties, and it was apparently through the Polish Communist Party that it was obtained by the CIA and then released by the State Department. But the discussion in Soviet party cells was strictly controlled, as local party officials tried hard to contain the potential wildfire of liberalization. At a party meeting in a Moscow physics institute Yuri Orlov, a young physicist, took a cue from the speech, rose to speak, and argued that Stalin was not to blame alone, that lower officials who were also guilty should now be brought to justice. When his point drew some sympathy from his colleagues, he was quickly expelled from the party and from his job. "When it became clear that they could not make only one man responsible, they began to falsify," said Lev Kopelev. Orlov left Moscow for Yerevan, where he was eventually elected to the Armenian Academy of Sciences. Twenty years later he was a leading dissident, organizing a committee to publicize Soviet violations of the human rights provisions of the Helsinki accords; in 1977 he was arrested and then sentenced to seven years in a labor camp and five years in internal exile.

For party *apparatchiki* most concerned about control and order, the denunciation of Stalin created unwelcome fluidity, internally and externally. It provided the context for the Hungarian uprising

that followed, the subsequent rift with China, the brief liberalization of Soviet literature, and, ultimately, the fall of Khrushchev.
Other factors were also central to each of these events, but the
process of de-Stalinization stood as a background to them all, intrinsic to the impression of declining party unity and authority that
allowed competing interests to work. After the release of political
prisoners; the posthumous rehabilitation of many others; the deletion of Stalin's name from every city, town, factory, school, and
mountain peak that had been thus honored; and the removal of his
body from beside Lenin's after a decision by the Twenty-second
Party Congress in 1961, the passion for de-Stalinization was spent,
overcome by the considerably greater passion for order. And since
his ouster in 1964, Khrushchev has been widely remembered by
Russians with distaste, as a crude and impulsive buffoon whose shoe
pounding at the United Nations (so frightening to America) caused
only embarrassment to his country. Stalin, by contrast, continues to
hold a popular image as solid, steadfast, determined, wise—a man
who was in command. His memory is a source of nostalgia to many
in a period of corruption, inefficiency, drift, and stagnation.

An old veteran moved furtively along the swaying corridors of
an overnight train bound for Moscow. At each compartment he
stopped briefly, holding something concealed in a cupped hand,
clandestinely offering it for sale. The price: one ruble; the illicit
merchandise: a small homemade calendar, each page bearing a
heroic photograph of Stalin. There was Stalin in his marshal's uniform, his chest laden with medals, Stalin speaking firmly from a
rostrum, Stalin sitting with Lenin on the famous white bench at
Gorki, Stalin on the mausoleum being hugged by a little Pioneer
girl, Stalin and the Politburo, Stalin with his mother, Stalin lifting
his hand in a wave that looked also like a blessing being given over
a vast crowd. These were banned pictures, evidently taken from old
books and put together in a household darkroom; the calendar
consisted of strips of photographic paper folded and stapled together at the fold, a bit of grass-roots homage to the memory of the
vozhd, the supreme leader, during the year 1979, 100 years after
his birth. It was being sold in trains and stations throughout the
country, and it was being bought.

On the morning that the treason trial of the Jewish dissident

Anatoly Shcharansky began in 1978, a trailer truck pulled slowly out of a small factory near the courthouse and turned a corner past a group of dissidents and foreign journalists standing in the street. Suddenly photographers began running alongside the truck, pumping hard until they got out in front; then they turned, pedaled backwards, and snapped picture after picture of a decoration that had been propped up facing forward through the big windshield: a portrait of Stalin. It took the bewildered driver a few moments to realize why his truck was so interesting to the foreign press corps, and then he quickly took the portrait down. Such pictures have appeared in more and more trucks and buses as the name Stalin has become a code word for Russians akin to "law and order" for Americans. A police investigator told of his admiration for Stalin as he argued for tougher tactics against criminals. A Muscovite asserted that there had been no juvenile delinquency in Stalin's day. Another contended that anybody who had shown up drunk at work would have been shot under Stalin, and he approved of the method as good medicine against widespread alcoholism and laziness on the job. "Under Stalin," a young man grumbled as he picked over a market of New Year's trees with nearly no needles, "these people would have been imprisoned for selling such things." Another Russian, pointing to a construction site, remarked, "See that building? It's been under construction for eleven years. See this one? Stalin built it in four years." In the museum at Stalin's birthplace in Gori, Soviet Georgia, a man passing a case displaying a letter to Stalin from Marshal Georgi Zhukov, the wartime general, shouted in despair, "Zhukov wrote a letter to Stalin! Everybody wrote to him! But still, Stalingrad is called Volgograd—why?" An engineer who lost both parents to Stalin's firing squads frequently raised a glass in a toast to the late dictator. A teacher whose father was executed chided Irina Brailovsky for bringing up her son to be "disloyal." The system, the teacher explained, had some faults but on the whole was very good. She forced the boy out of her class and out of the school.

Much of the regard for Stalin in retrospect is fostered by the very skepticism that de-Stalinization encouraged, the modicum of dissent and emigration that has been permitted, and especially the sense that the national leadership is less single-minded, more fallible, less resolute. Many Russians find all this an unsettling sign of weakness. "When Stalin had something to say, the whole country hushed down," a young linguist recalled admiringly. University classes stopped. Factory work came to a halt. Everyone hung on every word. "What is he saying? Shhh. Now when Brezhnev says something, there is just a weary sigh, 'Oh, he's at it again.' " Roy Medvedev told me once that he was struck by the difference as he was strolling in Gorky Park, where loudspeakers were broadcasting a Brezhnev speech. Stalin's voice would have had everyone in rapt attention. People had even listened to Khrushchev because he would often say things that were funny. But as Brezhnev droned on over the loudspeakers, the crowds went about their business as unaffected as if unintrusive background music were being played. "I have never come across any portraits of Brezhnev or Khrushchev in private apartments," said Roy. After Brezhnev died, Yuri Andropov addressed the broad yearning for discipline and efficiency with hard-hitting campaigns against corruption and absenteeism, but without restoring any Stalinesque grandeur to the party leadership.

The nostalgic affection for Stalin gets no official blessing, but it has been allowed to develop as the official portrayal of his rule has, over the years since Khrushchev, retreated into ambivalence. Even those who should be fluent in the official history find the line so equivocal and delicately drawn that they are afraid to discuss it. I once asked the principal of a middle school in Minsk how Stalin was taught in history classes. The principal was a history teacher, a party member. He replied smoothly with a recitation of the periods of history studied in each grade, through the Revolution, the civil war, the Great Patriotic War. He did not answer the question, so I asked it again. Again he dodged and weaved, but with the beginnings of discomfort. I pressed again, suggesting politely that perhaps he had not understood that I was asking specifically how Stalin's rule was dealt with: Were the purges described? Was the unpreparedness for war discussed? The poor man was in agony. His vice-principal, a woman, stood by watching in scarcely concealed enjoyment as her boss writhed. Every time I pushed him she almost smiled. Finally, exasperated, he said I should just read the textbooks.

There, Stalin is presented as a true Marxist-Leninist, the legitimate heir of Lenin. No mention is made of Lenin's Testament. The purges and the mass arrests and executions are treated with allusion and euphemism—the leader made a few "mistakes"; he fostered a "cult of personality." But the laws from his time are good laws, the history says. "In 1961 you could say more in school," Leonid Borodin remembered. "I talked about the purges, about the unpreparedness of the army, I talked in a rather detailed way about it."

In the middle of our discussion he called his tenth-grade daughter, Lena, and asked her what she learned in school against Stalin. "Only the cult of personality," she said. "In some congress, I don't remember exactly which, they talked about the personality cult."

"And about the purges, when millions perished?" her father asked.

"No, nothing."

" 'Several violations of the Leninist norms of party life,' that's the phrase they use," Borodin explained. "More than that, of course, they can't say."

"People don't know what happened," said another Russian friend. "Each knows only his own experience. People don't want to know: I cannot change it; if I know, I'll only live worse."

Furthermore, the basic structure of the system Stalin left behind —the heavily centralized government, the police apparatus, the woefully inefficient form of collectivized agriculture—is never challenged and seems immune to reform. And his supposed brilliance in guiding the nation to victory in World War II is unquestioned. No accurate account of his military blundering has been permitted in the post-Khrushchev era. In 1967, for example, three years after Brezhnev had replaced Khrushchev, the party expelled a historian named Aleksandr Nekrich, who had written a book under Khrushchev on the Soviet unpreparedness for the German invasion in 1941. Nekrich was allowed to emigrate in 1976, but his case carried a clear message. The war is too sacred; it cannot be tampered with in the self-adulation of historical propaganda.

The appropriate line was provided in a war novel by Vladimir Bogomolov, *In August of '42*. Published in the mid-seventies, it was reviewed favorably for the way it tiptoed around Stalin and for the peripheral treatment it gave him, in only one chapter. The journal *Nash Sovremennik* commented approvingly:

The author treats the character of Stalin only insofar as he has direct bearing upon the novel's principal plot. The characterization of Stalin includes nothing that is not derived from the memoirs of Marshal Zhukov and other military leaders. Bogomolov approaches his task very tactfully and strictly, never aiming beyond it at something more. He stresses the Supreme Commander's authoritativeness, decisiveness, and indomitable energy, and at the same time his ruthlessness and suspiciousness . . . yet the chapter does not contain the slightest hint of sensationalism.

Stalin's exaggerated wartime record is reinforced by popular, officially approved films, in which Stalin usually makes cameo appearances as a steady military commander of great wisdom. He is far superior to Roosevelt and Churchill, who are often portrayed as scheming and waspish; Stalin remains true, honest, and well above the tawdry maneuvers of the "allies."

In 1969 party authorities even laid the groundwork for an extensive commemoration of Stalin on the ninetieth anniversary of his birth. According to Roy Medvedev, Moscow art studios were ordered to produce busts of Stalin; printing plants were told to prepare an issue of large official portraits. The possible establishment of a Stalin museum in Moscow was discussed, his works were made ready for publication, the Institute of Marxism-Leninism was instructed to plan a special meeting dedicated to Stalin's memory, and a major editorial on Stalin was written for *Pravda* and the newspapers of foreign Communist parties. When the Polish and Hungarian parties were informed of the plans, Roy said, they protested vehemently, and just two days before the observance the Politburo in Moscow voted by a narrow margin to forgo most elements of the celebration. The busts were shelved; the portraits, filed away. The editorial was ordered withheld from all papers. "However," Roy wrote in a manuscript on the subject, "an employee of the Central Committee apparently forgot to call Ulan-Bator, where morning begins seven to eight hours earlier than in Moscow. Therefore, on December 22 in the Mongolian-language newspaper *Unen,* the large article and Stalin's portrait were published." *Pravda* ran only a small article devoted mostly to Stalin's errors and the personality cult. A similar one was printed a decade later, on December 21, 1979, the hundredth anniversary. It made Stalin into "a very complex and contradictory figure," with both "positive and negative aspects." It acknowledged that "serious violations of Soviet legality and wholesale reprisals took place" and that "many distinguished leaders of the party and the state, high-ranking military chiefs, honorable Communists, and nonparty people innocently suffered as a result." Roy told reporters that the 1979 articles were "about what was to be expected. They are not another step forward in the rehabilitation of Stalin." The day itself was observed in a low-key fashion, reflecting officialdom's mixed feelings. Komsomol representatives laid wreaths on his grave near the Kremlin wall as small groups of people clustered around. There was more exuberance in his hometown of Gori, Soviet Georgia; according to officials there, thousands of people paraded through the streets, waving flowers and portraits of Stalin as five marching bands took part. "Music is playing everywhere today—along the streets, on the squares and in the cafés," the Reuters news agency quoted the police spokesman in the town as saying. In Moscow, Roy Medvedev discounted the threat of a direct rehabilitation of Stalin. "But a new threat has arisen," he said, "that of the rehabilitation of Stalinism under another name. The edifice of Stalinism has been destroyed, but its foundations and building blocks, however shaken or scattered around, still exist. And there are still Stalinists today, people who support a harsher regime in our country or within the party, who want to use some of Stalin's methods without attaching his name to them."

Indeed, there are. Many of them are searching for heroes. "We need a god," said my friend Igor, the newspaper deliverer. He was drunk at the time, but he knew what he was saying. He admired Stalin even when he was sober. He admired his firmness, his swift and ruthless "justice," the fervent unity he commanded.

The admiration grows out of the ideological and economic stagnation, the absence of a single figure of strong authority, the declining sense of national purpose. "It is not nostalgia. It is something a little different," said a Moscow engineer. "It is a junction between positive recollections of the past and a decline of belief in the future. Under Stalin, talent and daring could advance your career —you could shoot up quickly. It was clear that if you violated the rules, you were through. Now different policies exist for different people and at different times." The society has ossified into layers and enclaves of elitism and special privilege; the hopes for a bright new era have flickered and died.

"We were Stalinists," explained Lev Kopelev, speaking of himself and his wife. "Our ideals were quite rational. We wanted to be a communist country, a communist world—happiness for all humanity, freedom for all humanity. We used barbarous means, but for a great number of us they were means for a good end. Now people have no official ideology. Now the leadership of today is very unpopular. Nobody knows them as individuals. They have no image. Social ideals are almost dead. Now, thanks to the loss of ideology and thanks also to the loss of senseless terror, people live more freely. Terror is no longer senseless, but ideology no longer exists. What remains is the structure of the society as it was built up in Stalin's time. It was built as a means, and now it exists for itself. We are ruled not by a communist party or by a fascist party, and not by a Stalinist party—but by a status quo party."

Lev saw the admiration for Stalin expressed in four contemporary myths about the dictator, which he called the Official Myth, the Popular Myth, the Georgian Myth, and the Nationalist Myth.

The Official Myth, the one perpetuated in textbooks, classrooms, newspapers, and films, permits the development of the others, for its silence denies the truth, allowing pseudotruths to grow and harden. And amid the silence of official history Russians are left to read great significance into even the subtlest shifts in the treatment of Stalin's memory by the political leadership. Just a passing mention of his name in a speech is enough to stir a smattering of applause and then a spate of excited, worried speculation about what it means. His portrayal in feature films is scrutinized by Russians for clues to the party's evolving views and policies. A Moscow woman remarked with fascination and disgust, "I'm seeing Stalin's face on television more and more," and she gave it ominous meaning.

Even the Central Committee's rejection in 1977 of an attempt to rehabilitate Bukharin was seen as much more than a historical curiosity. Bukharin was a close comrade of Lenin, who called him "the favorite of the whole party" in his Testament. In the early years of Soviet rule Bukharin and Stalin served as the co-leaders of the party, and differences between them over policy grew acute as time went on. Bukharin strongly supported the New Economic Policy, which permitted considerable private enterprise; he opposed Stalin's abandonment of the policy in 1928–29 and objected strongly to the "revolution from above," which imposed a highly centralized state-dominated structure on the economy. He opposed the forced collectivization of the peasantry. Stalin had him publicly tried and then executed by firing squad in 1938; more than twenty years later his widow, encouraged by Khrushchev's de-Stalinization, began working for his rehabilitation by the party. There was no answer for sixteen years, until June 1977, when a telephone call came to the family's apartment from a Mr. Klimov of the Central Committee. Bukharin's son, Yuri, took the call. "I am instructed to convey to you that your request for the readmission of Bukharin to the party and to the status of an active member of the Academy of Sciences of the USSR cannot be granted because the accusation of criminal activity for which he was convicted has not been dropped." The decision, though unpublicized, of course, was discussed with concern by people who heard of it in Moscow. It was interpreted as a coded affirmation of the legitimacy of the show trials of the 1930's, a refusal to reverse their verdicts, in essence a repudiation of any current liberalization—and a perpetuation of the Official Myth.

The Popular Myth sees "Stalin as a just statesman who ruled with a hard hand, but with order and military genius," Lev Kopelev said. "Now there is corruption in the country. Then prices were less each year, and enemies of the people and corrupt bureaucrats were seized and placed in the camps, and we were feared in the world." This is a spontaneous popularity, arising from a passion for order, a yearning for iron rule against the inefficiency, the constant shortages, the shoddy merchandise, the artistic and literary unorthodoxy, the dissent and emigration, the defilers of the motherland. So powerful is this hunger for firm leadership that it has even taken on a bizarre form among a few young Russians who tried, on the evening of April 20, 1982, to observe Hitler's birthday. Western news reports said they numbered anywhere from a dozen to over 100; they began to congregate in Moscow's Pushkin Square. Some wore high-shaven sideburns, black shirts, caps with swastikas. Other tough youths, having apparently heard that the demonstration was coming, were ready in large numbers to confront the fascists; a few fistfights broke out, and the pro-Hitler rally fizzled. Serge Schmemann of *The New York Times* wrote that "many adherents are said to be offspring of well-placed functionaries in the Communist Party and in the Soviet state, and their tenets seem to combine ill-defined yearnings for a strong leader and iron discipline in industry and agriculture, with elements of racism, anti-Semitism and anti-communism." The phenomenon "seemed to derive less from actual sympathy for Hitler and Nazi Germany," Schmemann continued, "than from a general sense of frustration with the absence of iron leadership in the Soviet Union, with the loss of incentives to work and with the general sense of stagnation."

As it applies to a renewed reverence for Stalin, this unsettled sense of disorder tends to blame whatever "mistakes" may have been committed on those around Stalin, not on the supreme leader himself. Many Russians blame Lavrenti Beria, Stalin's secret police chief, who was deposed, arrested, and shot after Stalin's death, well before the "secret speech." "They think Beria deceived Stalin," said a young Muscovite, "like under the czars, when people thought the czars didn't know how badly we lived."

In Lev's third myth, the Georgian Myth, Stalin is seen by ethnic Georgians as "the great hero of Georgia," the expression of a primitive, fiery patriotism by which the Georgians keep their distinctiveness of culture, language, food, song, and religion—and for some, national aspiration. In this small Transcaucasian republic, where the streets have a sultry Mediterranean style and the houses are graced with balconies of iron filigree, Stalin is embraced with false pride not for his methods but for his origins. He was Georgian ethnically, born in Gori, Georgia, as Iosif Vissarionovich Dzhugashvili. His father was a cobbler.

Georgia is where the portraits of Stalin are most prevalent. They aren't just propped up in truck windshields but are hung permanently in some stores and factories. A bas-relief of Stalin's profile hangs high on a wall of the Rustavi Factory of Chemical Fiber outside Tbilisi, the Georgian capital. Just south of Gori the director of a tomato-growing state farm, a man named Tskitishvili, took a couple of us into his office, where portraits of Brezhnev and Stalin hung, and offered us vodka and white wine, tomatoes, cucumbers, sweet walnuts, apples, and red caviar. Expansively he proposed a toast. It was just two days after the death of the defense minister Andrei Grechko, so Tskitishvili raised his glass and said, "Let us drink to the memory of Grechko and Stalin." A woman told me that she once visited the home of a Georgian whose parents were executed in 1938. Tears in his eyes, he told the moving story, then declared, "Now let's drink to Stalin, our hero." It seemed a combination of Georgian nationalism and an old reflex. The more perilous your situation, one Georgian dissident explained, the more loudly you drink to Stalin. "It is a psychological complex," he said, "something done out of fear, terror."

The one Stalin museum in the country is at Gori, which is a dusty provincial town of dull brick houses and earth-colored tile roofs. A manicured garden, contrasting vividly with the town, leads to the tumbledown house of Stalin's parents; the tiny one-room building where Stalin was born on December 21, 1879, is enveloped now in an elaborate pavilion. Visitors may see the bed of his parents, the wooden table where they ate, the other simple furnishings. Inside the main museum building, and up a flight of stairs past a huge marble statue of Stalin, five sedate rooms of memorabilia, letters, photographs, and sculpture portray him warmly, with no hint of the terrors or the madness. One learns that he was a winning youth with a poetic flair. As a boy he wrote a pretty verse called "Flowers of My Georgia." He served as a dedicated and central figure in the Revolution, a faithful disciple of Lenin. Only a fraction of the exhibits covers the period of his rule, from 1924 to 1953. Most of the displays show him as revolutionary: Heroic oils and drawings have him organizing a conference of coal miners, meeting with Lenin in Finland, attending the Fourth Party Congress in Stockholm and London. The impression is carefully created, through pictures and documents, that Stalin was handpicked by Lenin as his successor. When I asked a museum official about the omissions, she explained simply: "We have a memorial museum, and that is why we prefer not to mention negative factors. The purpose is to glorify him. That period was already discussed at the [Twentieth] congress; that's why it was decided to exclude it from the museum."

Georgians with clear memories regard Stalin as popular only among the less educated, common people, who were proud to have a native son in such power. After Khrushchev's speech in 1956, violent demonstrations erupted in Tbilisi among Georgians protesting what they saw as the denigration of their Georgian symbol by a Russian. But many Georgian intellectuals realize that the notion of Stalin as Georgian nationalist, as a local boy with a mystical love of his home soil, is pure legend. They recall his unpopularity in 1921 in his role during the Red Army's reoccupation of Georgia, which ended the three years of independence Georgia had achieved under the local Mensheviks. Nor have many intellectuals forgotten their hatred of him for the terror and the purges, which spared Georgia not at all. Otar Yoseliani, a brilliant Georgian film director, once found a canny answer to a tricky question from one of my colleagues. Could a film be made now about Stalin? "Stalin lived outside the republic," Yoseliani replied with a straight face. "That's why it's hard to produce a film about him in Georgia; the scenery here is different. He lived in Russia."

Lev Kopelev's final myth, the Nationalist Myth, touches one of the most important political undercurrents in the country. It goes like this, in Lev's words: "In spite of his Georgian origins, Stalin was a good general in the Russian state. He built up the Russian state. He was a good Russian statesman." Here is the confluence of several powerful streams: the official exaltation of nation, the hunger for strong leadership, and the search for Russian roots. In the absence of faith, in the suspension of motion, Russia now is "virgin ground," Lev says, "ground on which anything can be sown, without fear, without belief, without ideology."

The Lure of Russianism

An American who lives in Moscow for a time becomes gradually aware of a strange tension between order and disorder, between a superficial layer of control and a deeper, darker unruliness that churns silently beneath the surface.

Everyday life seems meticulously regulated. Every intersection is clearly marked and closely policed to minimize doubt, to lighten the burden of choice by requiring or prohibiting a turn this way or that; a driver who wants to be different by heading left must often continue straight for a long stretch before encountering a U-turn sign that lets him go back and then make a right. On the flat three-lane road north toward Leningrad, every foot is carefully painted with alternating solid and dotted lines barring or allowing passing, but without any perceptible reason for giving one direction of traffic preference over another at any given place; even where the road is straight and level, the lines make the decision for you, freeing you to pass here, locking you into your own lane there. All this is tightly enforced, with policemen materializing magically to wave down violators who think they've committed their transgressions unseen. The beauty of it lies in its senselessness. I was once chided by a policeman at a red light for having stopped in the left lane of a four-lane city street, rather than in the vacant curb lane. What did it matter? I asked innocently. The officer seemed surprised. If there is only one car, it must always be in the curb lane, he explained; you may not use the left lane when the curb lane is empty. As a poorly informed foreigner I was spared a penalty and released with nothing more than a courteous warning. And I was careful to use the curb lane from then on, meekly abandoning my propensity to use my own judgment. A middle-aged Russian with a keen eye for the absurd summed up this philosophy of regimentation in an acid comment on the Soviet Constitution. "What's not forbidden is compulsory," he said.

In every sphere, however, the control seems precarious to many Russians, especially to those on top. It never really satisfies the passion for order that struggles against whatever wildness it is they feel lurking within their society, within themselves. I saw this once in Ashkhabad, Soviet Central Asia, where I was boarding a plane to Moscow. Foreigners are usually taken on separately, but there I was dumped in with the crowd of about 100 passengers, a mixture of Russians and Asians. Their internal passports had been examined with their tickets during check-in, and at the departure gate the boarding passes, tickets, and passports were checked again. We were then herded out on foot to the plane. It was raining steadily, but at the bottom of the ramp we were made to wait for a long time while an imperious Aeroflot stewardess stood squarely across the steps and insisted on examining all tickets and passports for a third time. This forced each passenger to juggle carry-on baggage and fish around in pockets and handbags for documents that had been tucked away as no longer necessary. As individuals were thus cleared one by one and allowed up into the plane, the rest of us got steadily soaked. The unreasonableness of the procedure was so apparent that I wondered at the docility of the crowd. No one grumbled; no one raised a voice of protest. We all stood like whipped dogs. The stewardess was in complete command. Finally an elderly man suggested timidly that perhaps our documents could be checked in the shelter of the plane. At that the stewardess flew into a screaming rage. "Anarchy! Anarchy!" she shrieked at the poor man. "You're creating anarchy!" I stared in disbelief. We were all standing silently, sopping, but I could feel an edge of real panic in her voice. And suddenly I no longer minded the rain, for something about Russia had just snapped into focus, something about the low threshold of insecurity, the fear of what you cannot control.

I once saw passions boil up to sweep away authority; it was frightening and exciting. It happened at a poetry reading by Andrei Voznesensky, a mild and articulate artist in private who transforms himself onstage into a powerful man of bursting emotion and oratory. His poetry is literate and honest, sometimes moving, so his infrequent readings in Moscow are as popular as rock concerts in New York. The crowds were huge outside the Tchaikovsky Hall at Mayakovsky Square; we had tickets, but getting in was hard. The police had set up barricades to hold back the shoving mobs, and by the time we worked our way up to the entrance it was nearly time for the reading to begin. Finally inside the lobby, we joined a stream of young, well-dressed men and women, who must have used every ounce of pull and barter to get their precious tickets, racing for the doors to the auditorium. But just as we approached, the stout and solid elderly women on guard slammed the doors shut in our faces and stood in front of them, smug and immovable. We were too late.

Now, if there is any symbol of authority in the Soviet Union that is above question or argument, it is the sturdy *babushka* who takes tickets, hangs up coats, opens (and closes) doors, oversees the entrances of the higher-class apartment houses. One does not have to grow up in that country to know who really runs it, so when I saw the tough, bulldog expression of the *babushka* who faced us in front of that closed door, I knew I had missed Voznesensky. I was about to turn away when the young Russians ahead of us began to argue. They waved their tickets. They reasoned. They cajoled. They yelled. The woman, and her colleagues at the other doors, were about as responsive as bulkheads on a destroyer. The pitch of the young Russians' frustration and anger rose. They hurled slang expressions that I did not understand. The whole crowd pressed forward, on the brink of riot. And suddenly a couple of young men reached past a *babushka,* grabbed the handle of a door, and pulled it toward them. The woman, who must have weighed at least 250 pounds, leaned back against it and dug in her heels. The men pulled. She leaned. The door began to move, just slightly at first, then more and more until the woman, still bracing herself, started to skid along the floor, pushed out by the opening door. "Hooligans!" she screeched. "Hooligans! Hooligans! Hooligans!" She was joined in the chorus by other women, who rushed to her aid. But by then the door was open enough for the crowd, and us, to flow in like water.

This could all be a metaphor for intellectual disorder as well as physical turbulence. It is not exactly that the Russians derive any Germanic sense of satisfaction from regulating both thought and behavior, but that they deeply fear the alternative. Their history, as they repeatedly remind a foreigner, is replete with illustrations that authority cannot be eroded only a little but is swept away completely when weakened and overwhelmed, like the old *babushka* at the door. And in the milieu of Russia's upheaval and chaos, revolutions have been made.

Safety is sought in the sanctuary of a single idea, some truth that is comprehensive enough to exclude all others. "The West lives under a pluralistic system—he's right, and he's right, and he's right," said Pyotr Paliyevsky, deputy director of the Gorky Institute of World Literature. "We live under a general rule, a sense that there is a right path. And we are looking for it." Paliyevsky, speaking in the ease of his book-filled study, was an impassioned defender of the Russian classics against the mutilation he felt they were suffering in Moscow's contemporary theaters. His "right path" was an elevation of all that was inherently and historically "Russian," and his role was to fight to preserve a prerevolutionary Russian culture as embodied in the great literature. "I am defending the Russian classics not because they are Russian," he argued, "but because they are classics with enormous significance for our cultural future. It is an interest in the spiritual values of the past. People are wondering who they are, what they are doing, where we are going to go from here."

In wedding the past and the future, the thinkers who strike the broadest chord today are neither the Communists nor the dissident democrats like Sakharov, but those who profess a Russian nationalism, a Russian chauvinism, a Russian consciousness. This Russianism, as it can be called, draws a sharp distinction between what is Soviet and what is Russian, between a Soviet patriotism and a Russian identity. It views the Russian ethnic group, which represents just over half the country's population, as the guiding soul of the vast multinational state that the Soviet Union has become. It seeks a return to an idealized peasant morality, the simple honesty and piety that existed, at least in the imagination, with the common people at their roots in the prerevolutionary village. Like communism, Russianism seeks an all-embracing truth to explain the past and chart the future. Like communism, it envisions a society forged from the top into a homogeneous unit of shared beliefs and values, except bound by ecclesiastical authority.

The potential force of Russianism, whose best-known apostle is Solzhenitsyn, lies in its coincidence with the most powerful impulses of both the political hierarchy and the people. As it shares Soviet communism's devotion to political unanimity, it also taps the deepest Russian wellsprings of obedience to authority and such a visceral aversion to diversity that some liberal dissidents find the Russianists even more frightening than the Communists in power. Furthermore, Russianism is unlike any other of the multiple strains of dissent in the country, for it runs vertically, not horizontally: Its sympathizers extend all the way from the ranks of the society's outcasts, some of whom have served prison terms for their views, into the corridors of power. Enough influential figures in the Central Committee seem to share the reflexes of Russianism to lend a certain cast to policy, to make some difference in the art exhibits that are permitted and the books that pass censorship. It is a set of attitudes and emotions that accentuate all that is conservative and insular in the Russian character.

"The nationalist movement is the only mass movement in the country," said an aging writer. "These people believe that state, church, and nation are all the same, and that is a very dangerous myth." The man speaking had talked to me candidly for an hour or more about the dangers he saw in neo-Stalinism, the emptiness of the ideology, the self-serving rule of the party. He did not mind having his name published with those observations, criticizing the current leaders. But when we turned to the subject of Russianism, he asked to remain anonymous. He was more afraid of the "nationalists," as he called them, than of the KGB or the party. "We are ruled now by satiated wolves," he said, "but among these people are hungry wolves. Idealists can be such good terrorists. If these nationalists came to power, it would be very dangerous. The roots of nationalism can be very sound, but its fruits can be very bad."

Russianism embraces a spectrum of attitudes within itself, beginning from a diffuse sense that Russian history and tradition have been lost in the modern, godless wasteland of communism and extending into an aggressive, acute utopianism that denigrates all things non-Russian—religions, ideas, material goods, people. Its main advocates see authoritarianism as desirable and an intrinsic feature of Russian culture, but they reject Communist authoritarianism and set out to dramatize the foreign and profoundly anti-Russian origins of Marxism and Communist rule. Solzhenitsyn's 1973 letter to Soviet leaders, which declared, "Russia is authoritarian. Let it remain so," also described Marxism as a "dark, un-Russian whirlwind that descended on us from the West." His disciple Leonid Borodin branded communism "an original experiment to construct a social form alien to the roots of the people. Like any experiment," Borodin declared, "it has its beginning and its end. How can you boast about the results?" Igor Shafarevich, a mathematician and friend of Solzhenitsyn, denounced Marx and Engels as having "always displayed a special hatred for Russia and the Russians." Gennady Shimanov, an elevator operator who has written extensive underground essays on Russianism, emphasized the non-Russianness of Lenin and his first Politburo. Shimanov pointed out that Lenin's father, Ilya Nikolayevich Ulyanov, was not Russian ethnically, but came from a Mongolian people called the Kalmyks. His mother, Maria Aleksandrovna Blank, was Jewish, Shimanov asserted. Western scholars agree that Ilya Ulyanov was Kalmyk. He was born in 1831 in Astrakhan, then a Volga trading port with the East; his mother was from a Kalmyk family; his father had Mongolian features. Lenin's mother, Maria Blank, was apparently of German origin, whether Jewish or not seems unclear. But none of this non-Russian genealogy is mentioned very loudly in the Soviet Union. The Russianists' purpose in publicizing it, of course, is to discredit the Bolshevik leader racially and ethnically. Shimanov did the same with Lenin's five-man Politburo, formed on the eve of the Revolution. None of the members was Russian, he observed.

Trotsky, Zinoviev, and Kamenev were Jews, Stalin was Georgian, and Lenin was Kalmyk-Jewish, Shimanov wrote. Dzerzhinsky, the head of the secret police, "was brought up by his mother, a Polish nationalist, to hate Russians," Shimanov declared. "He ruthlessly exterminated the Russian national intelligentsia, aspiring to destroy the brain of Russia."

Shimanov, the worker, and Shafarevich, the mathematician, had similar views. Shafarevich spoke with me several times on the subject. I would go to his pleasant apartment, which he had obtained through his high position as a corresponding member of the prestigious Academy of Sciences. He would talk quietly but with a penetrating glare of intensity that added weight to every word. During one of these sessions he gave a dissertation on the destruction of Russian consciousness. "In one of his speeches, Trotsky ended with the exclamation 'Let patriotism be damned!' " Shafarevich reminded me. "It is possible to imagine what consequences followed from the realization of such views. They demolished monuments, churches and old buildings, reminders of Russian history. Streets were renamed so that now their names have no connection with their past. Children were raised on distorted Russian history, all of whose figures were depicted as greedy robbers, idiots, and syphilitics. An entire generation was raised in this atmosphere, which attached a complex of accusations to Russian history. Only by understanding that can you appreciate this dreadful crisis through which Russian national self-awareness survived: The right itself of a people to exist—spiritually, if not physically—was made unconscious." The popular reaction to that attempt at destruction has come "completely spontaneously," he said, "not in treatises or programs. And so clean an emotional outburst, a widespread gravitation toward a reunification with the lost national roots, an attraction to Russian culture, trips by groups of young people to old monasteries, collecting reproductions of icons, interest in Russian religious philosophy of the nineteenth century and the beginning of the twentieth, attempts to defend old buildings against demolition and efforts to save the manuscripts of dead priests for posterity."

In all this there runs a search for morality. "It may start with the preservation of monuments," said Leonid Borodin as we sat over tea, "but during the last ten years I know enough people who have moved toward a religious outlook, a religious view. It is easier to go to church now. The controls are not that harsh." He spoke as a man who had spent six years in a labor camp for his religious activism. As I began to write these words about him in May 1982, he was arrested again.

"It seems to me," he said when we were together in Moscow, "that if an unreligious nationalism develops, then it will not be any kind of nationalism to me. It is not possible today to talk about Russian culture, about the remembrance of Russian culture, about painting, architecture, history, literature, that did not come from Russian Orthodoxy and all of its culture. That, of course, is not desired by the authorities. They annihilated Russian national culture because it was deeply religious. Dostoyevsky said if there is no God, then everything is permissible. If there is no higher moral sense, then a person is not made in a like image."

Borodin was far from being a fanatic. He spoke as an intellectual, well read and quietly studious. But his careful thoughts were framed by passion, and once, his clear eyes filled with tears. He was speaking of morality, and of socialism's failure. "Socialism's objective is to create a new man, a new type, with higher morality," he said, "but it hasn't happened. Socialism has its own moral principles, borrowed partly from Christian principles—kindness, justice, love, do not kill, do not lie—and these have been preserved." But without the higher source of morality, they have no strength, no durability, he argued. "Russians have become so amorphous, have been so dispersed, you understand, because there are no roots, no foundations. 'Russian' is more spiritual than biological. And when we say that our spiritual foundation has been destroyed, we are speaking about something Russian. We stand now before the threat of transforming the Russian nation into some other social being. Any nation wants to protect its own existence. We are accused of nationalism, but it is not nationalism. It is a survival instinct." His voice rose. "We simply, today, suddenly realized that we were actually losing our existence. Why are we interested in history? Because our history is Orthodox, organically Orthodox, understand? We see the level of drunkenness, and so on, and a certain cynicism, not characteristic of our people, understand? We had humor, some skepticism, but cynicism was not present among our people, not even among the intelligentsia. It's not an attribute of our character."

Then came the other part of his argument. "Basically our nation has been a peasant nation," Borodin declared. "From our guts, our insides, our culture, our language, the most living elements of our conscience, outlook, you understand? And always this class—this peasant, landed class, which was the majority—was considered moral. What did the Revolution do? It rightly destroyed the ruling class. But what about the peasantry? The peasantry was the remaining class, moral and stable." He summed up, his voice emotional. "The roots of nationalism are Christianity, man, and his land. Man on the land." His eyes were brimming with tears. "There is a Soviet patriotism; there is a Russian patriotism. Soviet patriotism is a devotion to a social form, existing on a particular territory, a social patriotism. But Russian patriotism . . ." He could hardly speak. "Russia, yes. Russia, yes."

By dawn the line was already long. The people stood patiently, not in single file but in clumps and clusters that made a thick swath as wide as the broad sidewalk. The crowd began at the doorway of the Manezh, once a czarist riding school and now the Soviet Union's central exhibition hall, on Marx Prospekt just outside the Kremlin walls, and it grew rapidly before the doors were even open, until like a great serpent, it reached entirely around the huge city block on which the Manezh is situated and curled back on itself.

Moscow is a city of lines—lines for meat, lines for furniture, lines for shoes, lines for buses, lines for plays and concerts—but never had I seen anything like this. Day after day for a month Russians from all corners of the country came to wait and wait for a glimpse of something they had merely heard about from friends or friends of friends, something unreported on television and scarcely mentioned in newspapers. Twenty thousand a day were admitted through the doors of the enormous hall, and many thousands more were turned away. Such was the drawing power of an exhibit of paintings by Ilya Glazunov, who was trying to say something to them about the Russian soul. It was early summer 1978.

Glazunov's works included portraits and scenes that glorified the czars, the saints, the old Russia, that showed a barren Soviet landscape of neglected, ruined churches and stark high-rise city blocks. The centerpiece of the show, at least as the crowds judged it, was a large canvas entitled "The Return of the Prodigal Son"; against a background of Dostoyevsky, Tchaikovsky, and other writers, composers, soldiers, and saints from prerevolutionary Russia stood a Christlike figure, bearded and robed. Before him knelt a young man in jeans, seeking forgiveness, being blessed. Behind the youth, slobbering pigs rooted among the decaying rubbish of sacrilege and immorality. Kevin Ruane of the BBC overheard a teenage girl ask Glazunov whether the painting meant a return to God. "It means what you think," he replied.

A small boy pointed to the Christlike figure. "Who's that man?" His father answered, "That is the future."

The visitors' book recorded an outpouring of affection for Glazunov's message. "I congratulate all Russians on this great festival," someone wrote. "They won't see anything like this for a long time. This is a call to moral purification. Let's respond and cleanse ourselves of dirt." And there were others: "It's unbelievably difficult to be Russian in 1978. . . . Thank you for telling the truth about Russia. . . . Thank you for Holy Russia. . . . Thank you for 'The Return.' " One day a visitor stood up on a chair and began to praise Glazunov. When a policeman stopped him, the crowd objected loudly, and the man was allowed to go on, finally reciting the famous lines of Fyodor Tyutchev, the nineteenth-century poet who wrote with a Slavophile bent in his later years:

> You cannot understand Russia with your mind,
> She cannot be measured by the yard,
> She has a special stature,
> You can only believe in Russia.

Various theories were advanced about why party and governmental authorities would permit such a large, long-running, one-man exhibition in such a prominent hall, across the street from the Kremlin, when it addressed such a sensitive and explosive theme. When *Pravda* ultimately wrote about the show, it did so critically, and Glazunov told me that some ranking officials had complained about "The Return," thinking it showed Soviet life as piggish; he replied that the painting was meant as a positive statement, pleading for a return to Russia's traditions. But many Russians felt that the sentiments contained in Glazunov's work tapped sympathies high up in the hierarchy, where divisions and disagreements on such matters are generally assumed to exist. Some Russians claimed to be able to identify the Politburo members who were Russianists and who would have approved of the exhibit. Others attributed Glazunov's success to his deftness, charm, and political acumen, for he has cultivated a role for himself as a kind of court painter, doing portraits of high officials and wooing them with his slick friendliness and passionate devotion to Mother Russia. Even the late Mikhail Suslov, the Grey Cardinal of party ideology and probably an anti-Russianist, liked a portrait Glazunov did of him and therefore liked Glazunov. The painter's detractors, mostly among the liberal-minded Moscow intelligentsia, branded him an anti-Semite, a KGB agent, a superficial artisan, a man of technique but no taste, a sycophant willing to pander to whatever line suited his ambition.

I found him somewhat harder to categorize. He obviously used his official connections skillfully. He lived in an immense apartment and studio on the top of a building in a pleasant old quarter of central Moscow, with one vast room of dark wood walls covered with beautiful icons. A high, heavily hewn beam was lined with antique brass samovars. And he did his official duty, always making unctuous efforts to please his audience of the moment. He was sent to North Vietnam during the war to make drawings for a propaganda book, *The Days and Nights of Vietnam,* but when he gave me a copy, he made sure I understood that the text was not his. And he showed me a canvas he had done just for himself, and for his Russianist friends, I suppose. It was a racist painting of an American pilot being captured by North Vietnamese villagers. The pilot was blond and handsome, his face like many a Russian face; the Vietnamese villagers were swarthy, dusky, almost sinister, like Russians' images of the Mongol hordes. Glazunov gave a chilly, knowing smile as he pulled this work from behind a stack of paintings in his studio; apparently he thought I would like the noble portrayal of the American. He was also careful about masking his anti-Semitism in my presence; indeed, he went to lengths to create a pro-Semitic reputation, sweeping me up one evening from his kitchen table and whisking me off to a new, officially sanctioned Yiddish theater troupe, for which he was ostentatiously helping design scenery. He dashed into the workshop backstage, gave some rapid suggestions for a better way to make the Golden Calf, and dashed out again. Later I discovered through some remark he made to a colleague that he thought I was Jewish ("Shipler's not bad for a Jew," or some such crack).

Glazunov was an important force behind an unofficial and mostly hidden group of noted citizens who organized to lobby for the preservation of historical landmarks in Moscow. He gathered a few of them in his apartment one day, and I sat with them for hours, going over an album they had prepared to show the destruction of beautiful old buildings over the years. The album, containing photographs and maps, had been circulated among high government officials in a partially successful effort to put the brakes on the demolition. Glazunov and his group had counted 492 valuable pieces of architecture torn down between 1935 and the beginning of World War II, and the process was continuing. "In many ways," he said, "our architects are now continuing this destructive tendency. They do not respect the past. They do not love the monuments of Russia." Between the album and the testimony of the concerned citizens sitting around the table, the catalogue of destruction was impressive: The Church of Christ the Saviour, built in the early nineteenth century to celebrate the victory over Napoleon; on the wall by each icon the name of a Russian who had perished in the Napoleonic Wars had been inscribed. The Strastnoi Monastery, built between the sixteenth and nineteenth centuries; the Rossiya movie theater now stands in its place. The Pokrovsky Church of the seventeenth century, which Napoleon ordered saved because he liked it so much. A 300-year-old gate in Dzerzhinsky Square. Bas-reliefs on a church. An elaborate eighteenth-century arch called Red Gate. A Baroque-style church from the seventeenth century. A bronze bas-relief of the 1905 Revolution. Buildings where Pushkin, Tolstoy, Turgenev, Chekhov had lived, destroyed in the early 1970's. A round arcade at Taganka Square, built in the eighteenth century at Peter the Great's command. Almost all the city's picturesque houses of weathered wood. "Such barbarians," hissed one of the men at the table. He pointed to pictures of modern Chicago and Moscow's modern Kalinin Prospekt, with tall, steel and glass towers looking almost alike. "Are we going to copy capitalism and call it a new communist city?" he asked. "It's a paradox."

Glazunov declared, "If I don't love my mother, then why should my children love me? I am an example to them. Steps to the future are built of old stones."

The Russianist movement for preservation carries heavy political overtones; in literature and theater, for example, it becomes a vehicle of conservatism and is thereby useful to the political leadership's efforts to suppress avant-garde or critical fiction and drama. When Chekhov and Gogol are staged as biting commentaries on contemporary society, *Pravda* solemnly invokes its staid guardianship of the eternal and condemns the offending directors and actors who tamper with the Russian classics. While I was in Moscow, Aleksandr Vilkin was assailed for his production of Chekhov's *The Seagull* at the Mayakovsky Theater, where the stress and meaning of the original text had been manipulated to create cheap puns, *Pravda* intoned, provoking unseemly applause. The puns, of course, were made at the expense of today's Soviet society, and they pulled the play suddenly out of its convenient portrayal of the decadent czarist era. *Pravda* also denounced Yuri Lyubimov of the Taganka Theater for his collage of Gogol pieces entitled *Revizskaya Skazka,* taken from parts of *The Overcoat, Dead Souls, Diary of a Madman,* and other Gogol works. The production was a display of Lyubimov's deftness in translating commentary from another century into a critique of the present, a talent that some party officials fail to appreciate. *Pravda* called it Gogol "dismembered and mutilated." Another production by Lyubimov, with Gennady Rozhdestvensky, a conductor, and Alfred Snitke, a composer, was canceled by the Ministry of Culture in apparent response to Russian conservatives. It was to be a modernized version of the Tchaikovsky opera *Queen of Spades,* based on the Pushkin short story. *Pravda* called it an "Americanized musical" and used a religious lexicon to damn it. "To permit this is to issue an indulgence for the destruction of the great inheritance of the Russian culture," *Pravda* thundered. "To permit this means to bless a crusade against what is holy to us." Indulgence? Bless? Crusade? Holy? In the newspaper of the Central Committee of the Communist Party of the Soviet Union?

These are the emotions that mystical Russia stirs. In my years there, nineteenth-century Slavophile writers and philosophers who had not been published for a long time, such as Ivan Aksakov and Ivan Kireyevsky, reappeared as the subjects of articles. Popular writers such as Valentin Rasputin, whose novels and stories dwell on the soul of rural Russia in his native Siberia, were published extensively. Soviet rock music took on a double form, torn between Western rock and Russian folk songs, much as the country has always been pulled by both the outer and the inner worlds. And the authoritarian, insular character of Russia was distilled in this Russianism. Writers told me of a strange meeting at which a Stalinist, anti-Semitic novelist named Ivan Shchevtsov was invited to read a chapter from a novel. It described Stalin meeting a marshal, presenting the marshal with white roses (representing Russia). The marshal notices that Stalin has blood on his fingers and realizes that Stalin has gathered the roses himself, and the marshal weeps, and his tears mix with Stalin's blood on the white roses. Then Shchevtsov put the book down and talked about how Jews were everywhere, in the publishing houses and everywhere.

How quickly Russianism moves into anti-Semitism was illustrated at a general session of the Writers' Union, where Pyotr Paliyevsky began with a plea to preserve the Russian classics. He himself said nothing anti-Semitic; he merely deplored experimental productions of Chekhov, Gogol, and other great writers. He complained about the modern Palace of Congresses, built by Khrushchev inside the Kremlin walls to give the Bolshoi another theater besides its ornate czarist hall outside the walls. But performing Russian ballets in the modern theater, Paliyevsky said, was "like staging a tragedy of Sophocles in a circus." He criticized specific productions and specific directors. "How long are we going to listen to these People's Artists, professors?" Paliyevsky asked. "How long are we going to be present at such performances?" There were more than 1,000 people at the meeting, according to a couple of writers who were there. And Paliyevsky's remarks triggered an ugly response. One writer stood and quoted (in Russian) from the Jewish writer Sholem Aleichem, then commented, "In these lines there is only evil, not tragedy, since there is no purity. There was never such a thing in Russian classical poetry, and could not be." Anatoly Efros, a highly regarded director who is Jewish, then rose to address the hall. His avant-garde production of Chekhov's *Three Sisters* had come under attack. "I am very worried," he said, according to another writer who took notes. "Very rarely does this happen in this auditorium. It is dangerous, dangerous to play with such things." He said he had been passed a note, unsigned, from someone in the audience of assembled writers. He read it aloud: "Organize your own national theater, and there mutilate the Russian classic as you wish." The gathering dissolved into a babble of astonished voices, and an intermission was called.

Ironically, much of the conservative Russianist impulse springs from a discomfort over living in the ethnically heterogeneous society that Russian nationalism has produced, a distaste for the diverse fruits of the vast Russian, and now Soviet, empire. The Soviet Union is no melting pot. It holds more than 100 national, ethnic, and racial groups that maintain (in varying degrees of integrity) their own languages and alphabets, some elements of religious traditions, distinctive cultures, historical pride, and a few formal expressions of national identity such as music, folk dancing, and handicrafts. Some, including the Georgians, Armenians, Azerbaijanis, Estonians, Latvians, Lithuanians, Buryats, Tadzhiks, Uzbeks, and so on, have their own territories. Through skillful political and police work, however, the Russian-dominated power structure severely circumscribes their powers and curtails their nationalist activities, punishing harshly any anti-Russian or separatist tendencies. The most resilient and nationally conscious groupings, such as the Georgians and the Estonians, complain constantly about attempts at Russification, a process of assimilation that has enjoyed considerable success among the Moldavians, for example, and almost none at all among the Armenians. When new constitutions were written in Moscow for all fifteen constituent republics in 1978, thousands of Georgians took to the streets in Tbilisi to protest the proposed deletion of the previous constitution's provision that Georgian was the official language of the republic. Demonstrations also took place in Yerevan, Armenia, over a similar deletion with respect to the Armenian language. The significance was mostly symbolic, but the authorities backed down and restored the clauses in the Georgian, Armenian, and Azerbaijani constitutions, a rare case of those in power responding to those in the streets. The incident fed the popular conviction among working-class Russianists that other national groups in the country were treated better, lived more comfortably, and retained more coherence culturally than did the Russians. Such fantasies are woven into a general malaise about demographic trends; with a birthrate much lower than that of Central Asians, for example, the ethnic Russians are gradually slipping toward a minority status in the Soviet Union. They represented 54.6 percent of the population in the 1959 census, 53.4 percent in 1970, and 52.4 percent in 1979, according to the official figures. The apprehensions about this trend are profound.

Many Russians in Moscow grow uneasy when they see squads of Central Asians, whom they call by the derogatory term *Chuchmek*, brought into the capital to help build new apartment houses, for they think that crime and disorder are coming with them. I was once assailed in Tass by the party secretary of Buryatia for an article I'd done on the ambiguous relationships in that Siberian region between the local Buryats, a Mongolian people, and the ethnic Russians. I had written about the integration of schools and residential areas, on the one hand, and the social segregation, on the other, exemplified by the low rate of intermarriage. This prompted the party official to defend the record of tolerance and supposed unity and to deny any racism. It also prompted Vsevolod Sofinsky, then head of the Foreign Ministry's press department, to make a revealing remark to a mutual acquaintance. If I didn't think there were enough mixed marriages, he said, "Tell Shipler to go out there and marry one of those monkeys."

Similar racist attitudes are held about blacks, who are rarely seen by Russians outside Moscow, where there are African students and diplomats. A friend once spotted a peasant family on the Moscow subway, all standing around a black man and staring at him. They had obviously never seen a black person before; they seemed especially fascinated that the palms of his hands were lighter than the rest of him. "If we see a black student with a Russian girl," said an eighth grader, "We say, *'Vot nakhal'* ["There's an impudent fellow"]." And the language is full of antiblack idioms and epithets. If someone doesn't want to do the menial chores, he may say, "I don't want to be a Negro in this institute," or, "I don't want to be a Negro for you." Someone working hard is likely to hear youngsters chant, "Work, nigger, work, the sun is still high." A teenager who came from a liberal-minded dissident family told me seriously, "Although I have never met a nigger, I have very bad images of them." I asked for some adjectives, and he gave the following: lazy, stupid, unattractive. "Of course," he said, "Negroes are big." A black American student in Leningrad told me that she had gone several times for examinations by a Russian doctor, a very pleasant woman, who finally asked her, "Which of your parents is white?"

The American was taken aback. "Why, neither," she said. "They're both black."

"Really?" said the doctor, surprised.

"Yes, really. Why do you ask?"

"Because you're so beautiful," said the doctor.

Gennady Shimanov greeted me at his door with the firm hand-shake of a man who prides himself on staying taut and tough. He was short but sturdily built, muscular and broad-shouldered. He wore a neatly trimmed black beard and mustache and seemed practically humorless. Our conversation began on some of the familiar Russianist themes. "Belief in communism began to disappear after Stalin. . . . There is an enormous cultural hunger. . . . Young people look around and see that no one believes in anything. . . . The effect of antireligious propaganda in school is very superficial. . . . The Revolution, of course, was a frightening blow against Russian tradition, but it really just sped up a process that was taking place in Russian life and Western life." He moved quickly through this broad analysis of the past and present into a clear and frightening vision of the future. Shimanov had taken the diffuse feelings of loss and drift and had come to a militant ideology of Russian cohesiveness and exclusivity that disdained what was culturally impure and assaulted what was modern.

Shimanov was schooled in the virtue of uncompromising thought. His father was a Communist. His grandmother was an Orthodox churchgoer who had him baptized as a baby. During his school days he became a leader of his Pioneer organization and, later, the secretary of his local Komsomol committee. He served in the army, where he had a lot of time to read Dostoyevsky, Tolstoy, Shakespeare and to educate himself. Then he worked in menial jobs, and he was now an elevator operator, living simply and humbly by choice and by conviction while his wife worked as an architect. He instructed his elementary-school-age son, who was both a Pioneer and a churchgoer, to keep his two worlds separate, to say nothing in school about his religious practices.

"Each person has internal freedom," Shimanov explained. "To believe in God is very easy here, much easier than in the West. Material things are less important, and there is a thirst for belief. There will be a huge religious revival, such as in the fourteenth or fifteenth century. The state can't do anything—it's powerful and powerless."

Shimanov had developed a model of how he thought his society should look, and he talked about it at some length, supplementing his observations with thick reams of typescript *samizdat* (literally "self-published," or unofficial) essays that he had written and distributed among like-minded Russianists. He believed, with Solzhenitsyn, that Russia should spurn the use of Western technology, but he went farther. Solzhenitsyn had written in his 1973 letter to Soviet leaders: "We, the great industrial superpower, are behaving like the most backward country by inviting foreigners to dig our earth and offering them in exchange our priceless treasure—Siberian natural gas." Shimanov expanded on the virtue of insularity. Travel abroad, he said, was like making tours of brothels. The craving of foreign goods was disgraceful. Russians should avoid drinking foreign wine, he argued. "It is important to use the products of foreign origin as little as possible. You have to value the fruits of your own land, always giving them preference over the fruits from another's land. In this way we will not only show the proper respect for our land but develop our own holding in a healthy way. To drink foreign wine at a feast means simply not to notice one's own deformity. . . . And Russia is blessed. God has blessed it with bread and honey. . . . It is necessary to try to produce, as far as possible, all products at home, that is, within the boundaries of the region or country, including intoxicating drinks. . . . It's best to drink them out of a silver cup or goblet."

Shimanov argued that the essence of Russianness lay in the Russian Orthodox Church and in the attachment of man to his own land, a relationship with the soil that was destroyed when peasants were forced onto collective farms in the 1920's. He urged an exodus from the cities, a return to village life, an acknowledgment that "each citizen has the moral right by virtue of his birth to some minimal land, qualitatively equal for all citizens and enough for dignified living." The "simple peasant life," he said, counteracted the wider "fear and misfortune, wars, death, falseness, and cruelty of every kind. There were sources of certainty and peace, strength and courage: God and the church, one's home, one's own holding, one's own village, and the sympathy of close ones. The negative and the positive in life were contrasts, mutually strengthening each other. Therefore, life itself tried to become brighter and more valuable. But in the contemporary world these poles have almost completely disappeared, and everything is mixed up in a kind of unimaginable slop, in a greying and droning mass in which there is neither good nor evil, neither top nor bottom, neither someone else's nor your own, neither holiday nor ordinary day. . . . There is nothing better on earth than to work together with one's own family on one's own holding, especially in the fresh air, in one's own field or kitchen garden, when everyone can be taken in at a glance: mother and father and grandmother and sister and the neighbors. Here work becomes not only work but also like a general dance and choir. It makes the spirit peaceful and light, smooth and strong, satisfied with life. 'All the family is together and the soul's in its place,' goes the Russian saying. This family work and after-work unity have moral significance. It is genuine life, it is the genuine health and strength of the spirit; here are brought out the best features of character, and the truth of life makes itself known."

Shimanov's vision of the family was quite like the current Communists' prescription for the state. The family, he argued, must be characterized by "unanimity and authority," a firm patriarch, and an enhancement of "the masculine and military spirit" of the men and boys. Here were the same attributes sought for the political order. Then Shimanov called for a return to a traditional family structure. The women should not work, he said, but should stay home and care for their children. In one essay he provides rather detailed instructions on child rearing, arguing that youngsters should be kept at home, not sent to nursery school:

> . . . a child thus uprooted goes through an unhealthy metamorphosis, which affects society; he becomes nervous and capricious. Imagine apples which are still green and unripe, still drinking their mother's juice, being ripped from the apple tree, and the apples are ripened in unnatural conditions. Isn't this what happens with children? A child has the feeling of safety, the feeling of spiritual kinship, only from closeness with his parents, and especially with his mother. . . . And here this spiritual support unexpectedly collapses for him, causing a spiritual catastrophe. For almost nine hours a day, almost all his waking hours, he is among strangers, who command him as they wish, have him play senseless games, whether he wants to or not.

Shimanov denounced "most toys," which he said "repress a child, weaken his imagination. . . . These toys are really like narcotics. . . . There is something the same about all of them. They're made by machines and mechanical indifference, lifeless toys . . . any little machine breaks on the second day."

His idea of a proper ideological state was much like Solzhenitsyn's—an authoritarian theocracy—or, as Shimanov put it, an "ecclesiastical-state approach to the restructuring of the life of the whole society on eternal and wise human principles." A key element would be the purification of each nationality's culture, not by breaking up the Soviet Union into separate states but by moving its population around so that all Russians would live on Russian territory, Estonians in Estonia, Georgians in Georgia, Uzbeks in Uzbekistan, Ukrainians in the Ukraine, and so forth. The closest parallel in American terms would be to put all blacks in Alabama, all Chinese in lower Manhattan, all Italians in New Jersey, and all WASPs in Massachusetts. "When there is a mixture of either group," Shimanov insisted, "their culture is annihilated. It's a bad tendency that Buddhists, Christians, believers, dissidents all have one style of life." I asked him about the Jews, who have no territory of their own in the Soviet Union, unless one counts the synthetic "Jewish Autonomous Oblast" of Birobidzhan, in the Soviet Far East. Shimanov's answer was interesting, and it drew us into a discussion of racism. "I don't think the Jews have to go to Israel," he said, "but they need, along with the Russians, a parallel autonomy. They must have their own territory—not a better or a worse territory than the Russians'—so that the Jews have the chance to live autonomously and the opportunity for worldwide cooperation with Jewish society, to support contacts. I think that's the only solution to the Jewish problem, and I support it, although many consider me an anti-Semite." And what about Jews who don't want to be farmed off to some such territory? "I have a good friend who is purely Jewish; he considers himself a Russian patriot," Shimanov replied. "I am a decisive opponent of racism, and I regard nationhood as, first of all, spiritual, educational, and not a matter of blood. If a person, Jewish by blood, feels himself spiritually Russian, that means he is Russian. If you don't want to be Russian, by the grace of God, be Jewish. Here's your land; nobody will touch you. We must respect each nationality." But above all stood his aspiration for autocracy and unanimity. "And does the society have the right to expel from its midst members who negate its spirit and destroy its internal order?" he asked rhetorically. "Without this right, no social organization is possible. If you are not in agreement with its order, find yourself another society according to your standard."

These clannish reflexes produced some bizarre and vicious attitudes. Most notable was the anti-Semitic *samizdat* put out by Vladimir Yemelyanov, once an Arabic translator for Khrushchev and later head of the Arabic department at a prestigious language institute in Moscow. Although he wrote many anti-Zionist and anti-Semitic books and articles that were officially published, his *samizdat* contained some intricacies that were too much even for Soviet authorities. One essay detailed what he called the Jewish-Masonic conspiracy, contending that the B'nai B'rith was a Masonic organization, that President Carter was a 33rd-degree Mason, but of a lower order than the then Senator Jacob Javits, whom he named as the No. 1 Mason in America. Thus, logically, Carter was subordinate to Javits, and the sinister machinations of the Zionists emerged. Yemelyanov would undoubtedly have updated his conspiracy theory as both Javits and Carter lost their bids for reelection, but he, too, had troubles. In March 1980 Yemelyanov was expelled from the party for smuggling an anti-Semitic book abroad for publication by a Palestinian organization. According to Dan Fisher in the *Los Angeles Times,* the book claimed that Palestine "was Russian since olden times" and that the Slavic race, which he called the backbone of the Aryans, was "the greatest creative force of the ancient world." In official eyes, his offense was not in the book's content but in its publication abroad without party and state permission. His loss of party membership led to his dismissal from his teaching post, which in turn provoked his wife into an angry argument, during which he killed her, according to Fisher's account. After her charred body had been found in a garbage dump on Moscow's southwest side, Yemelyanov was arrested and held in a psychiatric hospital for criminals.

Other ugly manifestations of Russianism surfaced during my years in Moscow. Mimeographed pamphlets signed "Russian Liberation Movement" were distributed in apartment houses charging that control of the Politburo had been seized by Zionists and that the chief of all Zionists was Brezhnev himself. A mimeographed letter signed "Vasily Ryazanov," alleging that "a powerful Zionist lobby" existed in the Central Committee, was sent around. Since duplicating facilities are strictly controlled and unavailable privately, it was assumed that the pamphlet and letter were done by people with official connections.

An overtly official link between Slavic chauvinism and demented anti-Semitism occurred during an art exhibition in Minsk; among the works by Mikhail Savitsky was a lurid canvas entitled "Summer Theater," centering on a pile of naked Russian corpses in a concentration camp. A helmeted Nazi officer and a Jew wearing a Star of David stood over the bodies, leering sadistically. Not only was the painting part of an officially approved show, but it was printed in the journal of the Byelorussian Ministry of Culture, *Literatura i Mastatstva.*

Outside the courthouse where the Jewish dissident Anatoly Shcharansky was being tried, among the crowds of friends and fellow dissidents who were there to lend their support to the prisoner, I spotted a man I knew to be an extreme Russianist and anti-Semite. He used the pseudonym Maliuta Skuratov, the name of the chief of Ivan the Terrible's secret police in the 1500's. It seemed a rather peculiar place for this man. He was there lending his support to Shcharansky as well. I asked him why. "We support the emigration movement," he said evenly. "We think all Jews should leave Russia."

Russianism is unalterably opposed to pluralism. The antipathy is profound, rooted firmly in Russian soil, nourished by the hunger for a single truth. Gennady Shimanov writes:

The ideology of liberalization is the most vague, irregular, and undogmatic ideology, not knowing other values except the value of abstract freedom. . . . The spirit of liberalization . . . does not know any limits and does not contain within itself any constructive beginning, but only destructive: It is the destruction of all forms by a freedom having gone crazy. If a man is allowed to believe in anything he wishes, but not allowed to construct civil life on the foundation of his belief, if he is allowed to be, for example, a Christian, but is not allowed to live in a society constructed on Christian principles, then this impossibility to realize his belief socially, and the necessity to live in spiritually strange surroundings, undermine and gradually destroy even individual religious life. . . . Deprive a fish of water and give it the most complete freedom and it will suffocate. Put it in water, but not that water in which it is determined to live, and it will become sick. . . . To the accompaniment of the sweetest speeches about freedom, wittingly interpreted in the secular style, the democratic system unhurriedly penetrates and destroys religious social structures.

Like many Russians, Shimanov had an apocalyptic view of what any Soviet liberalization would produce. He asks:

What will the furthest liberalization of the Soviet Union lead to? Only to its failure. Why? Because the fund of contradictions in it—national, religious, and all others—is so great that emancipation will lead to an explosion which will destroy the regime, bringing the country to bloody chaos, forming a huge political vacuum in its place. Having destroyed the world balance of political forces, it will provoke a collision of the world powers. This outburst will inevitably detonate conflicts that are now restrained in the world, chiefly conflicts between America and China, which one way or another will draw in all the rest of the countries.

One does not have to agree with Shimanov, or even regard him as sane, to appreciate the significance of his fear as an expression of the fear that possesses all Russia. Leonid Borodin, much less of a fanatic, also put the dangers in graphic terms. "Sakharov is a wonderful person," Borodin declared. "He wants only goodness. But what he wants today, now, is just impossible. A man wants to talk, let him talk; he wants to organize, let him organize. But let's assume that such wishes were suddenly realized, just today, and that all who want to talk could speak as they liked, and go there, come here. You understand, at the level of consciousness that exists today it would be a national catastrophe, a slaughterhouse. Today, in our conditions, all classes, all groups are located in a kind of rigid goodwill. They are held in a balanced positiveness by the authorities. And imagine that today there was no authority. But give us a million copies of *Gulag*, understand? Let's not give any kind of positive thing except the slogan 'Freedom,' et cetera, et cetera, et cetera, without a moral basis, without any special systematic view of the world. And what would happen? People would begin to settle scores. It would simply be anarchy. People would begin to settle scores.

"It's fine, freedom of speech, it's fine," Borodin went on. "Freedom of assembly—excellent. But in our conditions in which popular consciousness is, all told, lower than before the Revolution of '17, how can this freedom be realized? Who will come to power? Sakharov? No. Today you'd find a new character who would be even worse. In our conditions, if we give freedom and that's all—well, give freedom, and the first who would perish under the guillotine's blade would be Sakharov. Liberals are always the first to go under the knife."

One of those liberals, Val Turchin, believed in Russia's ability to absorb democratization only gradually, step by step. "It is a question of abruptness," he said. "If today they dissolved the KGB and everyone could speak out, I admit there could be a sort of anarchy. There is no tradition of democratic values, and they are preventing us from developing these ideas. Nobody is for abrupt change. It would mean violence. The national element would be predominant, and there would be awful violence. Everything would fly apart. The Russian manner is either nothing or everything. Constructive, slow change is the most difficult for us. You can see it in our national character, our history. The system will be stable until the last moment, when it ceases to exist at all."

SEVEN
Beyond the Walls

I want to be where I'm not;
I want to see the whole wide world.

—Underground rock lyrics
Leningrad, 1980

Western Things

Russia for centuries has looked out upon the Western world
through a blended sense of infatuation and inferiority, drawn by the
material wealth and cultural novelty, repelled by the disharmony of
pluralism, terrified by the fluidity of ideas that rage outside the
gates. This has been no easy gaze of detachment but a raw obsession
driven by the Russians' conflicting emotions about themselves.
Gripped by an aching inadequacy, cloistered by an ancient chauvinism, Russia remains intrigued by Western life and largely immune
to it.

In the decade of the 1970's the openings provided by détente
exposed Soviet society to more Western, especially American, influence than at any other period since the Bolshevik Revolution.
American banks and businesses set up offices in Moscow to promote
trade. Tourists, students, scientists, scholars, performers, and journalists poured in from Western Europe, Canada, and the United

347

States. And a more restricted and selective flow of Russians went westward, bringing back an array of impressions unvarnished by the politics of their textbooks and newspapers. But the qualities in America that the Russians came to admire were not those that many Americans had hoped to export. A powerful lust developed for the material goods and popular styles of American society, a craving for the exotic artifacts of the consumer culture. In Moscow and other major cities a lucrative black market flourished in jeans, rock records, chewing gum, and American cigarettes. Faddish teenagers slapped English words into Russian slang and sported dungaree jackets with American flags sewn on the sleeves. The Voice of America, which the authorities stopped jamming from September 1973 to September 1980 and then again from May 1987, became a source of news for millions of Russians, including officials.

But the idea of democracy never gained much favor, even in the quiet of personal attitudes. Few Russians comprehended the principles of a free press, free elections, open debate, and individual liberties; few could grasp the curious American notion that government was to be distrusted and contained and kept out of private lives. And those who understood often found the ideas distasteful, productive only of disorder. Black-marketeering was much more popular than political dissent, though just as dangerous: Many more Soviet citizens were willing to risk imprisonment for buying and selling jeans than for advocating free speech.

The lessons of this came to me slowly. It is easy to be dazzled by the semi-illicit jazz concert, held in a trade union hall at the farthest outskirts of Moscow, the tickets passed out hand to hand by members and friends of the local bands and combos that are assembling for a long night of Dixieland and saxophone blues and tuneless improvisation. The kids are mostly college students with connections, dressed in denim and suede, jammed into the seats, where they listen intensely but impassively, letting whatever emotions the music rouses stir quietly beneath an implacable surface. A long-haired young man onstage, alone with his saxophone, begins to undress slowly as he warbles and screeches and toots and squawks. He has a bushy, Gabby Hayes moustache, and he is supposed to be funny, free, unrestrained, wonderfully impulsive. He takes off his dungaree jacket, revealing a raspberry red undershirt. He writhes, makes faces, yells into the microphone, gets down on his knees, and plays unmusically. The kids around me are intrigued, but many are contemptuous; they think it is stupid and undisciplined, and the applause he gets at the end is scattered, perfunctory. They have good taste; they like the accomplished groups. Above the stage hangs a red and white banner: "LET US FULFILL OUR PERSONAL TASKS IN THE 3RD YEAR OF THE FIVE-YEAR PLAN."

It is easy to be enthralled by the excitement of a crowd of Muscovites pushing, clamoring for places at a performance of the London Symphony. It is easy to imagine that in the craving of travel to the West, in the passion to read Western literature (even trash), in the stalwart lining up at dawn to get into a State Department exhibition on American life, Russians are expressing their rebelliousness, their discontent, their yearning for the freewheeling cultural and political values of the Western world. Only gradually did I see that the phenomenon did not often run that deep. "It is the only opportunity for them to look through a window," Irina Brailovsky explained to me. "It is as if you lived in a little room with the same people, the same point of view, and no visitors. All of a sudden there's a window, so you rush to it to look out, even if you don't like what's on the other side." The attraction to the tangible, the shimmering superficiality, leaves impulse and attitude at the depths unchanged.

This is a hard discovery for Americans, one we often resist, for its implications corrode our creed that freedom is man's natural state, that all other conditions are abnormal, that the innate reflex of human beings is to strive against their bonds. After a time in Russia we become embarrassed by the nakedness of our naïveté. And on some level, perhaps, we hate the Russians for giving the lie to our innermost assumptions about mankind.

The disjointed reactions to the outside world, the dissonance of infatuation and contempt, expressed themselves in several rather symbolic episodes. Irina McClellan, the Moscow schoolteacher who married an American, found herself vilified as *Amerikanka,* ("American woman"), by neighbors in her communal apartment, people who were anti-Semitic Russian nationalists, she said, but who shamelessly acquired every possible electronic or wearable item from the West and Japan. They talked about these goods constantly and seemed to see no inconsistency between their material and social views. Irina laughed about this in that wry fashion

349

that has become the trademark of the dissident who has learned how closely these bitter situations come to comedy.

One December, as the New Year approached, Russians in contact with Westerners began their annual rite of agitation and lobbying for the item of prestige and currency known as the business calendar, which was to be used in schemes of favoritism and bribery so complex that only a bazaar merchant could unravel them. Soviet employees of the American Embassy and news organizations put in their bids for Pan Am calendars. The annual shipment of Swissair calendars was stolen from Sheremetyevo Airport, as usual. And a carton of Chase Manhattan Bank calendars was delivered to the bank's offices in the Metropole Hotel near Red Square, setting off a remarkable chain of events. The bank's secretary in the outer office buzzed the bank's representative, David Buckman, on the intercom. She told him the calendars had arrived. Five minutes later she appeared in Buckman's office to explain, quietly, that the gentleman who listens to the telephones had heard the conversation about the calendars and wondered if he might have a few. "I figured I'd smoke him out," Buckman told me later. So he had his secretary tell the KGB man that he, Buckman, would present him with some calendars if he came personally to get them. Minutes later the man was there, shaking hands and smiling, receiving his calendars, taking Buckman down the hall to show him his room equipped with telephone paraphernalia and a reel-to-reel tape recorder. Thereafter, when Buckman came to work each morning, the KGB man would lean out of his room and wave greetings.

In the winter of the United States bicentennial year, plastic bags with the bicentennial seal were being given out at a mobbed American exhibition to all Muscovites who had the fortitude to line up long enough in the freezing cold to make it into the pavilion. The plastic bag became an instant sign of status, proof that the citizen who carried it had caught a glimpse through that window into the outside world. At the height of this frenzy, on a boulevard some distance from the exhibition, a traffic policeman spotted a black Chevrolet Impala with the distinctive license plate that designated a diplomat of the American variety—black numerals on white, beginning with the telltale code D-04. The Chevrolet was being driven by a Soviet chauffeur, and the policeman waved him over. The chauffeur got out, walked back to converse with the cop, then returned, explaining to his American Embassy passenger that he was being accused of crossing a solid line presumably painted somewhere beneath the snow.

"Did you get a ticket?" the passenger asked.

"I don't know yet," the driver replied. "He said if I got back here with a plastic bag before he goes off duty at two P.M., he'd tear the ticket up."

One cannot expect all uniformed or plainclothes guardians of Soviet insularity to maintain indifference as tantalizing fragments of American life flit past them. So relatives visiting prisoners sometimes slip the guards packages of American chewing gum in exchange for a longer time with their loved ones. Packs of Marlboros and Winstons become currency for favors from the most officious bureaucrats. A hapless tourist, ahead of me in a customs line, found his *Playboy* magazine intercepted at the airport as pornography; the customs inspectors (several were needed for such a serious purpose) leafed through the journal with considerable slowness, studying each page to be sure that the momentous step of confiscation, which they were about to take, was thoroughly justified. An American diplomat once had the temerity to offer a copy of *Playboy* to a KGB "militiaman" on guard outside his apartment house. The officer accepted it with alacrity. Later, as the American returned home, another officer, who had just come on duty, asked if he had another *Playboy* to spare. No, the diplomat apologized. "Well," said the guard, "do you have a gin and tonic?" The American got him one.

In certain suave circles of the middle elite, American styles became overt fads. A friend of mine whose parents were both medical professors told me that at her sister's fifteenth birthday party, all the boys and girls, who clustered separately, wore American jeans—every one of them. At a prestigious Moscow architectural institute's annual dance the students one year built a huge model of a pair of dungarees to tower over the dance floor—the centerpiece of their decorations and a totem in the idolatry of the age. An American woman shocked her Russian maid by removing and throwing away a leather Lee patch that was coming loose from a pair of jeans. The patch was the whole idea, the maid said, and snapped it up to sew on a pair of her son's. English words, especially American slang, also crept into the colloquial language of the urbane, as pretentiously as did French in Chekhov's day. Young English-speaking Muscovites were fond of salting their Russian with English nouns and verbs conjugated and declined according to the rules of Russian grammar. Thus the sentence "The girl comes, and he speaks to her" turned out *"Girla pricomaet i on ei speakaet."* This was just for fun, to show off a bit.

Despite periodic official campaigns against such displays of Americanisms, the fads have arisen in the context of high-level ambivalence and overall relaxation. The Komsomol activists who prowled the streets in the 1950's shortly after Stalin's death, guarding against ideological deterioration by rounding up youths who wore tight, narrow-legged pants in the Western fashion of the period, have grown into establishment members whose children now covet jeans and rock records and whose own rewards for conformity and obedience often involve the privileges of contact with Western goods and culture. In urban society at large, the virtue of Western styles has attained an unquestioned invincibility. On the opening day of the Twenty-fifth Party Congress, a woman called her husband at his office near the center of Moscow to ask if he could buy some American fashion magazines for her at one of the major hotels. Fashion magazines? Yes, she said. Surely the state would have put some on sale to impress the foreign Communist delegations, to show them that we're not backward. No, her husband told her. In the hotels he'd seen only literature about the party. "Oh," she said sadly, "only about the party." He later explained to me how devoted the social-climbing Muscovite can be to an object that just appears Western, as a status symbol. "The refrigerator should be, first, blue," he said, "and secondly, labeled 'Made for Export,' written in English. People put the labels on themselves. But I can tell when it's a fake by looking at the gasket around the door. Then there are people who have somehow gotten sheets with roses on them; when they have guests, they turn the bed back slightly."

The craving smolders, but it can also burn. I knew a young man in his late twenties, "Aleksandr," an intelligent and stimulating conversationalist who had good connections with young party activists and a perceptive candor about his society. I used to go see him to talk about the workings of the system, the values of the country. He was a deeply angry, though thoroughly private, dissident, yearning to see the West but wary of any overt protest. He knew none of the Sakharovs or Orlovs and didn't want to, and we both made some effort to conceal our meetings, for his protection. I never called him from my own phone, and he never called me; I would dial him up only from a random coin telephone in the street to ask quickly when I could come. I tried to make sure I wasn't being followed when I went. But one day he broke all the rules. He called my apartment and left a message, using his real name. When I got back to him, there was distress in his voice. I must come to him urgently, he said. He needed to see me right away. I was alarmed. The trouble must be serious for him to throw away the precautions. I walked into his two-room flat expecting to find the disorder of a KGB search. Aleksandr greeted me with warmth and relief, but it was a welcome laden with pain and panic. "What is it?" I asked.

"My stereo," he said. "It's broken."

On a low bookshelf against the wall, his sleek Japanese-made equipment sat idle. His racks of rock records stood in a silence that made the room seem empty, for his apartment usually swam perpetually in the mellow, biting, soothing, sour sounds of electric guitars and amplified voices. I knew of his addiction, and now I understood how his hunger gnawed at him. I knew his passion for this music, how thoroughly it seemed to take him out of his dismal world. An American student friend visiting a few years before had bought him the stereo from a special store that accepts only foreigners with hard currency. Now the amplifier had something wrong, requiring parts and technical expertise unavailable to Russians in Moscow. Would I go to the Beryozka, the special store, and buy him a new one? He had been there and had looked and had picked out the model. Here, he said, giving me a scrap of paper with the model number he wanted. They have it now, he said. And here, he added, holding out a wad of rubles.

It would be too much to say that Aleksandr and I were close friends, but I did not think him a provocateur; he came to me well recommended by someone I trusted. So I saw this plea to me as his own despair, nothing more. What he was asking of me was the kind of illegality performed by Russians for each other daily, and he had no reason to imagine that I would refuse. But it violated my guidelines, for I was determined to keep my behavior within bounds appropriate to journalism; if I were to be expelled from the Soviet Union, I wanted to be proud of the reason, not ashamed of it. So I told him as gently as I could that no, I could not buy him a new amplifier.

He refused to believe this for a moment. He offered me more rubles, beyond the official exchange rate. I explained that it was the principle, not the money, and told him of the authorities' pressure on correspondents then. He thought I was bargaining, and he changed the offer. Rubles, he conceded, were not of much value, and perhaps I would be more pleased with a couple of fine icons. His father (a party member) collected icons. No, no, I repeated and tried to explain again about being a journalist, sticking to journalism, keeping my nose clean. He could not grasp the notion that anyone would do anything out of pure principle. He seemed confused, distraught. As I made to go, he stuffed the wad of rubles into my coat pocket. I took them out, put them on his sofa, and left in a mood of annoyance and pity.

In the following weeks Aleksandr tried a couple of more times, with me and my colleague Craig Whitney, showing us icons and throwing in a sterling silver Turkish dagger in a handsome scabbard. Craig was equally adamant in avoiding such dealings, but Aleksandr just never understood us. He begged and coaxed, and ultimately his insistence destroyed our relationship, for neither Craig nor I ever felt comfortable with him again.

It is impossible to separate the allure of the West from its danger; even the authorities reinforce and combat the attraction simultaneously. A few students, children of the elite, gained the privilege once of guiding a group of American sports reporters on a visit to the Soviet Union. It was a rare chance for the kids to touch the outside world, and they used the opportunity with relish, becoming quite chummy with the Americans. After a few days the senior woman overseeing the guides called them together and told them that for their health and security they shouldn't be so friendly to the Americans and should stop dressing, acting, and chewing gum like them. The change was sudden and complete; the guides were cool and distant for the rest of the trip.

But the association with Americans also opens doors. At the popular Aragvi Restaurant in Moscow one evening, I had booked a table by going through the normal routine of writing a letter on *New York Times* stationery, sending my driver to deliver it, and seeing a place magically reserved—the blessings of *blat*. My colleague Flora Lewis, who was visiting from Paris, had invited two *Izvestia* correspondents, Vikenty Matveev and Melor Sturua, to have dinner with us there to talk about Soviet-American relations. Flora and I arrived first. A crowd hovered outside the restaurant, hoping to catch the attention of the crusty brute who worked as a doorman, slip him a couple of rubles, and get inside. I felt like an imperialist heel as I pushed up to the door and tapped my ring on the glass. The doorman turned his back. I rapped again and yelled. He walked away, into the recesses of the restaurant. We waited for a moment, until he had to open the door for someone leaving. I said, *"New York Times,"* into his fat face. He tried to push the door closed. I said, "We ordered a table—*New York Times."* Reluctantly, he consulted a miserable scrap of paper in the palm of his hand, found us on his list, and broke into a beaming smile of hospitality and welcome, ushering us in with a flourish.

We had been seated for a time when Matveev joined us. He is one of the most respected columnists in Moscow, with high party connections and an infallible instinct for the correct line. His colleague, Sturua, arrived a few minutes later. Flora asked them if they'd had trouble getting past the doorman. "No," Matveev answered. "I just said, *'New York Times,'* and he let me right in."

Then Sturua piped up. "When I said, *'New York Times,'* a woman in line spoke up. 'Mr. Sturua,' she said, 'shame on you! I know you. I've seen you on television. You're not from *The New York Times!"* At that point Sturua had to stop to explain that he was just a guest of *The New York Times.* So she asked him if he could get her in, too.

I could never reconcile myself to being vilified and coddled at the same time. But it was even stranger for some Russians. Here was a writer, let's say, whose novels or essays were politically unacceptable at home. So he smuggled his manuscripts to Paris or New York or London, and they were published there. His royalties on this contraband might very well have been permitted to reach him in hard currency (the Soviet Union having a great appetite for Western cash), which he could then convert into scrip known as certificate rubles. With these coupons, each bearing his name and barred legally from transfer to anyone outside his immediate family, the officially disgraced writer could make purchases in special, restricted stores, which carried Western and Soviet goods unavailable to the loyal, plodding citizen, who depended on the ordinary state stores, and other goods at lower prices than in the ordinary stores. Predictably a black market developed in the scrip—I was told that people were paying seven regular rubles for one certificate ruble.

Not all dissident writers received their royalties, of course. But some did, and enjoyed the privilege, just as diplomats and performers who work abroad and are paid there in hard currency hoard their money for its extra buying power. Several musicians at the Bolshoi explained the system: If you were doing a tour in the United States, for example, you received a stipend of $19 a day, $25 on concert days. The cash was supposed to go for lunch and dinner—you didn't have to pay for travel, hotels, and breakfast— so many musicians tried to survive with as little restaurant eating as possible, practically starving themselves by eating cans of fish and hunks of salami and cheese carried with them from the Soviet Union, saving as many of the dollars as they could to buy clothing, tape recorders, and stereo sets for themselves, friends, and acquaintances who did them favors back home. One clarinetist stocked up on clarinet reeds whenever he went abroad and made a lucrative little business out of selling them to colleagues when he returned. The same kind of trade grew up in strings, mouthpieces, and other essentials that were either unavailable or inferior in the Soviet Union. A trumpeter who did not own a trumpet, but who used one that was state-owned and American-made, longed for the time when he could gather enough dollars to buy a fine trumpet for himself. He was already in his fifties, and when he retired, he would have to relinquish his state-owned instrument, leaving himself with nothing to play. Any refusal to allow him to travel to the West with the orchestra, he told me, was "the biggest punishment" the authorities could level against him. And permission depended on the approval of the orchestra administration, the trade union, and the party; the party looks at your work record, your attendance at political lectures, and your relatives abroad, who disqualify you immediately out of a fear that you might defect.

Thus have the authorities deftly twisted contacts with the West into a new form of social control, more humane than labor camps but quite effective. The coveted trip to Western Europe or the United States, and the access to American records and films, are now enticements in some circles for good behavior at home; the denial of the privileges can be devastating.

For many dancers, musicians, actors, directors, and other performers and intellectuals, travel outside the walls of their own society becomes more than a way of getting Western goods—it is a compelling and essential experience of encounter with creativity and innovation. In the détente of the 1970's many came to feel dependent culturally on their tours to Western Europe and the United States, and once having tasted the exposure to cultural freedom, they were left unsatisfied by both their own restricted repertoires and the curbs on travel. The restrictions have provoked a number of emigrations and defections. Valery Panov, the ballet star, applied for an exit visa to Israel only after the authorities had deprived him of travel abroad and smothered his efforts to push his dance beyond the accepted, conservative norms on the Soviet stage. Rudolf Barshai, a well-known and popular conductor of the Moscow Chamber Orchestra, was driven to ask for emigration after he had been repeatedly denied permission to go on tour with his orchestra. Both Panov and Barshai were eventually granted exit visas. Mikhail Baryshnikov, the dancer, defected from the Kirov Ballet Company during a Western tour. He explained why: "If I had had the opportunity to leave Russia for one month, two months at a time, to work with different choreographers and return home to the Kirov, I would never have left. My homeland, my theater, my friends mean more to me than anything. But the time came for a choice: my art or my peaceful contentment."

These talented and sensitive artists are merely a tiny elite, however, with no political impact on their society and little opportunity to spread their admiration for cultural freedom. I spoke with many Russians who had traveled; the overwhelming impression they returned home with was one of material plenty. A simple man who visited Helsinki for a few days told me in wonder of his visit to Stockmann's department store. "The store was full of stuff," he said. "Briefcases, suitcases, shirts. But there were no lines. You could just pick things up from the counters and pay cash—just pay right there. No standing in separate lines for cashiers." Another Muscovite went to the United States and took pictures of a supermarket. "Strawberries and bananas in February!" he marveled. He bought a computer chess game named Boris.

A Russian woman visiting the New York area maintained a stoic "ours is better" attitude through a cruise around Manhattan, a tour of Lincoln Center, and a trip up the Empire State Building, until her hostess took her into a big, fancy supermarket. There the veneer of smugness cracked as the Russian woman stood amid seemingly endless aisles of fresh vegetables, red meat, and frozen foods —and wept.

"My friends," said a seventeen-year-old Moscow girl, "see the United States as a place to buy jeans and records. They don't seem to think of much else." Why don't they also think of it as a place of political freedom? I asked. "They don't have time," she explained. "Here, they are spending hours trying to find shoes to buy, so that is naturally what they think about in terms of America." She once overheard a conversation at a hospital where she worked: A woman who had just returned from a visit to the United States was asked by a surgeon whether there was enough meat in America. The woman said there was.

Western Ideas

In all aspects the United States looks chaotic to many Russians. Politically, because of its pluralism, it seems disorderly, directionless, frighteningly disharmonious. Economically, because of its diversity and decentralization, life seems insecure, uncertain, dangerously unpredictable. Socially, the country seems riven by street crime and racial conflict. It makes a terrifying spectacle.

Russians' propaganda plays to their natural affinity for order, planning, and authority, magnifying the discord in American life. And while some Russians suspect that their newspapers and television exaggerate American problems, the official themes of distaste find fertile and receptive ground in the population at large. The exhibitions that were sent to Soviet cities by the United States Information Agency (USIA) provided a good sampling of popular opinion among the ordinary Russians who crowded into the pavilions and spoke with the young American guides, who were usually graduate students fluent in Russian. Most of the Russians' questions were about money, salaries, prices, unemployment, expensive medical care, and the like. There was a general conviction that nobody except millionaires could afford the rather typical furnishings and appliances they were seeing on display. They couldn't believe that someone out of work wasn't starving on the streets or that someone who wasn't rich didn't simply die because he couldn't pay for medical care. They had never heard of unemployment insurance or medical insurance. "They all think every American has a giant set of ulcers, fearing he will be unemployed the next day," one guide remarked. "They think American life is incredibly insecure." When I asked a young woman what she thought the main differences were between American and Soviet societies, she said, "Here I feel secure. I know I will never starve. In the U.S. I could have a lucky day and an unlucky day." To many Russians, the American practice of job hunting seems frightening, and they wonder how Americans can possibly live without having such vital things done for them.

Much of the distaste also stems from racism. Realizing that so many blacks live in the United States and linking blacks with crime, many Russians see a scary picture. "They think slavery just ended about five years ago," said Carl Lee, a black guide at an exhibit. He was only half kidding. He had brought along a copy of *Ebony* magazine to show Russian visitors to his pavilion. "They are absolutely surprised that there are middle-class blacks," he said. "They don't believe I'm black—they think it's a trick. They have a really warped view of it, and they're all sure they know the truth."

Antiblack attitudes pervade the private and semiofficial portrayals of American life. A friend of mine once sneaked a tape recorder into a closed lecture at Moscow State University, where a Soviet journalist just back from a visit to the United States described the following scene:

"Not knowing all the customs and habits of American life, we started to walk up a Washington street, and from around the corner three Negroes advanced upon us. I carried a hammer, which I had bought earlier, and it had a chrome-plated handle. The working tools in America are excellent, and if it's a hammer, the handle will never break or fall off, and it gleams. So the only thing that I had in my hands was that hammer, and in confusion and apprehension

I thrust it into my pocket and then drew it out again. And it turned out that that was the most appropriate gesture I could make because the Negroes evidently saw that something flashed, black and long, and just as they were coming to us, they swerved around us, and we went in opposite directions. Should it have been otherwise," the journalist concluded, "I'm not quite sure that I would be delivering this lecture." So the stereotypes are confirmed: material excellence, dangerous streets, hostile blacks, terrifying disorder—a profound ambivalence about America.

The journalist's talk, to a group of selected students, combined a line of propaganda with a set of his own candid observations. "The climate of America is warmer than ours, and nature is beautiful," he said. "There are bright flowers, dazzling colors; everything is beautiful, and nothing smells! Not a lake, not the flowers, not the grass! I perceive natural beauty through smell, but in America there is none of that important ingredient of scenery as smell. I must say that American life, as well as its nature, is beautiful, especially if one looks at it in such magazines as *America, Newsweek, Time,* and others. But when you look at it more closely, it doesn't smell. There is no more than beauty. There is none of that coziness, that goodness and trust of one another, which can be observed on the other side, in the socialist camp. . . . We were struck most by American women. An American woman is always easily discerned from others. They are always confident. The whole American way of life works in that direction—to be sure of everything, to keep smiling. Smiling does not mean that she is merry, no. This shows that all your affairs are in order, that you are healthy, that you can still get credit. So American women always maintain their hair in excellent condition."

The lecturer followed the normal Soviet practice of taking only written questions, and as they were passed up on slips of paper, he read them out one by one. "What manifestations of American individualism struck you most?" one student asked.

"First of all," the journalist replied, "individualism manifests itself in the fact that another's life has no value there. This stems from a lack of respect for the human being, from the American TV's openly and brazenly promoting a cult of force. And the Americans feel themselves, to a degree, naked if they don't carry some kind of weapon. . . . What struck us most was that indifference to the victims of violence. . . . Then this individualism reveals itself in America in perverted form, in a barbaric attitude toward some things. Take, for example, a beach. There are cabins on it. And if a girl, say, of seven years of age would start changing her clothes without retiring to the cabin, the parents would have to pay a fine. Immediately around the corner there is a go-go club, and there, in the immediate vicinity of the beach with its strict moral code, you will see women dancing on the podium absolutely nude or, depending on the rules set by the state, sporting little pendants or having nothing at all. And everything is absolutely routine, come who wants, be it a child or a woman. This is a hypocritical approach."

He read another note from the audience: "You are wrong in placing such a stress on the absence of state ideals among Americans, for here in the Union, among the young people in particular, there is no belief in anything, and only fools believe in the bright future. If compromising questions are asked here, they meet only a rather ironic attitude. Better let the young men develop business-like qualities than indulge in drunkenness and laziness."

The journalist retreated into defensiveness. "You know, comrades, if I ask a question, if I hit somebody in the snout, I say honestly that I hit him in the snout. This note is not signed. This alone shows that the author does not believe in what he wrote. Let us sort this out. This is a serious matter. When I said that the Americans don't have common ideals binding them together, I said common ideals, I did not say state ideals. And what is a state ideal? This is a wrong way to put it, an illiterate way of describing it. Whoever wrote it, can he now explain what he had in mind? He is not here? Well, you understand. Now for the second part. He says they don't believe in anything in the Soviet Union. Well, how can that be? The fact that the USSR held out during the most destructive war with fascist Germany, who bore the brunt of it? In a considerable measure it was precisely the youth. Why did people give up their lives? Precisely for the bright future! . . . When you are abroad, you perceive very sharply the bright side of what we have and what we are developing in the USSR. I was not making up stories when I told you that even if I have, in America, good trousers and a good car, I am still afraid to drive it. I am afraid to park it near a Negro block because they will wreck not only my car, they will wreck me or, still worse, my son. So what would you prefer, to have a worse car, but use it and travel in it with absolute assurance, or to know that sooner or later some unpleasant thing will happen to you? To exist on a smaller salary than, say, an American, but to know for sure that your old age will be secure and that if you happen to fall ill, or your beloved wife or child does, you will be able to do everything to save them without regard to your financial situation? Everyone here can call an ambulance, can't he? And in America you will have to think it over a million times. Only when you are abroad are you aware of a whole series of things that show you what the Soviet way of life is. Here we somehow get accustomed to them and believe it is quite normal that I work, and I even work badly, and still they won't turn me out because my trade union will step in for me. It is very difficult for a common manager to get rid of a bad worker in the Soviet Union. And for Americans it is quite different. If you don't perform to the employer's taste, you will find yourself out in less than no time. You can put up a show of democracy and not bend your back before him, but as soon as he finds you unwanted in any way, he will throw you out, and no trade union will save you. Now, they wag their tongues about so-called civil rights. . . . But you must realize clearly and sharply that the concept of civil rights in the U.S.A. is different. The Americans believe that, first of all, these rights include full freedom of conscience, religion, and so on. But we promote the idea that at the foundation of civil rights lie the social rights. What use would I have with my complete freedom if I am hungry? If my child is dying? If my wife is ill?"

The enormous capacity to project their own world onto the West has shaped many of the Russians' images of America. A temporary Russian teacher we had in Moscow, a pleasant, limited woman who had worked as an Intourist guide, once asked Debby what was available in state stores in America. When Debby said that we didn't have state stores, the woman looked aghast. "Then where do you buy things?" she said. A fourteen-year-old schoolgirl in Minsk once asked me, "At what age do you admit children into Komsomol?" In the same city an American guide at a USIA exhibition found himself entangled in a baffling discussion with two Soviet women who were wondering whether Americans had internal passports, as Russians do. When the guide said no, one woman snorted in triumph. "You see?" she declared to her friend. "I told you Americans couldn't travel freely inside their own country." At a display of home appliances people often made comments such as "Well, what good is this washing machine going to do if you live in the countryside? You're not going to have plumbing."

The projection has considerable impact in matters of politics and civil liberties, for Russians who have developed a keen cynicism about the hypocrisy of their own society's platitudes and empty guarantees assume that others' are equally false. Many people who listened to newscasts on the Voice of America, or who lined up for hours to get into those American-sponsored exhibits on home furnishings or construction materials or American life-styles, viewed the information through the corrective lens of skepticism, as they did their own, treating it as propaganda and as *pokazukha,* a show representing Soviet-style unreality. When they asked about racial discrimination, and the guides explained that it was now prohibited by law, they were unimpressed, for their own laws guaranteeing rights have no effect. In other words, they were as canny with American images as with their own. But the skepticism often blocked understanding.

I remember a long talk Debby and I had one evening with two sisters, sixteen and twenty-one, who spoke English, read whatever they could get their hands on from the West, and were interested in informing themselves. Their parents were well established in the academic world and had no dissident impulses that I could discern. We spoke of revolutions, and I asked them what they knew about ours, the American Revolution. Their faces went blank. They had not understood the question.

"The what?" said the younger.

"The American Revolution," I repeated. "What do you know about the American Revolution?"

For a moment, the vacant look remained, then suddenly dissolved into a smile of recognition. "Oh, yes," said the girl. "But we don't call it a revolution. We call it the War of Independence."

She and her sister and a couple of other young Muscovites around the table explained that the American Revolution was just an anticolonial uprising that brought independence from Britain but made no revolutionary changes in man's economic or political condition. As I later learned from reading the pertinent high school textbook, entitled *New History,* it was merely a "bourgeois revolution" in which "the victory of the people was used by the capitalists and the slave owners to strengthen their supremacy." It was just a transfer of power from one exploitative class to another, from the British "landowning aristocrats to the trader-industrialist bourgeoisie of the North, which ruled in alliance with the plantation slave owners of the South." Through the prism of Marxism, the American Revolution appeared diminished, its noble slogans perverted. And in the medium of a Soviet citizen's appreciation of hypocrisy, the Declaration of Independence and the Constitution contained only fine, empty words. "The declaration proclaimed that the people themselves have the right to establish the power of state government," the textbook said, "that power springs from the people, that the people are sovereign. However, the foremost idea of the declaration was used by the bourgeoisie to strengthen the wealthy, and only the whites. The declaration did not abolish slavery and did not stop the ouster from the land and the annihilation of the Indians, but preserved the exploitation of hired workers."

These messages of Marxism and American hypocrisy make a potent brew. The young people around that evening table were unable to cite any of the political ideals that emerged from the American "War of Independence." The twenty-one-year-old sister thought the Boston Tea Party was a protest over poverty, against the taxes on tea, "which people were too poor to pay." She had never heard of the political dimension, the outrage against taxation without representation (although it was mentioned fleetingly in the textbook),* and she had trouble understanding it after Debby and I explained. None had heard about the principle of the separation of church and state, and as we talked about it, they began to smile knowingly, thinking of that Article 52 in the Soviet Constitution: "Citizens of the USSR are guaranteed freedom of conscience, that is, the right to profess any religion or not profess any. . . . The

---

*Lenin took a slightly different tack in his Letter to American Workers of 1918. "The history of the newest civilized America is opened by one of those great, really liberating and really revolutionary wars," he wrote, but in the subsequent 150 years an abyss had opened "between a heap of arrogant billionaires" on one side "and millions of working people who live eternally on the verge of poverty on the other side. The American people who gave the world an example of revolutionary war against feudal slavery found themselves in the newest, capitalist-hired slavery. . . . In the American people there is a revolutionary tradition which has been taken by the best representatives of the American proletariat."

church in the USSR is separate from the state, and the school from the church." Other articles bring a chuckle, such as number 49: "Every citizen of the USSR has the right to present, to state organs and public organizations, suggestions for the improvement of their work, criticisms of shortcomings in their work. . . ." Or, my favorite, Article 56: "The private life of the citizen, the secrecy of letters, telephone conversations and telegraph communications are protected by law." I once heard about a dissident called in by the KGB for an interrogation that contained a sketch of charges about to be brought against him. He started to argue by citing one article or another of the Constitution. "Please," the KGB man interrupted, "we're having a serious conversation." So the young Muscovites saw our constitutional guarantees as they saw theirs. "All men are created equal, and everybody has the same opportunity," the older sister sneered sarcastically. "But it's not true in America," she said. "There is segregation and discrimination."

She was right as well as wrong, of course. American violations of the principles help Russians misunderstand the principles themselves. And the official press and television project a mirror image of Soviet defects onto the United States, making Soviet problems into American ones. When the Soviet Union is hit somewhere by an earthquake, the nightly news in Moscow is full of vivid reportings on tremors in California. When a cold snap of 40 below strains the capacity of Moscow's gas mains and the heating falters, television viewers are smothered in films of blizzards in Chicago. Shortly after a Soviet satellite had crashed in Canada, spraying radioactive material around, Tass delighted in reporting the crash of an American weather balloon in Montgomery, Alabama; the balloon "carried on board, as the authorities admit, a 'small source of radioactivity,' " Tass declared.

In a more serious vein the propaganda portrays American democracy as a screen behind which virtually identical candidates trick the people into thinking that they have a real choice. "Police persecution in the USA," as Tass headlined one item, is a constant theme. "The main targets of police persecution by the FBI have been and remain the Communist Party of the USA," Tass wrote, "the progressive democratic organizations, all those who seek civil liberties and human rights for all Americans without any discrimination. Any means, including trials, forgeries, blackmail, intimidation, and physical suppression, are used against them." The CIA's misbehavior has given Soviet commentators a field day. "This spying agency has organized conspiracies with the aim of assassinating foreign politicians who didn't suit Washington," Tass declared, asserting that "these methods of international gangsterism" are combined with "massive infringement of elementary civil rights of Americans suspected of 'disloyalty.' " Indeed, the CIA has done more than probably any other American institution to damage the appeal of American principles. Its "dirty tricks," along with those of the FBI, have been a boon to Soviet propagandists, who don't have to stretch the truth quite as far as they might.

In its search for mirror images the Soviet press finds American "dissidents," usually antiwar or antinuclear protesters who are arrested for a day or two during demonstrations and who become heroes, "living in an atmosphere of unceasing threats, hounding, and persecutions." A Tass story about the arrest of Elizabeth McAlister and the Berrigan brothers during a demonstration at the Pentagon against the nuclear arms race began:

> American propaganda is fond of talking about "freedom of convictions," about "democracy" in American society. The facts, however, show that those are only declarations. At a distance of a thirty-minute car ride from downtown Washington where zealous advocates of "civil rights and liberties" sit in cozy offices, there is a gloomy building with bars on the windows. Over there, in the prison of Alexandria, Virginia, those who know full well the true value of the high-flown talk about the freest society are kept. Their names have been known throughout the land since the sixties, when the USA launched the dirty venture in Vietnam. [And so forth.]

Occasionally I heard a Russian voice skepticism about this heavy-handed stuff. Pyotr Reznichenko, a burly fitter in a poultry factory near Odessa, said to me, "Angela Davis, a black Communist, is a philosophy professor, and they reported that they found a gun registered in her name. That's discrimination? She's a philosophy professor and she can buy a gun? Some discrimination!"

I had the feeling at times that in these attacks on America I was reading an Aesopian effort at criticism of Soviet society, couched in terms acceptable to the authorities. Certainly Soviet journalists and scholars whose specialty is America enjoy a freedom to use their critical faculties as few other Russians do. The experts on America who work in the Kremlin's think tank, the Institute of U.S.A. and Canada Studies, enjoy the privilege of sitting among desks and tables overflowing with copies of *The New York Review of Books, The New Yorker, The New Republic, Commentary, The New York Times, Harper's,* and the like, all barred from circulation among ordinary Russians. In one man's office I even saw a Manhattan telephone directory. A Soviet friend who has had some association with the institute told me that its members often write of America as they would like to do of their own country. So on a certain level the portrayals of American life become parables.

But even Soviet Americanologists, fluent in English, well read in American periodicals and literature, frequent visitors to the United States—even these carefully selected men, who have more access and exposure to American life than almost any other Russians—always seemed to understand their subject in a most brittle fashion. As I spoke with them, I kept seeing in my mind a painting by Richard Estes, the American artist who practiced in a school known as Photorealism or Hyperrealism. His method was to photograph typical American scenes in the early morning, when hardly any people were around, and then to paint from the photographs with an exaggerated purity and precision. The work that kept coming to mind hung in Moscow's Pushkin Gallery for a while as part of an exhibition of American painting, assembled by the Metropolitan Museum of Art. It was a scene of Times Square, completely empty of people, without a soul. Every building and billboard and sidewalk and traffic light was vivid and clean and accurate, as if brandnew, freshly painted and seen through crystal mountain air. The gutters were not filled with trash; the storefronts and streets were free of grime. Its reality was perfect but incomplete, making a wonderful fantasy, and to anyone who knew Times Square, who could fill in the filth and the masses of variegated human beings jostling and pushing across those pavements, the painting brought laughter. And this, I often thought, was how the Soviet experts saw America; the geometry was perfect, every angle precise, each object in accurate relationship to every other—but no soul, no grime, no gut feeling for the emotions and attitudes that drive American political life. And there was no way that they could fill in these qualities from their own experience or backgrounds.

For years the experts believed and told Soviet policy makers that American business would soon force Washington to abandon the obstacles to most-favored-nation trade status for the Soviet Union. Congress had made the relaxation of trade restrictions contingent on Soviet relaxation of emigration restrictions for Jews, and those who studied America were fairly sure that the enormous power of business and its self-interest would eventually weigh decisively. They were as mistaken on this as they had been earlier, when they advised the Kremlin that President Nixon would survive Watergate. They simply did not have a good feel for the qualities of American democracy that cannot be drawn in a precise geometry.*

When the American Embassy invited groups of sophisticated, informed Soviet officials to watch videotapes of the televised debates between Jimmy Carter and Gerald Ford during the 1976 campaign, many of the Russians who came were disgusted by the spectacle, finding the sharp questions by reporters "humiliating" to the national leaders. When Marshall Goldman of Wellesley College taught a semester course at Moscow State University on the American economy, his free discussion of unemployment, inflation, racism, and other problems in the United States convinced some students that he was as much of a pariah in American society as a Russian who spoke so openly would be in the Soviet Union. "Some of the students thought I was a Communist," Goldman said. "I told them I wasn't a Communist—I was a bourgeois apologist, about as far as you can get from being a Communist in the United States." American guides at exhibitions disarmed hecklers and confused hostile questioners, just by speaking candidly. "They don't expect us to be honest," one American told me. "This is the biggest mistake they make. When we say yes, we have problems, this floors them." Another guide shocked a group of Russians who had gathered around him at an exhibit in Minsk. "One guy started talking about Gus Hall [head of the American Communist Party], and I said, 'Gus Hall is the biggest jerk in America,' " the guide recalled. "He got upset. A guy standing next to him said, 'You couldn't say

---

*Nor have Americans gained a feel for Soviet attitudes and priorities; Washington was wrong in its calculations that the Russians would drop the barriers to emigration in exchange for the freer trade.

that about Nixon,' so I said, 'I don't think that about Nixon; I think he's a criminal.' "

When a group of United States senators visited Moscow as the SALT II treaty of 1979 was running into Senate opposition, they encountered startling misconceptions about the American system from leading Politburo members. Aleksei Kosygin lectured them about how they wouldn't get reelected if they didn't vote for the treaty since public opinion polls showed the American people supporting it. Grigory Romanov asked why party leaders couldn't discipline their members and deny them money for their reelection campaigns. Both men imagined an order and logic more suitable to the Soviet than to the American system.

Robert Kelley, a history professor from the University of California at Santa Barbara, found significant blind spots among faculty and students he met at Moscow State University during a semester of teaching about nineteenth-century American politics. "They have absolutely no sense of what individualism is, what individual freedom is," he told me. "They tend to approach subjects formally, structurally—when studying William Jennings Bryan, they study the structure of the party. Teaching them is like trying to explain physical illness to a society that has never had it. They have never come down with democracy. They have never experienced physical illness, though they know that some other cultures have. They have developed a theory," he said whimsically, "that green paint will make it worse and red paint will make it better, but really inside, they think it is all due to the phases of the moon." Kelley tried to explain American individualism to his Soviet colleagues. After one attempt a medievalist said to him, "That's very undisciplined. That's bad for your army. You don't have an idea. Russians have an idea. Russians need an idea to believe in." This highly educated Soviet professor did not understand that the essence of the American idea is in the din of ideas.

Even where this alien notion finds its best support in Soviet society—in the dissident community—it is poorly understood and badly absorbed. Even those known loosely as democrats or Westernizers, who take great risks to protest political arrests and to advocate a liberalization of their system, rarely rid themselves of the deeply ingrained Soviet intolerance toward pluralism, toward the multiplicity of outlooks and opinions, which forms the central Western ideal of free thought. Many are political absolutists themselves, as dogmatic as the party *apparatchiki* with whom they went to school. Many see themselves in ideological combat with the authorities and so pursue their line with as definite a certainty as the authorities follow theirs. There is little delight in the babble of varied voices, no value placed in the free interplay of disparate views. The definitions imposed upon Russians and foreigners are startlingly clear: You are either with their cause or against it.

This was a disheartening discovery for me. I encountered some dissidents who detested and avoided others who took a slightly different position, some who manipulated facts as unabashedly as party *apparatchiki,* many who saw the Western press as a slavish conveyor of the dissident position, much as the authorities saw it and just as the Soviet press articulated the official Soviet stance. Among the notable exceptions to this inability to readjust perceptions were Roy Medvedev, Anatoly Shcharansky, Valentin Turchin, and Irina and Viktor Brailovsky, whose intellectual curiosity and open-mindedness allowed them a refreshing understanding of the world outside. I wish I could also count Andrei Sakharov among them, but it pains me to say that his towering courage and devotion to speaking for humaneness, which entitles him to all the immense respect he receives, did little to revise his Soviet-made impulses and preconceptions, which often proved more powerful than his contact with Western ideals.

In the fall of 1976, on the first anniversary of Sakharov's winning the Nobel Prize for Peace, Chris Wren of *The Times* thought of doing an interview with him on the state of the dissident movement. We went to see him in his simple flat. He was wearing his usual tattered sweater, and he and his wife, Yelena Bonner, invited us warmly into the kitchen for some steaming tea. They were devoted to each other—he like a lovelorn teenager, she as his spark and spirit, giving him a fire to complement his placid gentleness— and they were invariably hospitable, even through the veil of fatigue they suffered from being constantly under pressure and in demand. Chris pulled out his notebook, but Sakharov demurred. He would rather have the questions in writing, he said, to give them proper study before answering. This was a familiar tactic of Soviet bureaucrats, but we hadn't expected it of Sakharov. Chris agreed, went back to the office, and in a few days delivered the questions. A week or two later Sakharov called. He was ready.

When Chris arrived, Sakharov handed him a thin manuscript. The questions were typed, and the answers were typed below. Chris was nonplussed but took the paper and began going through it. Many of Sakharov's answers were incomprehensible to an average reader, consisting of long lists of last names of political prisoners, without further identification or explanation, as if the very act of publishing the names in *The New York Times* would somehow signal Soviet authorities of their prominence and perhaps help their cases, like lighting a candle for them at an altar.

A few days later Sakharov called. Had the interview run yet? No, Chris said, he'd been busy with other things and hadn't had time to write the article but would get to it soon. What article? asked Sakharov. There is no article. Just this interview, the text. Chris explained that *The Times* did not publish simple text without an accompanying article, that many of the answers required explanation, and that if part of the text were published in addition, it would be the editor's decision. Sakharov was adamant that there should be no article by Chris, that only his text should be published, in the precise form in which he wrote it and in its entirety. Chris tried to explain how that wouldn't work, but Sakharov, egged on by Yelena, whose voice Chris could hear in the background, insisted that the "interview" was his property and that it could not be printed except as he demanded. He told Chris to contact his editors; they would understand. "I am an unusual person," Sakharov said in an uncharacteristically immodest fashion. "I am not just an American movie star."

"And I am not a Soviet journalist," Chris shot back. Sakharov demanded the return of his "interview," and nothing appeared in the paper. Several years later, Tony Austin of *The Times* used patient coaching to solve a similar problem. When Sakharov again demanded that an interview be published only as a text, Tony made a counterproposal. He explained quietly that he would have to write an article but would be willing to show it to Sakharov before sending it to the paper, to reassure him that his words were not being distorted. This was quite a departure from *The Times*'s usual procedures, but Tony was sympathetic to Sakharov's concerns and felt he needed to be educated gradually in the ways of the Western press. Sakharov accepted the offer and read the article before publication. He suggested one minor change, but Tony talked him out of it, and the article was sent as written.

I knew Yelena Bonner as a shrill critic of those who disagreed with her. Once, after a press conference of the Helsinki Watch Committee, which dissidents set up to monitor Soviet violations of the 1975 European security accord signed at Helsinki, a group of unofficial artists announced to Western reporters that they were forming an organization to protect their freedom to paint. Yelena waited until most of the correspondents had left, then began shrieking at one of the young artists, "Who are you? We don't know you! How dare you use this press conference for your own ends!" The poor man was shocked into silence, as were the Westerners who had thought that the dissidents believed in free speech.

Yelena was involved in an ugly incident with the literary and film critics Vladimir Solovyov and Yelena Klepikova, who wrote a gloomy piece on the Op-Ed page of *The Times* after they had emigrated. Their theme was "the democratic movement's lack of roots in Russia, which at present has the government it deserves, and perhaps even better." They wrote: "The inability and unwillingness of Soviet dissidents to look truth in the face and acknowledge it as such underline their paradoxical resemblance to the Kremlin rulers, against whom they are in opposition on the essence of things, but not the form!" They asserted that "dissidence in Russia is living out its short life span," that the KGB had succeeded in "isolating and barricading Academician Sakharov and turning him into a general without an army," thereby "making the renowned academician helpless in the fullest sense of the word."

True to the style of journalists schooled in Soviet techniques, the piece was polemical and overstated. But it made a valid point about the vacuum in which the struggling rights movement operated, one that many dissidents did not want to hear. Sakharov's wife, in Rome at the time for eye treatment, reacted sharply, so sharply that Vladimir Maximov, editor of the émigré journal *Kontinent,* published in Paris, took her reaction to mean that the magazine should never publish a word by Solovyov. A manuscript Solovyov had submitted was rejected in a tart note from Maximov saying that Yelena Bonner had issued a "veto" over his work. Solovyov, taking this as an attempt by the premier defender of free speech to stifle free speech by putting him on a blacklist, wrote an open letter of protest to Sakharov. When I asked Sakharov about it, he denied having issued any veto, saying, "I think that *Kontinent* has the full right to publish or not to publish Solovyov. It's the right of every editorial office." Yelena denied any attempt to blacklist Solovyov, and in the face of imminent publicity, Maximov sent Solovyov a cable saying, "Unfortunately I completely misunderstood what has been told me by Mrs. Helene Bonner-Sakharov. Nevertheless the majority of the Russian members of our editorial staff still remain against publication of the material sent by you because of its form." It was, perhaps, a tempest in a teapot, an unattractive display of nasty émigré politics. But it also demonstrated the durability of the Soviet-taught instincts and the profoundly alien nature of the Western concept of free debate.

Even many of those who choose to leave the Soviet Union forever carry a heavy baggage of Soviet-made impulses and attitudes into their new lives in the United States and Israel. Even those Soviet Jews who have been drawn powerfully enough by the outside world to run the gauntlet of emigration often find, when they get to the West, that their Soviet-bred instincts shape their encounters with the free market of goods and ideas, causing them considerable discomfort, at least initially. I know many who find the acerbic debates of Israeli and American politics unbecoming and disturbing. They are confused and distressed by the irreverence and variety of the Israeli and American press, yearning for more orderly and respectful discourse. In disagreement they see weakness, danger. They have somehow imagined that the bipolar, black-and-white world as portrayed by their Soviet experience is indeed the reality and that now they have moved to the other side of the coin, where the West must be as unanimously anti-Soviet as the Soviet Union is anti-Western. They are peppered by the synonyms and antonyms of their Soviet upbringing, seeking structure by pursuing old patterns or by embracing rigid opposites. Thus some in Israel find Orthodox religious observance a useful substitute for the hierarchy of beliefs they rejected and left behind in Soviet society. Others, suddenly adrift in a seemingly chaotic political melee, swing to the extreme right of Israeli politics, finding in the ultranationalistic and militaristic passions a welcome ideology and commitment to replace the one they abandoned back in Moscow, Leningrad, or Kiev. I have found it more difficult to talk politics with some Russian friends in Jerusalem than I did in Moscow. There, while I recognized their "conservatism" in an American context, their opposition to the extremes of the system opened dimensions of Soviet society to view; in Jerusalem, their same opposition has in itself become extreme, flattening the contours of reality into a false replica of the Israeli social and political landscape. The line between good guys and bad guys, which they have learned to draw so neatly in their Soviet experience, some of them draw now between Jews and Arabs. A few think the Arabs should all be driven out of Israel and the West Bank.

By contrast, some Soviet émigrés dislike the ideological character of Israel because it seems to carry a whiff of what they deliberately and happily left behind. Others simply melt into the new society apolitically. But almost all those I know in both Israel and the United States have endured some confrontation between their Soviet perceptions and their Western environments. Often these are finally resolved; sometimes not.

Some newly arrived émigrés, for example, have continued their practice of using acquaintances for connections and personal gain, acquiring and discarding American and Israeli friends like pieces of Kleenex and offending in the process. Others are lost when they find no central government agency to assign them housing and jobs, and they interpret the inattention as they would in a Soviet context —as a rebuff. Some find it hard to shed the old sense of perpetual illegality in what they do and the old aversions to, say, free market activities that are considered natural and healthy in the West but illegal and morally wrong in the Soviet Union.

In Beersheba, Israel, one Thursday morning, I was wandering through the weekly Bedouin market with Micha Bar-Am, an Israeli photographer, when we spotted a middle-aged couple standing in the midst of the mostly Arab crowd, holding out swaths of cloth for sale. Micha guessed they were Soviet émigrés, and we went to talk with them. Our approach made them nervous. They looked suspiciously at Micha's cameras and resisted our attempts to open a conversation. Their Hebrew was quite broken, and when I began speaking Russian to them, a look of terror came over their faces. They backed away, and I tried to calm them, finally getting them to talk a bit. They told us a little about themselves, about the material and clothing they had brought with them from the Soviet Union to sell, apologizing embarrassedly for the fact that they were there in the market doing an improper thing. I explained that there was nothing wrong here in this, that private enterprise was not against the law, as it was "in the Union," and that they really had nothing to be ashamed of. The woman became more forthcoming than her husband; she even told Micha her name. But as we said good-bye and walked away through the swirling crowds, and Micha asked me for a piece of paper to jot down a caption (he had snapped a few shots surreptitiously), the husband, who had been watching us steadily, charged at us through the mobbed market to scream that we should not mention their names, and that he had seen me give Micha a piece of paper, and that he knew perfectly well who we were and what we thought and what we were going to try to do to him. Ghosts of the secret police.

Getting used to the marketplace can be especially hard for artists, musicians, performers, and writers whose creativity has never before been measured by its popular appeal, but rather by the official bureaucracy's judgments of politics or favoritism. Having to sell things, or having creative decisions made by box-office considerations, is thoroughly demeaning. And it is difficult to accept the hard lesson that what is suppressed in the Soviet Union is not automatically revered in the West.

Rudolf Barshai, a balding man with a pleasant calm about him, was the conductor of the Moscow Chamber Orchestra, known colloquially as the Barshai Orchestra. He was so popular that his name became the most prominent feature of the advertising posters, inscribed in letters much larger than those spelling out the title of the orchestra itself. "BARSHAI," the posters cried. This was remarkable in a system that tends to elevate the institution and to eclipse the individual.

When he received permission to emigrate to Israel, word spread rapidly through Moscow; his final concert was attended by some high-level Soviet officials and party members, in a kind of silent tribute. He left this fame behind. In the West he hoped to form his own symphony orchestra, not really appreciating the economic obstacles to doing so. He did build up a chamber orchestra in Israel, but he found the country parochial and the music of inadequate quality for his ambitions. He quickly accepted guest appearances in Europe and the United States and finally left Israel entirely. But he was repeatedly disappointed to find limits imposed on his repertoires.

He came one warm autumn afternoon before a concert to sit in our garden in Jerusalem and talk of his frustrations. The example he hit upon to symbolize them all was a work by an excellent Soviet composer named Aleksandr Lokshin, who had written a choral piece based on some Kipling poetry. Barshai had decided to perform it in Moscow. After rehearsals and just a week before the concert a party functionary had told him no, Kipling was representative of the imperialist ideology. Barshai had argued. "The chorus is all assembled," he had said. "The soloists have learned their parts. The posters are printed." The director of the Moscow Philharmonic had then proposed that the text be translated into Russian and that English soldiers be changed to American soldiers, and India to Vietnam, "and I guarantee that you'll win a Lenin Prize." Barshai had been too honest for that, and the work had gone unheard in Moscow. So, several years later in London, after a very successful reception of another Lokshin work, Barshai tried to get this Kipling piece onto a program he was conducting. The orchestra management refused, arguing that people wanted something a little different, a little avant-garde. In other words, the same result, different motives. Barshai, who had been so excited about being in a free society where he imagined that he could finally perform any work on its merits, was crushed and disillusioned and embittered.

But the man I found most profoundly unable to move into his new world was an angular-faced, eloquent painter in his seventies named Yefim Ladyzhensky. Debby and I first met him in his spacious Moscow studio, allocated to him by virtue of his membership in the official Union of Artists. He had begun as a thirteen-year-old in Odessa, entertaining small children by drawing pictures of Lenin in black pencil on their hands. One day a plainclothes secret policeman spotted him, grabbed him by the hand, and asked where he lived. "He took me to my apartment," Ladyzhensky recalled. "Mama opened the door, turned pale. 'Is this your son?' the Chekist asked. 'Yes,' she said. 'He's very talented,' he told her. 'Tomorrow I am going to take him to an artist's studio for training.' "

Ladyzhensky became a scenery painter by profession, but it was only his living, not his pleasure. "It is just as temporary as the play itself," he lamented to us. "Everybody bows and applauds, but then it's gone." And so his studio was filled with his more significant pieces: canvasses of naïve, colorful scenes from his boyhood in Odessa—streets and bakers and concerts and Jewish weddings and bar mitzvahs—and paintings on themes from the stories of the Jewish writer Isaak Babel. "To express and to preserve my inner feelings in paintings that would remain," he explained. He was good, I thought, very good, and some of his works did hang occasionally in official exhibitions, though with limitations. Those on Jewish themes were excluded. Once a pastoral scene was removed by an official who said "that it wasn't pretty enough," Ladyzhensky told us. "The secretary of the Union of Artists said it didn't present the Soviet Union in a good enough light." Another canvas of people cutting wood on a city street was rejected because it implied that people were so poor they had to use wood for fuel. A painting of a dog being hanged, a scene he remembered seeing as a child, "they wouldn't exhibit because they thought it had a hidden, symbolic meaning," he said.

Ladyzhensky decided to try to leave the country, to join his daughter, who had gone to Israel. His application for an exit visa was accepted and approved; the authorities seemed unconcerned about his going. The question was whether his paintings would go with him. If not, he told us, he was determined to burn them rather than allow them to be confiscated. There were protracted discussions, with the result that most of his brilliant Odessa scenes were allowed out, but only after he had paid an enormous export tax on each of them.

Because his painting, especially on Jewish subjects, had been largely suppressed in the Soviet Union, he expected it to be hailed in Israel. He thought the Israeli authorities would welcome him as a cultural hero, set him up in a studio, invite him to the Ministry of Culture, and hang his paintings more or less permanently in the country's leading museum. When none of this happened, he did not understand it as a function of the free market, nongovernmental system in an open society; he saw it as official and social rejection, and it cast him into a deep depression and anger. Nobody gave him a studio, naturally, and he could not afford to rent one. So he and his wife moved in with their daughter, and he used the empty apartment in which they would have lived as a place to paint. The rooms were small, the light was bad, it was in an outlying neighborhood of Jerusalem, and nobody came. He was up at dawn each day working alone, gnawing at his soul because there were no flocks of admirers at his door.

When the Israel Museum in Jerusalem organized an exhibition of his work, he took no pleasure in it because it all went wrong, he felt. First, they said they did not have room to hang everything he wished; secondly, they were not interested in Jewish themes, which were quite ordinary in Israel; thirdly, the catalogue was printed in black and white, not color, because of funding problems. Ladyzhensky saw all this, through his Soviet eyes, as a deliberate, official effort to play down his work. It was not that at all, of course. For the Israel Museum to give a one-man exhibition was rather special, and the local critics raved. But Ladyzhensky read everything through the veil of his other life, so he saw conspiracy where there was none. And this annoyed, infuriated those with whom he dealt, plunging him more deeply into isolation. He tried to see the minister of culture—who in Israel is the minister of education—and could not; he felt he had been slapped in the face, not understanding that the official had neither the authority nor the importance of his Soviet counterpart. He could not get a museum in New York to take an exhibition of his work because although the museum was interested, he placed such a high value on each painting that the insurance on them during shipping would have been prohibitive. When I asked him how he had come to a value of $10,000 to $15,000 each, he said simply that those were the assessments of the Soviet Ministry of Culture when it was figuring his export tax. I wanted to weep.

He could never accept or even grasp the concept of a free market in art. He didn't want to sell his paintings, but he did want people to be willing to pay huge amounts for them. He didn't want to hang them in private galleries for sale, but he did want them seen constantly and widely. "Do you know what the galleries do?" he asked me. "If they don't sell them right away, they lower the price; then they lower it again, and again!" He felt unclean, cheapened, by such squabbling in the marketplace. He showed me a letter once from a man in Texas who had been to see his work. The man was making an offer—quite handsome, but apparently less than Ladyzhensky had asked. I saw the letter as enthusiastic praise; the artist saw it as an insult. People who took an interest in him and tried to help did not take enough interest and did not help sufficiently, he thought. He once wrote me a rude letter after a month or so had passed without my visiting him —and had his daughter deliver it stone-faced to my door, turn on her heel, and walk away without a word. An Israeli woman who went to some pains to show slides of his work in New York, to generate interest, was rebuffed by Ladyzhensky, who seemed to think she was just playing with him.

He came to hate Israel. He thought it was the most anti-Semitic place in the world, a view apparently based on its indifference to his works on Jewish subjects. He told Debby and me that he wished he had remained in Moscow. And when I asked what work he was doing currently, he pulled out several large, powerful ink drawings he said he did not usually show people, just his friends. They were self-portraits, one of him holding his severed head under his arm, a nest of barbed wire protruding from the collar of his shirt, where his neck should have been. In others he was being hanged, his face contorted in various masks of death.

As time passed and his life remained unchanged, the corrosion continued. By the beginning of 1982 he was ready to show these horrible self-portraits to the public. It was the rainy season in Jerusalem, a raw, cold time of late February, early March. He hung his works on the top floor of a small artists' association building near the center of the city. Rain pelted the skylights, leaking in and making puddles on the cold floor. Ladyzhensky stood silently at the entrance to watch people amble in and look, and stop, and look again. Two large oils hung next to each other in the main room. On one, a red Soviet star against a background of the red brick Kremlin wall. From each of the five points, a head of Ladyzhensky was hanged with a noose around its neck. On the other oil, a blue Star of David against a background of the ancient Herodian stones of the Wailing Wall. From each of the six points, a head of Ladyzhensky was hanged with a noose around its neck. He could not survive in either world. In another room there were nostalgic portraits of his mother, done at various times throughout his long and painful life.

"Yefim," I said, "how can you turn your insides out so thoroughly?"

"Each morning," he replied, "I go to my studio planning to hang myself. This is what I do instead."

Several weeks later, early in the morning, Yefim Ladyzhensky's daughter found him hanging in the stairwell of his studio.

The fates played cruelly. Vitaly Rubin, a scholar and teacher of ancient Chinese philosophy, a leader of the emigration movement, and a founder of the Helsinki Watch Committee, managed to get an exit visa after long years of struggle. He adapted better in Jerusalem than anyone I knew, learning Hebrew so fluently that he could teach in it at the Hebrew University, making his friends among Israelis, becoming wholly and happily integrated into his new society. He had a lot of trouble learning how to drive a car, for he had never been able to get one in Moscow, and he failed the driving test in Israel several times. But he finally succeeded, and in October 1981, while driving too fast on a desert road in the Negev, this profoundly contented man crashed and died.

Western Influence

Historically the West has served as a haven for Russians with unapproved ideas, a refuge from which intellectuals and reformers could expound views that filtered back into the circles of the Soviet intelligentsia. Thus Aleksandr Herzen, living chiefly in London from 1847, founded and published the first Russian émigré paper, *The Bell,* whose liberal socialism stimulated considerable ferment inside nineteenth-century Russia. Marxism, of course, was a Western idea, and Lenin spent years in Western Europe, writing and organizing before the Revolution, as he could never have done in his own country. Now Solzhenitsyn, writing from his estate in Vermont, maintains a following inside the Soviet Union for his chauvinistic visions of a Russian ecclesiastical state. Indeed, the small Soviet communities of dissidents, fundamentalist Protestants, underground artists, would-be Jewish émigrés, experimental musicians, avant-garde dramatists, unorthodox writers, and others who exist beyond the brink of official acceptibility gain much intellectual, spiritual, and emotional sustenance from their tenuous ties to the free arena of the Western world. Science gains from Western inputs, and a new practice of empirical sociology has grown up using Western sampling and polling techniques.

But it would be difficult to say that any of the fertilization from the West had significant effects on Soviet political or intellectual life during the détente of the 1970's. The clusters of political and cultural dissidents remained peripheral, restricted, even discredited in some measure by their reliance on support from outside. Western thought—such as it was—had little notable success in penetrating the mainstream of Soviet attitudes. Where there was cultural seepage from the West into Soviet society, it failed to stimulate much more than imitation; one could rarely find significant Russian creativity—in literature, art, or music—that had been nourished by this new influx of Western ideas.

I remember, during my first months there, being so struck by the pervasiveness of Western music that I jotted down examples. In the Kiev airport I heard the Beatles' "Let It Be" on the public address system. I made a note. Somebody sang "Summertime" in a restaurant. I scribbled it down. In a Leningrad factory a videotape machine on display was showing a tape of a man singing "Lara's Theme" from the film *Dr. Zhivago.* (The irony seemed lost on the factory manager, who was proudly showing off his products.) A drummer once told me that bands and combos were given quotas of Western music, which they could not exceed during a performance; the majority of tunes had to be homegrown, not imported. Nevertheless, I stopped taking notes on Western songs; the entire country had been infiltrated by our music. Craig Whitney, who plays a pretty mean harpsichord, heard a band in a Yakutsk restaurant doing "Rah, Rah, Rasputin, Russia's Greatest Love Machine," which the Western European group Bony M, in a bit of self-censorship, had quietly omitted from its repertoire on a Soviet tour just a few months earlier. Craig found music the freest of all the arts, with more and more open performances of jazz and avant-garde works by Western composers, including even the strange atonal pieces of John Cage, which have influenced a few Soviet composers to do likewise.

However, the emulation of the modern dissonances being heard from the outside reminded me of the largely imitative painting by the "underground" artists, who copied the styles of Picasso, Monet,

Warhol, and others, but who produced little original of their own, from what I saw. There has been no contribution equivalent to that of the Russian avant-garde artists of the early part of the century; the abstract innovations of Marc Chagall, Vasily Kandinsky, Vladimir Tatlin, Kliment Ritko, and the others have not been absorbed into the currents of Russian creativity but have been suppressed and neutralized by a conservatism that leaves contemporary talent sterile. Except for Ladyzhensky, who had something to say, artists who are burning to speak in a new voice pore over slick, smuggled art books with full-color plates of the modern masters; the results seem often shallow and affected, their excitement lying in the simple fact that their imitated styles are officially banned and their content is officially taboo. A painter can cause a stir by including churches, crosses, and onion domes prominently in his work or by drawing a portrait of a somber reality in a gloomy city street scene that tells some truth beyond the bright, heroic optimism of the propaganda posters. Or he can poke fun at the system, as Alek Melamid and Vitaly Komar used to do before they emigrated. Their wittiest work, I thought, was a parody of a poster glorifying the power and nobility of heavy industry. Their painting showed a grey, polluted atmosphere being cleansed by clear blue sky pouring out of the smokestack of a pure white factory made to look like a Greek temple; the factory was bringing goodness to nature.

What this means is that the restrictions on art and drama, literature and music have introduced a dimension of creativity that the West does not have; in the Soviet Union there is exhilaration in the very act of pushing beyond the frontiers of the permissible, of treading on the edge of danger, of crossing a line, flirting with irreverence. When it is done cleverly and subtly, as it must be to survive the cold scrutiny of the authorities, it can be immensely exciting, often becoming a substitute for essential artistic creativity as we understand it. And in its most successful forms it seems wholly indigenous, borrowing nothing from the West that hasn't already been in the Russian bloodstream for generations.

At the Taganka Theater in Moscow, the director Yuri Lyubimov produced many such works, none finer during our years there than his own stage version of Mikhail Bulgakov's mystical, sardonic novel *The Master and Margarita.* Opening night was the most powerful experience Debby and I had had in any theater in a long time, anywhere.

Bulgakov, the son of a teacher at the Kiev seminary, wrote fantasies and allegories in the period of tightening Stalinism. In the late 1920's he came under official criticism, his plays were removed from the stage, his work went unpublished, and wherever he applied for a job, he was turned away. He finally wrote a plea to Stalin, the story goes, and the dictator telephoned him, advising him to try again at a certain theater. There he was hired as an assistant director. But *The Master*, which he completed in 1938 after a decade of work, was suppressed and never allowed to be published in his own country during his lifetime. It finally appeared in 1966–67, first as a serial in the magazine *Moskva* and later in book form. Ten years later it was on the stage.

The old Taganka was an intimate theater, and that April evening only the select with connections could get seats, the luminaries among Moscow's foremost actors, writers, and filmmakers. As each one approached the theater through the narrow street outside, hundreds of people crowded around, pleading to buy whatever extra tickets there might have been. The advance publicity had been mostly by word of mouth, through the grapevine that intertwines the elite and the aware, testimony to just the sort of privilege and stratification that Bulgakov's novel ridiculed. We pushed in through the crowds and settled into our seats; the audience seethed with excitement.

The story is a well-woven fantasy of a myriad of characters, all of whom seemed to end up on stage in Lyubimov's four-hour drama. The devil pays a brief visit to modern Moscow, playing a kaleidoscope of satanic tricks that evoke the greed of the city's residents, drive sane citizens into madhouses, corrode law and order, nourish shame, and leave everyone debased except the Master and Margarita. He is a writer devoted to the search for truth; she is his illicit and selfless lover. He has done a manuscript on Christ's death, with Pontius Pilate as a man tortured by his role in passing sentence. The work, the ultimate truth, is rejected by Soviet publishing authorities; the Master, the paradigm of honesty, is confined to a mental hospital. The action swings back and forth, back and forth between Satan's capers in Moscow and Pilate's dialogues with Jesus. A huge pendulum was suspended in front of the stage, swinging, swinging: Pilate, wanting to save Jesus, but weak in the face of his official duties. Pilate, representative of the state. Jesus discussing the temporal nature of state authority. Pilate and

Satan, Jesus and the Master, Satan and Stalin, the Master and Bulgakov—parallels crisscrossed complexly. The music wailed and echoed, strobe lights flashed, and smoke burst from the stage. Devil's helpers breathed fire and ate mice. The theater was electric, the audience poised on the edge of exultation as taboo after taboo fell away. Margarita, summoned by Satan to preside over a great ball for the dead, did so half-nude, her back to the audience. And Satan offered her a gift, anything she wished. She asked the devil to free the Master. And a great, revolving curtain swung back to reveal the writer, wearing hospital garb and clutching a pillow, standing against the cross where Jesus died. Then he walked from the cross to Margarita's embrace. He had burned his manuscript, or so he thought. But Satan had it all, and he sat turning its pages as the pendulum swung and the music roared, and the devil thundered, "Manuscripts never burn!"

Manuscripts never burn. It was not only the power of the literary and dramatic work that moved the audience; the political, social irreverence titillated and delighted where it would have simply drawn blanks from a Western crowd. "You are atheists?" asked an unsmiling Satan, played with exquisite coldness by Venyamin Smekhov. He had been sitting on a park bench speaking to a Muscovite who thought that there was neither a God nor a devil. "What kind of country is this?" Satan asked, staring out at the audience. "Whatever you ask about, there isn't any." The theater erupted in laughter at the allusion to the country's material and spiritual poverty. When a devil's helper appeared at Margarita's flat to invite her to the ball, she asked if he had come to arrest her. "Why," asked the helper, "does one only have to speak to a person for him to imagine he's going to be arrested?" Laughter again. The Master, freed by Satan but worried that official papers show him still an inmate of the mental hospital, watched as the devil's assistant tore them up, saying, "Remove the document, and you remove the man." Titters. At the curtain call the giant pendulum swung back and forth, a spotlight following it, illuminating first Jesus on the right, then Satan on the left. The actors gathered to take their bows. Eight of them picked up huge photographs of Bulgakov, and an eternal flame was lit onstage as the rest of the cast turned toward the portraits of the author and applauded. There was a soaring sense of freedom in honoring a man so long oppressed, in hearing the trueness of a lonely voice, a supernatural force, against the dead hand of the party.

In adapting Bulgakov's novel to the stage, Lyubimov and his scriptwriting colleague Vladimir Dyachin made some compromises, softening a little here and there to smooth the project's way through the conservative bureaucracy of the Ministry of Culture. Bulgakov's delicious mockery of the arrogant comforts enjoyed by official writers—fancy apartments, country dachas, a "members only" restaurant—was dodged onstage. When a show of black magic by Satan provoked an audience of Muscovites to fight over ten-ruble bills and clamor for free clothes, the greedy in the play were considerably less ugly than in the novel. The book portrays an apartment house at 302a Sadovaya Street, where Satan makes his temporary residence, as a long time scene of mysterious disappearances. People go off and simply don't return. The analogy to Stalin's secret police work is obvious, but the disappearances were dropped from the play. The state's capriciousness was also slightly less explicit onstage, where a nice line by Satan's assistant was omitted. "Who is official and who is unofficial these days?" the assistant asks in the novel. "It all depends on your point of view. It's all so vague and changeable. Today I'm unofficial. Tomorrow, Hey Presto! I'm official! Or maybe vice versa—who knows?"

It is an essential custom for dramatists and filmmakers to compromise where they must to say what they wish, or to create riddles in which the *apparatchiki* and *chinovniki* ("bureaucrats") who are previewing the productions become entangled and confused. Georgian directors are canny and skillful practitioners of this craft, particularly when they seek to convey some unwelcome Western idea, such as individualism. In Tbilisi I saw a film, *There Was a Singing Blackbird,* in which an endearing and free-spirited young man, an antithesis to the serious-minded Soviet ideal, becomes a hero or an antihero, depending on one's viewpoint. He plays the kettle drums in an orchestra but is forever chasing girls and daydreaming and turning up late to concerts, giving fits of furious anxiety to the conductor, who always starts the piece without him in the hope that he will show up in time for his part. Sure enough, as the piece moves toward the crescendo, our hero dashes into the theater, rushes to an old stage manager who likes him and always helps him into his tuxedo, and pops onstage behind his drums just at the right moment to pound them into a thunderous frenzy. I thought he had charm. He does small kindnesses for friends and keeps forgetting his larger obligations. He is his own man, and the nice, human people in the film like him a lot; the officious, serious, grey figures can't cope with his uniqueness and detest him. At the end, as he is turning to smile and wave at a pretty girl while crossing a street, a bus runs smack into him, knocking him dead.

The cleverness of this film, in a Soviet context, was its ability to let the party bureaucrats hear whatever melody they wanted, while sending the message home in a subtler key. A politically orthodox Intourist guide named Natasha, who saw the film with me, had an entirely different reaction from mine. I liked the young man for his freedom; she disliked him for it. She saw the film as a morality play against frivolity and irresponsibility, and his death as a kind of sad justice. "He would never have made anything of his life," she said scornfully. She could not see his death as a comment on her society's murderous ambition for conformity, on its inability to tolerate a happy-go-lucky man who wanted to watch a pretty girl as he crossed a street.

More heavy-handed compromises are inflicted on American works that reach the Soviet stage. At the Mayakovsky Theater in Moscow, a production of *A Streetcar Named Desire* by Tennessee Williams introduced some Soviet-style twists. It was not dirty or sweaty enough, not sick enough for Williams. Stella was too good, too upstanding. Mitch was turned from an object of ridicule, a mama's boy, into a hero who honored his mother. The searing birthday scene was played too much like a situation comedy, provoking laughter that was blind to the spectacle of people destroying each other. The coup de grâce came at the final curtain. The Soviet producers changed the ending. In the original, Blanche is dragged off to an insane asylum. In the Mayakovsky Theater, the doctor and nurse who came to get her, who chased her upstairs, who grabbed her suddenly relented when she shouted, "Let me go!" Mitch then picked her up and carried her off into the sunset. Happy ending. The audience, flushed with pleasure, burst into enthusiastic applause. Debby and I sat there stunned. Tennessee Williams had been turned into soap opera.

Kurt Vonnegut Jr.'s *Slaughterhouse Five* suffered a similar, though somewhat less extreme, misfortune when it was adapted to the stage and performed at the Red Army Theater in Moscow. Vonnegut's novel is a bizarre, dreamlike, hilarious tragedy of war and violence that follows a well-to-do middle-aged widower named Billy Pilgrim as he spins helplessly back and forth through time, in and out of the sweet and painful episodes of his life, through his capture by the Germans in World War II, his daughter's marriage, the fire-bombing of Dresden, his optometry office, a veterans' hospital, his kidnapping by a flying saucer from the distant planet of Tralfamadore. It is a strong psychological drama, a philosophical statement, a comment on America, a set of disturbing questions about free will and fate, time and logic. The play was none of these. It did not violate the book, but diminished it, converting the literature of the absurd into the theater of realism, reducing a universal antiwar, antiviolence statement to a specific anti-American exercise. Performed under the title *The Wanderings of Billy Pilgrim,* it was a slightly zany, but nonetheless realistic, story of a pitiable American driven mad by the horrors of his wartime experiences. Andrei Mayorov played Billy with the perfect benign casualness to death, the precise smile, the bumbling, good-natured weakness that was ultimately responsible for hindering his fellow soldiers and leading to their capture. But onstage, Billy was explained only in the context of the atrocity he witnessed in the fire-bombing of Dresden. His early encounters and fascination with violence were ignored; the deeper psychological dimensions of his character were blanked out. And he became a cardboard figure. The Soviet scriptwriters obliterated every trace of Billy's vaguely right-wing sympathies. There were no bumper stickers on his Cadillac reading "Support Your Police Department," "Impeach Earl Warren," "Reagan for President." The Billy in the book, proud of his son as a Green Beret in Vietnam, turned upside down at the Red Army Theater, where the son, in uniform, visited Billy in the hospital, and Billy mocked him, goose-stepping across the stage, ridiculing his medals; the son grabbed his father and tried to hit him. It was just politically impossible for anyone on a Soviet stage to express pride in a Green Beret in Vietnam. This erased some of the novel's cold irony, through which Billy's outward normality finally comes to seem insane and his inward madness attains a sort of sanity.

Thus do the styles and statements from the outside world pass through the distorting lens of Russian culture and Soviet conservatism. And so, what finally touches people are the things of their own making, the songs and poetry from their own hearts and the soil of their own land. Much more than the petty excitement of what comes from the West, these stir something profound.

Russia did have a kind of hero while I was in Moscow, but in testimony to the opaqueness of the place, I never knew much about him until he died, a year after I left. He was Vladimir Vysotsky, an actor-poet, a balladeer, "a true bard of the people," as Lyubimov called him, who killed himself with heavy drink at the age of forty-two. It was summer, and the public outpouring was full and unrestrained. On the day of his funeral, some 30,000 people crowded into Taganka Square, near the theater where he had sometimes performed, and for weeks afterwards his grave at the Vagankov Cemetery was the focus of a remarkable display of grief and affection, visited by a constant stream of young and old, simple and erudite admirers who came with flowers to add to the heaps already there, to stand a moment and look and leave. "Volodya wrote and sang about the grimy, gritty, poignant things that are not supposed to exist in our society, but that people live by," said his friend the poet Bella Akhmadulina to Tony Austin of *The Times.* "Their love for him is a sign of a profound weariness in our people for all the official gloss, a profound hunger to be told about things as they are."

The few records of his songs that the authorities allowed to be made were never given substantial distribution, and his concerts, unadvertised, were held mostly in the provinces. But the songs were taped and copied and taped again, and the cassettes given and sold and passed hand to hand. His concerts were jammed. "He sang," Tony Austin wrote, "of the desperate and the defeated, the victimized and the untamed, the reckless ones just this side of the law and sometimes on the other side. With a Russian feeling for the underdog and a Russian relish for tragedy, he could spend a night with an eccentric or a bum he met that evening. He listened, he remembered, and he drank."

He wrote a song called "Wonderland," which began:

> *There is much unclear in this strange country,*
> *You can get confused and lost,*
> *It even makes you feel creepy all over,*
> *If you imagine what can happen.*

> *Suddenly, a precipice, you need to jump,*
> *Will you be a coward, or will you leap bravely?*
> *Ah? Eh? Just so, my friend,*
> *That's the main point.*

Some of his work had a strange nostalgia and symbolism, like the opening lines of "The Ballad of the Struggle":

> *Among the melting candles and evening prayers,*
> *Among the trophies of war and the peacetime bonfires.*
> *Lived the bookish children, not knowing battle,*
> *Pining away in their small catastrophes.*
>
> *To children, age and life are eternally vexing,*
> *And we fought until scratched, to the deadly insult.*
> *But our mothers in time patched up our clothes,*
> *We devoured our books, drunk from their lines.* *

In the last years of his life Vysotsky tried to live in the world outside, as well as in his own at home, and could not. His wife was a French actress of Russian background, Marina Vlady. She tried unsuccessfully to find movie work in Moscow; he tried and failed to find a niche for himself in Paris. Finally they lived apart. And three days before he died, he wrote his last poem, to her:

> *O let the ice around me burst and crack.*
> *I'm country-pure though born to city curses.*
> *I will go back to you like ships go back,*
> *Remembering everything, the songs, the verses.*
>
> *I'm over 40 and my life, a dumb thing,*
> *Is in the care of God and your good sense.*
> *And if I'm brought before Him, I'll have something*
> *To sing to Him and say in my defense.*

This fatalism was reflected also in a poem by Bella Akhmadulina, her eulogy to Vysotsky, to her own people. Moved by the crowd that gathered to mourn him, she spoke for the soul of Russia, the

---

*"Wonderland" and "Struggle" translated by the author from Russian-language edition of *Vladimir Vysotsky, Songs and Poems* (New York: Literary Frontiers Publishers, 1981). Vysotsky's last poem to his wife and Bella Akhmadulina's eulogy were translated by Anthony Austin and first published in *The New York Times*.

soul of pain and hope. She wrote these lines for her great, brooding country in search of heroes:

> Our salvation is this: that they filled the square
> not like a mob come for food and spectacles
> but like an orderly congress of kinfolk eschewing
> all cheapness. Stranger, gape at this wonder
> that can be seen only here.
>
> The people in their fullness are not ignorant, are not,
> now or before, listeners to nonsense, buyers of trifles.
> Adoring the singer, we weep.
> Valorous requiem. To be or not to be, that is the question.
> How are we to be? Don't judge too severely.
>
> He who does not refuse the fateful chalice, him do I
> praise and love. In an embrace we journey,
> still further, still higher and purer.
> We don't stint, we don't mind that our hearts are breaking.
> It's only right. If not ours, then whose?

EPILOGUE

Gorbachev's Glasnost

The thaw of the society progresses slowly,
and it is not done yet.
Many good people wait. They don't hurry,
they wait.
—Roy Medvedev, Moscow, 1988

"Vysotsky," the boy in the second row said under his breath.

"Vysotsky," I repeated, so the whole class could hear. Nobody flinched. Nobody echoed the name.

I had asked the seventeen-year-olds, "Who are your heroes?" the same question I had put to a group of Komsomol teenagers in Moscow nine years before. And the same silence followed now as then, a long emptiness that lingered until the boy pronounced the name Vysotsky, which hung in the air like a solitary note of melancholy. Then, silence again. No one resorted to mentioning Lenin or Che Guevara or Fidel Castro, as the Komsomol kids had finally done in 1979.

Now, in 1988, still without heroes, the Soviet Union had entered a turbulent struggle against its own authoritarian tradition. Mikhail S. Gorbachev was striving to bring a renaissance to his country, to address the major elements of his society's distress:

the economic stagnation, the ideological emptiness, the alienation and hypocrisy of its most able citizens, the layers and enclaves of privilege and deficiency. He never presented himself as a Western-style democrat, but he sought to engage the brightest minds by giving them intellectual breathing space. To encourage a sense of participation and responsibility, he introduced contested elections for managers at work, delegates to the legislatures, and some officials of the Communist Party. This was a bold attempt to make a new revolution from above, no less dramatic than Stalin's but more difficult to achieve, for its success depended on the Soviet people's capacity to overcome their deepest political reflexes. Gorbachev was pushing in the opposite direction of Stalin, away from the tight centralization of economic and political authority, and against the grain of the society's aversion to public candor and diversity of thought.

Within limits, Gorbachev's policy of *glasnost*, or openness, broadened the scope of permitted criticism and debate, exposing certain spheres to an unprecedented pluralism of ideas. Soon after he came to power in March 1985, the official press and television began reporting more truthfully on corruption and alcoholism, then moved to other social ills, including police brutality, drugs, prostitution, homelessness, and teenage runaways. Even some crime statistics were published. Beginning in 1987, the press became a forum for competing arguments over the efforts toward *perestroika*, the "restructuring" that Gorbachev advocated in the economic and political systems. The incessant chant of empty slogans abated somewhat, most visibly in the streets of Moscow, from which the imperious red-and-white banners announcing the current platitudes were quietly withdrawn.

The country's chief cartographer admitted in 1988 that for fifty years, official Soviet maps had been routinely distorted, with towns, streets, rivers, and bridges deliberately misplaced. A KGB official declared in the ideological journal *Kommunist* that excessive secrecy had impeded scholarship and led to abuses of power. This calculated reduction in paranoia had an immediate impact in the field of arms control: To make new treaties possible, the Kremlin opened some Soviet military facilities to American inspection, and of course got similar concessions in the United States. Defense Secretary Frank Carlucci was even taken to see the most advanced Soviet strategic bomber, the Blackjack.

Then in December 1988, after a devastating earthquake in Armenia buried tens of thousands under the rubble of poorly built schools and apartment houses, the Soviet press exploded in angry accusations that state construction enterprises had mixed too little cement and too much sand into the concrete. Soviet journalists and officials openly complained about inadequate and bureaucratic rescue efforts. Ruthlessly, the press described thieves looting the remains of houses and pulling rings and bracelets off corpses. And most remarkably, the Soviet authorities hid nothing from the outside world, opening their borders to foreign rescue teams and journalists, many of whom arrived without visas and were admitted to the country on the spot. The customary travel notifications were waived for Moscow-based foreign correspondents, who hitchhiked and roamed at will through the areas of misery. The ancient scourge of xenophobia seemed to be abating, at least for the moment.

The Gorbachev leadership also broke the comfortable lie of historical silence, ordering a reexamination of some of the most sensitive facets of the Soviet past. A bold second chapter of de-Stalinization was written as historians and journalists were freed to attack most of the myths about Stalin. This went far beyond what Khrushchev had done. Capricious arrest and exile, mass execution, famine, and even Stalin's failures in the sacred endeavor of World War II were opened to scrutiny. Some of the most prominent victims of Stalin's show trials were officially rehabilitated, fifty years after they stood before firing squads.

In a rush to taste every forbidden fruit, Soviet editors took advantage of the open atmosphere to publish long-suppressed writings. Boris Pasternak was readmitted posthumously to the official Writers' Union, his *Doctor Zhivago*—which had led to his expulsion from the union in 1956—was serialized in the journal *Novy Mir* in 1988, and a biography by his son, Yevgeny, was cleared for publication. Authorities published *We*, the anti-utopian novel by Yevgeny Zamyatin; Vasily Grossman's novel *Life and Fate*, written in 1960, which was serialized in *Oktyabr* magazine; and several other works set amid the evils of Stalinism, including Anatoly Rybakov's *Children of the Arbat* and Aleksandr Bek's *New Appointment*. A month before Yuli Daniel's death in 1988, the monthly magazine *Yunost* published his story *Atonement*, which explores a man's sense of guilt over having denounced others during Stalin's time. The story was one cause of Daniel's arrest in 1965 and his trial with Andrei D. Sinyavsky in a case that marked the end of the Khrushchev thaw. Some émigré writers such as Vasily Aksyonov—previously relegated to the invisible status of nonpersons by virtue of their departure from the motherland— began to appear. Lev Kopelev was mentioned favorably. George Orwell and Franz Kafka, long banned for their surreal allegories of totalitarianism, were suddenly publishable. Orwell's *Animal Farm* was serialized in a youth newspaper in Riga. A chapter of Orwell's *Nineteen Eighty-Four* appeared in *Literaturnaya Gazeta*, the weekly of the Writers' Union, apparently in preparation for the publication of the entire novel. *Neva*, a literary journal in Leningrad, ran Kafka's *The Castle*. Solzhenitsyn's *Cancer Ward* was scheduled for publication in *Novy Mir*, but then canceled after the Kremlin's leading ideologist, Vadim Medvedev, said that "to publish Solzhenitsyn's work is to undermine the foundation on which our present life rests."

Increasingly, prominent émigrés were invited to return. Some Jewish refuseniks, who had suffered for years to get out, went back for a week or two at a time to see relatives. Lev Kopelev, whose small box of Russian earth had been confiscated, was allowed to visit. Yuri Lyubimov of the Tanganka Theater visited Moscow in the spring of 1988, reconnecting emotionally with his native soil and his old colleagues in the theater. But his success and freedom in the West could not be matched in Moscow, he felt, and he declined friends' pleas to stay without some guarantees that the authorities would not interfere with his travel abroad and his artistic judgments at home. Solzhenitsyn also received an invitation to return, from a private group sponsoring a monument to the victims of Stalin. From his Vermont retreat, the writer declined, saying that he would not go back without the restoration of his citizenship and the possibility of participating in the civic life of his country.

Film, theater, music, and painting began to flourish in the widening circle of the permissible. Ten verses by Aleksandr Galich, the late émigré balladeer, appeared in the journal *Oktyabr*; he was restored posthumously to membership in the Writers' Union, from which he had been expelled in 1972. Even the irreverent, gravelly voice of the late Vladimir Vysotsky was reproduced officially in records and tapes for wider distribution than during his lifetime.

He was brought out of the shadows of black-market popularity by the country's spate of truth-telling and by Gorbachev's calculated appeals to the nation's youthful, restless spirits. On January 26, 1988, *Pravda* reported that a plaque had been placed on Vysotsky's house in Moscow on the fiftieth anniversary of his birth.

And so the boy who named Vysotsky as his hero was not being all that rebellious, nothing like a boy who might have dared to do so nine years before. My conversation with his tenth-grade classmates contained many of the contradictory currents of attitude that ran through this uncertain time. The Russians were at odds with themselves in a conflicting mood of exhilaration, hesitation, excitement, and anxiety. They were like Michelangelo's unfinished "slaves" in Florence, rough-hewn figures struggling to break out of the heavy stone from which they were created.

I met with two classes of tenth graders at Middle School No. 6 in Pereslavl, a small city about eighty-five miles north of Moscow. It was a city of deep history and shabby charm, founded in 1152 by Prince Yuri Dolgoruky of Vladimir. Many of its streets were still lined with quaint, sagging wooden houses decorated with carved window frames painted in bright blues, greens, reds. Here, the traditional flow of power from above seemed as durable as the walled monasteries, which were two hundred to seven hundred years old. They were crumbling into disrepair, but their graceful onion domes still dominated the skyline of Pereslavl.

The slogans had not all disappeared from these streets. Across the yard of a factory that manufactures photographic paper, near a stretch of log cabins and wooden houses, and under the silhouettes of domes crowned with golden crosses, a red-and-white banner declared: "THE PEOPLE AND THE PARTY ARE ONE!"

The teenagers rose to their feet as I entered, then took their seats, sitting erect, their desks bolted in straight rows to the floor. A few had broken with the rigidity of the school uniform, wearing nonregulation sweaters or blouses or jeans. And their views, too, were a mixture of the orthodox and the individual.

When I asked how they imagined *perestroika* would affect their lives, a girl in the back jumped into the question as if she had been waiting for it all week. "I think *perestroika* is essential," she said enthusiastically. "Without *perestroika* our society would have died. Our industry, our economy is revived, and people have become more responsible and started to pay more attention to each other and have started to talk more about history. History is either attacked too much or praised too much. Even if Gorbachev leaves his post, the process will be continued."

Another girl, wearing glasses, spoke up in a similar vein of hopeful expectation. "I think our life will be different from our parents'. That's just an optimistic view. Our parents still spend much time at home in front of television, but I think we'll go out more to movie theaters, and so on." A few other youngsters agreed happily that *perestroika* ought to invigorate Pereslavl's dull night life by bringing in more movie theaters.

And through it all ran a deep dissatisfaction with the present, a yearning for change. "I want my life to be different from my parents'," another girl declared. "I would like to travel more. I want to know more than the school can give me." Here were some restive seekers.

However, when I asked what wrongs they saw in the world that they wanted to set right, most of the youngsters had nothing to say. One girl mentioned racism, chauvinism, the problem of war and peace. I prompted them to talk about the Soviet Union, and the same girl, saying there were "many problems," listed a few tasks: to ease tensions between ethnic groups, "to improve the economy, to uproot bureaucracy, arrogance, both in industry and in Komsomol." This was certainly more candid than the Komsomol kids from nine years before. She had obviously been reading the newspapers.

But the revised history of Stalinism being discussed in the press had not penetrated this classroom. "We have already passed that period," the girl in the back of the room explained. "Very little has been said."

"We both talk with our parents and read ourselves," another girl added. "We don't get information in school, so we need to talk to our parents."

"Do you disagree with your parents?" I asked, remembering the Komsomol kids who had denied having any disagreements at all.

"My parents are highly skilled specialists," she said, "but they are indifferent, apathetic."

And again from the back of the room: "My parents think their own opinion is the only one that is right. From our point of view, we are better informed than they are. In history, for example. My parents were born at the end of the war. This was the time when the bureaucratic machine took form."

Dissonance with parental authority, dissonance with the past, emerged as themes in discussions with the second class as well. "I think our life has already changed," said one girl. "I think we express our thoughts even more openly than our parents."

"I think our life will turn better," said a boy with a steady gaze, "because discipline will be better in the Soviet Union, because there will be more incentives to work."

Discipline. The notion of liberalization promoting discipline seemed paradoxical, but it laced many Russians' hopes for *perestroika*. They came to this out of their gnawing concerns over an eroding work ethic, a corrosive amorality, and a flagging sense of national purpose. And contrary to the Western assumption that liberalization would foster individualism, many Russians expected the changes to enhance authority and reinforce collectivism. This was nicely put by Tatyana Vasyutina, whose eager, scrubbed face and blond-brown hair made her look like one of those propaganda posters of wholesome Russian children. "The person will grow in moral terms and spiritual terms when he expresses his ideas," she said. "When everything is open and there is full *glasnost*, there will be more collectivist sense and more mutual understanding among people. We know the mistakes of adults and we are not going to repeat them."

"You're going to make your own, right?" said Sergei Amelin, who was standing beside me at the front of the classroom. The kids burst into laughter. Sergei, my guide, was a twenty-eight-year-old member of the Communist Party Committee of Pereslavl; he was listening with enormous fascination to this exchange across cultures.

The boy who had spoken of discipline began talking about the party "moving to become more democratic," and he said, "I think in ten years, we'll catch up with the States." His classmates laughed derisively at his optimism. "Everything takes time," he said then, revising his estimate. "I don't think it will take less than twenty years to catch up with the States in cultural development."

"Do you mean that you want to have a political system like the

United States, with multiple parties?" I asked. All the youngsters in the class shook their heads and said no.

"I was speaking of the economy," the boy explained. "I think our political system here is better. Here, someone is elected because of his authority. In the U.S.A., a candidate can buy his way into office."

"Is that true?" Sergei whispered to me. I shook my head.

"The Democratic and Republican parties are the same," the boy went on. "We have one party that expresses the will of the whole people, so why do we need another party? There should be more democracy within the party."

Here was a combined expression of new admiration and old contempt for the United States as a land of technological prowess and political injustice. The political side of the boy's discourse was heavily familiar. But I was about to be surprised.

At the end of our session, Sergei scolded the youngsters. "Do you know how to make steel? No?" So you wouldn't presume to explain the process, the party official told them. "Then why, when you know nothing about America, do you say that the candidates buy their positions? We can learn much from America."

I felt like pinching myself. They are speaking Russian, I thought, and this certainly looks like the Soviet Union. But here is a Soviet Communist Party official telling a class of teenagers that they had a lot to learn politically from America. Something was wrong with this picture.

Old habits and expectations die hard, not only for most Russians but even for Americans who absorbed the Soviet climate in a less liberal time. When Bill Keller of the *New York Times* Moscow Bureau asked me one morning if I'd like to go to a press conference by Fazil Iskander, the Soviet writer, I said sure. I had known Iskander casually during the 1970's as a member of the official Writers' Union but also as a rather recalcitrant thinker who used to hold forth around his friends' kitchen tables. So, as we hopped in Bill's car and drove along Moscow's Sadovo Ring Road, I assumed we were going to some dissident's apartment to hear what the writer had to say. Suddenly, Bill made a U-turn and pulled up in front of the Foreign Ministry Press Center. This was an officially sponsored press conference, under the auspices of the Foreign Ministry! Unbelievable.

There was Iskander, at the front of a small conference room filled with Soviet, as well as Western, reporters, and a Foreign Ministry man beside him. I must have looked like a country bumpkin whose mouth hangs open on his first visit to the big city. And Iskander was true to himself, uttering a nice assortment of heresies. He talked in flattering terms about some émigré writers whose names had become taboo since they left the country. He supported the idea of creating private, cooperative publishing houses, despite the government's recent decision to leave publishing entirely in state hands. He criticized the authorities for failing to provide enough Armenian schools and Armenian-language books in the Nagorno-Karabakh Autonomous Region, a largely Armenian-populated area of Azerbaijan that had erupted in demonstrations a short time before; going against the government's decision, he urged a plebiscite among the region's residents to decide whether it should be shifted into the adjacent Armenian Republic's jurisdiction, as the demonstrators had demanded. At this point, I thought I detected a flicker of discomfort in the serene expression of the polished Foreign Ministry man. But Iskander also declared himself a proponent of Gorbachev's *perestroika*, adding his guess that only about 15 percent of the population supported the policy. "As a rule, it's the most educated people," he remarked.

Two months later, following the Reagan-Gorbachev summit meeting in Moscow, something of a repeat performance took place, but this time with Andrei Sakharov, the dean of the dissidents. He was invited by the Foreign Ministry to hold a news conference at the ministry's press center, in the same hall where Gorbachev had held his two days earlier, and just a few days after Sakharov had attended an American embassy dinner for Gorbachev and Ronald Reagan. Now, as the scope of permitted discussion expanded at a dizzying rate, Sakharov was able to utter, in an official setting, words that had once drawn long prison sentences for others. Sakharov, exiled to the closed city of Gorky in 1980, released in December 1986 after a telephone call from Gorbachev, now played his role in the drama with his usual calm reason, supporting Gorbachev's policies but urging further reforms, pressing for free emigration, free religious observance, multiple political parties, the release of political prisoners. Many of Sakharov's positions were Gorbachev's as well, which explained the sudden official tolerance. Banished because of his outspoken opposition to the war in Afghanistan, Sakharov was brought back from exile largely because of Gorbachev's own opposition to the war and desire to withdraw the Soviet troops. But Sakharov also deviated from Gorbachev in praising President Reagan's meeting with dissidents during the summit, and criticized the official press for using "old methods" to attack the session.

Then, three weeks later, Roy Medvedev made an appearance at the Foreign Ministry's press center. Many of his views, especially his anti-Stalinism, also coincided with Gorbachev's, and he was now invited to sit on a panel of historians to discuss the Stalin era before a packed hall of Soviet and foreign journalists. It was a dramatic reemergence for Roy, who had been cut off from visits by foreigners for fifteen months when the regime of Konstantin Chernenko stationed a policeman at his door to turn people away. Now, as David Remnick of *The Washington Post* reported, the official setting did nothing to erode Roy's methodical candor. He described the techniques of torture used during the purges and compared Stalinism with Orwell's *Nineteen Eighty-Four*. He did not seek reinstatement in the party, he said, quoting Mikhail Bulgakov's warning: "Never ask those in power for anything in this world, or they will give you what you deserve." Roy added: "If they give me back my party card, I will accept it without trouble. But I won't apply." The party readmitted him a year later, after he won a legislative seat in the 1989 elections.

The irreverent, the unorthodox, the unthinkable were suddenly spread out like a delectable smorgasbord to be sampled by the hungry. And the delicious dissonance between the expected and the actual could be disorienting. In Pereslavl, when I asked to see some of the old monasteries, Sergei Amelin, the party official, arranged for a young Komsomol activist named Natasha to give a tour. She turned out to be quite a church buff, despite her Komsomol connections, and she knew her history. In fact, at Pereslavl's Komsomol headquarters, they were taking up a collection to finance the restoration of a nearby church, and they prevailed upon me to put a dollar bill into the box. The monasteries were in severe disrepair. Behind broken walls, weeds reigned. At the Nikitsky Monastery, built in the eleventh century, Natasha called my attention to a dome that had collapsed a few years before.

As we drove from one site to another, I asked her why the

structures were not being restored and preserved. Sergei was in the car, along with a Soviet translator from the *Times* Moscow Bureau and Paul Hosefros, a *Times* photographer. It was hardly a private conversation. In an earlier time, the answer would have been predictably soothing: Restorations are being done elsewhere (true), only a small number of craftsmen have the skills for this work (also true), and there are plans to restore these monasteries as well (false). In this time, however, my question triggered an explosive answer from Natasha.

"Why aren't they being preserved?" she repeated my question acidly. "Because our leadership was brought up with a barbarian attitude toward monuments. The Nikitsky Monastery was a cattle yard, a tractor depot, a prison. I don't see any way of persuading them that it's important. The enthusiasts do not have enough force. I think nobody is interested," and she pointed upward.

Sergei, offering a lame explanation, fell back on his country's poverty. "When a person has a bit of bread, he can think of other things," he said.

Natasha shot back: "We can't wait until we are rich—everything will fall apart." They discussed and argued in front of me; he wondered whether the city party committee, of which he was a member, would take it up; she was driven by an angry sense of hopelessness. I was nonplussed. This felt like another planet, where the laws of gravity had been revised. Nothing seemed to behave the way it was supposed to, the way it used to. I was having normal conversations with official people, and they were having normal conversations in my presence. The sense of artificiality was gone. That invisible, impermeable sheet of glass that used to stand between me and almost every official, that used to block every attempt to reach out and make real contact, had suddenly disappeared. There was contact, and it felt genuine.

It did not take very long to get past the euphoria and see the pockets of resistance to this. Or perhaps the resistance was more significant, a groundswell against the small eddies of libertarian behavior. Sometimes the deeper, conservative aversion ran in a hidden current below the sparkling surface of exciting talk, like an ominous undertow. You could occasionally feel that cold reverence for unanimity and authority filtering into the most freewheeling discussion, like the tenth grader's remark about liberalization leading to "discipline," and his support of "democracy" resting on the conviction that the party "expresses the will of the whole people."

Still, Russians were flexing their minds, trying out new ideas, testing the limits of debate. At the city Komsomol committee of Pereslavl, five Komsomol officials in their twenties sat around a table answering my questions. They made little attempt at unanimity, although their comments fell mostly within the broader guidelines now set down in the official press. They conceded that membership in Komsomol, once considered an unwritten requirement for access to higher education and decent jobs, had suffered a sharp decline. Only about 60 percent of the city's fourteen- and fifteen-year-olds were joining, they said, compared with 90–95 percent just a few years before. "That's directly connected to the social, political situation in the country," said Aleksandr Skorospelov, chief of the Komsomol department of primary cells. "People are more free to express their opinions. Earlier, nonmembership might have influenced the kind of institute he was able to enter."

"Under democratization," said Yuri Merkulov, chief of staff of the Komsomol organization on construction sites, "a person must decide for himself whether to be a Komsomol member or not."

Sergei Amelin, who had previously been First Secretary of Komsomol in Pereslavl, ventured the heretical notion that membership in the organization was irrelevant in most jobs. "If you're a captain of a vessel, it doesn't matter if you're a Komsomol or not," he said. "What matters is if you can sail the ship."

Sergei, with a soft face that melted easily into smiles, struck me as Gorbachev's kind of party man: idealistic and educable, candid and well liked around town, his views tinted by the irreverence of the time but tempered with a realistic appreciation for the existing structure of authority. He was no revolutionary. He did, however, have the sort of puritanical streak reflected in Gorbachev's policies. He did not take a single drink of vodka, wine, cognac, or other alcoholic staples of the Soviet table during all the restaurant meals I ate with him, testifying to the effectiveness of Gorbachev's antialcohol campaign, at least within officialdom. It helps to be at the top of an authoritarian system if you are going to try to change ingrained practices. Privately, the high prices and short hours in liquor stores provoked such widespread home brewing that sugar shortages resulted, and the liquor restrictions were finally relaxed somewhat. But in official circles, Gorbachev's admonitions were being taken seriously. Sergei also had a straightlaced answer when I asked what major problems Pereslavl faced. "The low level of culture," he said. Workmen wear their oily, dirty work clothes on buses, he observed with disgust, and curse words are heard often in the streets. People are not educated in a proper level of morality.

Sergei was an advocate of more open discussion, and he was startlingly free with his opinions. He embraced the notion of democracy inside the Communist Party. "The system doesn't allow people to display their best qualities," he said. "That's why the image of the party functionary is a person without a soul who strictly follows the party line." After a couple of days of this sort of stuff, I asked him whether he would mind if I quoted him. He thought for a moment, then said fine. If it ever affected his ability, say, to travel abroad, he mused, he would just put his words side by side with Gorbachev's to prove his own correctness. The dictates of relatively free speech still came from on high.

With Sergei sitting in, the Komsomol officials around the table presented a mixed assortment of views. They spoke of the need to hold truly competitive elections to the Supreme Soviet, as advocated by Gorbachev, although they seemed not to understand the accompanying need to enhance the legislature's real authority, even at the expense of the Politburo's power, if the elections were to mean anything. Most of them opposed multiple parties to compete with the Communist Party. "In our country, it's not needed," said Skorospelov.

"We have always been guided by Leninist principles," declared Merkulov, "and the positions our leaders have followed have always been basically the same." Even a couple of years earlier, nobody would have thought to ask this question. Or, if asked, it would have been met with derision, not taken seriously. And in a group such as this, two authoritative members' categorical answers, falling precisely along the accepted official line, would have been enough to end the discussion. But now Grigori Kovalenko, chief of the Komsomol department of working youth, spoke up in disagreement with his colleagues.

"The process of democracy provides for the emergence of other parties," he said simply. Nobody chastised him, at least not then.

Similarly, Kovalenko took a dissenting view on Afghanistan, as did several others who thought it had been wrong to send Soviet troops there in 1979. This was just a month before the Soviet withdrawal began, so the subject had been exposed to the liveliest debates seen on a foreign policy issue.

"I think it was a mistake," said Skorospelov, the senior official in the room. "It was a dirty war like Vietnam."

"I think the troops should have been sent," countered Merkulov, the supporter of Leninist unanimity.

"There might have been other options," Kovalenko suggested.

"Maybe there were other ways, without bloodshed," said Yulia Nikitina, who heads an international club. "Three from Pereslavl were killed there, fifty-six have served. Eight serve now." Her eyes reddened.

Merkulov came back defensively. "Based on the information we had at that time, this was not a mistake," he said firmly. "When the troops entered, the United States also wanted to get in there. Now that we see this can be settled, that the Soviet Union can pull out the troops, I think we'll settle all the problems there."

Sergei added an observation. "It was difficult for the previous leadership to admit a mistake," he said. Here was a touchstone of the Gorbachev era, the denunciation of the immediate predecessors for faults that would, in time, come very close to the faults of the current leadership. Some Russians would see it as self-criticism by analogy. But Sergei, an ardent supporter of Gorbachev's program, had a more direct complaint, which he made boldly in front of the Komsomol officials. "I am very unhappy," he declared, "that in three years I haven't heard a single word of criticism of Gorbachev. That reminds me of the Brezhnev era. Everyone should be subject to criticism."

Sergei got his wish about a year later, in May 1989, when live television showed newly elected legislators accusing Gorbachev of amassing personal power. Even the taboo on knocking Lenin was broken by a few critics, beginning in April 1988 with an article in *Sovietskaya Kultura* by Nikolai P. Popov, a historian; he noted that it was under Lenin that the party began to acquire extraordinary power, laying the groundwork for Stalin's "perfect totalitarian state." Popov then rushed to neutralize his barb by asserting that Lenin understood the danger of concentrated authority but was too ill in his last years and too beset by his colleagues' maneuvering to reverse the trend. Another historian, Yuri Afanasyev, called for a reduction in Lenin's status as a "demigod" and urged critical examinations of both Lenin and Marx.

To help citizens sort things out, the recent Soviet past was divided into periods with neat, derogatory labels. Although Gorbachev permitted more positive portrayals of Khrushchev than were allowed under Leonid Brezhnev, Yuri Andropov, and Konstantin Chernenko, the Khrushchev era was dubbed the "Period of Voluntarism" to suggest the impulsiveness of some of Khrushchev's attempted reforms. Then came the "Period of Stagnation," presided over by Brezhnev, who died in 1982; Andropov, who died in 1984; and Chernenko, who died in 1985. The Soviet Union entered a phase of "pre-crisis" during the last part of the Period of Stagnation, a term applying primarily to the alarming economic difficulties that Gorbachev inherited, and from which he sought to save the nation. Resistance to his radical program of "new thinking," especially by vested bureaucratic interests, was labeled the "braking mechanism." Thus, the unsettling flow of competing ideas was channeled into some structure, providing a measure of solace for Russians who needed clear definitions by which to interpret public issues.

These contradictions between critical and restricted discourse were contained in a documentary film, *More Light*, shown first in movie theaters and then broadcast on prime time television in April 1988. With old, long-suppressed newsreels and still photographs, it extolled the prosperity under Lenin's New Economic Program of the 1920's, creating an image of immense well-being with scenes of plush stores and well-dressed street crowds. The policy, which permitted considerable private enterprise, served as a model for some of Gorbachev's ideas about loosening central planning and encouraging the play of market forces. The film also showed Bukharin and Trotsky for the first time in more than half a century; they were described as among "the most talented members of the Politburo at the time."

The documentary skirted the hardships of rural collectivization, a Stalinist policy with which the Gorbachev regime had not come to terms. But some oppressive practices of the 1930's were detailed. There were dramatic scenes of crosses being knocked off the onion domes of churches. In one, a bell crashed to the ground and shattered. The famous Church of Christ the Savior, whose land proved too marshy for Stalin to erect his towering Palace of Congresses, was shown being demolished in a terrible explosion of dynamite, the ornate walls collapsing in a roar of dust. Statistics were offered on the purge of the Soviet officers' corps, a long-hidden offense by Stalin. Film of Khrushchev making his secret speech was included, without a sound track.

The narrator, a mocking irony in his voice, quoted Khrushchev as predicting that communism would arrive in twenty years, propelling the Soviet Union past the United States in the production of meat and other commodities. In the 1970's, the narrator sneered, there were "no problems, no defects." The film attacked Brezhnev for getting "more medals than Marshal Zhukov."

But when it came to the present, there seemed to be no problems, no defects in the current policy. The film portrayed this as a bright new era and, some Muscovites grumbled, the self-congratulatory tone was reminiscent of the very lack of self-examination that the film deplored about the past. "Our course is clear," the narrator boomed at the conclusion: "More socialism. More democracy. More light."

This was the propaganda of openness. It was exhilarating in its truth-telling about the past. But in romanticizing the present it drew the viewer into a chamber of mirrors, reversing images and creating its own illusions of reality.

"The Soviet system has been based on some restrictions, which created a circle of permitted activity," said the dissident Lev Timofeyev. "Everything that was outside of this circle was prohibited. The only thing they did up to now, they widened this circle. They didn't take it off, they just widened it. We have some icons which are untouchable—Lenin, socialism." He might have said Gorbachev as well, although at times even Gorbachev allowed himself to be shown on the television news shaking hands in crowds that shouted complaints about long lines and scarce food supplies.

Timofeyev, who looked like a lumberjack in his red flannel shirt and salt-and-pepper beard, was sitting in his small living room at the outer edge of Moscow, surrounded by the papers and type-writers with which he put out his unofficial journal, *Referendum*. He described himself as a member of the "loyal opposition," for which he had done some time in a labor camp; Gorbachev freed him as part of a release of many political prisoners, and Timofeyev was campaigning now for the release of all. "The widening is useless," he said, continuing his metaphor of the circle. "The exit from the crisis is to eliminate the circle entirely." But it cannot be done all at once, he cautioned, returning to that old theme of Russia as vulnerable to the disruption of suddenness, to the cross-winds of revenge. "If you eliminated the circle today, at one mo-ment, it would be a tragedy here."

Both the circle of limitation and the large political landscape that it defined were visible in the letters that poured into the offices of *Ogonyok*, a slick, brash, official weekly magazine that became a pioneering force at the front rank of Gorbachev's *glasnost*. Re-markably, the vast majority of letters, including sharply worded complaints, were coming in signed with names, addresses, and sometimes even telephone numbers—an indication of a sea change in Russians' inhibitions, an ebbing of fear.

A man from Lvov wrote urging that Solzhenitsyn's works be published. A woman from Moscow complained about poverty. A man from Sverdlovsk wrote sardonically about the prohibitions on the technology of communication. Carbon paper, he noted "is hardly used at all in the West. As a rule, one copy is typed on the typewriter, and a necessary number of copies is Xeroxed. Copying machines are not kept behind iron doors with a sign 'admission forbidden,' but they are located in any convenient corner. . . . We have a totally different situation in our multiplying technology. It is entangled by the darkness of prohibitions and instructions. Ear-lier, all this necessity was explained by the fights against ideological diversions and dissemination of pornography, sinister stories were exposed about the fact that spies would start to gather around our Xeroxes. . . . Only recently, at the end of the last year, rules appeared prohibiting copying nonsecret materials of outside or-ganizations. Today the personal computer is starting to replace the typewriter in developed countries. . . . What is destiny pre-paring for it? What will a genius bureaucrat create for it?"

An elderly woman from Krasnodar complained about privileges

for the upper ranks, writing, "For high officials and the top spheres, high technology is used for turning out food products. . . . For those at the top, there is nothing resembling a deficit of good products."

A man from Leningrad wrote that in elections to the soviets, or legislatures, "voters get just a row of second-rate actors." He went on to say: "Crimes have become the norm of behavior for the majority of the people in the leadership—bribes, special hotels, special saunas, special shops, special conveyor belts for producing foodstuffs, special houses, special recreation zones, and special streets for special cars. Everything for the select few, but not for the people."

Others attacked the system of *nomenklatura*, by which the party assigns members to key jobs. Some advocated multiple political parties. Making the argument, N. N. Myagkov, an engineer from Gomel, wrote:

> We cannot avoid a cult under our current political system. If it's not a cult of personality, then it's a cult of just one party, which will inevitably grow into a personal cult of some sort, as it happened during all of Soviet history. . . . This may happen tomorrow or the day after tomorrow, and there are no guarantees that this will not happen under the current system. Moreover, there are all reasons to fear that the society can roll over to dictatorship. As is known, Lenin was an opponent of any factions in the party. But he was, if I'm not mistaken, at some period quite patient with the possibility of participation in the government of representatives of other parties. Suppose, in the present, these are just different kinds of Marxist-Leninist parties, like a Workers' Party, a Socialist Party, a Communist Party. The democratic foundations of the society won't shrink after that, and our Communist ideals won't weaken, but rather vice versa.

Such a letter "I am not prepared to publish," said Valentin Yumashev, *Ogonyok*'s letters editor. "As a small boss, I understand what the situation is around me, and I'll probably wait until *Pravda* publishes it first." He smiled apologetically.

Yumashev, a boyish-looking thirty years old, was a frustrated investigative reporter for ten years at *Komsomolskaya Pravda*, the newspaper of the Young Communist League. He had that fire in the belly that makes a relentless muckraker, not the most popular sort of journalist at traditional Soviet papers. "I was always suspicious of the bosses who were always afraid of something," he said, "and I'm trying to fight this bosses' feeling in myself now." His best articles never appeared. "At *Komsomolskaya Pravda*," he said, "I had terrible relations with my superiors. I wrote against corruption in the police, about where the party apparatus was suppressing young people. Five years ago, when all drug addicts lived 'only in the West,' I tried to write about this problem, which Soviet youth had too. I had quite a lot of stories unpublished." He spent three months in 1981 investigating a scandal at a Young Pioneer camp that was supposedly reserved for the most exemplary youngsters; he documented a system of bribery by parents to get their children in. "The story never saw the light," he recalled with a sad smile. "It was much easier in my section of the newspaper to write how the Soviet police were fine and that they received awards."

Then Yumashev got this job giving him a window on the angers and yearnings of his countrymen. He wore that eager, hopeful grin of fascination that I came to recognize as the badge of the *glasnost* gang. Their eyes shone with bright wonder at the delicate miracle they seemed to be living in. But there was a glimmer of the tentative, too, a sense that the structure of change might be no more solid than the translucent fragility of an eggshell. Could all this heady liberalization endure? I asked Yumashev. "*Glasnost* is irreversible," he said buoyantly. But then he added, "To tell you the truth, I don't quite understand how it could happen at all."

Ogonyok's offices vibrated with the irreverent air of an underground journal, the staff exulting in their newly acquired liberation from suffocating orthodoxy. One evening in November 1988, at a party thrown by *Ogonyok* in a Moscow cooperative restaurant, I felt as if I had been transported back to a dissident's gathering in the 1970's. An editor complained loudly that when Stalin died, he left a powerful machine that was still in operation; "Now, they are just changing the wheels on the machine," he said of the Gorbachev policies. "We need to break the machine." Another editor, who had traveled extensively in the United States, was asked if he had seen American poverty. Yes, he replied. Then he grinned. "*U nas bolshe*. We have more. We have more poverty." It was a delightful twist on the usual Russian boast about having more of everything.

Yumashev, in jeans, sneakers, and a sweater, sat in his tiny office, which was practically submerged under stacks of letters, piled precariously on desks and spilling onto the floor. The explosion of debate brought a surge in mail to *Ogonyok*, from 15,000 letters in 1986, to 50,000 in 1987, to a projected 100,000 or more in 1988. The magazine was running about sixty a month. Yumashev pulled out letters he thought would interest me, both those he could print and those he could not. Could he run the one about Solzhenitsyn? I asked. He reddened, and said no. (Just four months later, however, a Moscow book review printed a literary critic's plea for the restoration of Solzhenitsyn's citizenship.) Nor could he publish letters about ethnic minorities in the Soviet Union at that moment, given the demonstrations and violence that had been occurring between Armenians and Azerbaijanis. "We don't want to whip up emotions," he said. The 300 to 400 letters *Ogonyok* received in support of Boris N. Yeltsin were not fit to print just then, he explained. Yeltsin was ousted as Moscow city party chief and Politburo member after delivering an acerbic speech to the Central Committee in 1987 criticizing the slow pace of the reform; many Muscovites liked his aggressive style of cleaning house and dictating change. "We couldn't publish anything on Yeltsin," Yumashev explained, "because the party organization decided there could be no discussion of this."

Those considered publishable dealt with issues Gorbachev and his colleagues wanted criticized, including the patterns of privilege for the upper political levels. Gorbachev moved to curb the perquisites, cutting down on limousines, curtailing access to special stores. It was not a popular policy with many of the politically powerful, and was slow to take hold. "Of course, they receive special privileges," said Roy Medvedev, who kept in close touch with the inner workings of the party through liberal Communist friends, "but the number of family members entitled to such privileges has been cut." He cited the example of one key party official who had been provided with access to special stores for twenty-eight of his relatives, including children, nephews, cousins, and the like. Now, Roy said, it was available to only the official and his wife.

How far one could go in writing an article or publishing a letter was a question of extreme uncertainty. There may have been a circle, as Timofeyev said, but the line was blurry, smudged in places, and constantly shifting. Yumashev said that he usually relied on his own instincts to choose letters, and his senior editors rarely had to check with Central Committee authorities; they had a knack for knowing. His staff, most of them in their twenties, selected thirty to forty letters for each issue. "Two of us discuss them," he said, "and I choose about twenty letters. The twenty letters, with my signature, are sent to the chief editor. Two deputies to the editor read the mail. Out of twenty, they select about fifteen to eighteen."

Vitaly Korotich, *Ogonyok*'s editor, once phoned the propaganda department of the Central Committee seeking guidance on a letter from a worker about Sakharov, who had just been released by Gorbachev from exile in Gorky. The letter raised the possibility that Sakharov was a decent man, Yumashev recalled, since Gorbachev had spoken with him by telephone, and since Sakharov had expressed opposition to President Ronald Reagan's scheme to create an antimissile system in space. "We were told to put it aside," Yumashev said, "and it was published a little bit later." By November 1988, Korotich was able to have Sakharov at a small roundtable conference of Soviet and American journalists and scholars and to publish Sakharov's critical remarks about Gorbachev's political reform concentrating too much power in one man's hands.

When Yegor Yakovlev, editor of *Moscow News*, dispatched a reporter to cover a fire in the monastery at Zagorsk, the reporter phoned him from the scene with a problem. "A holy father was against publication," Yakovlev said. "I called him and said it was necessary to publish. He asked if I had approval from the Central Committee." Yakovlev insisted that he needed no such approval, something the "holy father" found impossible to believe. The article appeared. "There are quite a few holy fathers," Yakovlev said acidly, "and not only in the Church."

Journalists had their own inhibitions, especially in the provinces, where Russians who read the local papers said there was no sign of *glasnost* at all. The inertia prompted the Union of Journalists to conduct seminars for regional and local editors on what was allowed and what was not. Nor were all of Moscow's influential editors comfortable with a freer atmosphere. When the young West German pilot Mathias Rust landed his light plane near Red Square, *Moscow News* was the only paper to decide immediately to publish a story and a picture of the embarrassing event. "Nobody interfered with our publication," Yakovlev insisted. "I didn't ask anybody for permission. But I know one editor who was calling ten places for advice. Finally he got a negative response, and he was very glad. It is not difficult to find somebody to say no. There are a lot of people who know how they should not act, but don't know how they should."

That seemed to be the case with Vsevolod Marinov, senior researcher at the Institute of Sociology. My *Times* colleagues and I were drawn into protracted negotiations with him over what questions we could ask in a poll of Muscovites that the institute was doing in May 1988 for the *The Times* and CBS. We wanted to probe people's attitudes toward democratic ideas, foreign policy, Gorbachev's economic restructuring, and other sensitive issues. Marinov was excited and nervous. Such a poll would have been unthinkable just three years earlier, he noted. As a sociologist who had labored during his entire career under the impediments of a system geared to good news, he was anxious to get the data. But he told me that he was also worried about inadvertently treading across that ill-defined line and possibly losing his job. He knew that the director of his institute would have to approve the questionnaire, and he frankly did not want to be put in the position of having a question rejected because it seemed too daring politically. So he drew some lines of his own.

He thought up all kinds of reasons for doing away with some of our most interesting questions. Pointed inquiries would be seen as "provocative" by already suspicious respondents, he argued, and would distort their answers. He was probably right. Although the interviewing was to be done by phone, the numbers randomly generated by computer so the names of the respondents would not be known, no Soviet citizen would believe in his anonymity when somebody called him at home to ask his political views. Still, the results, after 939 Muscovites were polled, showed a healthy willingness to take positions that dissented from the offical view.

Marinov was very upset by our desire to have people judge current and past Soviet leaders on a scale from positive to negative. We had listed Gorbachev; Viktor Chebrikov, then head of the KGB; Lev Zaikov, Moscow party chief; Yegor Ligachev, who was seen as an opponent of many features of *glasnost*; and Boris Yeltsin, who had lost his position on the Politburo after attacking Ligachev. Marinov adamantly rejected this; nothing we could say would budge him. He was also uncomfortable about inviting evaluations of Brezhnev, Khrushchev, Stalin, Bukharin, and Trotsky, but finally gave in and let us ask about the dead. A plurality thought negatively of Brezhnev, Stalin, and Trotsky and positively of Bukharin. Those willing to express an opinion of Khrushchev split almost evenly.

Marinov did approve a question on whether people supported Gorbachev's domestic policies (78 percent said "completely," 19 percent said, "less than completely.") But he did not want to ask for an overall evaluation of President Reagan, fearing that a negative rating would appear inhospitable on the eve of Reagan's visit to Moscow later that month. He finally allowed it. (Half did not offer an opinion; 24 percent viewed Reagan favorably and 18 percent unfavorably.) Marinov mustered all sorts of ingenious ways of explaining why a question on reactions to possible price increases would not work; it was a sensitive issue because of Gorbachev's desire to end subsidies of food and other commodities, and Marinov said he did not want to be the first to ask the question. It was worded too vaguely, he argued. It would provoke conversations with the interviewers, not precise answers. People would hedge their responses, making them so conditional that the data would be muddy. In the end, however, he relented. (Forty-six percent said they might be willing to pay higher prices if the quality improved significantly, 43 percent said they would "probably" or "definitely" refuse to pay more for improved goods.)

He refused to ask whether it was a mistake to send Soviet troops into Afghanistan. But he allowed a question on whether the goals of the war had been fulfilled. (Forty-eight percent said yes, completely; 10 percent said no; and 23 percent said partially.) He tried hard to avoid a question on whether Soviet troops should be sent to countries that ask for military help, probably out of the old instinct to steer clear of military issues. When the question was translated into Russian, we noticed that "send troops" had been changed to "interfere in internal affairs." As a standard propaganda line, that would have drawn virtually unanimous opposition, making the Soviet people seem unduly pacific. We persuaded him to change the question back. (Sixty percent said the Soviet Union should send troops, 20 percent said it should not.) He told us that he saw no point in asking whether private, cooperative publishers should be allowed to publish books and magazines, since the government had already decided to prohibit private publishing. In other words, Why should anyone have an opinion after the government has ruled? The question was asked, and a majority favored cooperative publishers.

Even after all the negotiations, the questions on a multiparty and multicandidate system, on the acceptability of street demonstrations and the like so alarmed the State Committee on Printing that it refused to run off copies of the questionnaire for interviewers without an official stamp of approval from Glavlit, the agency that censors published material. Finally, Marinov told Bill Keller, "Glavlit gave us a stamp saying no stamp was necessary."

The poll results could be read either as a showing of broad support for liberalization or of deep conservatism about change. They reflected the divisions that were delineated as the Gorbachev policies set into motion a boisterous process of debate and search, of intellectual combat between those who favored and those who feared a relaxation of restrictions on debate itself. A majority of 54 percent, for example, said that it was not acceptable for people with grievances to hold street demonstrations. But 35 percent said it was acceptable, a significant minority in a society where the unplanned demonstration has not usually been seen as a legitimate tool of political activism. Similarly, a slim majority of 51 percent agreed with the statement: "The one-party system in the U.S.S.R. promotes the development of democracy." But 28 percent disagreed, hinting at a new political restiveness among a people without any experience in a multiparty system. Moreover, older respondents gave more conservative answers than those eighteen to twenty-nine, suggesting that the major constituency for change had yet to attain political power.

Of course, Moscow is about as typical of the Soviet Union as

New York is of the United States. It is a center of authority and a cauldron of ideas, which makes it both more important and less respresentative in the country's overall scheme of attitudes. Across the sweep of the entire Soviet Union, the population has a vast capacity for political apathy and a sense of powerlessness. This Gorbachev was trying to attack, and many Russians certainly warmed to the practice of introspection and self-appraisal that his policies encouraged. But the affection for unanimity and the discomfort with criticism that I found during the late 1970's also remained in evidence during the late 1980's, mixed into the swirling debate. The question was which set of impulses would prevail.

One handicap was the culture's inexperience with public criticism. Not everyone rejoiced in seeing problems turned into the sunlight for scrutiny. A Komsomol official in Pereslavl said he was afraid of "anarchy." A young linguist told me that the newspapers were so full of negative stories that she felt dirty after reading them. "Why can't they write about the good things?" she asked plaintively.

A masseuse reported that her clients invariably complained that the criticisms in the press were making no dent in the deficiencies of the economy. "People talk a lot when they take their clothes off," she said with a laugh. They were asking what the use was of all the criticism when the shelves in the stores were still empty. Russians had a one-liner about the contrast between the excitement in the papers and the drabness of their lives: "It is more interesting to read than to live."

Then there was the joke about the Soviet dog meeting the American dog, who asked, "How is *perestroika?*"

"They've lengthened the chain by two meters," the Soviet dog replied, "and they've put the food bowl five meters farther away. But they let you bark all you want."

Given the Russians' political culture, there seemed to be a dangerous tendency here to see criticism as a direct, pragmatic tool of reform, rather than as a long, oblique process of creating a forum and generating ideas. Many Russians delighted in being able to speak publicly the way they used to talk only around their kitchen tables. But a mood of impatience also accompanied *glasnost*, which, to some minds, would be tested by its tangible results in living standards. "The Russians talk more, and think this will turn into sausage and shoes," Sergei Amelin said caustically. As an end in itself, the multiplicity of ideas seemed to appeal to only a small segment of intellectuals.

The avant-garde of the most open press—*Ogonyok* and *Moscow News*, for example—received some nasty mail on the damage they were allegedly doing to "socialist norms" and the patriotic cause. A sixty-five-year-old woman from Kiev, who ostentatiously identified herself as "Russian," told *Ogonyok* that what was being put in her mailbox every week was not a magazine but a venomous cobra.

Furthermore, as Roy Medvedev pointed out, a great many people had a vested interest in nonchange, and these included more than the bureaucrats who were jealous about retaining their powers and privileges. "Here it is necessary to understand the structure of our intelligentsia," he said as we sat over tea and Easter cakes in his apartment. "Only a part of the intelligentsia supports *perestroika* in the full sense of the word. The creative intelligentsia is an elite, and they are not everybody. There exist only a million of us: propagandists, party workers in the field of ideology, professional teachers of social science in institutes, who have been used to teaching during the last twenty years by the old methods. Ninety-five percent of these people don't know how and don't want to change their personal, old viewpoints. This layer of people sees the past: Everything was good. They don't grasp the new thinking at all. They don't comprehend the new criticism. Among professional historians, there is a frightening displeasure. In general, all professional workers in the social sciences, who already have their academic honors and are candidate members of the Academy of Sciences, received their privileges based on the old concepts. They don't want to accept new concepts. They don't want their books to be thrown out."

In the Soviet tradition, the liberalization was balanced with a containment of that liberalization. Nothing proceeded in a straight line. Nothing was unequivocal. Every step had its compromise. In the heyday of irreverent discourse in the press, the Communications Ministry put restrictions on subscriptions to the most daring newspapers and magazines, freezing them at the previous year's levels and placing them beyond the reach of most prospective readers. People lined up before dawn at newsstands to buy *Ogonyok*. Elaborate barter deals were struck for previously banned books. Copies of *Novy Mir* were passed hand to hand. The official explanation, a national paper shortage, was ridiculed in some of the publications that were subjected to limited circulation, such as *Moscow News*, which published a literary critic's suggestion that paper should be diverted from "propaganda sheets and pseudo-scientific works that no one needs."

A celebrated attack on *glasnost* came in March 1988 as a kind of manifesto from the party's conservative establishment headed by Ligachev. Published in the Moscow party newpaper *Sovietskaya Rossiya* in the form of a long letter from a Leningrad chemistry teacher, it was laced with the darkest appeals to chauvinism, anti-Semitism, authoritarianism, and intolerance. It sent shock waves of anxiety through circles of Gorbachev supporters, and three weeks later was rebuffed in a thumping counterattack by *Pravda*, providing a rare glimpse into high-level party politics. In fact, as Roy Medvedev was told by Gorbachev people, the "letter" from the teacher, Nina Andreyeva, had been rather brief; it had been expanded by Ligachev's staff into a full-blown state-ment of dismay and anger at what it called "the nihilistic attitudes among some students, moral and ideological mishmash, a shift in political bearings, and sometimes even ideological omnivorous-ness," which apparently meant the acceptance of all kinds of ide-ology. The manifesto defended Stalin and attributed much of the liberalism to a subversive mixture of "professional Western anti-Communists" and "scions of the classes overthrown by the Great October Revolution." It revived the insidious, Stalinist term "cos-mopolitan" to brand what it called "leftist-liberals" with the mark of being Jewish, alien, highly educated, and apart. The letter seemed a throwback to an earlier era, a reminder of the undertow that still ran darkly beneath the surface. It was full of statements whose full import snuck up on you, sometimes long after you had finished reading. For example: "Another specific feature of the 'leftist-liberals' is their obvious camouflaged cosmopolitan trend, some kind of nationless 'internationalism.' I read somewhere that after the revolution, when a delegation of merchants and plant owners came to the Petrograd Council to Trotsky as to a 'Jew' complaining about abuses by the Red Guard, Trotsky said that he 'was not a Jew but an internationalist,' which greatly puzzled the applicants."

The publication of the letter was carefully timed to appear

just as Gorbachev was beginning a visit to Yugoslavia. This was Ligachev's technique, to take advantage of the leader's absence. Ligachev then met with a group of top Soviet editors—excluding those of *Ogonyok, Moscow News*, and other "liberal" journals—to extol the letter as authoritative. When Gorbachev returned, he waited until Ligachev was out of Moscow, in Vologda, and convened a special meeting of the Politburo, which reportedly issued Ligachev a warning and gave Gorbachev and his program a formal vote of confidence—at least that was the story the Gorbachev people leaked to the Western press. Six months later, Ligachev was demoted to the thankless job of heading a commission on agriculture.

Whatever the actual maneuvering in the Kremlin, the appearance of such a manifesto suggested how well established the virulent insularity and intolerance were in the upper reaches of power. Ligachev reinforced this message himself immediately after the Reagan-Gorbachev summit in June 1988, when he accused mysterious, unnamed foreign forces of trying to use political and economic liberalization to subvert the Soviet Union. "Foreign voices want the USSR to have a political opposition and are dishing up to us the idea of a multiparty system," he told workers at an automobile plant, perhaps in an allusion to the Voice of America and other Western radio stations. "But if we consider the 'advice' that our country's economy be placed on the footing of Western market economies, little remains of socialism. All that is aimed at weakening the political stability in the country, upsetting social justice and stimulating a far-reaching stratification in the society."

Gorbachev was also capable of expressing a xenophobic intolerance toward dissenters. Inside the circle of shared values, which meant support for socialism, debate was welcomed, he said in a May 1988 interview with *The Washington Post* and *Newsweek*. "Our problem has been that for many years there was no such debate in the society, in the party, not in the Central Committee, not in the government itself or in the Politburo," he said. "The absence of debate led to many losses, mistakes, and omissions." Therefore, he explained, "We want our decisions, at least our principal decisions, to be prepared with the involvement of the whole society, the intellectual forces of our society. . . . This, we believe, is the main guarantee against mistakes. So that is why we are so persistent in developing the process of democratization and openness and public debate, *glasnost*, in our society." He went on to insist that "the whole country is now an enormous debating society," and that the process "will bring forward new, interesting forces, new, interesting people, new, fresh faces."

But Gorbachev had another message for those outside his defined circle of values, and it was reminiscent of the most corrosive indictments of dissidents through the decades of Soviet rule. It came in the *Post* interview after his glowing statements on the virtue of open debate. He was asked about Sergei Grigoryants, a wiry, tough-minded human rights campaigner who persisted in exposing the plight of political prisoners, the violations of rights, and the shortcomings in Gorbachev's *glasnost*. Grigoryants had just spent a week in jail after offering support to a quickly suppressed group that tried to organize as an alternate political party. When he was released, he discovered that the KGB had destroyed files and confiscated equipment that he used in putting out an unofficial magazine. It was a lively journal full of acerbic challenges to the Soviet leadership to make good on its noble ideals of openness. One issue, for example, reported policemen breaking up an impromptu street concert on the Arbat pedestrian mall because two young men were singing in English. "Walking on, we found a smaller group singing a fervent youth-hiking song," the journal said. "But no one was being chased away. Another militia major was overheard telling a companion, 'Those are students from the Moscow Institute of Aviation. They're singing good songs—let them sing.' They also didn't bother a choir singing Russian folk songs nearby. . . . That's the Arbat for you. That's democracy. That's freedom. Now everything is sedate and respectable. A woodwind group plays, people stroll in twos and threes. It's just like a park before the war. Only there are no portraits of Stalin on the walls." The name of Grigoryants's magazine: *Glasnost*.

"People here," Gorbachev said, "know that the Grigoryants 'organization,' in quotation marks, is tied not only organizationally but also financially to the West, that his constant visitors and guests are Western correspondents. Therefore, people think of him as some kind of alien phenomenon in our society, sponging on the democratic process, sponging on the positive aspects of *perestroika*. This happens. It happens in nature, too. There are such parasites living off healthy organisms and attempting to harm them."

Again, the Soviet organism was rejecting uncomfortable words as if they were alien, foreign bodies. And since this was being done by the apostle of openness, it raised the question of how thorough this process could be, how long it could last. Russians were debating this endlessly. Some argued that a word was like a sparrow; once loosed, it could never be caged again. Some thought it could all be closed down tomorrow, possibly even with the approval of most of the country's population. Others struck a middle position, believing that the advances could be curtailed, even turned back somewhat, but not all the way, and only at the great cost of losing the commitment and bolstering the cynicism of young people whose formative years were being spent in this more open atmosphere.

If the liberalization continued long enough, a generation of youth who had not been conditioned to fear would mature as bolder, more outspoken individuals. Even many of my Russian friends had let their guard down and spoke more freely on the phone and in their apartments than they had when I was living in Moscow. Roy Medvedev, always the most precise litmus test of the political environment, had adjusted his behavior considerably. He used to have an understanding with correspondents that we would not put him in the position of using his home telephone to talk with us, lest it be cut off. So if we needed to know that he was home before going to see him, he asked that we call from a pay phone, and if he answered, just hang up without saying a word. For fifteen months under Chernenko, a policeman had been stationed at his door to keep foreigners away. But now, in the era of *glasnost*, Roy was happy to give on-the-record interviews by phone, which he did not only to Western reporters but to the Soviet press as well.

This relaxed atmosphere made my colleagues less cautious, I noticed. They tended to talk on the phone and in their offices and apartments less cryptically, and while they still protected certain Russian acquaintances by phoning from pay booths, the practice became less extensive and the atmosphere considerably less anxious. Access to officials, including the party apparatus, was enormously improved, providing a healthier journalistic climate. Yet the Moscow correspondents were perfectly aware that the KGB continued to monitor their activities, perhaps even with more success now that conversations were less guarded.

Many Russians, even those who delighted in the new spirit of *glasnost*, were canny enough to know that the dossiers were still being kept and had probably become even thicker and more numerous than before. This produced caution in some, often out of old habits. In one striking case, Paul Hosefros, the *Times* photographer who was visiting from Washington, received permission from the official Novosti press agency to spend time photographing a Moscow family in their apartment. Despite the official clearance, however, the grandmother wrote to the police asking if it would be all right. The police said yes.

A little rhyme on this theme circulated in Moscow. Based on a Pushkin verse, it went like this:

> *Vot i nastala era glasnosti,*
> *Tovarishchi, ver, proidet ona,*
> *I v komitete bezopasnosti,*
> *Zapishut nashi imena.*

Or, in a rough translation, with only slight poetic license to make it rhyme:

> *Now, the era of* glasnost *has begun,*
> *Believe, comrades, it will soon be done,*
> *And in the Commmittee of Security,*
> *They jot down the names of you and me.*

A young professional who wrote under the initials "B.P." for Timofeyev's journal *Referendum* described the limits of his boldness. He wrote often about what he called "economic democracy," a private economy that would give people real choices in the marketplace. "A person who has no choice about where to work or how to work, to express his initiative, is not free," he said. But he asked to remain anonymous. "I have a child, and my wife has very good work," he explained. "I can't risk my job. I am afraid we will not have any job in our profession. We are economists, and all economists work for the state." And so B.P. reflected on the most difficult part of the process of change, the process of change in people's minds. "Every time you say something direct and you are not punished, it helps you speak more directly. Every

421

time I write something for our journal, it is so difficult to say direct words. Your mind tries to say something that is not punishable."

The distance between freedom of speech and freedom of action, one Russian observed, is as great as the distance between no freedom of speech and freedom of speech. And as the Russians began to move out of the most restricted realm into a broader landscape of ideas, they began to discover the long road they still had to travel. Now they could talk about many of their problems, but they could not do much about solving them. Their ponderous political and governmental machinery, with its intricate affection for the alignments of higher authority, trimmed and compromised and reprocessed the concept of competitive elections in a skillful effort to avoid a genuine redistribution of power. In this task of change without reform, the bureaucracy found a willing partner in the minds of many Soviet citizens, for whom the notion of political choice remained alien and uncomfortable.

As Gorbachev's program of liberalization gained ground, the Communist Party became both catalyst and opponent, for the party itself had become a multiparty party, a container of multiple policies and factions embroiled in maneuver and intrigue. The disputes were put on remarkable public display in June 1988 at the Nineteenth Party Conference, called by Gorbachev to codify his recommendations for competitive elections, limited terms of office, the creation of a powerful presidency, and a shift of authority from the party toward the soviets. Such meetings are normally austere pageants of carefully orchestrated unanimity, and whatever disagreements occur remain behind closed doors.

But the eruptions of discord at this conference were broadcast in videotaped excerpts on national television. Millions of Soviet citizens watched a party official from the Urals, Vladimir Melnikov, call for the ouster of Brezhnev cronies. (He had been prompted to do this by superiors in the hierarchy, one Gorbachev adviser told me.) When Gorbachev, sitting behind him on the dais, interrupted to ask whom he had in mind, Melnikov named four senior figures: Andrei Gromyko, the veteran former foreign minister and then president; Mikhail Solomentsev, a Politburo member responsible for party discipline as head of the Party Control Committee; Viktor Afanasyev, editor of *Pravda*; and Georgi Arbatov, head of the Institute of U.S.A. and Canada Studies. Vitaly Korotich, editor of *Ogonyok*, shocked the conference by charging that four party delegates from Uzbekistan had criminal records. He turned and handed a document with their names to Gorbachev. (Prosecutors, frustrated by party interference in the cases, had chosen Korotich as the best route to Gorbachev. It worked: The four were later arrested. "Our Watergate," an *Ogonyok* editor beamed victoriously.) A Moscow delegate urged that Boris Yeltsin, the ousted Moscow party leader, be given a chance to defend himself before the conference. And the next day he was, attacking the conservative Yegor Ligachev and pleading, "Rehabilitation after fifty years has now become habitual. But I am asking for political rehabilitation while I am alive." Ligachev in turn denounced Yeltsin as a "destructive force." In a tumultous final session, interrupted repeatedly by delegates' demands for amendments to various resolutions, the conference approved Gorbachev's program with the first divided votes seen in the Kremlin since the 1920's.

The greater play given to these internal conflicts constituted the first sign of "democratization." But this new politics of the party also took on an ad hoc quality, governed by no rules and no systemic guarantees. As Gorbachev opened decision making to lower levels, conservative *apparatchiki* moved to thwart the liberal agenda. In the selection of delegates to the 1988 Communist Party conference, middle-level bosses imposed many of their own people on the rank and file, blocking the seating of many Gorbachev allies and provoking angry protests at public meetings. "The party apparatus," Aleksandr Bovin wrote bitterly in *Izvestia*, "has taken the preparation for the conference in its skilled hands, and, with minor exceptions, it smashed the young seedlings of party democracy. As before, the lists of candidates went from the top down."

Three months later, at a hastily arranged Central Committee Plenum and Supreme Soviet session, Gorbachev engineered the retirement of Gromyko and promoted himself to Chairman of the Presidium of the Supreme Soviet. There were no debates and no dissenting votes. Ostensibly it was a defeat for the opponents of liberalization, but in the old dictatorial style that had reformers worried about the amount of power being concentrated in one man's hands. Paradoxically, given the Soviet system and the Russian culture, the country could be pushed toward "democratization" only by undemocratic means.

Gorbachev and his allies also wanted the party out of the daily operation of the government and the economy. They spoke of relieving party committees of their roles as efficiency boards and management groups, leaving those tasks to a leaner establishment of government officials. Reviving Lenin's battle cry, "All Power to the Soviets," Gorbachev urged that some authority be given to the country's network of legislatures, which stretched from the Supreme Soviet on down to neighborhood soviets, bodies that had long served as compliant rubber stamps for party decisions. The first inconvenient result took place when recalcitrant members of the Supreme Soviet, testing their independence, rejected a stiff tax rate that the Gorbachev leadership had proposed on the income of private cooperative enterprises, such as restaurants. Next came a vote by the Armenian Republic's Supreme Soviet to transfer the heavily Armenian-populated region of Nagorno-Karabakh from Azerbaijan to Armenia in the wake of clashes between the Christian Armenians and the Muslim Azerbaijanis. The Nagorno-Karabakh soviet voted for the shift as well, but the Azerbaijani Supreme Soviet opposed the transfer, which was referred to the Supreme Soviet in Moscow for final decision. There it was rejected. This jockeying among independent-minded soviets was a brand new experience for the country's politicians. So was the overt expression of ethnic tensions that had long been muted under the weight of authority from above.

Those tensions took specific political form in the Baltic republics of Estonia, Latvia, and Lithuania, where "Popular Fronts" were created as alliances of citizen groups with the acquiescence of the local Communist Party committees. The fronts, which began to look like alternate political parties, planned to field candidates and put forth programs of economic autonomy, cultural integrity, and even political independence. Some of their proposals had an anti-Russian tinge—a demand, for example, that immigration by ethnic Russians into the republics be limited. In a burst of desire for autonomy, the Estonian Supreme Soviet even passed a law declaring Moscow's decrees invalid unless ratified by the Estonian legislature. This came amid a blossoming of Estonian political movements advocating independence, candid talk about Soviet "occupation" of the tiny country, and open writings on aspects of Estonian history that had been barred from public discussion during the entire forty-five years under Soviet control. The long-banned national flag of independent Estonia, with its horizontal stripes of blue, black, and white, suddenly appeared on the town hall of Tallinn, in street demonstrations and shop windows, and pinned on the lapels of Estonian nationalists.

Given the society's historical inability to change gradually, the sudden relaxation of limits raised the specter of anarchy for some conservatives who feared that the permissiveness would set loose uncontrollable centrifugal forces. There was always that deep passion for control. This was Gorbachev's most acute vulnerability: that the political culture would not be sufficiently supple to adapt to the struggle among competing views, that it would prove too brittle, that opponents of liberalization would point to disruptions along ethnic, political, or economic lines and argue, "You see, this is what your *glasnost* has brought us."

In Roy Medvedev's view, the early signs of democratic impulse could be seen less in the formal political structure than in the proliferation of informal groups of citizens organized around various causes and ideas. There were a couple in Moscow that campaigned successfully for the release from prison of Mathias Rust, the West German pilot who landed his light plane near Red Square. Environmental groups sprang up, determined to preserve natural resources from the ravages of industry. Russian nationalists organized to save historical monuments, especially churches, from the ravages of the Soviet state, and their best-known group, *Pamyat*, meaning "Memory," contained all the elements of ethnocentric xenophobia and anti-Semitism that had run through the Russianism of earlier years. "There are several tens of thousands of big and small informal groups outside Komsomol, outside the party," Roy said. "They don't arrest these people, don't disband them. They give them the possibility to do this. There are no repressions. These groups gather, discuss, put out their journals. Now, in Moscow alone dozens of different journals are being published. If in the sixties you did this, it would be a pretext for your immediate arrest. This is already an element of democracy in an embryonic form. The KGB observes these people, of course, studies them. But the KGB doesn't have the right to arrest them."

Boris Kagarlitsky, a slender, smiling intellectual, was part of a group that put out the journal *Left Turn*, which advocated what he called "democratic socialism," including economic self-management, freer debate, and elections in which the party would have to prove itself in competition with other alternatives. But he was also sensitive to the weight of history. "The level of politicization in the country is very low, but it's growing rapidly," he said. "It's not a problem of the last twenty years, as some people say—twenty years of Brezhnevism. It's not a problem of the years of Stalinism, it's not only a problem of seventy years of Soviet power, or the three hundred years of the Romanovs' czarism. It's maybe a problem of the whole Russian history, from the very beginning." He laughed with an air of futility. "Maybe the tradition of politically conscious citizens was finished already by Ivan IV, who destroyed the Novgorod Republic in the fourteenth century. Maybe even earlier, I don't know. But somehow it was deep in the past."

So you're swimming against a tide? I asked him. "It's not a tide," he answered with a grin. "It's a kind of vortex, where everybody's swimming, you see." Then he added, "I think there are some social currents, currents of culture, which are objectively very favorable to the left. Some ideas of self-management are gaining ground, and also there are a lot of ideas about workers' rights that are gaining ground. But at the same time, there is a deep-rooted authoritarian culture. This is one of the most complex societies in the world. It is quite modern, Westernized. On the other hand, you can go to some places where you'll find a medieval society. The most important problem is that on the one hand we have thousands of contradictions, and on the other hand, we have no democratic or even liberal mechanism of solving the contradictions, which makes it very dangerous. We better think about some positive solution or we'll have another Stalin very soon. The radical, authoritarian, emergency solution will be implemented from the right."

The powerful affection for authority, and the tender inexperience with pluralism, were illuminated by the Russians' first experiments with elections. Even some who welcomed the freer spirit did so in an outburst of deference to the strong leader. One

Moscow woman, interviewed on the street by American television during the 1988 summit, declared, "This is the first time in forty years I have felt like a human being." Then she added fervently, "I will kneel before Gorbachev!"

Boris Bakumov, a Moscow worker who served as party secretary in a metallurgical plant, embraced "democratization" in precisely the same terms that I used to hear workers embrace authoritarian unanimity. He had a short grey beard and an impish cheerfulness as he sat at a table with colleagues from the Volgogradsky district's party committee. "Everything Gorbachev says finds a harmonious response," Bakumov declared. "Forgive the informality, but the guy does what's needed. Everything he says you accept as it is. I think what the party says is our ultimate goal is right and very sincere. Following the path of *perestroika* and *glasnost*, the party's authority should be reinforced and grow. We have to get rid of those party members who have stained the pure name of communism." And what qualities does a pure Communist have? I asked him. "First of all, honesty," he replied. "Discipline. Responsibility. Much knowledge. An orderly person."

This theme of liberalization strengthening party authority appeared in many comments. Authority had been undermined by the ritualistic lies of the Period of Stagnation, officials explained. "It's difficult to imagine a greater decline in the authority of the leadership than what we learn from the papers today happened in the past," said Sergei Amelin, the liberal party man from Pereslavl. "Authority has grown from the fact that the party has told the truth, although I don't know that we have learned all the truth. It's impossible to become a literate person all at once. It takes time." It helped that Gorbachev presented himself as a vigorous, decisive leader, exuding power and control. Even in the midst of debate over his policies, his manner gave people a sense of security that was absent in the previous era of frail senility.

In the beginning, the assortment of elections that evolved under his tutelage were hardly models of democracy, but they were true reflections of the country's political instincts. The Russian word for "elections" is *vybory*, which means "choices." But Russians had been having "elections" without choices for decades—ceremonies in which a single candidate named from above was offered for each position and elected unanimously, usually with a show of hands. Gorbachev, advocating multiple candidates, secret ballots, and limited terms of office, was pushing against the weight of tradition. And middle-level bosses, intent on preserving their power, made effective use of that traditional habit of playing charades with directives from above.

The State Research Institute for the Exploitation of Machines and Tractors in Moscow exists to investigate ways of prolonging the life of agricultural machinery, a noble task that one would imagine could be free of politics. But politics reared its ugly head when the institute's party secretary got word that he was to be transferred to another job. In keeping with the Gorbachev catechism, he decided to hold an election for his successor. He named as his candidate Galina Kozhevnikova, a matronly party worker who was dutifully endorsed by the party committee at the institute. A clean process, it seemed: one candidate, one job, one meeting at which she would be voted in—by secret ballot, of course. As she told the story, however, the efficient operation was complicated by higher authority, and not for the best of motives, either. "The director of our institute, a man of solid age and a serious view, was not sure that a woman was able to occupy such a post," she explained, blushing. He nominated a male laboratory chief, Anatoly Novikov.

A three-month campaign ensued, complete with meetings in party cells and speeches by the candidates. "My competitor came up with a substantive program of how to develop the institute in the next five years," she said. "My speech was rather brief. I came up with just a few proposals, referring to the democratization of the inner life of the institute, that elections should be held for managers at every level." Then it was time for the members of the party committee to vote by crossing out the name of the candidate they did not want and dropping their paper ballots into a box. "My competitor and I sat side by side, deciding how to vote," Kozhevnikova said, "and we decided that each of us should cross out himself, so as not to influence the result." She gave a humble smile, which she could afford to do, since she won, 123 to 81.

There was something charming about Russians who used to claim that they had taught the world democracy now tiptoeing tentatively into that alien culture, abandoning their ideological arrogance and even asking Westerners modestly how it was done. They made you want to root for them, hoping that the flirtation with democracy would not prove too delicate, too fragile to survive a hostile climate.

"People are still afraid," said Sergei Amelin, who had his hope and his skepticism, "and they ask questions of the type, 'Has it got approval at the top?'" And even if they didn't ask, they were instructed by the evolving electoral system, which preserved the downward flow of power. In general, anyone elected had to be approved by his superior, and this created conflicts. In a Moscow truck factory, workers elected a director who was rejected by the responsible ministry. Workers elected him again. Again he was rejected. And again they elected him. Another ministry simply harrassed and badgered and refused to cooperate with a man who was elected director of a Moscow ceramics factory. When a factory in Kiev put up a candidate whom the ministry disliked, officials went from Moscow for a long, heart-to-heart talk with the man, who came to understand that he was not sufficiently qualified for the job. He withdrew. The same technique was used with a large group of candidates for the first party secretary's job at UPDK, the agency for servicing foreigners. After a series of intensive discussions with their superiors, the candidates stood up one by one and modestly withdrew; an outsider was brought in to be unanimously elected to the post.

Occasionally, however, truer elections took place. Sergei, as first secretary of the Komsomol committee in Pereslavl, presided over one to replace his deputy, the second secretary, who left to become editor of a local newspaper. The first step was to get permission to fill the job through a contested election. Sergei applied to the Communist Party committee of the city, which in turn asked permission from the party committee of the *oblast*, or county. "They replied, 'Well, it's the fad now. Let them try it.'" Sergei recalled.

The procedure demonstrated the care with which control was maintained. Each Komsomol cell was invited to nominate a candidate, who then had to submit a program to the thirteen-member political bureau of the city Komsomol committee. From seven candidates, the bureau chose three. The others could have continued, Sergei said, but the lack of endorsement by the bureau would have been enough to defeat them, and they all dropped out. One of the three finalists withdrew after being promoted to chairman of a collective farm, making it a two-man race. The election turned out to be a classic contest between an old-guard member of the inner circle, a Komsomol functionary named Leonid Sobolev, and an innovative outsider, a museum worker named Andrei Sukin. In an effort to make Komsomol more attractive to teenagers, Sukin had grand ideas for a lighted cross-country ski track, hobby clubs, and a sports center. Sobolev offered only a dull program of increased discipline; he was worried about members who failed to pay dues, attend meetings, or pursue political schooling.

As the candidates toured Komsomol cells to speak and answer questions, Sergei was pleased to see that the imaginative Sukin was the favorite. He fit Sergei's notion of the kind of person who should be attracted to a revitalized party apparatus. Certain that he would win, Sergei withheld his own endorsement to avoid influencing the outcome. But the attitudes expressed in the cells were not reflected in the voting, because not all Komsomol members were entitled to vote; only the fifty-one members of the city Komsomol committee could cast ballots. It was typical of the hierarchical structure of party elections, which minimized the impact of the rank and file membership. And when the ballots were counted, Sobolev the functionary had won by a single vote. Sergei lamented his reluctance to make an endorsement, but he figured that a lot of people had last-minute doubts about Sukin's grand plans. "Before, it happened that many things that were promised were not fulfilled," Sergei observed sadly in what could have been a universal comment on political campaigns. Moreover, it just seemed safer to go with a conservative insider.

Conservative, antidemocratic forces learned quickly how to take advantage of the burgeoning democratic processes, to use the greater latitude for debate to advance people and programs aimed at stifling debate. When the liberalized Union of Cinematographers tried to liberalize the Institute of Cinematography, which teaches filmmaking, the effort backfired. "When they wanted to change the leadership and put in a more progressive person," Roy Medvedev said, "they gathered the professors and instructors, who elected an old-fashioned person worse than the one before." In general, however, the limited electoral process was aimed at promoting a sense of responsibility and harmony, not at giving voice to competing interest groups or varied policies; it was not conceived as a vehicle for the campaigns of conflicting constituencies. So the choices were usually blurry, inarticulate.

The nominating process for candidates to the Supreme Soviet in 1989 became a struggle between the old traditions of one candidate for one seat and the new urgings to give voters some real choices. The party leadership began by setting a poor example, convening a Central Committee session without telling members the purpose, which was to approve dutifully the Politburo's recommendation of a list of 100 candidates for 100 seats reserved for the party apparatus. It was done.

But ordinary voters rebelled occasionally, jeering the party's chosen candidates out of stormy caucuses or denying them victory on election day. Some high officials who ran unopposed, including two senior military commanders and at least six city party secretaries, failed to win the required majority because most voters crossed their names off the ballots. The gadfly Boris Yeltsin won 89 percent of Moscow's vote against a party stalwart.

Active aversion to some elementary democratic principles, such as universal suffrage and secret ballots, also flourished, however. At a computer institute in Pereslavl, where a director and a council of scientific workers had just been elected, a twenty-nine-year-old mathematician complained haughtily that even clerks and secretaries had been allowed to vote for the director. "It's not a good idea that everybody has a vote," he said. "It should be only those with Ph.D.'s." A young linguist in Moscow raised her nose slightly in the air and pronounced the working classes unqualified to vote intelligently for managers.

Alfred Ailamazyan, who had just been elected director of the computer institute by secret ballot (albeit unopposed), had a certain moral objection to voters selecting candidates clandestinely and skulking over to slip the unseen, folded ballots furtively into the ballot box. "I think an open vote is preferable," he declared. "If you want to have real democracy and citizen responsibility, why should I hide my point of view?" Sergei countered with the obvious argument that not all bosses were as "democratic" as Professor Ailamazyan; many would put pressure on their workers to vote for them, and punish those who did not.

The exercise in workplace democracy was going full blast at Ailamazyan's Institute for Programming Systems, which he had founded four years before, under the Academy of Sciences, to write educational programs for schools and develop software for industry. Housed on a small campus of blue-painted wooden buildings in a tranquil birch grove, the institute was an insulated scientific enclave. A young, casually dressed staff, with an average age of twenty-nine, worked in cramped offices on a motley assortment of personal computers. For a few years, they had "elected" a "scientific soviet" of researchers who served as an impotent advisory council, but the elections were like the ones for our PTA at home. Hardly anyone wanted to run, and we were lucky to draft even one person for each position. But now the programmers and mathematicians were being asked to wake up from their political slumber and regard the council as something potentially significant. It worked. The 150 researchers nominated 56 candidates for 29 positions. The council convened for the first time the day I visited the institute.

Ailamazyan, as director, was chairman of the council, and he presided over the meeting—another typical feature of workers' representational bodies to make sure that democracy doesn't go to anyone's head. He was fifty-one, a short, stocky man with close-cropped grey hair. Because of his age, his position as founder, and his role as mentor and teacher to the young staff, Ailamazyan was a revered figure who did not invite opponents to his candidacy for the directorship. His election, unopposed, was ratified by the Academy of Sciences. The academy had also approved the twenty-nine members of the scientific soviet, he announced as he brought the meeting to order.

The session displayed curious crosscurrents of diverse participation and firm command. Ailamazyan was subjected to some intensive criticism, but he also radiated authority. He began by reminding the council—and the sixty or seventy nonmembers who had assembled to observe the meeting—that it was merely an advisory body, without decision-making power. That struck at the nerve of uncertainty surrounding the entire effort toward workplace democracy, for only in feeling influence would workers get involved. And it was not at all clear how much influence they would have. Ailamazyan took some hard blows on the inadequate numbers of computers in the institute, and on his distribution of them. When he announced plans to computerize the institute's accounting, there were sharp words from the council members who wanted their research fully equipped before sharing scarce hardware with the bookkeepers. Ailamazyan chided them as well, commenting acidly on one or another laboratory's work, praising, cajoling, and finally decentralizing. Announcing plans to delegate financial authority to laboratory chiefs, he declared: "Don't come to me for money. I don't have any money." There was a good give and take, a lot of laughter, and an air of collegial respect. I asked him later whether the level of criticism was new. No, he said. In private, they criticized him before. The only thing new was that before, they would not have done it with an American correspondent in the room.

There was tentative evidence that in bureaucracies elsewhere, the warming trend of *glasnost* had begun to thaw the frigid imperiousness of those in command, making them more sensitive to subordinates as the subordinates gained some measure of confidence. "For many years we were educated in an authoritarian system, and it was much easier," said Sergei Potapov, second secretary of the party committee in Moscow's Volgogradsky district. "We could invite the secretaries of the party organizations and say, 'You have to act this way.' The effects were instantaneous, but the results were negative. Now we have to find ways to convince people. This way is more difficult, but the results are better."

A question is how deeply these notions are absorbed into the political bloodstream. Ailamazyan professed commitment to democratization, for example, both in his institute and in the country at large. But he also assumed that as the man in power, he would have a great deal to say about who inherited his authority. "In five years, when I stand for reelection," he said, "I think my colleagues will be mature enough and there will be another candidate. One of my tasks is to create such a person. I think one of the most important things is to prepare a person to take over."

Tentative steps in the direction of democracy were being taken by pupils and teachers at PTU Vocational School No. 6 in Pereslavl. There was something earnest, inquiring, modest, charming about their venture as they dipped their toes into the vast sea of uncertainty. But my visit may have shaken them. We sat in the office of the principal, Konstantin Malyshev, a man with a bushy black moustache and an expansive cheerfulness. He and a few of his teachers informed me proudly that the pupils had elected a student soviet, in accordance with the thrust of *perestroika*. I asked if anyone had been elected whom the teachers opposed. "From time to time they elect somebody we don't even want in the school!" exclaimed a teacher, Lyudmilla Vinogradava, to a chorus of approving laughter.

The inconvenience was kept under control. First, the chairman of the student soviet was not a student but a young Communist who worked in the library. Secondly, the soviet had no more power than most student councils in the United States, except that under assiduous guidance from teachers it organized the cleaning of the school and played a role in dealing with pupils' misbehavior— listing the offenders publicly or deciding to notify parents.

"We have to teach the children democracy," the principal declared. "You can imagine how difficult it is to teach them this." But it turned out that democracy was a foreign language that nobody in the school knew how to speak.

I sat with five members of the soviet, bright-eyed sixteen- and seventeen-year-olds, and asked about procedures. The council had forty members, they explained, with each classroom nominating two or three students. "Each group nominates one person for each position," said Olga Migachova, sixteen. "Each group nominates two or three and sends two or three."

"If each group nominates two or three, how many candidates are there altogether?"

"Forty," Olga said.

I asked Mikhail Pinigin how many were nominated from his group. "Two," he said.

"There were two nominated and two sent to the Soviet?" I asked. He looked at me with bewildered fascination, probably wondering why an American did not understand how elections worked. "Did any of you have more candidates than positions?" They all said no, and being polite children, they did not scoff at the absurd question. But they did seem intrigued, as if they had just been asked why gravity pulled things down instead of up.

"In other words," I said, "in all of your groups, the names of only the correct number of candidates were put up. So, in other words, when people voted, they really didn't have a choice." The youngsters nodded thoughtfully.

"Do you think that's a good way to do it?" I asked. "Or do you think there should be more candidates than there are places on the soviet so the students have a choice?"

The teenagers reacted with nervous giggles. "That's a difficult question," said Mikhail. "Like for forty places, sixty candidates?" He and the others looked thoroughly puzzled.

"Let's say, for example," I explained, "there were four people who were nominated and you could send only two to the soviet. Would that have been a better system or too complicated?"

Mikhail was baffled by this, and none of the others came to his rescue. Finally the principal, from the side of the room, prompted: "Which form suits you better?"

"It would have been better to send four," said Mikhail.

"No," I tried again, "to send two, but to elect from four. Whoever gets the most votes."

Laughter erupted over the novel idea. Wide-eyed and bemused, Mikhail asked, "So all four wouldn't get the same number of votes? So whoever got the most number of votes would win?"

"Right," I said. The youngsters paused, absorbing this.

"Well," Mikhail finally conceded with a smile, "that strikes me as also good."

I pressed further. "How come you nominated only two people in your group?" I asked.

"In this group," Mikhail replied, completely misunderstanding the question, "the students nominated and elected the best comrades and those who were trusted the most."

"And if there had been three candidates?"

"There should be only a certain, fixed number of members of the soviet."

Sergei, my trusty guide, tried to help. "Misha," he said to the boy, "we are now six people. Let's say this group has to elect one person to go with David to America. By what means today are you going to elect that person? By what criteria? And by that we can see how you could elect people to a council."

"By his activism, first of all," said the boy.

And Olga, the realist, declared, "We don't know how such a situation could arise."

Then they asked me questions about student council elections and students' rights in the United States. They and their teachers seemed surprised that student council presidents were students. And at the end, several teachers told me the session had been extremely interesting for them. "We are studying, studying," declared Malyshev, the principal. "We have to teach the children democracy."

In any society, schools convey the mainstream values, and Soviet schools were among the slowest institutions to adjust to the upheaval of ideas at the beginning of the Gorbachev era. The patterns of authority, the interplay between collective conformity and individualism, the sloganeering, the power of declaration over reality—all these possessed an immense durability in the face of the country's gradual awakening.

The inertia in the classroom was dramatized by the revision of history in the press, which left textbooks entombed in their own lies. Banished names of purged Bolsheviks, so carefully excised from books over the years, were suddenly restored to historical significance. Stalin's misdeeds were suddenly more extensive and explicit than just the "cult of personality." Teachers were at a loss. Some hastened quickly through the Stalin era, pupils and parents told me, others stuck to the old texts, some embraced the new candor with alacrity by basing lessons on the newspaper attacks against Stalinism. In many cases, teenagers read the papers on their own and leaped way out in front of where their teachers were prepared to go. In one tenth-grade history class, a student asked the teacher, "How should I answer the question—according to the textbook or according to the newspaper?"

"Keep close to the textbook," the teacher replied. "In one class a boy answered according to the newspaper, and it sounded so terrible."

The renditions of history were in such flux that at the end of the 1987–88 school year, the State Committee on Education cancelled the written final examinations in history, replacing them with oral discussions that were ungraded. The decision prompted one Moscow student to make a delicious comment to a *New York Times* reporter: "History is changing."

Virtually all the elements of the official myth of Stalin were officially destroyed, some of them by Gorbachev in an address marking the seventieth anniversary of the Bolshevik Revolution, then more extensively by historians, journalists, and ordinary Soviet citizens in the columns of the country's most authoritative official newspapers and magazines. Bukharin was formally rehabilitated, his conviction thrown out, his widow interviewed in the press and praised in a compassionate poem by Yevgeny Yevtushenko. The figure of Trotsky appeared favorably in a play, *Onward . . . Onward . . . Onward*, by Mikhail Shatrov. A *Pravda* article then exonerated Trotsky of the charge of being "an enemy of the revolution and socialism" and suggested what had long been deduced in the West—that Stalin had him murdered. Lev Kamenev, Grigory Zinoviev, Aleksei Rykov, and other early Bolsheviks, victims of Stalin's purges, were rehabilitated. Out from behind the veil of silence came the figure of 20 million dead in the purges, Stalin's nonaggression pact with Nazi Germany, his purge of the officer corps, and even the cruelties of collectivization and the famine in the Ukraine. A vivid and terrible description of the famine was published in *Literaturnaya Gazeta*. Yuri Chernichenko, whose grandfather died of starvation, wrote: "My mother kept me in my room so I wouldn't be kidnapped because of cannibalism. . . . I recall an old lady who came to my mother, saying, 'Don't throw away the water after you wash up. I'll drink it.' I asked her to tell me some fairy tales, but this old woman could remember only her children who had died."

One day in the offices of the magazine *Ogonyok*, the letters editor, Valentin Yumashev, showed me a remarkable letter that had just come in, signed with the initials K.A. It was a kind of confession, a wrenching cry of pain and guilt shaken loose by the rush of public denunciation of that time.

Issue No. 4 of *Ogonyok* carried a letter from a former Gulag security guard, A. Arbuzov, who had lost his health doing this "thankless" work. For people like him—not very bright or educated—it is easy to live. They understood nothing, they understand nothing today. But what about me, a former NKVD and KGB investigator, an educated man, an intellectual, as I always thought of myself? I cannot sleep at night, and it is not just old-age insomnia. It would have been better for me to have been convicted, just to finish this nightmare. My wife has gone long ago. My children and grandchildren do not know the whole truth about me, and I am afraid to be ashamed in their eyes. That is why I do not name my name.

I was twenty-six when I started working in the NKVD "organs" in a central Russian town. The first "enemy of the people" whose case I was assigned to investigate was an arrested first secretary of the city committee of the VKP [the Communist Party]. Fifty years have passed, but I can see this man as if it happened yesterday. His smashed, swollen lips moving with difficulty, he says, "The time will come and you will be cursed by the people." I exploded with anger. "I will be recommended for a decoration, an order for you, but you, dirty snake, won't even have a grave of your own." The days passed, and he did not confess. And then he was tied down to a bench, on his naked stomach a saucepan was placed with a live rat under it. Then we started hitting the pan with sticks. In five minutes he confessed to everything and signed the testimony.

People, can you forgive me? I am ready to kneel in front of you, to crawl at your feet. I was not a sadist or a killer, though there were such characters among us. I really thought that I was carrying out my duty and that all means were acceptable in the struggle with the treacherous enemies. I trusted the wise leader, Comrade Stalin. . . . But I will be completely sincere. The more "enemies of the people" passed through my hands, the less belief I had. When I finally saw the things as they actually were, the only choice was: either they or you will be destroyed. If you do not unmask the enemies, that means you have lost vigilance, or become their accomplice. This sounds terrible, wild, but we had a plan, a quota for "enemies of the people" to fulfill.

After the 20th Party Congress I wanted to shoot myself. I thought revenge would follow. But I remained in the "organs." I was only offered a change in my place of residence. And I moved from one city to another, trying not to recall the past, and until lately I managed. But now the people in the cases I investigated visit me at night, and instead of fear in their eyes I see that they despise me. How can I tell these

people I tortured, how can I explain that my damned life was
a tragedy, too? But this will help neither me nor them.

K.A.

The letter could not be published because it was anonymous,
Yumashev explained, and its authenticity could not be verified.
But he believed it to be genuine, for other, similar letters had
come in signed and would appear.

The treatment of Stalin in history became a touchstone of the
Soviet Union's most anguished politics, and a citizen's reaction to
the truth grew into a test of his political values, his sense of himself
and his country and his future. The new candor provoked a disturbing outcry from Russians at all levels who yearned to protect
their myths, to close off scrutiny, to keep their grip on the suspension of disbelief. Letters poured into the Central Committee,
the newspapers, the magazines, many of them in defense of Stalin,
or in pain that his reign was being painted "all black," as many of
them put it. "Recently," a man from the Dagestan region wrote
to *Ogonyok*, "they are saying that allegedly Stalin was a cruel person
and that he illegally killed many people. If this is true, then why
at that time didn't we talk about this? On the other hand, the cruel
and difficult time demanded cruel measures from a personality.
The situation demanded this. He was strict with the *enemies* of the
Soviet people, traitors of the Motherland. . . . We should not go
into so many details on these questions. Stalin did what needed
to be done."

Even more deeply than under Khrushchev, the attacks on Stalin
shattered the belief in belief itself. Even more severely than under
Brezhnev, the vacuum of ideology ate away at the people's sense
of purpose. The search for a single Truth continued.

Superficially, the term *perestroika* became a slogan with a blurry
meaning equivalent to "progress." But many imagined it as some
kind of deliverance anticipated from above, not a prescription for
a hard passage through a realignment of the social order. It was
like good weather. People waited for *perestroika* to happen to them,
and they grumbled when it didn't. It was merely policy, not ideology. It did not grip the populace with fervor or commitment. It
did not grow naturally out of a national ethic, nor did it fit into

an ideological or moral superstructure that would interpret and justify and bolster its principles. In some minds, the exhortations of *perestroika* must have sounded as hollow as the earlier slogans of utopian communism turned out to be, and one could easily imagine the sardonic way in which this grand program of "Restructuring" would be denounced in the official pronouncements of some future Soviet regime.

Perestroika was also personified by the figure of Gorbachev, even though the policy emerged from a broader consensus of leadership. If Gorbachev disappeared, it was thought, so would his policies. But they were derived from a larger context, largely generational. Gorbachev and many of his advisers, in their twenties when Khrushchev shattered the icon of Stalin, must have been deeply affected by the sudden destruction of all that they had been raised to believe. Just out of school, perhaps not yet cynical in their experience with the world, these young people were the most likely bearers of the long-term impact of that earlier de-Stalinization. Now that they were coming to power, the reverberations of the Khrushchev effort were being magnified. And a new generation of Soviet citizens was maturing in a new environment of questioning debate. The longer it lasted, the more difficult it would be to reverse entirely, even after Gorbachev's departure. After a decade or more, too many young people would be used to integrating their private and public views, and would have to learn that peculiar Soviet schizophrenia that marked the behavior of their elders for more than half a century. Oppression might then have a sharper edge, drawing less support from the enveloping conformity that once ruled. One Russian friend found a religious metaphor to express his hope for the durability of the liberalization. "Exorcism is a difficult process," he said. "Maybe Gorbachev is a transitional figure who has to take the devil out of us and then leave."

But there were many devils, some given more play by the Gorbachev phenomenon. The combination of the search for a Truth and the relative openness also released the ugliest in Soviet society: the bigots, the chauvinists, those who used openness to campaign against openness. Among those with the most potential power were the Russianists, who were so plentiful that if multiple political parties were allowed, Roy Medvedev speculated, many of them would be like fascist parties. *Pamyat*, the organization ostensibly devoted to preserving Russian historical architecture, was noted for its crude anti-Semitism. At its meetings, speakers suggested that non-Russians be exiled to non-Russian republics and that Russians and non-Russians be prohibited from intermarrying.

A cooperative that made political buttons produced one against *Pamyat*; it pictured a church's onion dome crowned with a swastika instead of a cross. Leonid Borodin, who had served a prison sentence between the time I had last seen him in 1979 and our reencounter in 1988, said that although he had nothing to do with *Pamyat* himself, he understood that many Communist Party members were involved. Gennady Shimanov, who had mellowed since our last contact nine years before, shunned *Pamyat* after attending several meetings that disgusted him for their virulent anti-Semitism. Shimanov heard Ilya Glazunov, the painter, speak at a meeting, despite Glazunov's insistence to foreigners that he had no association with the organization. Significantly, Yegor Ligachev attended a Glazunov art exhibition, reinforcing some Soviet citizens' suspicions that Russianism's dark intolerance had sympathy in the upper reaches of the leadership. One Leningrad man's answer to this was decidedly undemocratic. He wrote to *Moscow News* that *Pamyat* meetings should be banned.

As this is written, the yearning of Russia takes much the same form as before. It is a search through the available systems of belief: patriotism, religion, socialism, ethnocentrism. An optimist might add democracy to the list, although it is still a poorly understood idea. Nothing in the Gorbachev phenomenon has fulfilled this yearning or provided an answer to this search. And so the easy answers—the xenophobic and intolerant answers—remain as much a danger as before. Inside the mind of Russia, the struggle is far from over.

One spring evening in Pereslavl, when the muddy remnants of winter were drying and the first fragrances of warmth touched the city, Alfred Ailamazyan invited a few of us to his private sauna. This was one of the perquisites of being director of the computer institute: a house on the campus, among the graceful birches, and a wood-paneled *banya* in which to entertain his male guests. Sergei, Paul Hosefros, a translator, and I brought our own beer, and Ailamazyan left most of the drinking to us.

As the masseuse said, when people take their clothes off, they tend to talk. So we did some naked philosophizing late into the night as we alternated between the heavy heat of the sauna, pungent with the smell of birch branches, and the cool showers and refreshing beers.

We talked about authority, free choice, technology, children, skiing, and the requisites of civilized human beings. It was a generous evening, marked by a large scope of common ground and the essential humanity of a few men stripped of their outer roles and obligations. Ailamazyan seemed to admire Western political systems, and at one point said that having decisions come constantly from the top made you feel as if you were inside a keg. His dream, he said, was that my grandson and his would be able to sit at home and send computer messages back and forth to each other and wonder why the American and Soviet peoples used to be separated.

But the most telling remark he made was toward the end. It touched the question of systems of belief, of the weightlessness and drift that the country was enduring. Where in this exhilarating change could you get a foothold to feel solid ground again? What, I asked him, should be believed in? Communism? Christianity? Patriotism? Democracy?

He was silent for a moment. Then Paul added, "Self? Belief in self?"

"That's it," Ailamazyan declared. "Self."

Another kind of vision emerged some months later, when I returned to Moscow for *Ogonyok*'s roundtable discussion with Andrei Sakharov and other prominent Russians. A painful incident occurred that revealed how much poison had been put into the country's veins by long generations of living in a culture of secret police.

Sakharov had participated boldly in the conference and had departed. And the next evening, during an extended exchange of toasts at a small dinner with a few Americans and a few members of *Ogonyok*'s staff, a young reporter for the Soviet magazine stood and told a bitter little story.

He had been put in charge of administering the conference, the young man said, and so when it was done, it was his duty and pleasure to see Sakharov and his wife, Yelena Bonner, to the door.

He held Yelena's coat for her and then held Sakharov's. And at that moment, without looking at the young reporter, Sakharov said to his wife, "This man's profession could be something other than what it appears." In other words, his youth, his perfect grooming, his proximity to the veteran dissident at this official gathering suggested KGB connections.

The young man, who seemed to admire Sakharov deeply, was truly wounded by the comment. He could understand it, he said, after all that Sakharov had suffered. But he straightened proudly as he continued the story. "I said, 'You are mistaken. I am only a journalist.' "

And then the young man turned to us and raised his glass in a toast to the day when his country would "no longer be a place where people suspect each other."

Index

FOR THE BEST IN PAPERBACKS, LOOK FOR THE

In every corner of the world, on every subject under the sun, Penguin represents quality and variety—the very best in publishing today.

For complete information about books available from Penguin—including Pelicans, Puffins, Peregrines, and Penguin Classics—and how to order them, write to us at the appropriate address below. Please note that for copyright reasons the selection of books varies from country to country.

In the United Kingdom: For a complete list of books available from Penguin in the U.K., please write to *Dept E.P., Penguin Books Ltd, Harmondsworth, Middlesex, UB7 0DA.*

In the United States: For a complete list of books available from Penguin in the U.S., please write to *Dept BA, Penguin, Box 120, Bergenfield, New Jersey 07621-0120.*

In Canada: For a complete list of books available from Penguin in Canada, please write to *Penguin Books Ltd, 2801 John Street, Markham, Ontario L3R 1B4.*

In Australia: For a complete list of books available from Penguin in Australia, please write to the *Marketing Department, Penguin Books Ltd, P.O. Box 257, Ringwood, Victoria 3134.*

In New Zealand: For a complete list of books available from Penguin in New Zealand, please write to the *Marketing Department, Penguin Books (NZ) Ltd, Private Bag, Takapuna, Auckland 9.*

In India: For a complete list of books available from Penguin, please write to *Penguin Overseas Ltd, 706 Eros Apartments, 56 Nehru Place, New Delhi, 110019.*

In Holland: For a complete list of books available from Penguin in Holland, please write to *Penguin Books Nederland B.V., Postbus 195, NL-1380AD Weesp, Netherlands.*

In Germany: For a complete list of books available from Penguin, please write to *Penguin Books Ltd, Friedrichstrasse 10-12, D-6000 Frankfurt Main I, Federal Republic of Germany.*

In Spain: For a complete list of books available from Penguin in Spain, please write to *Longman, Penguin España, Calle San Nicolas 15, E-28013 Madrid, Spain.*

In Japan: For a complete list of books available from Penguin in Japan, please write to *Longman Penguin Japan Co Ltd, Yamaguchi Building, 2-12-9 Kanda Jimbocho, Chiyoda-Ku, Tokyo 101, Japan.*